APPLIED ECONOMETRICS

APPLIED ECONOMETRICS

J. L. BRIDGE
Faculty of Economic and Social Studies
University of Manchester

1971

NORTH-HOLLAND PUBLISHING COMPANY - AMSTERDAM • LONDON
AMERICAN ELSEVIER PUBLISHING CO., INC. - NEW YORK

Library of Congress Catalog Card Number: 73-157039

North-Holland ISBN: 0 7204 3052 6

American Elsevier ISBN: 0444 10098 9

13 graphs, 127 tables

Published by:

NORTH-HOLLAND PUBLISHING COMPANY — AMSTERDAM

Sole distributors for the U.S.A. and Canada:

AMERICAN ELSEVIER PUBLISHING COMPANY, INC.
52 VANDERBILT AVENUE, NEW YORK, N.Y. 10017

PRINTED IN THE NETHERLANDS

To the Memory of
David Bugg

ACKNOWLEDGEMENT

The permission to use previously published material is gratefully acknowledged. In all cases reference is made to the original publication. A full bibliography can be found in the reference list.

PREFACE

This book developed from a course of lectures given at Manchester University to graduate students who, though trained in the standard methods of econometrics, needed some introduction to the many ways in which these methods had been used. I also felt that in certain fields there were now so many applied studies that students and general economists needed a guide and quick reference to the methods and results of these studies. With these two aims in mind, the level of mathematical and econometric difficulty has been kept to that of J. Johnston's "Econometric Methods" although readers may find chapters 3 and 5 a little tedious.

Applied econometrics involves the use of a priori and statistical information to answer questions of economic policy and forecasting. This has determined the arrangement of the material in each chapter. After a short discussion of the types of questions that the empirical studies are or should be answering, the economic theory relevant to them is reviewed in order to explain the a priori information used in the empirical studies. When empirical studies are looked at in this way, the micro–macro distinction becomes one of the degree of aggregation. This is why the actual studies are arranged according to the type of data they use. Little time is spent on estimation since it is assumed that readers will be aware of the standard methods. Unusual methods are outlined so that readers can assess the results but anyone wishing to use a particular technique should refer to the original article. The section of fields was rather arbitrary but it is hoped that the ones chosen cover as many different aspects of applied econometrics as any other selection of manageable size.

Without the kind permission to use tables and diagrams of the authors whose work I am reporting, this book would not have been possible. I have tried to present their methods and results with as little distortion as possible – if I have failed, my apologies to them. In writing this book I have had help and encouragement from a number of colleagues and students. I would especially like to thank Varnar Ambalavanar, David Colman, Micheal Kennedy, Anna Koutsoyiannis, David Laidler, Leslie McClements, Michael Pearson, Leighton Thomas and John Zerby, all of whom read and commented on sections of an earlier version of the book. Special thanks are also due to Mrs. Watts and Mrs. Furlong, who provided invaluable assistance in the preparation of the manuscript.

CONTENTS

CHAPTER 1

THE STRUCTURE AND USES OF MACRO ECONOMETRIC MODELS

1.1. Introduction

1.1.1

During the last thirty years or so governments have taken upon themselves responsibility for the overall position of the economy. The major aim for most governments has been the preservation of full employment for which a high level of aggregate demand has been considered necessary. More recently governments have been concerned with increasing the rate of growth of aggregate income. Most governments would like to achieve these aims without departing too radically from the existing modes and conventions. It is questions concerning these types of policy that macro econometric models are designed to answer. From macro econometric models, the quantitative effects of changing certain aggregate variables on other aggregate variables can be derived. In order to get a good measure of these effects, it is necessary to have some data of previous changes in the variables, which implies that similar policies must have been used before. A typical question is what effect will an increase of 10% in government spending have on (a) the level of national income, or (b) the distribution of income. A more refined question is what level of government spending would give us the most desirable combination of the level and distribution of income. Of course, the government has other variables that it can change, and probably other aims. Thus, the questions become more complex, but basically of the same type.

1.1.2

A simple approach would be to take a time series of each variable designating an aim and regress it on one or all of these policy variables. This method ignores any ideas we might have gleaned from economic theory on, for instance, the relationship between consumption and income, and so is rather inefficient (see Klein, 1960). Furthermore, the method will work provided nothing is changed but the policy variables (see Marschak, 1953). If other things do change we have no way of adjusting this method to take account of these changes. It is for these reasons that the applied econometrician prefers to estimate these policy relationships on the basis of models.

1.1.3

The economic theory that appears most relevant to the questions we posed is the Keynesian theory and its extensions. The simple Keynesian theory is a macro theory although research since 'The General Theory' has developed the connection between this macro theory and the traditional micro theory. In this chapter we shall only consider it from the macro angle. Later in the book the relevance of micro theory will be developed. Keynes stressed the importance of aggregate expenditure in determining the level of national income and hence employment. Consumption expenditure, he assumed to be related to income leaving investment expenditure mainly dependent on expectations, which themselves were related to the level of income, although the rate of interest would have some effect on investment expenditures. The rate of interest, he explained, was determined by the supply and demand for money, which was related to income and the rate of interest. Thus Keynes developed a highly interdependent system which can be represented by a set of simultaneous equations. Samuelson and others combined the theory of the accelerator into the Keynesian framework to produce a dynamic model showing how these aggregate variables moved through time. It is from this base that aggregate econometric models have developed. Samuelson's technique for handling the interaction of the consumption function and the accelerator was a set of linear difference equations. The use of linear difference equations does restrict the model but there is considerable gain in convenience in manipulation and estimation especially since most economic statistics are published at discrete time intervals. Some simple examples will illustrate the properties of linear difference equations and at the same time introduce the terminology of macro models.

1.2. **Exogenous and endogenous variables in simultaneous equations**

Consider first a simple linear Keynesian system represented by the following five equations

$$Y = C + I + G \tag{1.1}$$

$$C = \alpha_0 + \alpha_1 Y \tag{1.2}$$

$$I \;\; = \beta_0 + \beta_1 i \tag{1.3}$$

$$M_D = \gamma_0 + \gamma_1 Y + \gamma_2 i \tag{1.4}$$

$$M_D = M_s \tag{1.5}$$

where

C is consumption;
I is investment;
G is government expenditure;
i is rate of interest;
M_D is the demand for money;
M_s is the supply of money;
Y is income.

Here, eq. (1.1) is a definitional equation and eq. (1.5) an equilibrium condition, whereas eqs. (1.2), (1.3) and (1.4) are behavioural relations. There are seven variables altogether, but since the system is a set of simultaneous equations it is possible to eliminate all but three variables, thus expressing either C, I, Y, i, or M as functions of G and M_s. The first five variables are called endogenous variables and G and M_s are exogenous variables. Endogenous variables are those determined within the model. In general, policy instruments will be exogenous variables and policy aims endogenous. This model is static, the only change in the endogenous variables can stem from changes in the exogenous variables. This gives rise to the concept of an instantaneous multiplier, i.e., given a unit change in an exogenous variable e.g., G, what will be the effect on an endogenous variable.

1.3. **Recursive difference equations**

Consider next the following system

$$Y_t = C_t + I_t \tag{1.6}$$

$$C_t = c Y_{t-1} \tag{1.7}$$

$$I_t = b(Y_{t-1} - Y_{t-2}) \tag{1.8}$$

where subscripts reflect time periods. This model is no longer simultaneous, since the feedback of Y onto C takes time. This system is called a recursive system. Since causation involves time, recursive systems would seem to be the most useful in economics; however, more on this later. Eqs. (1.6)–(1.8) do not include any exogenous variables at all, only lagged endogenous variables. Normally econometric models have exogenous variables as well as lagged endogenous. If we accept the proposition that causation takes time, theoretically we only need to consider recursive systems, which we shall now do. Consider the system (1.6)–(1.8), by substituting (1.8) and (1.7) into (1.6). We get

$$Y_t = (b + c)\, Y_{t-1} - bY_{t-2}\,. \tag{1.9}$$

Hence, the system can be shown to generate a time series for Y (and for C and I) given two initial values of Y. This is a single difference equation of the second order (i.e., its longest lag). It can be solved by finding the roots $(\lambda_1 \lambda_2)$ of

$$\lambda^2 - (b + c)\lambda + b = 0 \tag{1.10}$$

which are then substituted into

$$Y_t = A\lambda_1^t + B\lambda_2^t \tag{1.11}$$

where A and B are chosen to satisfy the initial conditions (see Baumol, 1959, pp. 169–174). The time paths generated by this system will not be explosive (with or without fluctuations) provided the roots are less than the modulus of one. This is called a stable system. Most economists believe that the economic system is stable and hence tend to ignore the possibility of unstable system. Certainly very little econometric work has been attempted without the assumption of stability being either explicitly or implicitly made. If one has to deal with large systems the difference equation corresponding to (1.9) tends to be of a higher order than 2 and the characteristic equation corresponding to (1.10) involves more than 2 roots. As usual it becomes more convenient to work in matrix algebra for general systems. In this case the advantage is that by working in matrix terms we can always reduce the lag to one period. Consider (1.6)–(1.8) again, substituting (1.6) into (1.7) and (1.8) we get

$$C_t = cC_{t-1} + cI_{t-1} \tag{1.12}$$

$$I_t = bC_{t-1} + bI_{t-1} - b(C_{t-2} + I_{t-2})\,. \tag{1.13}$$

Let

$$Z_t = C_{t-1} + I_{t-1}$$

then

$$C_t = cC_{t-1} + cI_{t-1}$$

$$I_t = bC_{t-1} + bI_{t-1} - bZ_{t-1}$$

$$Z_t = C_{t-1} + I_{t-1}$$

or

$$\begin{bmatrix} C \\ I \\ Z \end{bmatrix} = \begin{bmatrix} c & c & 0 \\ b & b & -b \\ 1 & 1 & 0 \end{bmatrix} \begin{bmatrix} C \\ I \\ Z \end{bmatrix}_{t-1}$$

Let

$$\mathbf{y} = \begin{bmatrix} C \\ I \\ Z \end{bmatrix}$$

$$\mathbf{A} = \begin{bmatrix} c & c & 0 \\ b & b & -b \\ 1 & 1 & 0 \end{bmatrix}$$

then $\mathbf{y}_t = \mathbf{A}\mathbf{y}_{t-1}$.

The roots of this difference equation will be the roots of the characteristic equation $|\mathbf{A} - \lambda\mathbf{I}| = 0$ i.e. the roots are the eigenvalues of the matrix $\mathbf{A}$. In this case $|\mathbf{A} - \lambda\mathbf{I}| = 0$ reduces to $\lambda^2 - (b+c)\lambda + b = 0$. We have shown how to reduce a recursive difference equation of any order to a system of first order equations of the form $y = Ay_{t-1}$ and hence how to find the roots which will determine $\mathbf{y}_t = \mathbf{A}\mathbf{y}_{t-1}$ whether it is explosive or not.

1.4. The nature of macro models

Although the nature of cause would suggest that we only need to consider recursive systems, most macro econometric models are a mixture of a simultaneity and recursiveness. One justification for this stems from the form of the data available for estimation. Since observations are seldom collected on a basis which reflects exactly the decision lags embodied in our functions, it is necessary to misspecify the model in order to make it compatible with the data. Thus we might feel that a lag of one month is the correct lag to have in a certain function, yet we only have annual data available. In this case we have to assume a lag of zero or of 12 (original) periods. In most cases a lag of zero is assumed and the result is a simultaneous model with lagged endogenous variables. The following is such a model

$$Y_t = C_t + I_t + G_t$$

$$C_t = c_1 Y_t + c_2 Y_{t-1}$$

$$I_t = b_1 [Y_t - Y_{t-1}] + b_2 [Y_{t-1} - Y_{t-2}]$$

which can be written as

$$\begin{bmatrix} 1 & -1 & -1 \\ -c_1 & 1 & 0 \\ -b_1 & 0 & 1 \end{bmatrix} \begin{bmatrix} Y_t \\ C_t \\ I_t \end{bmatrix} + \begin{bmatrix} 0 & 0 & 0 \\ -c_2 & 0 & 0 \\ b_1 - b_2 & 0 & 0 \end{bmatrix} \begin{bmatrix} Y_{t-1} \\ C_{t-1} \\ I_{t-1} \end{bmatrix}$$

$$+ \begin{bmatrix} 0 & 0 & 0 \\ 0 & 0 & 0 \\ b_2 & 0 & 0 \end{bmatrix} \begin{bmatrix} Y_{t-2} \\ C_{t-2} \\ I_{t-2} \end{bmatrix} + \begin{bmatrix} -1 \\ 0 \\ 0 \end{bmatrix} G_t = \begin{bmatrix} 0 \\ 0 \\ 0 \end{bmatrix} . \qquad (1.14)$$

From (1.14) it is easy to see that the general form of linear macro models is

$$\mathbf{B}\mathbf{y}_t + \mathbf{C}_1 \mathbf{y}_{t-1} + \mathbf{C}_2 \mathbf{y}_{t-2} + \ldots + \mathbf{C}_n \mathbf{y}_{t-n} + \mathbf{N}\mathbf{z}_t = \mathbf{0} \qquad (1.15)$$

where $\mathbf{B}$, $\mathbf{C}_i$, and $\mathbf{N}$ are matrices of parameters and $\mathbf{y}_t$, and $\mathbf{z}_t$ are vectors of endogenous and exogenous variables. If in (1.15) $\mathbf{B}$ is triangular (zeros below the main diagonal) the system is recursive; (1.14) is obviously not recursive. Most macro models are of this form and can be interpreted as we have done, i.e., in terms of an approximation to a recursive system. An alternative intepretation is that they represent an equilibrium model, i.e., a model where certain economic reactions are assumed to have been completed. Assuming $\mathbf{B}^{-1}$ exists it is possible to solve for the current endogenous variables, i.e.

$$\mathbf{y}_t + \mathbf{B}^{-1}\mathbf{C}_1\mathbf{y}_{t-1} + \mathbf{B}^{-1}\mathbf{C}_2\mathbf{y}_{t-2} + \ldots + \mathbf{B}^{-1}\mathbf{C}_n\mathbf{y}_{t-n} + \mathbf{B}^{-1}\mathbf{N}\mathbf{z}_t = \mathbf{0}\,. \quad (1.16)$$

To perform this manipulation, however, tends to pass over the difficulties of interpretation of the model. If this is an equilibrium model, for there to be much chance of it being in equilibrium, one would imagine it must be a stable equilibrium. This puts extra restrictions on the $\mathbf{B}$ matrix over and above those necessary for $\mathbf{B}^{-1}$ to exist. The same thing seems to apply if one considers this model to be an approximation for a recursive system. However, little attention has been paid to the restrictions on $\mathbf{B}$, although most model builders assume that their models are stable for the purpose of estimation. Eq. (1.16) can be viewed as a set of difference equations whose stability can be analysed in a similar manner to that of the previous section.

1.5. The stochastic term

1.5.1

The econometrician can never hope to include all the factors affecting any variable or set of variables in his function. It is for this reason that he appeals to the concept of probability and assumes that the total effect of all the variables not appearing in his model can be approximated by a random variable. Thus, to the general model should be added a vector of random variables, i.e.,

$$\mathbf{B}\mathbf{y}_t + \mathbf{C}_1\mathbf{y}_{t-1} + \mathbf{C}_2\mathbf{y}_{t-2} + \ldots + \mathbf{C}_n\mathbf{y}_{t-n} + \mathbf{N}\mathbf{z}_t = \mathbf{u}_t \quad (1.17)$$

where $\mathbf{u}_t$ is a vector of random variables.

The assumptions one makes about the behaviour of the disturbance terms are very important when considering how to estimate the model since such phenomenon as correlation over time or between equations can have considerable effect on the properties of the estimators. The assumption of no correlation between the disturbance terms $\mathbf{u}_t$ and the exogenous and lagged endogenous variables lead to a special role in the statistical estimation process for the form

$$\mathbf{y}_t = -\mathbf{B}^{-1}\mathbf{C}_1\mathbf{y}_{t-1} - \mathbf{B}^{-1}\mathbf{C}_2\mathbf{y}_{t-2} - \dots - \mathbf{B}^{-1}\mathbf{C}_n\mathbf{y}_{t-n} - \mathbf{B}^{-1}\mathbf{N}\mathbf{z}_t + \mathbf{B}^{-1}\mathbf{u}_t \tag{1.18}$$

or

$$\mathbf{y}_t = \mathbf{\Pi}\mathbf{x}_t + \mathbf{v}_t \tag{1.19}$$

where

$\mathbf{x}_t = [\mathbf{y}_{t-n}\mathbf{y}_{t-2} \dots \mathbf{z}_t]$

$\mathbf{v}_t = \mathbf{B}^{-1}\mathbf{u}_t$

as it is usually written. This is called the reduced form and it shows all endogenous variables written as a function of predetermined, i.e., lagged endogenous and exogenous variables and disturbance terms. Perhaps most importantly it can be shown, given certain assumptions concerning the disturbances $\mathbf{u}_t$, that for a sample of values of $\mathbf{y}$ and $\mathbf{x}$ there exists only one possible $\mathbf{\Pi}$ matrix. In other words, the values of $\mathbf{\Pi}$ are always identified. Stronger conditions are necessary for the same to be said of the elements of $\mathbf{B}$, $\mathbf{C}_i$ and $\mathbf{N}$. The first methods developed for the estimation of simultaneous models, were in fact based on the principle of maximising the probability of the joint occurrence of the sample values of $\mathbf{x}$ and $\mathbf{y}$ subject to the conditions that $\mathbf{B}$, $\mathbf{C}_i$ and $\mathbf{N}$ were exactly identified. It was in connection with the concept of identification that the Cowles Commission authors defined the words 'model' and 'structure'. Essentially a structure is a model with the numerical constants of both the stochastic and systematic parts specified. However, the terms are not generally used as precisely as this.

1.5.2

The introduction of the stochastic terms complicates the stability discussion since the interaction of the disturbance terms has to be taken into account. Chow (1968) has used spectral techniques to show that the stability of the whole model can, in general, not be decided on the parameters of the systematic part alone. Thus, the use of estimated coefficients of systematic parameters, though common practice, is dubious. It would seem that this complication does not affect the use of estimated econometric models to analyse the effects of a policy change, since the random drawings would be the same with or without the policy change.

1.6. The uses of econometric macro models

1.6.1

Assuming that it is feasible to obtain 'good' estimates of the parameters of a macro model, let us consider how the framework we have considered fits the original questions with which we started. Let us assume we are at the beginning of a period, for simplicity say a year, and that we have a model, or rather a structure, relating this period's policy aims to current policy instruments, other exogenous variables and all lagged variables. If we wish to ascertain the expected effects in the coming period of changes in certain policies we can look at the reduced form of the structure. We can also take into account any forecasts of other exogenous variables that we may have if it is felt that these will not be constant, provided these exogenous variables are specified in the systematic part of the model. The first period effects of policies have been designated impact multipliers (see Goldberger, 1959). It will be readily appreciated that forecasting without reference to policy instruments is exactly the same. For instance, say a businessman wishes to know what the level of consumption is likely to be in the coming year and we have some idea of what government policy and other exogenous variables will be, then the reduced form will again provide the answer.

1.6.2

Forecasting (or policy analysis) is not necessarily limited to the current period. Often one wishes to forecast a number of periods ahead. In this case it will be necessary to distinguish lagged endogenous variables from the exogenous and solve the difference equation embodied in the model. In many cases, because of the size of econometric models, the difference equation is iterated on a computer rather than solved analytically. Either way it will be possible to generate time paths of the endogenous variables given the values of the exogenous variables. These delayed reactions can be considerably more important than the immediate impacts.

1.6.3

So far we have only considered economic policy by looking at the effects on the system given certain policy changes. It is conceivable that by trial and error we may stumble upon the optimal policy. Theil (1964) has formulated an analytical approach for deriving optimal policies using econometric models. In order to arrive at optimal decisions it is necessary to have some objective function which is to be maximised. This, in the general form, would be a complete welfare function for the policy maker reflecting the utility derived from all possible combinations of policy aims and instruments. However, less general forms can be specified, for instance, in Theil's actual example he minimises the sum of squared deviations of the actual level of the variables from some previously specified desired level. Given an objective function relating utilities, instruments and aims, the reduced form of an econometric model can be seen as a set of linear constraints which the aims and instruments must satisfy. Thus the problem reduces to that of finding a constrained maximum. The econometric model that Theil uses in his example was first presented by Klein (1950).

In order to illustrate the ideas of this introductory chapter we also shall use this simple model. However, before doing that, the reader may wonder why econometricians bother about estimating the structural parameters as opposed to the reduced form parameters when the uses declared above only involve the reduced form. The reasons have been suggested earlier, but no harm will be done by repeating them here. The a priori information regarding the size or sign of a parameter gleaned from economic theory will almost always refer to the structural parameter: thus, if we wish to use this information, we usually need to concentrate on the structural parameters. The use of a priori information may be explicit or, more often, implicit. Implicit use of a priori information is made, for instance, when regressions are discarded because of 'unreasonable' estimates. A further reason stems from this one. Consider a situation where one wishes to forecast and one knows that although a certain parameter has been constant throughout the sample period, it is likely to change in the forecast period. If the parameter is a reduced form parameter, then one does not need to know the structural parameters to adjust the forecast. However, such knowledge usually refers to a structural parameter. If one only has estimates of the reduced form parameters, it will probably be impossible to adjust the forecast stemming from the estimated model.

1.7. **An example, Klein I**

1.7.1

In this chapter we shall not try to survey Klein (1950), but rather use his first model as an illustration of the ideas of this chapter. In doing so we shall probably give a distorted picture of Klein's own approach, i.e., we shall not consider how he derived his model from micro economic ideas, nor shall we refer to his other models.

Let us suppose that we are interested in three major policy aims, the level of aggregate consumption, C, as an indicator of present wellbeing; the level of investment, I, as an indicator of probable growth, and, for the sake of social justice, some distribution of income measure. Some idea of this last concept can be obtained by consideration of the level of profits π and the level of wages W. Furthermore, suppose that the government is prepared to alter not only its own incomings (i.e., the level of tax receipts, T) but also its outgoing in the form of government expenditure, G, and the wage payments to government employees, W_2.

1.7.2

Keynesian theory suggests that consumption is related to people's incomes; thus we can write in the most simple linear form

$$C = \alpha_0 + \alpha_1 W + \alpha_2 \pi + u_1 \,. \tag{1.20}$$

Notice that in this form Klein has preferred not to assume that profit earners and wage earners have the same propensity to consume which he would have done if he had written the function as

$$C = \alpha_0 + \alpha_1 (\pi + W) + u_1 \,.$$

The second equation he postulated is that investment is determined by present and past profits relative to the stock of capital. Heuristically this implies that the higher the profitability of capital, the more businessmen will invest. The second equation is

$$I = \beta_0 + \beta_1 \pi + \beta_2 \pi_{-1} + \beta_3 K_{-1} + u_2 \tag{1.21}$$

where π_{-1} is profits in the last period and K_{-1} capital stock at the end of the last period. The third equation arises from the equality between the wage rate and the marginal product of labour. In it the wage bill is related to the current period's output, last period's output and a time trend. The trend is included to take account of the growing strength of trade union, whereas the other variables stem from an implicit production function

$$W = \gamma_0 + \gamma_1 Y + \gamma_2 Y_{-1} + \gamma_0 t + u_2 \,. \tag{1.22}$$

To these three behavioural equations are added three definitional equations. Total output must equal total expenditure. Total income, which equals total output is also the sum of profits and wages. Finally, investment equals the change in the capital stock. Thus

$$C + I + G = Y \tag{1.23}$$

$$\pi + W = Y \tag{1.24}$$

$$\Delta K = I \tag{1.25}$$

1.7.3

The model as it stands, however, would not allow us to consider the effect of a change in the government's wage bill, since only the total wage bill is determined and this is endogenous. Furthermore, neither would it allow analysis of taxation changes. To correct these faults the two type of wages are introduced as are indirect business taxes. Direct taxation should be taken into account in the consumption function, but because of data limitations this is not done. This illustrates a point that often occurs in applied econometrics, namely, that we often have to adapt our models to fit the form of the data available. This is sad but usually unavoidable. After these modifications the model is

$$C = \alpha_0 + \alpha_1(W_1 + W_2) + \alpha_2\pi + u_1 \tag{1.26}$$

$$I = \beta_0 + \beta_1\pi + \beta_1\pi_{-1} + \beta_3 K_{-1} + u_2 \tag{1.27}$$

$$W_1 = \gamma_0 + \gamma_1(Y + T - W_2) + \gamma_2(Y + T - W_2)_{-1} + \gamma_3 t + u_3 \tag{1.28}$$

$$Y + T = C + I + G \tag{1.29}$$

$$Y = W_1 + W_2 + \pi \tag{1.30}$$

$$\Delta K = I\,, \tag{1.31}$$

All the modifications are obvious except for (1.28). This equation substitutes $(Y + T - W_2)$ for Y in (1.22). From (1.29), $(Y + T - W_2)$ equals $C + I + G - W_2$, i.e., total expenditure on goods, i.e., the receipts of the private business sector.

1.7.4

Although this system is clearly a simultaneous system, it is instructive to trace through a possible candidate for the underlying recursive system to the model (see Section 1.4). The recursive monthly system implied in the Klein I model could look like this. The lag of 12 periods reflects a lag of one period in the Klein model.

$$C = \alpha_0 + \alpha_1(W_1 + W_2)_{-1} + \alpha_2\pi_{-1} + u_1$$

$$I = \beta_1 + \beta_1\pi_{-1} + \beta_2\pi_{-12} + \beta_3K_{-12} + u_2$$

$$W_1 = \gamma_0 + \gamma_1(Y + T - W_2) + \gamma_2(Y + T - W_2)_{-12} + u_3$$

$$Y + T = C + I + G$$

$$\pi = Y - W_1 + W_2$$

$$\Delta K = I\,.$$

This recursive model is represented in flow chart form in fig. 1.1. From this it can be seen very clearly that π, K, C, I, W_1, Y are endogenous variables, since all of their boxes have an input, whereas G, T, and W_2 have no input and are

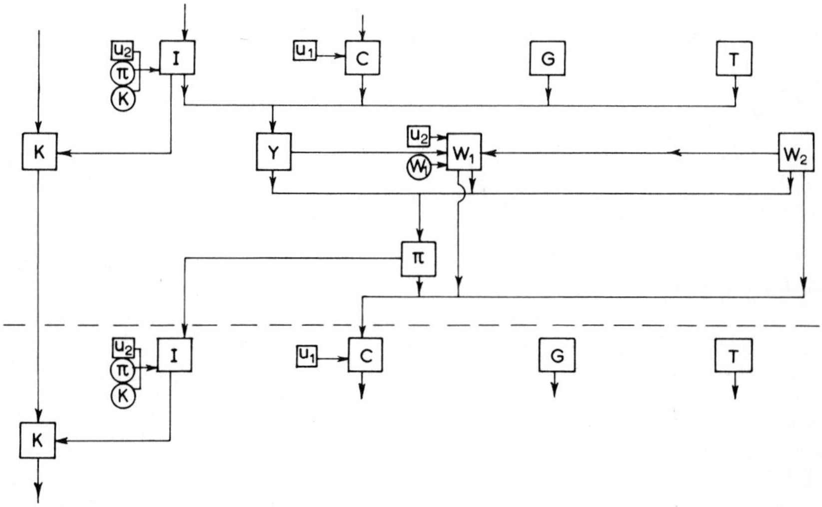

Fig. 1.1. Flow chart of a possible monthly recursive system for Klein's model. ○, indicates variables from 12 periods previous; - - -, indicates end of time period.

therefore exogenous. Similarly, u_1, u_2 and u_3 can be considered exogenous. It will be noticed that disturbance terms only enter three equations. This is because the final three equations are exact definitional equations. Thus all final expenditure can be classed as output; profits are defined as a residual left out of total output after wages have been paid; and implicitly assuming depreciation to be zero, the change in the capital stock equals investment.

1.7.5

With only annual data available, it would seem reasonable to approximate this recursive system by the Klein model. However, once the contraction has taken place the distinction between endogenous and exogenous becomes much less obvious. Klein's model can be thought of as a set of six equations with perhaps seven endogenous variables. Notice that T could be considered endogenous. The consideration of the recursive model enables us to dismiss this interpretation as not meaningful.

1.7.6

Using a sample of 22 annual prewar observations, Klein estimated the parameter of this model by three different methods; full information maximum likelihood, limited information maximum likelihood and ordinary least squares. We shall consider only the FIML estimates which are

$$C = 16.78 + 0.02\pi + 0.23\pi_{-1} + 0.80(W_1 + W_2) + u_1'$$

$$I = 17.79 + 0.23\pi + 0.55\pi_{-1} - 0.15K_{-1} + u_2'$$

$$W_1 = 1.60 + 0.42(Y + T - W_2) + 0.16(Y + T - W_2)_{-1} + 0.13(t - 1931) + u_3'$$

$$Y + T = C + I + G$$

$$Y = \pi + W_1 + W_2$$

$$\Delta K = I\,.$$

1.7.7

Theil (1964, p. 86) has calculated the reduced form coefficients for this structure and these are reproduced in table 1.1. From them we can see what the immediate expected effect of a unit increase in government spending,

Table 1.1
Numerical values of the reduced-form coefficients of Klein's model I.

	Constant term	Current instruments			Current noninstrum. exogenous:	Lagged instruments	
		W_2	T	G	$t-1931$	$(W_2)_{-1}$	T_{-1}
C	41.816	0.666	−0.188	0.671	0.155	−0.189	0.189
π	38.059	0.224	−1.281	1.119	−0.052	0.063	−0.063
W_1	30.338	−0.162	−0.204	0.811	0.195	−0.237	0.237
I	26.581	−0.052	−0.296	0.259	−0.012	0.015	−0.015
Y	68.397	0.614	−1.484	−1.930	0.143	−0.174	0.174
K	26.581	−0.052	−0.296	0.259	−0.012	0.015	−0.015

	Lagged endogenous			Structural disturbances		
	π_{-1}	Y_{-1}	K_{-1}	u_C	u_I	u_W
C	0.743	0.189	−0.098	1.671	0.671	1.148
π	0.863	−0.063	−0.164	1.119	1.119	−0.386
W_1	0.626	0.237	−0.119	0.811	0.811	1.445
I	0.746	−0.015	−0.184	0.259	1.259	−0.089
Y	1.489	0.174	−0.283	1.930	1.930	1.059
K	0.746	−0.015	0.816	0.259	1.259	−0.089

which amounts to a 10% increase, would be on any of the endogenous variables. Consumption, for instance, would rise 0.671 above what it would have done, investment by 0.259 and income 1.930. Calculated at the average of the sample period, the respective elasticities are 0.122, 1.869 and 0.323. The reduced form of this model has a special form which enables us to look at the dynamic properties with very little extra effort.

Rearranging the reduced form equations we can write

$$\begin{bmatrix} \pi \\ Y \\ K \\ C \\ W_1 \\ I \end{bmatrix} = \begin{bmatrix} 0.863 & -0.063 & 0.164 & 0 & 0 & 0 \\ 1.489 & 0.174 & -0.283 & 0 & 0 & 0 \\ 0.746 & -0.015 & 0.816 & 0 & 0 & 0 \\ 0.743 & 0.189 & -0.098 & 0 & 0 & 0 \\ 0.626 & 0.237 & 0.119 & 0 & 0 & 0 \\ 0.746 & -0.015 & -0.184 & 0 & 0 & 0 \end{bmatrix} \begin{bmatrix} \pi \\ Y \\ K \\ C \\ W_1 \\ I \end{bmatrix}_{-1} + [\mathbf{Z}] \tag{1.32}$$

where **Z** reflects the effects of exogenous and stochastic variables. This system can be partitioned into two sets of equations

$$\begin{bmatrix} \pi \\ Y \\ K \end{bmatrix} = \begin{bmatrix} 0.863 & -0.063 & 0.164 \\ 1.489 & 0.174 & -0.283 \\ 0.746 & 0.015 & 0.816 \end{bmatrix} \begin{bmatrix} \pi \\ Y \\ K \end{bmatrix}_{-1} + \mathbf{Z}_1 \tag{1.33}$$

and

$$\begin{bmatrix} C \\ W \\ I \end{bmatrix} = \begin{bmatrix} 0.743 & 0.189 & -0.098 \\ 0.626 & 0.237 & 0.119 \\ 0.746 & -0.015 & -0.184 \end{bmatrix} \begin{bmatrix} \pi \\ Y \\ K \end{bmatrix}_{-1} + \mathbf{Z}_2 \tag{1.34}$$

where $\mathbf{Z}_1$ and $\mathbf{Z}_2$ represent the effects of exogenous and stochastic variables.

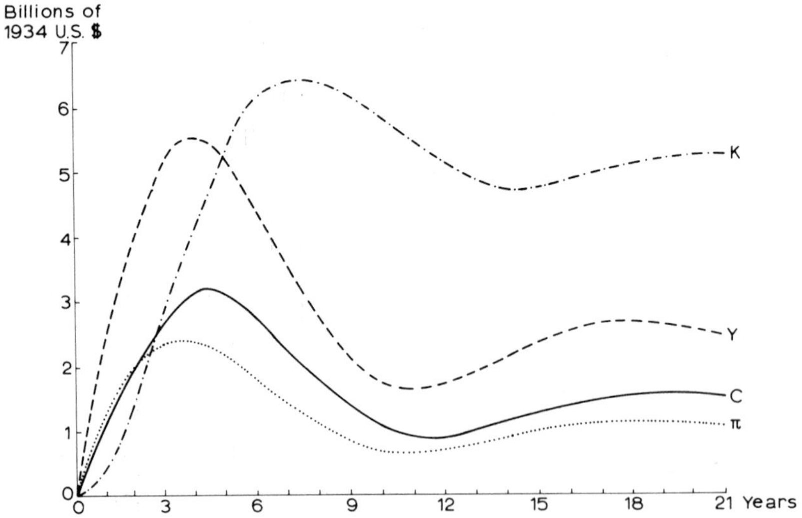

Fig. 1.2. The increase in K, Y, C, and π stemming from a shift of one unit to a new maintained level of G.

Hence the set of simultaneous difference equations (1.33) will determine the time paths of the endogenous variables and the roots of

$$\begin{vmatrix} 0.863-x & -0.063 & 0.164 \\ 1.489 & 0.174-x & -0.283 \\ 0.746 & 0.015 & 0.816-x \end{vmatrix} = 0$$

are required to test the stability of the model (see Section 1.5.2). This characteristic equation can be written as

$$x^3 - 1.853\,x^2 + 1.2082\,x - 0.23 = 0$$

and its roots are

$$\lambda_1 = 0.321$$

$$\lambda_2 = 0.770 - 0.360\,i$$

$$\lambda_3 = 0.770 + 0.360\,i \; .$$

Hence the time paths are fluctuating but damped.

1.7.8

To derive the general solution we need to take account of the initial conditions. However, more often than not we are only interested in the first few periods of the time path, rather than the whole of it. This is often simpler to do by iteration. These truncated paths give the answers to the second question on policy that we posed at the start of this section, namely, what will be the effect over time of a maintained unit increase in government expenditure on income and consumption. These effects can be seen from fig. 1.2 which shows the effects on four endogenous variables for the first 20 years after the change. From this it can be seen that the first period's impact gives very little indication of the longer run effects. A policy maker ignoring these latter consequences of his policies could produce effects which were far from those he desired.

1.7.9

So far we have only considered a change in one instrument but we could use the same techniques for a combination of policies. The problem of finding an optimal policy is more difficult and discussion of it here would sidetrack us too far. Fortunately, Theil (1964) has used this very model as an example of his technique for finding the optimal policies so that the interested reader can easily pursue this aspect of Klein's model there.

1.8. Conclusion

In this introductory chapter we have shown how macro models are set up to answer certain questions and how they can be manipulated to achieve these answers. A simple econometric model was introduced to illustrate these points. We could now proceed to review the many large scale models that are available but a more enlightening approach is to consider some of the individual sectors which play a large part in such models. By taking the latter course we will see the relationship between economic theory and econometric models much more clearly.

CHAPTER 2

CONSUMPTION

2.1. Introduction

Economists have long been interested in consumption since the satisfaction of the wants of individuals is one of the major aims of any economic system. However, following the tradition established by Keynes, considerable interest has been shown in consumption as a component of aggregate demand in models aimed at explaining fluctuations in aggregate income and employment. Thus if a policy maker wishes to attain a certain allocation of goods or to stabilise the economy, the economist must be able to produce for him models, which explain how consumers decide on their total expenditure and how they allocate it to different goods. Although these two decisions are related, economists have found it convenient to consider them separately, i.e., they have postulated models involving an individual taking two decisions, i.e., a savings decision, which determines his total expenditure and an allocation decision which determines the pattern of his expenditure on the many different commodities available to him. In spite of the fact that the economist makes postulates concerning the behaviour of an individual it is with concepts of a more aggregate nature he is usually concerned, i.e., the market demands for particular commodities or the level of aggregate saving, because the relevant problems are usually aggregative in nature and so are the data available. Quite obviously most econometric studies which start from a theory of the individual involve considerable aggregation problems. Theil (1954) among others has studied the effects of aggregation and produced some results, however, enormous problems still remain. In some econometric studies these problems are faced but more often they are stated and then ignored. These problems occur not only with functions aggregated over goods, e.g. consumption functions, but also with functions aggregated over individuals, e.g. market demand functions for specific goods. These two types of functions reflect the two decisions which we assume a consumer makes. This is the important distinction that has to be made in consumption analysis rather than a macro–micro distinction. Indeed, how individuals split their expenditure between durable and non-durable goods may be a very important decision for macro economics. In this chapter we shall deal with econometric studies relating to the savings decision, i.e., the consumption function, leaving those concerned with the allocation decision, i.e., demand functions, to the following chapter.

2.2. Early consumption functions

We have already indicated in the previous chapter the role played by aggregate consumption in macro models designed to help the management of the economy. The most obvious determinant of aggregate consumption is the level of aggregate disposable income. Assuming a simple linear form and applying least squares regression we can produce a consumption function. Furthermore such a consumption function may appear statistically significant and economically meaningful. Indeed, such functions were estimated in the early forties with the data then available. Unfortunately, when these functions were used for forecasting post World War II consumption in the U.S. very poor forecasts were obtained. Davis (1952) has analysed the predictions from a number of consumption functions fitted to 1929–1940 annual data. The prediction errors for three such functions are presented in table 2.1 along with the 'naive' no change prediction errors and the sample period R^2.

Table 2.1
Errors of prediction from three consumption functions and three naive models.

		Prediction errors (billions of current dollars)				
	R^2	1946	1947	1948	1949	1950
Undeflated variables						
CF	0.994	– 4.1	–13.8	–10.0	–14.0	–12.2
Naive		–23.8	–18.7	–12.3	– 2.3	–13.4
Deflated for price change						
CF	0.986	– 4.9	–12.9	– 8.8	–12.9	–11.9
Naive		–13.4	2.4	0.5	– 4.1	–11.5
Deflated for price and population changed						
CF	0.986	– 4.4	–11.9	– 7.5	–11.0	– 9.6
Naive		12.0	5.7	3.5	– 1.0	– 8.3

Detailed discussion of Davis's results would be out of place here but table 2.1 does indicate that good statistical fits are no guarantee of good forecasts and that we should doubt the usefulness of the simple Keynesian function. Doubt was also thrown on these simple consumption functions by data produced by Kuznets (1942). These indicated that there was no tendency for the average propensity to consume to fall over a long period, as would be the case with the simple consumption functions with a positive intercept. The history of early econometric consumption functions should be a warning to take great care in accepting and using apparently successful functions. The care referred to is consideration of the economic theory and checking whether the results are consistent with all data.

2.3. The theory

When we review the economics of saving, a number of competing hypotheses present themselves. The absolute income hypothesis, i.e., measured consumption is a function of the absolute level of measured income, is the one suggested by Keynes. In its modern version other variables would be added such that it fits all the relevant data. The relative income hypothesis was developed by Duesenberry (1949) and it states that an individual's consumption depends on his position in the income distribution. In the mid-fifties Modigliani and Brumberg (1954) attempted to derive the consumption function from utility analysis and developed a theory of saving which showed how important total life income is for a rational individual under certainty. Friedman (1957) produced a similar model indicating the importance of 'permanent' income. Both the 'permanent income' and the 'life cycle' hypotheses lead to some interesting thoughts. For instance, given that consumption is determined by some long run mechanism does it make sense to try to explain short run, e.g. monthly or even quarterly variations in consumption by systematic factors? Should consumption be measured exclusive of durables? Purchases of consumer durables net of depreciation may be thought of as savings. However, it should be remembered that purchases of durables are income generating and need to be explained if we are concerned with stabilisation policy.

The appeal of these hypotheses is reduced slightly when uncertainty is introduced for further motives for saving become apparent. More recently Spiro (1962) and Ball and Drake (1964) have proposed a wealth hypothesis based on the assumption that individuals like to keep a fixed ratio of consumption to non-human wealth. However, wealth is not a homogeneous commodity and Watts and Tobin (1960) suggest that individuals try to keep the different types of wealth in the same proportions. It could be that certain types of wealth have different effects on consumption than others since capital markets are not perfect. If this is so our savings decision becomes involved with what we might call a wealth portfolio decision. So far little work has been done on these aspects and so we will not consider them.

2.3.1. *The relative income hypothesis*

Duesenberry's (1949) starting point is the classical theory of demand which he believes is deficient for analysis of demand through time because tastes cannot be considered fixed. He puts forward ideas on how habits are formed and new goods accepted in a consumption oriented society. Basic to his ideas are the concepts of interdependence, i.e., one consumer's utility is affected by the consumption of others, and asymmetry, i.e., getting used to having goods is psychologically easier than getting used to doing without them. More formally he states that instead of a consumer maximising a utility function

$$U = F(C_1, C_2, ..., C_n, \quad A_1, A_2, ..., A_n)$$

where C_i is consumption in period i, and A_i is assets in period i.

He maximises

$$U = f\left(\frac{C_1}{R}, \frac{C_2}{R}, ..., \frac{C_n}{R}, \quad \frac{A_1}{R}, \frac{A_2}{R}, ..., \frac{A_n}{R}\right)$$

where R is a linear combination of all other people's consumption, subject to the constraints imposed by actual and expected incomes, assets and interest rates. This results in a consumption function involving current income, current assets, expected future (non interest) income, expected future interest rates and current consumption of other people, i.e.,

$$\frac{C}{R} = f\left(\frac{Y_1}{R}, \frac{Y_2}{R}, ..., \frac{Y_n}{R}, \quad \frac{A_1}{R}, \frac{A_2}{R}, ..., \frac{A_n}{R}, \quad r_1, r_2, ..., r_n\right).$$

Comparing two equilibrium positions, one with a higher per capita income but with (1) the income distribution, (2) interest rates and expected future rates, (3) the relation between actual current income and expected future income, (4) the population age distribution, all the same, he shows that the ratios Y_i/R and A_i/R are the same and hence so is C/R. In fact, what has happened is that all present and future incomes have increased by a factor k say, and with them all assets, and so all individuals have increased their current consumption by k. Thus the aggregate savings ratio, i.e., savings divided by income is the same, even though aggregate income has increased. This is Duesenberry's first conclusion, namely, that the savings ratio is independent of the absolute level of income. The other important conclusion that he draws from his discussion of interdependent utility functions is that people at the upper end of the income scale have higher savings ratios than those at the lower end. This then is the relative income hypothesis.

All of this discussion has been in terms of equilibrium situations and hence does not refer to cyclical changes in the savings ratio. Turning to the cyclical changes in the savings ratio, Duesenberry considers different sections of the community. The rich in a depression suffer a loss of income, but their expected incomes will probably not fall as much. This, together with the influence of habit and the desire to maintain living standards, should mean that their consumption does not fall as much as income. Thus, in a depression, the last highest level of income is important in determining consumption. Depending on the level of past accumulated savings, this level of consumption will be maintained for some years. Poor people and those moving in and out of employment will find it less easy to maintain their standard of living at the previous peak. Duesenberry's conclusion is that 'the income or consumption of the last cyclical peak will carry a special and very heavy weight in determining consumption at a given (lower) level of income' although 'in principle a weighted average of all the incomes from the peak year to the current year ought to be used'.

I.e.,

$$C = f\left(\sum_{i=0}^{n} w_i Y_{t-i}\right) \tag{2.1}$$

where Y_{t-n} is the last peak year's income.

$$0 \leqslant w_i \leqslant 1$$

$$\sum_{i=0}^{n} w_i = 1 \, .$$

2.3.2. The life cycle hypothesis

Modigliani and Brumberg (1954) and Ando and Modigliani (1963) consider a consumer with a life span of L periods of which N are earning periods and M are retirement periods. The consumer knows his future income with certainty and his aim is to spread his income throughout his life according to a utility function

$$u = u(c_t, c_{t+1}, ..., c_L)$$

where c_t is consumption, excluding durables, in tth year of his earning span. Assuming the rate of interest is not expected to change, the consumer in his tth year has to choose his set of

$$c_i (i = t, t+1, ..., L)$$

subject to

$$a_{t-1} + y_t + \sum_{\tau=t+1}^{N} \frac{y_\tau^e}{(1+r)^{\tau-t}} = \sum_{\tau=t}^{L} \frac{c_\tau}{(1+r)^{\tau-t}} \tag{2.2}$$

where

a_{t-1} is the value of the consumer's assets at the beginning of the tth period;
y_t is the non-property income in period t;
y_τ^e is non-property income expected in period τ;
c_τ is consumption in period τ.

Modigliani and Brumberg assume that the utility function is such that the consumer keeps his pattern of optimal consumption through the years the same, regardless of the size of his income, i.e., $c_{t+1}^* = k_1 c_t^*$, $c_{t+2}^* = k_2 c_t^*$, etc. where c_t^* represents the optimal consumption in period t. (A sufficient condition for this is that the utility function is homogeneous to any positive degree.) Hence substituting into (2.2) we can write,

$$a_{t-1} + y_t + \sum_{\tau=t+1}^{N} \frac{y_\tau^e}{(1+r)^{\tau-t}} = c_t^* \sum_{\tau=t}^{L} \frac{k_{\tau-t}}{(1+r)^{\tau-t}} \tag{2.3}$$

$$\therefore c_t^* = \gamma_t \left(a_{t-1} + y_t + \sum_{\tau=t+1}^{N} \frac{y_\tau^e}{(1+r)^{\tau-t}} \right) \tag{2.4}$$

$$= \gamma_t a_{t-1} + \gamma_t y_t + \gamma_t (N-T) y_t^e \tag{2.5}$$

where

$$y_t^e = \frac{1}{N-T} \sum_{\tau=t+1}^{N} \frac{y_\tau^e}{(1+r)^{\tau-t}}$$

Thus we have a function explaining the planned (desired, optimal, normal or permanent) consumption of an individual in his tth period of earning. Aggregation of (2.5) over all individuals aged t gives

$$C_t^* = \sum c_t^* = \sum \gamma_t a_{t-1} + \sum \gamma_t y_t + \sum \gamma_t (N-T) y_t^e$$

$$= \alpha A_{t-1} + \beta Y_{t_L} + \delta (N-T) Y_{t_L}^e \qquad (2.6)$$

where

Y_{t_L} is aggregate non-property income of individuals aged t;
A_{t-1} is the aggregate net worth of individuals aged t;
α is the weighted average of the γ_t when the asset values are used as weights;
β is the weighted average of the γ_t when the y_t are used as weights,
δ is the weighted average of the γ_t when the y_t^e are used as the weights.

Aggregate consumption in any one period is the total consumption of all ages, thus it is necessary to aggregate over ages. Unfortunately, assets and income are correlated with age and so the aggregation process is not easy. However, if α, β and δ, the age structure and the distribution of income are constant through time then we can write

$$C^* = \alpha' A_{-1} + \beta' Y_L + \delta' Y_L^e \qquad (2.7)$$

and α' β' δ' will be constants, while
C^* is aggregate optimal consumption;
A_{-1} is aggregate net worth;
Y_L is aggregate non-property income;
Y_L^e is aggregate expected non-property income.

2.3.3. *The permanent income hypothesis*

Friedman also assumes a homogeneous utility function and a resources constraint and as a result finds permanent consumption has a proportional relationship to resources, i.e.,

$$c_p = k(u, i)iW = k(u, i)y_p \tag{2.8}$$

where

c_p is permanent consumption;
W is level of resources;
i is the rate of interest;
u is variable which will vary with the age and family composition of individuals;
y_p is permanent income.

In the case of certainty the life cycle and the permanent income hypotheses amount to the same thing. When the future is uncertain, however, there is an asymmetry with regards to time, for the past is certain. Thus the calculations which relate past income levels to W are different from those which relate it to future income streams. The life cycle hypothesis explicitly recognises this by including A_{-1} to take account of past income streams. Friedman adjusts his model by introducing the ratio of assets, i.e., non-human wealth to human wealth which is discounted future income streams, into the function which determines k. Thus,

$$c_p = k(i, w, u)y_p \tag{2.9}$$

where w is the ratio of non-human wealth to permanent income.

This adjustment takes account of the fact that with uncertainty there is an extra reason for saving until one has a large stock of wealth with which to cushion any unexpected loss of income. Friedman also aggregates this function realising that the aggregate function can only be an approximation. Although the equation proposed by Friedman is a proportional one between permanent consumption and permanent income he has acknowledged the role of non-human wealth (see Friedman, 1958).

2.3.4. *Some measurement problems*

Two of the theories outlined above involve non-measurable variables and so further assumptions are necessary if the theories are to be analysed empirically. Transitory consumption, i.e., the difference between actual consumption and permanent consumption, is assumed to vary randomly. Friedman similarly assumes that transitory income varies randomly in such a way that permanent and transitory income are not correlated. Formally,

$$y = y_p + \eta \tag{2.10}$$

$$c = c_p + \epsilon \tag{2.11}$$

$$\rho_{\eta\epsilon} = \rho_{y_p\eta} = \rho_{c_p\epsilon} = 0 \tag{2.12}$$

where

η is transitory income;

ϵ is transitory consumption;

ρ_{rs} is the correlation coefficient between r and s.

If one wishes to estimate a consumption function it is necessary to make the variables, permanent and expected income, more specific. The standard approach is to relate permanent income to past and present levels of income, i.e.,

$$y_p = w_0 y_t + w_1 y_{t-1} + w_2 y_{t-2} + \dots \qquad 0 \leqslant w_i \leqslant 1\,, \quad \sum w_i = 1\,. \tag{2.13}$$

This, however, would introduce too many parameters to be estimated. Friedman's own suggestion amounts to assuming that the weights decline geometrically, in which case the consumption function can be written as

$$c_t = (1-\lambda)ky_t + \lambda c_{t-1} + \epsilon_t - \lambda\epsilon_{t-1}\,. \tag{2.14}$$

It is possible, given the assumptions (2.9)–(2.12), to analyse empirical consumption functions based on the absolute and relative income hypotheses as misspecifications of the permanent income consumption function. If a and b are the least squares intercept and slope coefficients in the regression of consumption on income, then it is possible to show for large samples that

$$b = k\,\frac{\sum (y_p - \bar{y}_p)^2}{\sum (y - \bar{y})^2} = kP_y \tag{2.15}$$

$$a = \bar{c} - kP_y\bar{\eta} + k(1 - P_y)\,\bar{y}_p\,. \tag{2.16}$$

Eq. (2.15) shows that we would expect a group like farmers, who have large transient elements in their income, to have a lower value of b than non-farmers.

A similar analysis can be performed for the relative income hypothesis. The relative income hypothesis has two empirical forms. One of these is the regression of the ratio of consumption to income on the ratio of income to average income. Friedman (1957, p. 160) shows on his assumptions that

$$\frac{c}{y} = kP_y + k(1 - P_y)\frac{\bar{y}}{y} . \tag{2.17}$$

The other empirical form of the relative income hypothesis relates the consumption ratio to the percentile position of income in the income distribution. This is difficult to handle analytically, but if we assume that the income distribution is approximately normal, then

$$y \approx \bar{y} + g\sigma_y \tag{2.18}$$

where σ_y is the standard deviation of y; and g is the deviation of income from its mean in standard deviation units.

Substituting (2.18) into (2.17) produces

$$\frac{c}{y} \approx kP_y + k(1 - P_y)\frac{\bar{y}}{\bar{y} + g\sigma_y} \tag{2.19}$$

$$= kP_y + k(1 - P_y)\frac{1}{1 + vg}$$

where $v = \sigma_y/\bar{y}$.

Thus, by Taylor series approximation

$$\frac{c}{y} \approx kP_y + k(1 - P_y)(1 - vg)$$

$$= k - k(1 - P_y)vg . \tag{2.20}$$

Performing the regression on the percentile position will be very similar to performing the regression on g, since g varies with the percentile position. From (2.20) the slope coefficient of such a regression will vary P_y. This type of analysis is of little use with aggregate time series data, but it is useful in explaining cross section results.

2.3.5. *The influence of wealth*

Although both the life cycle and permanent income hypotheses do involve the influence of wealth, the emphasis has not primarily been on the precautionary motive but on the smoothing of consumption through time. Ball and Drake (1964) introduced a model which reverses this emphasis by letting the individual choose an optimal level of present consumption and wealth. Wealth is now seen more as a precaution against a rainy day than as a source of future consumption. The ith individual's utility function is

$$U_{it} = F_i(W_{it}, C_{it})$$

where W_i is the stock of assets in terms of consumption goods; and C_i is the volume of consumption goods.

Assuming this utility function is homogeneous of degree one, maximising it subject to

$$Y_{it} = C_{it} + W_{it} - W_{it-1}$$

results in desired levels of wealth and consumption such that

$$W_{it} = k_i C_{it} \,.$$

Aggregating this relation for all individuals leads to the relation $W_t = kC_t$, which will contain an unknown amount of bias. Combining this with the aggregate identity $Y_t = C_t + W_t - W_{t-1}$ produces the following consumption function

$$C_t = \frac{1}{1+k} Y_t + \frac{k}{1+k} C_{t-1} \,.$$

This function is similar to that derived from Friedman's hypothesis, however, in this case an extra restriction on the coefficients is obtained, i.e., they sum to unity.

Independently Spiro (1962) developed a more general statement of this principle. Spiro proves that for a consumption function of the form

$$C_t = e_t^* + B\,W_t + By_t + \sum_{i=0}^{\infty} a_i y_{t-i} \tag{2.21}$$

where

W_t is the level of wealth at the beginning of period t;

y_t is total net earnings of all factors of production received at the beginning of period t;

e_t^* represents all other influences other than wealth and income;
B and a_i are constants.

If consumption increases when wealth increases, and for any given values of $y_t, y_{t-1}, ..., y_{t-\infty}$ and e_t^* there is some level of wealth at which saving will be zero; then the function can be written

$$C_t = E_t + \sum_{i=0}^{\infty} b_i y_{t-i} \tag{2.22}$$

where $\sum b_i = 1$, and E represents the effects of current and lagged values of e^*.

He shows that the Duesenberry type consumption function

$$\frac{C_t}{P_t} = \frac{AC_0}{P_0} + \frac{BW_t^*}{P_t} + \frac{a^* y_t}{P_t}$$

(where P_t is a price index; and C_0 is last peak consumption) reduces to

$$C_t = \frac{AP_t C_0}{P^0} + BW_t^* + a^* y_t \ ,$$

and thus has the form of (2.21) where $e^* = AP_t C_0 / P_0$. In addition he shows that (2.21) can be written

$$C_t = \left[\frac{B(W^* + y)}{\sum_{i=0}^{\infty} a_i y_{t-i}} + 1 \right] \sum_{i=0}^{\infty} a_i y_{t-i} \ . \tag{2.23}$$

This can be interpreted as one form of Friedman's permanent income hypothesis, i.e.,

$$C_p = k(i, u, w) \ Y_p$$

where $Y_p = \sum_{i=0}^{\infty} a_i y_{t-i}$. In fact in the empirical discussion of his theory Friedman takes k to be constant as a working hypothesis. Incidentally, if Friedman's function $k(i, u, w)$ is assumed to be equal to kw, the permanent income hypothesis is empirically equivalent to that of Ball and Drake's. Thus Spiro has highlighted the similarity of the models before us as well as provided a useful constraint.

Although wealth, human and non-human, plays a large part in the theoretical explanation of consumption, it has not featured so strongly in empirical studies. The reason stems from the shortage of data on total assets, including stocks of durable goods. Data on liquid assets have been available and these have been used although most authors stress that 'wealth' should refer to total assets.

2.4. The stochastic term

The use of the permanent consumption variable implies the presence of a stochastic term in the consumption relation. Complete specification of a model implies that the stochastic properties of this variable be established. Later we shall report on a study by Zellner and Geisel which emphasizes the importance of the stochastic specifications. For the moment we wish to remind that transformation of equations involving stochastic terms also transform these terms which may or may not be desirable. Linear combinations of values at different points of time are likely to lead to serially correlated disturbances, but an equation set up in ratio form may lessen the possibility of heteroscedasticity which could be important in consumption studies.

2.5. Summary

Let us summarise this theoretical section. We have a number of hypotheses that have been suggested: the absolute income, the relative income, the permanent income, the life cycle and the wealth hypotheses. Some of these hypotheses are very similar and we may not be able to distinguish between their empirical implications. Each suggests a possible aggregate consumption function which we can estimate by aggregate time series. However, the hypothesis should satisfy all the data available including cross section data and particular studies. We shall first turn our attention to some aggregate time series studies.

2.6. Aggregate time series

2.6.1. *Duesenberry* (1949)

Duesenberry does not believe that aggregate data can really test the relative income hypothesis, but his aim is to show that it is not inconsistent with such data. Using data for the U.S., 1929–1940, taken from the *Survey of Current Business* converted to a per capita basis and deflated by the Bureau of Labour Statistics consumer price index, he calculates the following regression which is a special form of (2.1)

$$\frac{S}{Y} = 0.196 + 0.25\frac{Y}{Y_0}$$

$$R^2 = 0.81$$

where

S is aggregate real per capita savings;

Y is aggregate real per capita income;

Y_0 is the last highest real per capita income.

Using this relation, he shows that if income were to grow steadily at 3%, i.e., $Y_t/Y_{t-1} = 1.03$, then $S/Y = 0.06$, i.e., a little less than 10% which is not inconsistent with Kuznets (1942) 1880–1930 data. His function also forecasts a savings ratio for 1947 of 4.1%. Since the actual ratio for 1947 was 5.1% he again takes this to be not inconsistent.

2.6.2. *Friedman* (1957)

In a small section concerning aggregate time series Friedman shows how the results of Duesenberry (1949), Modigliani (1949) and Mack (1948) can be interpreted in terms of the permanent income hypothesis. These three authors produced regressions of consumption on the present year's, the previous year's, and the past highest level of income in various forms. Eq. (2.13) indicates that this is equivalent to regressing consumption on permanent income when certain weights are taken as zero and the others estimated from the data. Table 2.2 contains the value of these weights and the ratio of permanent consumption to permanent income for these results and those of Ferber (1953) who recomputed the regressions on comparable data.

Friedman also presents three regressions (see table 2.3) based on Goldsmith's data. Expected income is calculated using geometrically declining weights in (2.13). The goodness of fit suggests that the highest previous income is the best specification, but given the errors inherent in econometric work, table 2.3 really provides no basis on which to dismiss any of the specifications.

2.6.3. *Ando and Modigliani* (1963)

Ando and Modigliani set out to test the life cycle hypothesis and to esti-

Table 2.2
Selected measures derived from regressions of consumption on current and past income computed by Modigliani, Duesenberry, and Mack, and recomputed by Ferber.

Country, years covered, income variable	Ratio of permanent consumption to permanent income (k)	Weight attached, in computing permanent income, to: Highest previous income (w_1)	Current income (w_2)	Preceding year's income (w_3)
Modigliani				
1. United States, 1921–1940, disposable income	0.90	0.14	0.86	
2. United States, 1921–1940, income = disposable income plus corporate savings	0.90	0.14	0.56	0.30
3. Canada, 1923–1939, gross national product	0.79	0.32	0.17	0.51
4. Sweden, 1896–1913, 1919–1934, national income	0.85(0.93)†	0.41	0.59	
Duesenberry				
1. United States, 1929–1940, disposable income	0.95	0.20	0.80	
Mack				
1. United States, 1929–1940, disposable income	0.86(0.97)†		0.93	0.07
Ferber recomputations (all United States, disposable income)				
1. Following Modigliani				
a. 1923–1940	0.96	0.16	0.84	
b. 1923–1930, 1935–1940	0.96	0.10	0.90	
2. Following Duesenberry				
a. 1923–1940	0.96	0.16	0.84	
b. 1923–1930, 1935–1940	0.96	0.10	0.90	
3. Following Mack				
a. 1929–1940	0.79(0.97)†		0.96	0.04
b. 1923–1940	0.82(0.97)†		0.90	0.10
c. 1923–1930, 1935–1940	0.96		0.87	0.13

† Value allowing for significant constant term.

Table 2.3
Three consumption functions for the United States: regressions of consumption on current and past incomes, non-war years 1905 through 1951.[a]

Regression	Ratio of permanent consumption to permanent income (k)	Weight attached, in comparing permanent income, to:				Square of multiple correlation coefficient (R^2)	Standard error of estimate as a % of average value of measured consumption
		Highest previous income	Current income	Preceding year's income	All prior years combined		
Highest previous income[b]	0.88	0.45	0.55			0.98	2.8
Preceding year's income[b]	0.90		0.64	0.36		0.94	5.0
Expected income[c]	0.88		0.33	0.22	0.45	0.96	4.0

[a] Excluded years are 1917–1918, 1942 through 1945.

[b] Although the war years 1942 through 1945 were excluded from current income in computing these regressions, 1945 was used as the highest preceding income and as the preceding year's income for the 1946 current income observation, since 1941 was so far out of line. For World War I, since no break was introduced, 1917–1918 was omitted for the other variables as well.

[c] The weights for 17 individual years to three decimals are as follows, starting with the current year and going backward in time: 0.330, 0.221, 0.148, 0.099, 0.067, 0.045, 0.030, 0.020, 0.013, 0.009, 0.006, 0.004, 0.003, 0.002, 0.001, 0.001, 0.001.

Note: Consumption = real consumption per capita. Income = real disposable income per capita.

mate the aggregate consumption function, i.e.,

$$C_t = \alpha_1' Y_{Lt} + \alpha_2' Y_{Lt}^e + \alpha_3' A_{t-1} .$$

Their first step is to derive a priori estimates of the order of magnitude of these coefficients which are then used to judge the 'reasonableness' of the regression estimates. They suggest three assumptions which they claim make the three parameters, i.e., α_1', α_2' and α_3', functions of the rate of return on assets and the overall rate of growth of income. Their defence for the assumptions is that even when they are changed the numerical values do not seem to be unduly affected. The a priori estimates they derive appear in table (2.4).

Before statistical analysis can take place on eq. (2.7) a method of measuring Y^e must be decided. Ando and Modigliani use two such measures.

Hypothesis I

$$Y_{Lt}^e = \beta Y_{Lt} \tag{2.24}$$

where $\beta \approx 1$

Hypothesis II

$$Y_{Lt}^e = (\beta_1 - \beta_2) Y_{Lt} + \beta_2 \frac{L_t}{E_t} Y_{Lt} \tag{2.25}$$

where E_t is the number employed and L_t is total labour force.

Hypothesis II stems from the different income expectations of employed and unemployed people. If the average employed person expects $\beta_1 Y_{Lt}/E_t$ where $\beta_1 \approx 1$, i.e., approximately the present average wage, and the average unemployed considerably less, i.e., $\beta_2 Y_{Lt}/E_t$ where $\beta_2 < 1$, then the total expected income Y^e will be

$$Y^e = E_t \beta_1 \frac{Y_{Lt}}{E_t} + (L_t - E_t)\beta_2 \frac{Y_{Lt}}{E_t} ,$$

Table 2.4
Coefficients of the life cycle consumption function under certain assumptions.

Yield on assets	0	0	0	3	5	5	5
Annual rate of growth of income	0	3	4	0	0	3	4
$\alpha_1 + \alpha_2$	0.61	0.64	–	0.69	0.73	–	–
α_3	0.08	0.07	0.07	0.11	0.13	0.12	0.12

Thus

$$Y_L^e = (\beta_1 - \beta_2) Y_{Lt} + \beta_2 \frac{L_t}{E_t} Y_t .$$

Using the two hypotheses, i.e., (2.23) and (2.24) we obtain

$$C_t = (\alpha_1' + \beta \alpha_2') Y_{Lt} + \alpha_3' A_{t-1} \tag{2.26}$$

$$= \alpha_1 Y_{Lt} + \alpha_3 A_{t-1}$$

where $\alpha_1 \approx \alpha_1' + \alpha_2'$

$$C_t = \alpha_1 Y_{Lt} + \alpha_2 \frac{L_t}{E_t} Y_{Lt} + \alpha_3 A_{t-1} \tag{2.27}$$

$\alpha_1 \quad = \alpha_1' + \alpha_2'(\beta_1 - \beta_2);$

$\alpha_2 \quad = \alpha_2' \beta_2;$

$\alpha_3 \quad = \alpha_3';$

$\alpha_1 + \alpha_2 \approx \alpha_1' + \alpha_2'.$

The data are all in current dollar values. They are taken from Ando et al. (1963) where the derivations of the series from Goldsmith (1955), the *Survey of Current Business*, and the *Economic Report of the President* are fully described. The consumption variable excludes durables purchases but includes their depreciation. Net worth of consumers is used for A_{t-1}. The data for 1929–1955 are derived from Goldsmith's bench marks with savings added or subtracted to obtain the annual figures. For 1945–1959 they used figures produced by Goldsmith.

Because the authors expect that all the standard econometric problems will be present they decide to try a number of approaches applied to both hypotheses I and II. The ordinary least squares estimates appear in row (1) of table (2.5). The coefficient of A_{t-1}, α_3, is too low and $\alpha_1 + \alpha_2$ is too high. The coefficient of multiple correlation is high but the DW statistic suggests serial correlations in the residuals. Similar results follow from the use of hypothesis II. Although the constant term is significant Modigliani and Ando justify its suppression by reference to their theory and by suggesting that the

Table 2.5
Coefficients of the life cycle consumption function (annual U.S. data 1929–1959).

Row	Hypothesis	Constant	α_1	α_2	α_3	R^2	DW
(1)	I	8.1	0.75	–	0.042	0.998	1.26
		(1.0)	(0.05)	–	(0.009)		
(2)	I	–	0.56	–	0.081	0.997	0.33
			(0.09)		(0.015)		
(3)†	I	–	0.52	–	0.072	0.929	1.85
			(0.11)		(0.018)		
(4)†	II	–	0.44	0.24	(0.049)	0.936	1.74
			(0.12)	(0.15)	(0.022)		

† First difference form.

O.L.S. estimate is probably biased upwards on account of the simultaneous bias. Row (2) which contains the hypothesis I results, presents values closer to the a priori magnitudes but also, unfortunately, evidence of considerable serial correlation. At this point they try a first difference transformation. The results of this (row (3)) are quite encouraging. This transformation has probably eliminated much of the trend influence in the variables and hence helped to reduce the multicollinearity. When we consider the results of hypothesis II so transformed, i.e., row (4), both the coefficients of Y and A fall vis-à-vis those of hypothesis I. Ando and Modigliani interpret this by suggesting that although $Y_{Lt}L_t/E_t$ is an 'income' variable its changes will be correlated with the changes in A_{t-1} since both are cyclically stable. Their conclusions are that these results by and large support the basic hypothesis, especially the role of assets, but that serious difficulties exist in estimating the individual influences of wealth, income, and expected income. They are aware that their estimates are subject to simultaneous bias and see no real solution to this problem although they do make two unsuccessful attempts to get some idea of the bias.

Comparing the 'life cycle' equation to a modern Keynesian formulation which distinguishes two types of income one sees a remarkable similarity. The Keynesian form is

$$C = \gamma_0 + \gamma_1 Y_L + \gamma_2 P$$

where P is property income, i.e., $\Delta C = \gamma_1 \Delta Y_L + \gamma_2 \Delta P$; whereas the 'life cycle' is

$$\Delta C = \alpha_1 \Delta Y_L + \alpha_3 \Delta A \ .$$

Is it that ΔA is a proxy for ΔP or vice versa? Ando and Modigliani suggest that since the Keynesian form is statistically less satisfactory, they believe ΔP is acting as a proxy for ΔA. The regression result for the Keynesian form is

$$\underset{}{\Delta C =} \underset{(0.07)}{0.93\ \Delta Y} + \underset{(0.29)}{0.07\ \Delta P} \qquad R^2 = 0.86\ .$$

Having shown that their equation is satisfactory with regard to the short-run time series, the authors show that the long run implications do not conflict with Goldsmith's (1955) evidence on the long run stability of the consumption total income ratio. Total income is the sum of property and non-property income. Furthermore, property income will be related to wealth via the rate of return. Thus

$$Y_t^* = Y_{Lt} + P_t$$

$$P_t = r A_{t-1}$$

thus

$$\begin{aligned} S_t &= Y_t^* - C_t = Y_{Lt} + P_t - C \\ &= Y_{Lt} + P_t - (\alpha_1 + \alpha_2) Y_{Lt} - \alpha_3 A_{t-1} \\ &= (1 - \alpha) Y^* - (\alpha_3 - \alpha r) A_{t-1} \end{aligned}$$

where $\alpha = \alpha_1 + \alpha_2$. However $S_t = A_t - A_{t-1}$

$$\therefore \frac{A_t - A_{t-1}}{A_{t-1}} = n + (1 - \alpha) \left[\frac{Y^*}{A_{t-1}} - \frac{(n + \alpha_3 - \alpha r)}{1 - \alpha} \right]$$

where, for the moment, n is an arbitrary number. If

$$\frac{Y^*}{A_{t-1}} > \frac{n + \alpha_3 - \alpha r}{1 - \alpha}$$

then assets, A, grow faster than n. If n is the rate of growth of Y^* then Y^*/A_{t-1} falls. If

$$\frac{Y^*}{A_{t-1}} < \frac{n + \alpha_3 - \alpha r}{1 - \alpha}$$

then Y^*/A_{t-1} rises. It follows that, in the long run, $Y^*/A_{t-1} = h$ where $h = (n + \alpha_3 - \alpha r)/(1 - \alpha)$ and $n = (A_t - A_{t-1})/A_{t-1}$

$$\therefore \frac{S_t}{Y^*} = \frac{A_t - A_{t-1}}{A_{t-1}} \circ \frac{A_{t-1}}{Y^*} = \frac{n}{h}.$$

Similarly,

$$\frac{Y_t}{A_{t-1}} = \frac{Y_t^* - rA_{t-1}}{A_{t-1}} = h - r$$

and

$$\frac{C_t}{Y_t} = \frac{Y^* - S_t}{A_{t-1}} \cdot \frac{A_{t-1}}{Y_t} = \frac{h - n}{h - r}.$$

The results from the regression analyses suggest $\alpha \approx 0.7$ and $\alpha_3 \approx 0.06$. For estimates of n and r Ando and Modigliani use 0.03 and 0.04 which are based on data from Ando et al. (1963). From these $h \approx 0.2$, $h{-}r \approx 0.16$ and $n/h \approx 0.15$ which are consistent with the data in Ando et al. (1963) as well as Goldsmith's findings on the savings to income ratio.

They also consider the cyclical implications of their theory and show how similar they are to the relative income hypothesis of Duesenberry and thus claim that any cyclical evidence that is consistent with the relative income hypothesis is consistent with theirs.

2.6.4. *Spiro* (1962)

Spiro's empirical sections are concerned with checking whether the type of function he suggests is consistent with time series data. As we pointed out earlier, see (2.22), the function he suggests is

$$C_t = E_t + \sum_{i=0}^{\infty} b_i y_{t-i}$$

where $\sum_{i=0}^{\infty} b_i = 1$;

y_{t-i} is net earnings of factors;
E_t reflects the effect of all non-income and wealth factors, wealth being defined as the sum of past savings.

With this framework the effects of capital gains and losses are reflected in E_t. Spiro assumes E_t is zero but hopes his measure of y tends to offset the error involved in this assumption. The measure of y is disposable personal income plus retained corporation profits. His concept of consumption excludes durables except for a depreciation element. Using geometrically declining weights for the b_i the function collapses to

$$C_t = b_0 y_t + (1 - b_0) C_{t-1} \, . \tag{2.28}$$

Spiro estimates (no details are given) that $b_0 = 0.162$ with $R^2 = 0.98$. Notice that only one degree of freedom has been used up and that the fit is very high. Spiro claims that this fit is considerably better than any (relevant) trend lines and as good as any other consumption functions, in spite of it using few degrees of freedom. The graph of the actual and calculated values of consumption reveal considerable serial correlation as one would expect if E_t were a stochastic term with expectation zero.

The use of the geometrically declining weights imply that the wealth–consumption ratio is constant. This is obvious for the Ball and Drake model, to which Spiro's model reduces. Spiro shows that for his model

$$\frac{W_t + y_t}{C_t} = \frac{1}{b_0} \, .$$

$W_t + y_t$ represents the stock of wealth immediately after the income distribution at the beginning of period t. This ratio, using Spiro's estimate of b_0, lies between 6.1 and 6.2. The average wealth–consumption ratio for 1905–1949 was 6.1 and all but one of these ratios fell within 10% of 6.1. Spiro was fortunate to have seven post-sample observations which he uses to forecast consumption for 1950–1956. The predictions all underestimate the actual values but the average error is less than 3% of consumption in spite of the fact that the data used was from a spliced series. Spiro takes the results to be strong evidence for his consumption function in which wealth is a major factor.

2.6.5. *Ball and Drake* (1964)

As we have seen, Ball and Drake present a model virtually the same as Spiro's but they do not restrict the parameters to add to unity. Again capital gains have been excluded and the income concept is personal disposable income. Consumption is measured by both total consumption and non-durable consumption. U.S. data allow for the depreciation of consumer durables but this is not possible for the U.K. The authors use two estimation methods, ordinary and two stage least squares. Their model is

$$C_t = \alpha Y_t + \beta C_{t-1}$$

where $\alpha = 1/(1+k)$; $\beta = k/(1+k)$; $k = W/C$.

In table 2.6 we report only their results for non-durable consumption since those for total consumption tend to conflict with the hypothesis as one might expect.

Ball and Drake then use estimates of personal wealth for selected years to estimate k, and from this calculate values for α and β (table 2.7).

The regression results show considerable stability with regard to both the method of estimation and the time period. The wealth data estimates are also quite stable but differ from the regression results. However, the TSLS 1929–1960 result does come closest to the wealth estimates, and Spiro's result of $\alpha = 0.16$, which is based on a longer sample period, is entirely con-

Table 2.6
Non-durable consumption functions based on time series.

			α	β	$\alpha+\beta$	R^2
U.S.A.	1929–1941	LS	0.38 (0.06)	0.60 (0.06)	0.98 (0.01)	0.96
		TSLS	0.36 (0.09)	0.63 (0.10)	0.99 (0.01)	0.93
U.S.A.	1946–1960	LS	0.50 (0.14)	0.44 (0.16)	0.94 (0.02)	0.99
		TSLS	0.36 (0.22)	0.61 (0.26)	0.97 (0.06)	0.98
U.S.A.	1929–1960 (excl. 1942–1950)	LS	0.31 (0.05)	0.67 (0.06)	0.98 (0.01)	0.99
		TSLS	0.25 (0.09)	0.74 (0.10)	0.99 (0.01)	0.99
U.K.	1950–1960	LS	0.29 (0.06)	0.68 (0.06)	0.97 (0.01)	0.99
		TSLS	0.29 (0.06)	0.68 (0.07)	0.97 (0.01)	0.98

Table 2.7
Non-durable consumption functions based on wealth data.

		α	β
U.S.A.	1929	0.15	0.85
	1939	0.15	0.85
	1945	0.14	0.86
	1949	0.17	0.83
	1953	0.15	0.85
U.K.	1954	0.25	0.75

sistent. When Ball and Drake use the constraint $\alpha + \beta = 1$ the TSLS results for the U.S. are $\alpha = 0.30$, 0.18 and 0.19, respectively for 1929–1941, 1946–1960, and 1929–1960, which are more or less consistent with the wealth estimates. Thus Ball and Drake conclude that their wealth hypothesis is consistent with the time series data available and suggest that more attention should be paid to the asset adjustment process.

2.6.6. *Stone* (1964)

Stone proposes a model of personal saving which involves the wealth hypothesis and has a permanent income flavour. Income, consumption and wealth all have permanent and transient components.

Thus

$$Y = Y_p + Y_T, \qquad C = C_p + C_T, \qquad W = W_p + W_T. \tag{2.29}$$

Furthermore,

$$Y_{pt} = \lambda Y_t + (1 - \lambda) Y_{p\,t-1} \tag{2.30}$$

and

$$W_{pt} = \lambda W_t + (1 - \lambda) W_{p\,t-1}.$$

Permanent consumption is assumed to be related simply to permanent wealth and income,

$$C_p = \alpha_1 W_p + \beta_1 Y_p \tag{2.31}$$

whereas transitory consumption depends only on transitory income,

$$C_T = \beta_2 Y_T \, . \tag{2.32}$$

From these relations and the identity $S = Y - C$, it can be shown that

$$S = [1 - \beta_1\lambda - \beta_2(1-\lambda)]\, Y - \alpha_1 \lambda W + \beta_2(1-\lambda)\, Y_{t-1} - (1-\lambda) C_{t-1} \, .$$

To take account of exogenous influences, let G^* denote the normal level of an index of government measures to discourage spending, where $G^* = \lambda G + (1-\lambda) G^*_{t-1}$. Then transitory consumption can be assumed to be affected by deviations from the normal level of this index. Hence,

$$C_T = \beta_2 Y_T + \delta(G - G^*) \, . \tag{2.33}$$

Thus, using (2.33) in place of (2.32),

$$S = [1 - \beta_1\lambda - \beta_2(1-\lambda)]\, Y - \alpha\lambda W + \beta_2(1-\lambda)\, Y_{t-1}$$

$$- (1-\lambda) C_{t-1} - \delta(1-\lambda)\Delta G \, . \tag{2.34}$$

Stone prefers to divide through by Y, thus the estimating equation is

$$\frac{S_t}{Y_t} = a' + b' \frac{W_t}{Y_t} + c' \frac{Y_{t-1}}{Y_t} + d' \frac{C_{t-1}}{Y_t} + e' \frac{\Delta G}{Y} \, . \tag{2.35}$$

The data used are mainly taken from the *National Income and Expenditure Accounts*. All variables are in 1958 prices. Income is 'personal disposable income', consumption includes expenditure on durables. Saving is 'personal saving' plus 'additions to tax reserves' minus 'personal provision for depreciation'. A wealth series is constructed using annual savings to adjust a benchmark figure for 1961 of £55,500 M. The index of government measures to discourage spending is represented by the minimum percentage down payment in purchasing contracts of radio and electrical goods. The ordinary least squares estimates are

$$\frac{S}{Y} = \underset{(0.084)}{0.413} - \underset{(0.0168)}{0.0464} \frac{W}{Y} + \underset{(0.157)}{0.130} \frac{Y_{t-1}}{Y} - \underset{(0.210)}{0.366} \frac{C_{t-1}}{Y} + \underset{(2.06)}{7.24} \frac{\Delta G}{Y}$$

$$R^2 = 0.97; \quad \text{DW} = 1.96$$

$\alpha_1 = 0.0732$
$\beta_1 = 0.721$
$\beta_2 = 0.355$
$\lambda = 0.634$
$\delta = -19.8$

All these coefficients are of the right sign and have reasonable values. The coefficient of Y_{t-1}/Y_t is not significant which is consistent with transient consumption not being related to transient income.

In view of this he re-estimates (2.34) with $\beta_2 = 0$ resulting in

$$\frac{S}{Y} = \underset{(0.077)}{0.439} - \underset{(0.0108)}{0.0570}\frac{W}{Y} - \underset{(0.116)}{0.222}\frac{C_{t-1}}{Y} + \underset{(1.99)}{6.93}\frac{\Delta G}{Y}$$

$$R^2 = 0.969; \quad \mathrm{DW} = 1.76.$$

$\alpha_1 = 0.0732$
$\beta_1 = 0.721$
$\lambda = 0.778$
$\delta = -31.3$

Stone also considers a model where income is divided into income 'from employment and small transfers', Y_L, and all other income, Y_0. The results are

$$\frac{S}{Y} = \underset{(0.095)}{0.395}\frac{Y_L}{Y} + \underset{(0.181)}{0.573}\frac{Y_0}{Y} - \underset{(0.0133)}{0.0631}\frac{W}{Y} - \underset{(0.127)}{0.183}\frac{C_{t-1}}{Y} + \underset{(2.06)}{7.22}\frac{\Delta G}{Y}$$

$$R^2 = 0.971; \quad \mathrm{DW} = 2.03.$$

$\alpha_1 = 0.0773$
$\beta_{1L} = 0.741$
$\beta_{10} = 0.523$
$\lambda = 0.817$
$\delta = -39.3$

Note that the model only allows a different response with regard to permanent income for the two groups, the wealth reactions are assumed to be the same. However, again the results are quite encouraging.

For his quarterly model Stone uses the original form because previously Stone and Rowe (1962) had found the Government measure influence to be insignificant. The data used to estimate this model are taken from the Central Statistical Office's *Economic Trends* in which income and saving are defined before deducting depreciation. In this case the data run from 1955(ii) to 1963(i). The results are

$$\frac{S}{Y} = \underset{(0.121)}{0.472} - \underset{(0.0060)}{0.0130}\frac{W}{Y} + \underset{(0.111)}{0.394}\frac{Y_{t-1}}{Y} - \underset{(0.145)}{0.684}\frac{C_{t-1}}{Y}$$

$$R^2 = 0.89; \quad \text{DW} = 2.17$$

$\alpha_1 = 0.041$
$\beta_1 = 0.411$
$\beta_2 = 0.583$
$\lambda = 0.316$

Stone then uses this quarterly equation to forecast personal gross saving in 1961, 1962, 1963 and 1964 (table 2.8). To forecast it is necessary to know the level of income. At the time of writing this was known for 1961 and 1962, however, for 1963 and 1964 Stone assumes an annual 4% growth of income. His forecasts are quoted for the whole year rather than for individual quarters.

Table 2.8
Annual consumption forecasts from quarterly permanent income consumption functions U.K.

	Actual	Calculated
1961	1826	1799
1962	1555	1595
1963	1701†	1700
1964		1847

† Last quarter calculated

Turning to the more long run implications of his ideas Stone calculates the equilibrium savings to income ratio for different rates of growth of income. For this he uses his second annual model. Thus for 2, 3, and 4 percentage rates of growth of income the corresponding savings percentages are 3.4, 6.1 and 8.4. Stone concludes that since the present British savings percentage is about 6%, a 4% rate of growth is hardly possible.

2.6.7. *Evans* (1967a)

All the empirical studies of Sections 2.6.3–2.6.6 acknowledge the importance of wealth but this study by Evans attempts to show that this emphasis is wrong. The basis of his attack is the operation of the wealth models in the long run, i.e., during periods of steady growth, income, consumption and wealth all growing at rate λ. Expressing the Ball–Drake function as

$$C_t = \frac{k}{k+1} Y + \frac{1}{k+1} C_{t-1}$$

where $k = C^{\dagger}/W$ then in steady growth

$$\frac{C}{Y} = \frac{k}{k + \lambda/(1+\lambda)} \ .$$

The average value for k in 1947–1964, when only non-durables are considered, was 0.16. Evans calculates the C/Y ratio for the Ball–Drake and the Ando–Modigliani functions for several rates of growth. His findings are reproduced in table 2.9.

Table 2.9
Long run consumption – income ratios for two models.

λ i.e. rate of growth	0.02	0.03	0.04
Ball–Drake	0.89	0.84	0.80
Ando–Modigliani	0.90	0.85	0.80

The average C/Y ratio for the period was 0.80 although the average rate of growth of consumption was 3.1%. Evans considers that this throws considerable doubt on the wealth hypothesis. Furthermore, the yearly marginal propensity to consume, i.e., $k/(k+1)$ calculated directly from k, is 0.14. Spiro's estimate is consistent with this but Ball and Drake tend to have higher values.

Evans also takes exception to Ball and Drake's deflation process. Both income and consumption should be deflated by the same series. Evans believes that the relevant deflator for income is a consumption price series because income would thus reflect a purchasing power concept. Ball and Drake have used a total income deflator and this causes bias. When the Ball and Drake function is re-estimated with a consumption deflator the sum of the coefficients are significantly different from unity. The sum of the coefficients and the relevant standard error is 0.985 and 0.006 while the similar estimates, using an income deflator, are 0.991 and 0.007. Evans also presents similar results for functions involving different consumption definitions, with and without constant terms, using quarterly and annual data.

† Note that Ball and Drake use $k = W/C$

Evans' second line of attack on the wealth hypothesis is that the short-run marginal propensity to consume is much smaller for this function than for many other functions. These include a Duesenberry type function,

$$\frac{C}{Y} = a + b\,\frac{Y^0}{Y} + d\left(\frac{C}{Y}\right)_{t-1},$$

a Friedman–Mincer function,

$$\frac{C}{Y} = a + b\,\frac{L}{Y}$$

and Evans' own version of the Friedman function,

$$\frac{C}{Y} = k + f\left(\frac{\Delta Y - \overline{\Delta Y}}{Y}\right) \tag{2.36}$$

where $\overline{\Delta Y}$ is the average change and $f\{(\Delta Y - \overline{\Delta Y})/Y\}$ reflects the effect of transitory income on the consumption ratio. Using a geometric lag function he transforms this to

$$\frac{C}{Y} = k^* + a\,\frac{\Delta Y - \overline{\Delta Y}}{Y} + \left(\frac{C}{Y}\right)_{t-1} \tag{2.37}$$

He then assumes $\overline{\Delta Y/Y}$ to be constant which results in the following equation

$$\frac{C}{Y} = k^{**} + a\,\frac{\Delta Y}{Y} + \left(\frac{C}{Y}\right)_{t-1}.$$

All Evans' yearly results appear in table 2.10.

Spiro's estimate of the yearly marginal propensity to consume was 0.162 as was Ball and Drake's estimate based on wealth data; and although their unrestricted regression results were in the same range as those in table 2.10, the restricted ones were much lower. The Ando–Modigliani model cannot be dismissed on these grounds. It turns out however, that Evans also tested their model on post war annual data and the wealth variable was insignificant. This leads Evans to believe that wealth was important during the depression but not in the post war years. These results do not appear in his article but he does present the complete set of post war quarterly results (see table 2.11). In these he has replaced all one period lag terms by a retrogressive four period

Table 2.10
Yearly functions, 1929–1941, 1947–1962.

	R^2	DW	Yearly m.p.c.	Long-run m.p.c.
Total consumption (C):				
(1) $C=4.95+0.6640\ Y+0.2752\ C_{-1}$	0.998	2.15	0.664	0.909
(1.71)(0.0631) (0.0736)				
(2) $C=0.5834\ Y+0.3875\ C_{-1}$	0.998	1.73	0.583	0.941
(0.0640) (0.0706)				
(3) $C=-4.84+0.5839\ Y_g+0.4170\ C_{-1}$	0.997	1.31	0.584	0.987
(2.04)(0.0809) (0.0876)				
(4) $C=0.5600\ Y_g+0.4202\ C_{-1}$	0.997	1.11	0.560	0.952
(0.0868) (0.0947)				
(5) $C/Y_L=0.7998+0.0567\ W_{-1}/Y_L$	0.849	0.93	0.664	0.946
(0.0045)				
(6) $C/Y=0.6777+0.2405\ L/E$	0.571	1.87	0.678	0.946
(0.0389)				
(6a) $C/Y=0.5697+0.2062\ L/E+0.1542\ (C/Y)_{-1}$	0.564	2.07	0.716	0.946
(0.0610) (0.2102)				
(7) $C/Y=0.5534+0.2105\ Y^0/Y+0.1885\ (C/Y)_{-1}$	0.759	1.99	0.732	0.946
(0.0325) (0.1276)				
(8) $C/Y=0.2115-0.3140\ \Delta Y/Y+0.7832\ (C/Y)_{-1}$	0.792	2.66	0.638	0.946
(0.0430) (0.0935)				
$\overline{(C/Y)}=0.946,\ \lambda=0.02$				
Non-durables and services (C_n):				
(1) $C_n=6.23+0.3945\ Y+0.4960\ C_{n-1}$	0.999	1.16	0.395	0.768
(1.64)(0.0450) (0.0634)				
(2) $C_n=0.2795\ Y+0.6757\ C_{n-1}$	0.998	1.09	0.280	0.828
(0.0408) (0.0518)				
(3) $C_n=-0.80+0.3155\ Y_g+0.6839\ C_{n-1}$	0.998	0.86	0.316	0.844
(1.68)(0.0563) (0.0737)				
(4) $C_n=0.3229\ Y_g+0.6252\ C_{n-1}$	0.998	0.81	0.322	0.834
(0.0534) (0.0669)				
(5) No equation †				
(6) $C_n/Y=0.3433+0.4397\ L/E$	0.792	1.45	0.343	0.834
(0.0424)				
(6a) $C_n/Y=0.2513+0.3380\ L/E+0.2454\ (C_n/Y)_{-1}$	0.798	1.73	0.456	0.834
(0.0855) (0.1801)				
(7) $C_n/Y=0.2086+0.2669\ Y^0/Y+0.4229\ (C_n/Y)_{-1}$	0.864	1.38	0.561	0.834
(0.0406) (0.0970)				
(8) $C_n/Y=0.1045-0.4015\ \Delta Y/Y+0.8840\ (C_n/Y)_{-1}$	0.962	2.05	0.440	0.834
(0.0286) (0.0381)				
$\overline{(C_n/Y)}=0.834$				

Table 2.10 (continued)

	R^2	DW	Yearly m.p.c.	Long-run m.p.c.
Consumption except durables+depreciation (C^*):				
(1) $C^*=3.43+0.3925\ Y+0.5673\ C^*_{-1}$ (1.48)(0.0439) (0.0545)	0.999	1.16	0.393	0.884
(2) $C^*=0.3352\ Y+0.6494\ C^*_{-1}$ (0.0391) (0.0447)	0.999	1.21	0.335	0.923
(3) $C^*=-3.08+0.3096\ Y_g+0.6977\ C^*_{-1}$ (1.62)(0.0525) (0.0606)	0.998	1.03	0.310	0.980
(4) $C^*=0.3192\ Y_g+0.6718\ C^*_{-1}$ (0.0574) (0.0618)	0.998	0.84	0.319	0.935
(5) $C^*/Y_L=0.6018+0.0846\ W_{-1}/Y_L$ (0.0033)	0.959	1.53	0.495	0.924
(6) $C^*/Y=0.4106+0.4597\ L/E$ (0.0504)	0.746	1.06	0.411	0.924
(6a) $C^*/Y=0.3318+0.3732\ L/E+0.1893\ (C^*/Y)_{-1}$ (0.1075) (0.2077)	0.744	1.28	0.504	0.924
(7) $C^*/Y=0.3143+0.3302\ Y^0+0.2958\ (C^*/Y)_{-1}$ (0.0442) (0.0974)	0.881	1.00	0.588	0.924
(8) $C^*/Y=0.1710-0.4747\ \Delta Y/Y+0.8263\ (C^*/Y)_{-1}$ (0.0271) (0.0330)	0.971	2.21	0.460	0.924
$\overline{(C^*/Y)}=0.924$				

Note. All variables in constant dollars, except equation (5) in current dollars.
Y = Personal disposable income deflated by the consumption deflator
Y_g = Personal disposable income deflated by the GNP detlator
Y_L = Personal disposable labor income, cash concept, current dollars
W = Net worth of households, current dollars, end of period
L = Labor force
E = Employment
Y^0 = Peak previous income, constant dollars

† The Ando–Modigliani hypothesis is not formulated explicitly for C_n. Since we are following the exact series used by Ando and Modigliani in order to draw the strongest possible conclusions about their results, this form of the function is not tested.

moving average. This is an attempt to find a more convenient lag distribution than the geometric.

Evans takes these results to imply that wealth should not be included in consumption functions. This will be certainly contested by other workers in the field. Of course care is necessary in comparing the results of different models. Because most economic time series are subject to trend one would

Table 2.11
Quarterly functions, 1947–1962.

	R^2	DW	Short-run m.p.c.	Long-run m.p.c.
Total consumption (C):				
(1) $C=5.41+0.531\ Y+0.417\ \frac{1}{4}\Sigma_{i=1}^{4}C_{-i}$ (2.94)(0.088) (0.192)	0.993	1.10	0.531	0.900
(2) $C=0.466\ V+0.590\ \frac{1}{4}\Sigma_{i=1}^{4}C_{-i}$ (0.082) (0.091)	0.993	0.99	0.466	0.932
(3) $C=-11.84+0.482\ Y_g+0.549\ \frac{1}{4}\Sigma_{i=1}^{4}C_{-i}$ (3.29) (0.085) (0.085)	0.993	1.06	0.482	1.046
(4) $C=0.315\ Y_g+0.681\ \frac{1}{4}\Sigma_{i=1}^{4}C_{-i}$ (0.078) (0.084)	0.992	0.86	0.315	0.952
(5) $C/Y_L=1.0919+0.0029\ W_{-1}/Y_L$ (0.0222)	−0.016	0.65	0.919	0.933
(5a) $C/Y_L=0.1653+0.0031\ W_{-1}/Y_L+0.8468\ C_{-1}/Y_L$ (0.0142) (0.0890)	0.584	2.32	0.139	0.933
(6) $C/Y=0.849+0.0800\ L/E$ (0.1604)	−0.012	0.87	0.849	0.933
(6a) $C/Y=0.3548+0.0589\ L/E+0.5533\ (C/Y)_{-1}$ (0.1347) (0.1064)	0.287	2.27	0.871	0.933
(7) $C/Y=0.2510+0.4178\ Y^0/Y+0.2819\ \frac{1}{4}\Sigma_{i=1}^{4}(C/Y)_{-i}$ (0.0600) (0.1143)	0.530	1.31	0.513	0.933
(8) $C/Y=0.2887-0.5977\ \Delta Y/Y+0.6959\ \frac{1}{4}\Sigma_{i=1}^{4}(C/Y)_{-i}$ (0.1416) (0.1335)	0.346	1.05	0.340	0.933
Non-durables and services (C_n):				
(1) $C_n=-1.22+0.212\ Y+0.756\ \frac{1}{4}\Sigma_{i=1}^{4}C_{n-i}$ (1.32)(0.032) (0.043)	0.998	1.26	0.212	0.824
(2) $C_n=0.222\ Y+0.738\ \frac{1}{4}\Sigma_{i=1}^{4}C_{n-i}$ (0.030) (0.038)	0.998	1.76	0.222	0.807
(3) $C_n=-8.40+0.203\ Y_g+0.806\ \frac{1}{4}\Sigma_{i=1}^{4}C_{n-i}$ (1.42)(0.032) (0.037)	0.998	1.26	0.203	0.976
(4) $C_n=0.117\ Y_g+0.874\ \frac{1}{4}\Sigma_{i=1}^{4}C_{n-i}$ (0.035) (0.044)	0.997	1.27	0.117	0.828
(5) No equation				
(6) $C_n/Y=0.6058+0.1894\ L/E$ (0.1580)	0.007	0.49	0.606	0.803
(6a) $C_n/Y=0.1575+0.0380\ L/E+0.7546\ (C_n/Y)_{-1}$ (0.1053) (0.0832)	0.570	2.31	0.765	0.803
(7) $C_n/Y=0.0819+0.4697\ Y^0/Y+0.3127\ \frac{1}{4}\Sigma_{i=1}^{4}(C_n/Y)_{-i}$ (0.0420) (0.0712)	0.826	1.19	0.333	0.803
(8) $C_n/Y=0.1079-0.6645\ \Delta Y/Y+0.8717\ \frac{1}{4}\Sigma_{i=1}^{4}(C_n/Y)_{-i}$ (0.0895) (0.0749)	0.721	1.06	0.143	0.803

Table 2.11 (continued)

	R^2	DW	Short-run m.p.c.	Long-run m.p.c.
Consumption–durables+depreciation (C^*):				
(1) $C^*=3.31+0.302\ Y+0.691\ \frac{1}{4}\Sigma_{i=1}^{4}C^*_{-i}$ (1.28)(0.045) (0.050)	0.998	1.50	0.302	0.941
(2) $C^*=0.286\ Y+0.695\ \frac{1}{4}\Sigma_{i=1}^{4}C^*_{-i}$ (0.046) (0.053)	0.998	1.83	0.286	0.902
(3) $C^*=-11.87+0.271\ Y_g+0.767\ \frac{1}{4}\Sigma_{i=1}^{4}C^*_{-i}$ (2.05) (0.044) (0.043)	0.998	1.42	0.271	1.100
(4) $C^*=0.076\ Y_g+0.936\ \frac{1}{4}\Sigma_{i=1}^{4}C^*_{-i}$ (0.035) (0.039)	0.997	1.52	0.076	0.945
(5) $C^*/Y_L=0.8152+0.0456\ W_{-1}/Y_L$ (0.0141)	0.130	0.68	0.686	0.896
(5a) $C^*/Y_L=0.2013+0.0108\ W_{-1}/Y_L+0.7661\ C^*_{-1}/Y_L$ (0.0095) (0.0780)	0.658	2.09	0.169	0.896
(6) $C^*/Y=0.4535+0.4207\ L/E$ (0.1094)	0.180	1.20	0.453	0.896
(6a) $C^*/Y=0.3034+0.2607\ L/E+0.3553\ (C^*/Y)_{-1}$ (0.1169) (0.1215)	0.269	1.92	0.622	0.896
(7) $C^*/Y=0.3085+0.2889\ Y^0/Y+0.3324\ \frac{1}{4}\Sigma_{i=1}^{4}(C^*/Y)_{-i}$ (0.0494) (0.1327)	0.380	1.09	0.606	0.896
(8) $C^*/Y=0.2714-0.7043\ \Delta Y/Y+0.7372\ \frac{1}{4}\Sigma_{i=1}^{4}(C^*/Y)_{-i}$ (0.1047) (0.1389)	0.445	1.22	0.198	0.896

expect a better R^2 for equations involving levels than one using ratios. One aspect of time series analysis of consumption that his results do bring out clearly is the apparent ease of explaining annual data as opposed to quarterly data. We shall now turn our attention to other quarterly studies beginning with Griliches et al. (1962) which compares Zellner's (1957) function with that of Duesenberry et al. (1960).

2.6.8. *Griliches et al.* (1962)

Duesenberry et al. presented a quarterly model of consumption where the desired consumption ratio $(C_t/Y_{t-1})^*$ depended on the past highest level of income previous to period $t-1$, Y^0_{t-1}. Thus

$$\frac{C_t^*}{Y_{t-1}} = \alpha + \beta \frac{Y_{t-1}}{Y^0_{t-1}} .$$

They also hypothesised a lagged adjustment process.

$$\frac{C_t}{Y_{t-1}} - \frac{C_{t-1}}{Y_{t-2}} = \gamma \left(\frac{C_t^*}{Y_{t-1}} - \frac{C_{t-1}}{Y_{t-1}} \right) .$$

This resulted in the following estimating equation.

$$\frac{C_t}{Y_{t-1}} = a + b \frac{Y_{t-1}}{Y_{t-1}^0} + c \frac{C_{t-1}}{Y_{t-2}} .$$

Notice that for the steady state $\alpha + \beta$ is both the average and marginal propensity to consume. Griliches et al. re-estimate this model using revised data and compare this result to the original. Table 2.12 compares the results stemming from both the revised and the original data.

Although the fits appear low, the R^2 of 0.55 for a ratio regression implies that about 99% of the variation of the level of consumption is explained. Griliches et al. believe that the high value of R^2 for the original equation must be a computing error since the data revisions should not have made so much difference when the variables are in ratio form. The use of the revised data does not seem to affect the estimates much. The same cannot be said of the Zellner study. The Zellner functions involve current income, lagged consumption and liquid assets. The coefficients of the liquid assets variables are significant but too high for a reasonable interpretation. It appears that liquid assets are acting as a proxy for permanent income. We will not reproduce the Zellner results here but rather turn to a methodological point.

Table 2.12

Original and revised estimates of the Duesenberry et al. function.

		a	b	c	R^2	Long-run m.p.c.	DW
Original	1948–1957	0.822	−0.625 (0.032)	0.784 (0.053)	0.866	0.91	1.8
Revised	1948–1957	0.898	−0.617 (0.158)	0.697 (0.111)	0.553	0.93	2.52
	1958–1960	0.617	−0.241 (0.314)	0.597 (0.375)	0.244	0.93	2.24
	1948–1960	0.839	−0.565 (0.134)	0.705 (0.099)	0.533	0.93	2.47

Table 2.13
Regression residuals – number of cases.

	Positive at t	Negative at t
Positive at $t-1$	13	5
Negative at $t-1$	5	16

This article provides an example of the dangers of using the Durbin–Watson statistic as a test for serial correlation when the function includes a lagged variable. Using 1951 to 1960 data the following simple permanent income equation is estimated.

$$C = -3.37 + 0.524Y + 0.451\,C_{t-1} \qquad R^2 = 0.993; \quad \mathrm{DW} = 1.51\,.$$

The DW statistic indicates no correlation in the residuals, however, a graph of the residuals shows positive correlation. In fact the residuals when arranged into a contingency table (table 2.13) and tested by a chi-squared test, show significant positive correlation.

Griliches et al. also consider the predictions from the Duesenberry et al. equation, the liquid assets equation and the simple permanent income equation. The latter performs best but all predictions are within 1% of consumption, however, it should be noted that the actual change in consumption is only about 1% anyway. This study though it has a negative flavour, does highlight the difficulties involved in disentangling the wealth effect from the permanent income effects and also the special care needed with regard to the error term. Zellner et al. have been concerned with the first of these problems and Zellner and Geisel with the second.

2.6.9. *Zellner et al.* (1965)

The aim of this study is to explore the role of habit, inertia, expectation and wealth in the consumption function. They propose initially four forms.

$$C_t = k_1 Y^{\mathrm{e}} + u_{1t}\,, \tag{2.38}$$

i.e., a simple permanent income hypothesis.

$$C_t = k_2(Y_t^{\mathrm{e}} + \beta Y_{t-1}^{\mathrm{e}} + \beta^2 Y_{t-2}^{\mathrm{e}} + ...) + u_{2t}\,. \tag{2.39}$$

This form attempts to allow for inertia in reactions to changes in permanent income.

$$C_t = \pi C_{t-1} + k_3 Y_t^e + u_{3t} \,. \tag{2.40}$$

Here habit persistence enters through the lagged consumption term. The fourth hypothesis is the expectation generating equation.

$$Y_t^e - Y_{t-1}^e = (1-\lambda)(Y_t - Y_{t-1}^e) \,. \tag{2.41}$$

Thus, substituting (2.41) into (2.38), (2.39) and (2.40) they derive the following equations.

$$C_t = \lambda C_{t-1} + k_1(1-\lambda) Y_t + u_{1t} - \lambda u_{1t-1} \tag{2.42}$$

$$C_t = (\lambda+\beta) C_{t-1} - \lambda\beta C_{t-2} + k(1-\lambda) Y_t + u_{2t} - (\lambda+\beta) u_{2t-1} \tag{2.43}$$

$$C_t = (\lambda+\pi) C_{t-1} - \lambda\pi C_{t-2} + k_3(1-\lambda) Y_t + u_{3t} - \lambda u_{3t-1} \,. \tag{2.44}$$

Eqs. (2.43) and (2.44) are indistinguishable except for the disturbance terms. However, both two stage least squares and ordinary least squares produce insignificant coefficients for C_{t-2} thus the authors concentrate on the simple permanent income equation. Previous studies stress the role of saving and an adjustment to a desired level of wealth, to allow for this the authors suggest

$$C_t = k_5 Y_t^e + \alpha(L_{t-1} - L_t^d) + u_{5t} \tag{2.45}$$

where L_t^d is the desired level of wealth and L_{t-1} is the previous period's actual level of wealth. In fact liquid assets are used for this variable, justified by the statement that they are probably the most strategic form of wealth. One further assumption is made, i.e.

$$L^d = \eta Y_t^e \tag{2.46}$$

Using (2.45), (2.46) and (2.41) they derive,

$$C_t = \lambda C_{t-1} + \alpha L_{t-1} - \alpha\lambda L_{t-2} + (k_5 - \alpha\eta)(1-\lambda) Y_t + u_{5t} - \lambda u_{5t-1} \,.$$

This equation embodies a non-linear restriction on the parameters, namely, that the coefficient of L_{t-2} is minus the product of those of C_{t-1} and L_{t-1}. The unconstrained estimates are

$$\text{OLS} \quad C_t = \underset{(3.606)}{-1.082} + \underset{(0.110)}{0.273}\, C_{t-1} + \underset{(0.172)}{0.560}\, L_{t-1} - \underset{(0.181)}{0.296}\, L_{t-2} + \underset{(0.085)}{0.517}\, Y_t$$

$$\text{TSLS} \quad C_t = \underset{(4.315)}{-9.104} + \underset{(0.140)}{0.531}\, C_{t-1} + \underset{(0.193)}{0.696}\, L_{t-1} - \underset{(0.200)}{0.468}\, L_{t-2} + \underset{(0.108)}{0.300}\, Y_t \,.$$

It will be noticed that the TSLS estimates are not inconsistent with the constraint. The authors then estimate the coefficients by a non-linear technique which forces the constraint to be satisfied. The results for α and λ are given in table 2.14. This shows that the liquid assets variable is very significant. In order to see whether this result is very sensitive to the specification used, further modifications are introduced, (2.46) is replaced by

$$L^{\mathrm{d}} = \eta Y_t^{\mathrm{e}} - \delta i_t \tag{2.47}$$

where i_t is the rate of interest, and the disturbance term of the resulting equation is assumed to follow a first order recursive system,

$$v_t = \rho v_{t-1} + \epsilon_t$$

where $v_t = u_{5t} - \lambda u_{5t-1}$ and ϵ_t is a non-autocorrelated random variable with zero mean, and variance σ^2.

The estimating equation that results from these modifications is

$$C_t = (\lambda + \rho)C_{t-1} - \lambda C_{t-2} + \alpha(L_{t-1} - \lambda L_{t-2}) - \rho\alpha(L_{t-2} - \lambda L_{t-3})$$

$$+ \alpha\delta(i_t - \lambda i_{t-1}) - \alpha\delta(i_{t-1} - \lambda i_{t-2}) + (k_5 - \alpha\eta)(1 - \lambda)(Y_t - \rho Y_{t-1}) + \epsilon_t \,.$$

Then they use non-linear ordinary least squares and two-stage least squares estimation procedures to obtain table 2.15. The value of λ determines the weighting pattern for the lag function which relates expected income to

Table 2.14
Non-linear OLS and TSLS estimates of α and λ.

	NL-OLS		NL-TSLS	
	Without constant	With constant	Without constant	With constant
λ	0.3778	0.2419	0.8729	0.5242
	(0.1062)	(0.1051)	(0.0480)	(0.1258)
α	0.2263	0.3758	0.7879	0.4992
	(0.0447)	(0.0502)	(0.2015)	(0.0968)

Table 2.15
Non-linear estimates of a quarterly consumption function including liquid assets.

	Without constant	With constant	Without constant	With constant
λ	0.3837	0.3253	0.8732	0.8152
	(0.1417)	(0.1254)	(0.0410)	(0.0746)
α	0.2818	0.3834	0.6974	0.6971
	(0.048)	(0.0509)	(0.1531)	(0.1435)
δ	24.825	2.574	10.168	8.797
	(11.92)	(10.29)	(7.251)	(7.330)
$k_5 - \alpha\eta$	0.7064	0.7551	0.4045	0.5294
	(0.0411)	(0.0401)	(0.1195)	(0.1232)
ρ	−0.0814	0.1002	−0.3213	−0.2892
	(0.1584)	(0.1386)	(0.1241)	(0.1248)
constant	–	−140.13	–	49.57
		(49.69)		(52.52)

actual income. The NL-OLS estimate produces an average lag of only 0.48 quarters whereas that of TSLS is 6.9 quarters. This latter value seems more reasonable. The estimate for α also seems more reasonable in that a higher value reflects a quicker reaction to an inbalance in the liquid asset position. A further reason for satisfaction with the TSLS estimates is that if $\eta = 0.764$, which is the sample average ratio of liquid asset to income, then the estimate of k_5, the property to consume, is 0.937 which is a reasonable value.

Zellner et al. conclude that there is no evidence for habit persistence or inertia in consumption over and above that already accounted for by expectational effects. However, they do find a strong influence by liquid assets which is evident in different formulations.

2.6.10. *Zellner and Geisel* (1968)

In this article the authors, in illustrating different ways of estimating distributed lagged models, present results for the simple permanent income model with varying stochastic specifications. Thus

$$C_t = kY_t^e + u_t$$

$$Y_t^e - Y_{t-1}^e = (1-\lambda)(Y_t - Y_{t-1}^e)$$

hence

$$C_t = \lambda C_{t-1} + k(1-\lambda)Y_t + u_t - \lambda u_{t-1} .$$

Four alternative assumptions regarding the disturbance term are considered. In each case ϵ_t is distributed normally and independently, with constant variance σ^2. The four assumptions are as follows,

I $\quad u_t - \lambda u_{t-1} = \epsilon_t$

II $\quad u_t = \epsilon_t$

III $\quad u_t = \rho u_{t-1} + \epsilon_t$

IV $\quad u_t - \lambda u_{t-1} = \gamma(u_{t-1} - \lambda u_{t-2}) + \epsilon_t$

Only if assumption I is valid can the parameters k and λ be estimated consistently by regressing C_t on C_{t-1} and Y_t. Zellner and Geisel present maximum likelihood estimates of these parameters under the different assumptions. We reproduce their table of results in table 2.16.

The data used are U.S. quarterly price deflated, seasonally adjusted series on personal disposable income and consumption expenditure taken from

Table 2.16
Maximum likelihood estimates of parameters in the consumption function with alternative disturbance terms.

	λ	k	b	ρ	γ	$\lambda/(1-\lambda)$
Assumption I	0.670 (0.108)	0.91 (0.031)	0.300 (0.095)	–	–	1.9155
II†	0.45 (0.029)	0.94 (0.16)	0.515 (n.c.)	–	–	0.8182
III	0.66 (0.085)	0.94 (0.46)	0.321 (n.c.)	0.69 (0.079)		1.9412
VI	0.772 (0.091)	0.96 (0.014)	0.218 (n.c.)	–	−0.13 (0.14)	3.3860

† The likelihood function had two maxima, the global maximum was ignored because it led to an unrealistic estimate of k^*.

Griliches et al. (1962). Notice that k is rather insensitive to differences in the disturbance assumptions, but λ is not. Assumption III indicates that the disturbances are strongly autocorrelated but that $\rho \approx \lambda$ and therefore assumption III collapses to assumption I. A similar conclusion stems from the assumption IV results where $\gamma \approx 0$.

These results suggest that assumption I is the most strongly supported by the data. In the rest of their paper Zellner and Geisel develop a Bayesian approach to estimating this function, and they find a measure of the extent to which the alternative assumptions are supported by the data. The fact that the simple permanent income function with a strongly correlated disturbance term fits the data well suggests a regularity which could be explained systematically rather than stochastically. Thus one conclusion of this study is that something more than a simple permanent income model is necessary to explain aggregate consumption.

2.6.11. *Conclusion*

We have seen that there are a number of theories of the savings decision but that it is very difficult to decide between them using time series data. The reasons for this are varied but probably the most important is that the estimating forms of the theories are very similar. What differences there are seem very slight when one considers the problems involved in any econometric estimation or testing procedure. The measurement error of net worth let alone permanent income is considerable. Low variation in the series of postwar consumption has heightened the econometric problems of serial correlation, lagged variables, least squares bias, etc. With such problems accompanying the use of time series it is not surprising that econometricians have looked to other types of data for help.

2.7. **Cross section studies**

Cross-section data in which different characteristics of consumers are isolated appear to be an ideal source for testing consumption theories. Friedman devoted most of his book to cross-section studies. Using (2.15) he was able to show that the permanent and relative income hypotheses are consistent with the findings of previous cross-section studies relating current consumption to current income whereas the absolute income hypothesis is not. Furthermore, he used (2.17) and (2.20) in a similar way to analyse the evidence of studies supporting the relative income hypothesis to show that their results tend to favour the permanent income slightly more. In addition he suggested some implications of the permanent income hypothesis which have been rigorously developed into tests by Eisner (1958). Modigliani and Ando (1960) extended these tests to the life cycle hypothesis. Because of the diverse nature of the cross-section data available, we will limit our discussion to these two studies using the Bureau of Labour Statistics and the Wharton School's survey of consumer expenditures. As the tests in the two studies are described other possible tests will become apparent for other data.

In 1950 the Bureau of Labour Statistics collected savings, income and expenditure data from 12,500 U.S. urban families. These data were analysed and published in Friend and Jones (1960). Since such characteristics as education, age and occupation of the principal earner in each household were registered, these data are apparently a rich source of material for testing savings theories. Modigliani and Ando (1960) show that the estimates of household savings are very unreliable and so the study is of much less value than would at first appear. Be that as it may, Eisner, and Ando and Modigliani, while not forgetting the weakness of the data, do feel that some analysis is possible.

2.7.1. *Eisner* (1958)

The tests that Eisner suggests stems from the fact that with this large sample it is possible to group the data according to various characteristics. Then three possible regression estimates of the marginal propensity to consume are available, namely: (a) the overall regression estimate; (b) a weighted average of regression estimates derived from each group; and (c) an estimate using the regression of group means. In his appendix which we reproduce, he develops the relationship between these estimates for a large sample under the permanent income hypothesis. Let,

C_{ig} = consumption of the *i*th household in *g*th group;
Y_{ig} = income of the *i*th household in *g*th group;
n_g = number of households in *g*th group;
$\overline{C}_g$ = mean consumption of *g*th group;
$\overline{Y}_g$ = mean income of *g*th group;
$\overline{C}$ = mean consumption of all groups;
$\overline{Y}$ = mean income of all groups;
n = Σn_g ;
G = Number of groups;
b_{CY} = regression coefficient of C and Y all combined;
b_{CY}^{iG} = weighted average of coefficients within group regression coefficients.

Let

$$c_{ig} = C_{ig} - \overline{C} \qquad y_{ig} = Y_{ig} - \overline{Y}$$

$$c_{i.g} = C_{ig} - \overline{C}_g \qquad y_{i.g} = Y_{ig} - \overline{Y}_g$$

$$c_g = \overline{C}_g - \overline{C} \qquad y_g = \overline{Y}_g - \overline{Y}\,.$$

Since

$$\sum_{g=1}^{G} \sum_{i=1}^{n_g} y_{ig} = \sum_{g=1}^{G} \sum_{i=1}^{n_g} (y_{ig}^p + y_{ig}^t)^2 = \sum_{g=1}^{G} \sum_{i=1}^{n_g} (y_{i.g}^p + y_g^p + y_{i.g}^t + y_g^t)^2$$

and

$$\sum_{g=1}^{G} \sum_{i=1}^{n_g} c_{ig} y_{ig} = \sum_{g=1}^{G} \sum_{i=1}^{n_g} (c_{i.g} + c_g)(y_{i.g} + y_g)$$

$$= \sum_{g=1}^{G} \sum_{i=1}^{n_g} c_{i.g} y_{i.g} + \sum_{g=1}^{G} n_g c_g y_g$$

$$b_{CY} = \frac{\sum_{g=1}^{G} \sum_{i=1}^{n_g} c_{i.g} y_{i.g} + \sum_{c=1}^{G} n_g c_g y_g}{\sum_{g=1}^{G} \sum_{i=1}^{n_g} y_{i.g}^2 + \sum_{g=1}^{G} n_g y_g^2}$$

Furthermore,

$$b_{CY}^{i.G} = \frac{\sum_{g=1}^{G} \left[b_{cy}^{i.g} \left(\sum_{i=1}^{n_g} y_{i.g}^2 \right) \right]}{\sum_{g=1}^{G} \sum_{i=1}^{n_g} y_{i.g}^2} = \frac{\sum_{g=1}^{G} (n_g - 1) S_{c_{i.g} y_{i.g}}}{\sum_{g=1}^{G} (n_g - 1) S_{y_{i.g}}^2}$$

$$= \frac{\sum_{g=1}^{G} \sum_{i=1}^{n_g} c_{i.g} y_{i.g}}{\sum_{g=1}^{G} \sum_{i=1}^{n_g} y_{i.g}^2}\,.$$

Since

$$\sum_{i=1}^{n_g} c_{i.g} y_{i.g} = (n_g - 1) S_{c_{i.g} y_{i.g}}$$

$$\sum y_{i.g}^2 = (n_g - 1) S_{y_{i.g}}$$

and

$$b_{\overline{CY}}^g = \frac{\sum_{g=1}^{G} n_g c_g y_g}{\sum_{g=1}^{G} n_g y_g^2} .$$

If $r_{y^p y^t} = 0$, which is assumed by Friedman, where r is the correlation coefficient, then,

$$E\left[\frac{1}{n-1} \sum_{g=1}^{G} \sum_{i=1}^{n_g} y_{ig}^2\right]$$

$$= E\left[\frac{1}{n-1}\left(\sum_{g=1}^{G} \sum_{i=1}^{n_g} (y_{i.g}^p + y_g^p)^2 + \sum_{g=1}^{G} \sum_{i=1}^{n_g} (y_{i.g}^t + y_g^t)^2\right]\right.$$

$$= E\left[\frac{1}{n-1}\left(\sum_{g=1}^{G} \sum_{i=1}^{n_g} (y_{i.g}^p)^2 + \sum_{g=1}^{G} n_g (y_g^p)^2\right.\right.$$

$$\left.\left.+ \sum_{g=1}^{G} \sum_{i=1}^{n_g} (y_{i.g}^t)^2 + \sum_{g=1}^{G} n_g (y_g^t)^2\right)\right]. \qquad (2.48)$$

Similarly

$$E\left[\frac{1}{n-1}\sum_{g=1}^{G}\sum_{i=1}^{n_g} c_{ig}y_{ig}\right]$$

$$= E\left[\frac{1}{n-1}\left(\sum_{g=1}^{G}\sum_{i=1}^{n_g}(c_{i.g}^p + c_{i.g}^t)(y_{i.g}^p + y_{i.g}^t) + \sum_{g=1}^{G} n_g(c_g^p + c_y^t)(y_g^p + y_g^t)\right]\right.$$

$$= E\left[\frac{1}{n-1}\left(\sum_{g=1}^{G}\sum_{i=1}^{n_g}(c_{i.g}^p y_{i.g}^p + c_{i.g}^t y_{i.g}^p + c_{i.g}^p y_{i.g}^t + c_{i.g}^t y_{i.g}^t)\right.\right.$$

$$\left.+ \sum_{g=1}^{G} n_g(c_g^p y_g^p + c_g^t y_g^p + c_g^p y_g^t + c_g^t y_g^t)\right]. \tag{2.49}$$

Furthermore if

$$r_{c^t y^t} = r_{c^p c^t} = r_{c^t y^p} = 0$$

also assumed by Friedman, then (2.49) becomes

$$E\left[\frac{1}{n-1}\left(\sum_{g=1}^{G}\sum_{i=1}^{n_g} c_{ig}y_{ig}\right)\right] = E\left[\frac{1}{n-1}\left(\sum_{g=1}^{G}\sum_{i=1}^{n_g} c_{i.g}^p y_{i.g}^p + \sum_{g=1}^{G} n_g c_g^p y_g^p\right)\right] \tag{2.50}$$

which shows that b_{CY} is the ratio of (2.50) to (2.48). Thus,

$$\underset{n\to\infty}{\text{plim}}\, b_{CY} = \lim_{n\to\infty} \frac{\sum_{g=1}^{G}\sum_{i=1}^{n_g} c_{i.g}^p y_{i.g}^p + \sum_{g=1}^{G} n_g c_g^p y_g^p}{\sum_{g=1}^{G}\sum_{i=1}^{n_g}(y_{i.g}^p)^2 + \sum_{g=1}^{G} n_g(y_g^p)^2 + \sum_{g=1}^{G}\sum_{i=1}^{n_g}(y_{i.g}^t)^2 + \sum_{g=1}^{G} n_g(y_g^t)^2} \tag{2.51}$$

Similarly,

$$\underset{n\to\infty}{\text{plim}}\, b_{CY}^{i.G} = \lim_{n\to\infty} \frac{\sum_{g=1}^{G}\sum_{i=1}^{n_g} c_{i.g}^{p} y_{i.g}^{p}}{\sum_{g=1}^{G}\sum_{i=1}^{n_g} [(y_{i.g}^{p})^2 + (y_{i.g}^{t})^2]}$$

and

$$\underset{n\to\infty}{\text{plim}}\, b_{CY}^{g} = \lim_{n\to\infty} \frac{\sum_{g=1}^{G} n_g c_g^{p} y_g^{p}}{\sum_{g=1}^{G} n_g [(y_g^{p})^2 + (y_g^{t})^2]} \, .$$

If the covariance of c^p and y^p is not related to the variable of classification,

$$k = b_{c^p y^p} = \lim_{n\to\infty} \frac{\sum_{g=1}^{G}\sum_{i=1}^{n_g} c_{i.g}^{p} y_{i.g}^{p}}{\sum_{g=1}^{G}\sum_{i=1}^{n_g} (y_{i.g}^{p})^2} = \lim_{n\to\infty} \frac{\sum_{g=1}^{G} n_g c_g^{p} y_g^{p}}{\sum_{g=1}^{G} n_g (y_g^{p})^2} \, . \tag{2.52}$$

Friedman claims that the ratio of permanent income to total income variance is likely to be less within groups than the ratio of the overall variances, i.e.,

$$\lim_{n\to\infty} \frac{\sum_{g=1}^{G}\sum_{i=1}^{n_g} (y_{i.g}^{p})^2}{\sum_{g=1}^{G}\sum_{i=1}^{n_g} (y_{i.g}^{p})^2 + (y_{i.g}^{t})^2}$$

$$< \lim_{n\to\infty} \frac{\sum_{g=1}^{G}\sum_{i=1}^{n_g} (y_{i.g}^{p})^2 + \sum_{g=1}^{G} n_g (y_g^{p})^2}{\sum_{g=1}^{G}\sum_{i=1}^{n_g} [(y_{i.g}^{p})^2 + (y_{i.g}^{t})^2] + \sum_{g=1}^{G} n_g [(y_g^{p})^2 + (y_g^{t})^2]} \, .$$

For this to hold it is necessary that

$$\lim_{n\to\infty} \frac{\sum_{g=1}^{G}\sum_{i=1}^{n_g} (y_{i.g}^p)^2}{\sum_{g=1}^{G}\sum_{i=1}^{n_g} (y_{i.g}^p)^2 + (y_{i.g}^t)^2} < \lim_{n\to\infty} \frac{\sum_{g=1}^{G} n_g (y_g^p)^2}{\sum_{g=1}^{G} n_g[(y_g^p)^2 + (y_g^t)^2]} . \tag{2.53}$$

A sufficient condition for this is that the variable of classification is related to permanent income but not to transitory income, i.e.,

$$\lim_{n_g\to\infty} \bar{Y}_g^t = 0 \qquad (g = 1, 2, ..., G)$$

$$\therefore \quad \lim_{n\to\infty} \bar{Y}^t = 0$$

and

$$\lim_{n\to\infty} \frac{1}{n} \sum_{g=1}^{G} n_g (y_g^t)^2 = 0 .$$

If Friedman's assumptions are valid and the covariance of c^p and y^p is not correlated with g, multiplying (2.53) by (2.52) gives

$$\lim_{n\to\infty} \frac{\sum_{g=1}^{G}\sum_{i=1}^{n_g} c_{i.g}^p y_{i.g}^p}{\sum_{g=1}^{G}\sum_{i=1}^{n_g} (y_{i.g}^p)^2 + (y_{i.g}^t)^2} < \lim_{n\to\infty} \frac{\sum_{g=1}^{G} n_g c_g^p y_g^p}{\sum_{g=1}^{G} n_g[(y_g^p)^2 + (y_g^t)^2]} . \tag{2.54}$$

i.e.,

$$\lim_{n\to\infty} b_{CY}^{i.G} < \lim_{n\to\infty} b_{\overline{CY}}^{g} .$$

Comparing (2.42) and (2.39) we see that,

$$\operatorname*{plim}_{n\to\infty} b_{CY}^{i.G} < \operatorname*{plim}_{n\to\infty} b_{CY} < \operatorname*{plim}_{n\to\infty} b_{\overline{CY}}^{g} .$$

Thus, if we have a large sample and can classify the observations such that the expected permanent income varies from group to group but expected transitory income does not, then the regression coefficient based on group means should be bigger than that based on all observations, which itself should be larger than the weighted average of coefficients derived from within each group. Furthermore, if the expected mean transitory income is the same in all groups, i.e.,

$$\lim_{n\to\infty} \frac{1}{n} \sum_{g=1}^{G} n_g (y_g^t)^2 = 0$$

then

$$\operatorname*{plim}_{n\to\infty} b_{CY}^{\underline{g}} = \lim_{n\to\infty} \frac{\sum_{g=1}^{G} n_g c_g^p y_g^p}{\sum_{g=1}^{G} n_g (y_g^p)^2} = k\,.$$

Thus the regression based on means produces an estimate of k.

The importance of these results lies in the fact that they are different from the results one would get from the absolute income hypothesis. In that case the regression estimates should be the same regardless of whether the data comprises actual observations or cell means.

Some of Eisner's linear regression results are reproduced in table 2.17. Each group contains 567 observations with the exception of the city classification which contains 81. All households in the category are used, that is he does not exclude those whose heads are either young or old. With the

Table 2.17
Marginal propensities to conclude estimated from cross-section data.

Variable of classification	Within $b_{CY}^{i.G}$	Overall b_{CY}	Between $b_{CY}^{\underline{g}}$
Age	0.661	0.681	0.975
Occupation	0.654	0.679	0.806
City	0.686	0.691	0.935
Age by city	0.656	0.681	0.949
Occupation by city	0.650	0.679	0.808

exception of the city classification the differences between the coefficients are significant at the 0.001 level of significance. The ordering of these coefficients for each classification is consistent with the relations derived by Eisner. Notice also that the within group coefficient falls when the classification becomes finer, i.e., the elements are more homogeneous. This is also consistent with the permanent income hypothesis since it can be shown that the regression coefficient is influenced by the proportion of transient income variance to total income variance. This will be indicated below in the discussion of Modigliani and Ando's work. Eisner also considers the log linear regression coefficients but these are dealt with more thoroughly by Ando and Modigliani.

2.7.2. *Modigliani and Ando* (1960)

Originally in this article the authors intended to differentiate the life cycle and permanent income hypotheses and test the differences using the BLS–Wharton survey. Unfortunately, they discovered sufficient measurement errors in the data to make it impossible to distinguish these hypotheses. As a result they concentrate on showing that the two hypotheses have similar implications and testing whether the data are consistent with these implications. In fact they show that both theories result in a log–linear relation between measured consumption and measured income and that the between group regression coefficients should be greater than the overall regression and equal to unity. The derivation of these results for the life cycle theory is quite tedious, so in this brief summary we will only outline their approach with reference to the permanent income hypothesis. Although they follow the same test procedure as that of Eisner they set up the model as follows

$$C = kY_p^m U'$$

$$Y = Y_p V'$$

where U' and V' are stochastic variables. Then

$$\log C = k_1 + m \log Y_p + \log U$$

$$\log Y = k_2 + \log Y_p + \log V$$

where k_1 and k_2 are constants, and $\log U$ and $\log V$ are stochastic variables with zero expected values, and all the covariances between them and $\log Y_p$ are also zero.

Then

$$\underset{n\to\infty}{\text{plim}}\, b_{\log C \log Y} = \underset{n\to\infty}{\text{plim}} \frac{\text{cov}(\log C \log Y)}{\text{var}(\log Y)}$$

$$= \frac{m \,\text{var}(\log Y_p)}{\text{var}(\log Y_p) + \text{var}(\log V)}.$$

This shows that the regression coefficient of the log regression depends upon the variance of the transitory income, since V reflects the transitory components of income. Any occupation or group which has a stable income should show a higher elasticity than one with a less stable income. Friedman has used this implication to test his theory by considering different groups of earners.

Modigliani and Ando also consider the data being classified into G groups in such a way that

$$E(\overline{\log V_g}) = 0$$

and

$$E(\overline{\log Y_{pg}} - \overline{\log Y_p})\, \overline{\log U_g} = 0$$

and

$$E(\overline{\log V_g^2}) = \frac{\text{var} \log V}{n_g}$$

where barred terms represent means, i.e., $\overline{\log \boldsymbol{Y}_{pg}}$ is the mean log of permanent incomes in group g ($g = 1, 2, ..., G$).

From these assumptions they develop an approximate relation

$$E(\overline{b_{\log C \log Y}}) \approx \frac{m \,\text{var}\, \overline{\log Y_{pg}}}{\text{var} \log Y_{pg} + (G/n)\, \text{var} \log V}.$$

Although this result is in terms of means of logarithms, i.e., logarithms of geometric means, Modigliani and Ando show that the corresponding result holds for the regression involving the logarithms of arithmetic means, provided the variances of consumption and income tend to be the same in each class. Thus as n gets larger the log regression on all means provides an estimate of m, the elasticity of permanent consumption to changes in permanent income. If the life cycle and strict permanent income hypotheses hold, m should be unity. A further result is that as n increases $b_{\overline{\log C}\,\overline{\log Y}}$ increases whereas $b_{\log C \log Y}$ does not and the overall regression coefficient $b_{\log C \log Y}$ should be lower than $b_{\overline{\log C}\,\overline{\log Y}}$. Thus, provided we have a large sample and can find classifications which satisfy the above conditions, we can test these implications.

The first classification they consider is by income, this definitely does not satisfy the criteria necessary for the test to be valid. However, they use the regression on cell means as a way of estimating $b_{\log C \log Y}$ since in this case cell means should more or less lie on the overall regression line. Because the lowest income group has a large variance, which conflicts with the assumption necessary to work in arithmetic rather than geometric income, this group is omitted when the value of $b_{\log \overline{C} \log \overline{Y}}$ is calculated.

As in the Eisner study the classification criteria imply that permanent income and permanent consumption should vary between the groups but that transitory income should not. Furthermore, mean permanent income and mean transitory consumption should not be correlated between the groups. This latter would occur if the value of k varied from group to group in contradiction to the test's implicit assumption that it does not. Ando and Modigliani present results based on a number of classifications, namely by city; education; occupation; age, all households; age, only households containing at least one full time earner; expenditure on housing, renters; expenditure on housing, owners bought prior to 1946; and expenditure on housing, owners bought post 1946. The variance of log Y gives some indication of the variance of permanent income but, for the other two criteria, we have to rely on a priori ideas. Classification by city, education, occupation (provided the 'not gainfully employed' are excluded) and expenditure on housing, one should expect to be satisfactory on these accounts. Age, however, one would not expect to be satisfactory since young people tend to earn less than their permanent income. In as much as education and age are correlated this too could be unsatisfactory. Some of the results presented by Modigliani and Ando are reproduced in table 2.18.

In all cases except income the group mean regression coefficient is higher than the overall regression coefficient (i.e., that of income group). However, only the city, which in any case has a low variance, and expenditure on housing groups are consistent with $m = 1$, i.e., that the ratio of permanent consumption to income is independent of income. The coefficients of the education regressions are much lower than 1 and need some explanation. If educa-

Table 2.18
Income elasticity of consumption and the variance of income derived from group means.

Classification by	$b_{\log \overline{C} \log \overline{Y}}$	var $\overline{Y}$
Income	0.847	0.0464
City	0.975	0.0014
Education	0.858	0.0067
Occupation excluding 'not gainfully employed'	0.880	0.0088
Age – all	0.880	0.0081
excluding families with no full-time earner	0.963	0.0021
Expenditure on housing renters	1.033	0.0178
pre 1945 home owners	0.972	0.0168
post 1945 home owners	0.975	0.0134

tion is correlated with k, the consumption income ratio, perhaps through the influence of age, then this could produce the low value for $b_{\log \overline{C} \log \overline{Y}}$. We can, however, test whether k is correlated with income within the education groups in exactly the same way as we have done for the total sample. The important education difference is that of college education or no college education, thus the sample has been divided into those who have had thirteen or more years of education and those who have had less. In order to eliminate some of the effects of age and unemployment only families who have at least one full-time earner aged between 20 and 65 have been included. This group of families was then sorted into those who rented and those who owned houses in order to make the samples more homogeneous with regard to type of tenure. Thus, in effect Ando and Modigliani have four sets of data, one of which is, for instance, 'Home owners with more than 12 years' education'. Each of these sets are then classified by income, to gain an estimate of the overall elasticity, and by housing expenditure. The results appear in table 2.19.

Thus, when the data are cleansed, as it were, from the effects of education and to some extent age, they are seen to be consistent with the life cycle and permanent hypothesis. Ando and Modigliani similarly distinguish 'self employed' and 'non-self employed' with similar results.

This study besides showing that the so called 'new consumption' theories are consistent with the BLS–Wharton survey data, emphasizes the use of

Table 2.19
Tests based on within education classes regression coefficients.

	Classification by income	Housing expenditure
Renters		
12 yr and under	0.91	1.08
13 yr and over	0.89	0.96
Owners		
12 yr and under	0.83	1.02
13 yr and over	0.75	0.95

cross section data to adjust for certain characteristics which are impossible to isolate in time series data. Of course, if this is to be done to any extent, the total sample size must be large or else each cell will have few observations. Before considering the global conclusions of this chapter it should be remembered that usually cross section data imply data for one time period only which, given the dynamic nature of many economic models, limits their general use – see Section 3.5 and Grunfeld (1961).

2.8. Conclusion

In the field of consumption functions we are faced with a number of competing hypotheses concerning behaviour. The relative income hypothesis is based on an idea of consumers adjusting the quantity of their consumption because of interaction with their neighbours. The permanent income and the life cycle hypothesis are based on consumers smoothing their consumption throughout their lives. The wealth hypothesis puts more emphasis on the role of uncertainty and consumers' desire to hold wealth for security. Although the central themes of the wealth and the permanent income/life cycle hypotheses differ, supporters of these views have borrowed from each other such that their final empirical forms involve elements of both consumption smoothing and risk reduction. The time series studies do not really provide evidence to choose between the empirical specifications in which the hypotheses have been proposed. Use of the simple absolute income form has been in disfavour following the early forecast errors using it, but probably this disfavour stems more from the lack of success in explaining cross section data. The cross section studies do not allow us to choose between the other specifications though perhaps the permanent income/life cycle hypotheses might have a slight edge on the relative income hypothesis. With the exception of the absolute income hypothesis the decision really has to be made on a priori grounds.

In the time series studies some authors have used variables in current prices and others in constant prices. Duesenberry (1949, p. 23) emphasises the role of quality changes and, if price changes reflect this quality change, then there may be an argument for using consumption measured in current prices. If price changes reflect inflation rather than quality changes, deflated variables are the most appropriate since all the hypotheses are based on theories involving real quantities. Evans (1967) raised the question of whether a consumption or an income deflator should be used. A convincing answer to the deflator problem would probably involve a careful discussion of the aggregation processes which as yet is lacking in the literature. Recently Branson and Klevorick (1966) have suggested that, contrary to the theories above, in the short run consumers suffer from money illusion. They estimate a consumption function involving the consumer price index for the U.S. and conclude that money illusion exists. Given the form they suggest, regressions involving variables in current and constant prices can both be viewed as mis-specifications, and the argument becomes one of which leads to less bias. Consumption functions play their major roles in economics as part of macro models and because of this it is difficult to discuss their uses in isolation. We started the chapter showing how poorly the simple Keynesian functions forecast. This has been one aspect which authors have reported and there does seem to have been some improvement. The consumption function prediction errors of table 2.1 are of the order of 6% whereas those of Spiro (1962) are of the order of 3%. Griliches et al. refer to prediction errors for the quarterly model which they re-estimate of less than 1%, although the growth of consumption itself is only of the order of 1% anyway.

Few studies have stressed the policy implications of their work although Stone is one exception to this rule. The general conclusions one would draw from this chapter are that income changes have delayed reactions on consumption and that policies aimed at affecting the level of consumption via income changes should take account of this.

The discussion in this chapter also indicates the rather special role of consumer durables, which have tended to be excluded by the theories of this chapter, although for short run stabilisation policies an understanding of their determinants would be most useful. In the next chapter durables are considered in more detail, but, again, the analysis is not wholly satisfactory.

CHAPTER 3

DEMAND FUNCTIONS

3.1. Introduction

Although the savings decision determines the level of aggregate consumption the impact of this consumption on the economy can have different effects according to its composition. For instance, some items of consumption have a greater import content than others, thus a given level of aggregate consumption could involve different levels of total imports. The composition of aggregate consumption is also important for investment planning both for government and industry. Although any particular industry is often only interested in the demand of its particular commodity, it should be borne in mind that all the final consumer demand for these individual commodities should add up to aggregate consumption. Indeed the recent econometric approach to demand functions has been in terms of a complete set of equations explaining the demand for every commodity (or group of commodities). The advantage of the complete set of equations approach is that consistency of each equation with the total expenditure is usually assured and hence, the resulting model can be used in a model of the whole economy. An example of this is Stone's linear expenditure system which is very convenient for his growth model (see Stone, 1962b). A further advantage is that estimation of demand equations is more efficient because more a priori knowledge can be incorporated. In addition to these obvious reasons for studying the allocation decision of consumers, there are more less obvious ones. In this category would appear such items as the measurement of utility and the comparison of tastes differences between countries. Classical consumer theory is invoked to relate these unobservable quantities to observable quantities, i.e., prices, incomes and expenditures. The classical theory of demand conceives of an individual consumer facing a perfect market equipped with a fixed income which he allocates to a particular set of commodities whose prices he knows. In order to do this the consumer is assumed to have a choice index or utility function which reflects his ranking of the commodities. Assuming that he maximises his utility it is possible to derive demand functions, i.e., functions relating the quantity of each good that he buys to prices and income. Notice that this theory relates only to one period of time and that all income is spent. This theory has been found useful as a consistent framework for the allocation decision especially where total expenditure is the 'income' being allocated.

Although the classical theory of the consumer is aesthetically appealing it does have serious drawbacks. In order to derive market demand functions it is necessary to aggregate over individual functions although this problem is often ignored. A further problem stems from the fact that the underlying theory is static and as a result econometric functions based on it have been found wanting with regard to the explanations of durables and goods strongly affected by habit. Demand functions where dynamic considerations are important have been developed but usually on a more or less ad hoc basis. The theory also does not allow for stochastic factors influencing demand although there have been some recent attempts to incorporate them into the classical framework.

The number of published econometric demand studies is enormous. Our aim in this chapter will be to present the major lines of approach from the point of view of providing a set of demand functions covering the different components of aggregate consumer expenditure. We shall not pursue the topics of welfare measures, optimal index numbers or analysis of individual commodities although much of the material of this chapter will have relevance to such matters. We shall cover first the approaches which stem from the static theory and later look at the studies based on a dynamic approach.

3.2. The static theory of the consumer

As stated previously one of the advantages of the classical approach is that it provides a number of constraints on the parameters of the demand functions which are of considerable help in their estimation. Presumably the theory of consumer behaviour is familiar to the reader but we shall take some time to develop these constraints, presenting them in a number of different ways. In doing this we shall practically reproduce a survey article on the functional forms of demand functions by Goldberger (1967). Indeed much of the discussion of static demand functions will be based on Goldberger's paper digressing to present the empirical results whenever convenient.

Essentially Goldberger presents three relations connecting the slopes of the demand curves. Then these are transformed to present the corresponding relations between the elasticities and, by a further transformation, those between the average budget shares. Houthakker (1960) has shown that the price effect can be separated into an income effect, a specific substitution effect, and a general substitution effect. This separation of the income effect enables one to consider the slopes of the demand function after they have been compensated for the income effect. There are similar income compensated concepts for the elasticities and the average budget shares. Goldberger then presents the constraints in terms of these concepts. However, because of Houthakker's development of the Slutsky equation it is possible to derive the slopes which have been compensated for the income effect and the general substitution effect, and also the corresponding elasticities and average budget shares. Once more the constraints can be set out in terms of these new concepts. The advantage of doing so is that the corresponding demand functions can be derived and the constraints expressed in a very simple manner. Furthermore, the inter-relationships stemming from the utility function are more clearly apparent as will be seen later.

3.2.1.

Let $\mathbf{q}$ and $\mathbf{p}$ be n dimensional vectors of quantities and their corresponding prices. Let $u(\mathbf{q}')$ be the utility function with $\mathbf{u}_q$ the vector of first order partials and $\mathbf{U}$ the matrix of second order partials which is symmetric and negative definite.

Maximising

$$u(\mathbf{q}') - \lambda(\mathbf{p}'\mathbf{q} - y)$$

gives the set of demand functions

$$\mathbf{u}_q = \lambda\mathbf{p} \qquad \mathbf{p}'\mathbf{q} = y \tag{3.1}$$

where λ and y are scalars representing a lagrangian multiplier and income.

Since we know that (3.1) can be written in the form $\mathbf{q} = \mathbf{q}(\mathbf{p}', y)$ we can write,

$$\mathrm{d}\mathbf{q} = \mathbf{q}_y \,\mathrm{d}y + \mathbf{Q}_p \,\mathrm{d}\mathbf{p} \tag{3.2a}$$

$$\mathrm{d}\lambda = \lambda_y \,\mathrm{d}y + \boldsymbol{\lambda}_p' \,\mathrm{d}\mathbf{p} \,,$$

i.e.,

$$\begin{bmatrix} \mathrm{d}\mathbf{q} \\ -\mathrm{d}\lambda \end{bmatrix} = \begin{bmatrix} \mathbf{q}_y & \mathbf{Q}_p \\ -\lambda_y & -\boldsymbol{\lambda}'_p \end{bmatrix} \begin{bmatrix} \mathrm{d}y \\ \mathrm{d}\mathbf{p} \end{bmatrix} \tag{3.3}$$

where

$$\mathrm{d}\mathbf{q} = \begin{bmatrix} \mathrm{d}q_1 \\ \mathrm{d}q_2 \\ \vdots \\ \mathrm{d}q_n \end{bmatrix} \qquad \mathrm{d}\mathbf{p} = \begin{bmatrix} \mathrm{d}p_1 \\ \mathrm{d}p_2 \\ \vdots \\ \mathrm{d}p_n \end{bmatrix}$$

$$\mathbf{q}_y = \begin{bmatrix} \dfrac{\partial q_1}{\partial y} \\ \dfrac{\partial q_2}{\partial y} \\ \vdots \\ \dfrac{\partial q_n}{\partial y} \end{bmatrix} \qquad \boldsymbol{\lambda}_p = \begin{bmatrix} \dfrac{\partial \lambda}{\partial p_1} \\ \dfrac{\partial \lambda}{\partial p_2} \\ \vdots \\ \dfrac{\partial \lambda}{\partial p_n} \end{bmatrix}$$

$$\mathbf{Q}_p = \begin{bmatrix} \dfrac{\partial q_1}{\partial p_1} & \dfrac{\partial q_1}{\partial p_2} & \cdots & \dfrac{\partial q_1}{\partial q_n} \\ \dfrac{\partial q_2}{\partial p_1} & \dfrac{\partial q_2}{\partial p_2} & \cdots & \dfrac{\partial q_2}{\partial q_n} \\ \vdots & & & \vdots \\ \dfrac{\partial q_n}{\partial p_1} & \dfrac{\partial q_n}{\partial p_2} & & \dfrac{\partial q_n}{\partial p_n} \end{bmatrix}$$

$$\lambda_y = \frac{\partial \lambda}{\partial y}.$$

Differentiating (3.1) gives

$$\mathbf{U}d\mathbf{q} = \mathbf{p}d\lambda + \lambda d\mathbf{p}$$

$$dy = \mathbf{p}'d\mathbf{q} + \mathbf{q}'d\mathbf{p}$$

i.e.

$$\begin{bmatrix} \mathbf{U} & \mathbf{p} \\ \mathbf{p}' & 0 \end{bmatrix} \begin{bmatrix} d\mathbf{q} \\ -d\lambda \end{bmatrix} = \begin{bmatrix} \mathbf{0} & \lambda\mathbf{I} \\ 1 & -\mathbf{q}' \end{bmatrix} \begin{bmatrix} dy \\ d\mathbf{p} \end{bmatrix} . \tag{3.4}$$

Thus by substituting from (3.3) and comparing coefficients

$$\begin{bmatrix} \mathbf{U} & \mathbf{p} \\ \mathbf{p}' & 0 \end{bmatrix} \begin{bmatrix} \mathbf{q}_y & \mathbf{Q}_p \\ -\lambda_y & -\boldsymbol{\lambda}'_p \end{bmatrix} = \begin{bmatrix} \mathbf{0} & \lambda\mathbf{I} \\ 1 & -\mathbf{q}' \end{bmatrix} . \tag{3.5}$$

Taking the inverse of the first matrix by partitioning and using this to pre-multiply both sides of (3.5) gives

$$\begin{bmatrix} \mathbf{q}_y & \mathbf{Q}_p \\ -\lambda_y & \boldsymbol{\lambda}'_p \end{bmatrix} \tag{3.6}$$

$$= (\mathbf{p}'\mathbf{U}\mathbf{p}^{-1})^{-1} \begin{bmatrix} \mathbf{U}^{-1}\mathbf{p} & (\mathbf{p}'\mathbf{U}^{-1}\mathbf{p})\lambda\mathbf{U}^{-1} - \lambda\mathbf{U}^{-1}\mathbf{p}(\mathbf{U}^{-1}\mathbf{p})' - \mathbf{U}^{-1}\mathbf{p}\mathbf{q}' \\ -1 & \lambda(\mathbf{U}^{-1}\mathbf{p})' + \mathbf{q}' \end{bmatrix}$$

hence

$$\lambda_y = (\mathbf{p}'\mathbf{U}^{-1}\mathbf{p})^{-1} \tag{3.11}$$

$$\mathbf{q}_y = \lambda_y\mathbf{U}^{-1}\mathbf{p} \tag{3.12}$$

$$\boldsymbol{\lambda}_p = -(\lambda\mathbf{q}_y + \lambda_y\mathbf{q}) \tag{3.13}$$

$$\mathbf{Q}_p = \lambda\mathbf{U}^{-1} - \lambda\lambda_y^{-1}\mathbf{q}_y\mathbf{q}'_y - \mathbf{q}_y\mathbf{q}' . \tag{3.14}$$

In order to see the meaning of (3.14) consider a typical element

$$\frac{\partial q_i}{\partial p_j} = \frac{\lambda \text{ co-factor of } u_{ij}}{|\mathbf{U}|} - \frac{\lambda(\partial q_i/\partial y)(\partial q_j/\partial y)}{\partial\lambda/\partial y} - q_j \frac{\partial q_i}{\partial y}.$$

This shows how the price effect can be broken up into three elements. The last term is obviously the income effect, thus the first two represent the substitution effect. Houthakker has called the second term the general substitution effect and it involves no utility terms. This shows that goods can be substitutes because they are competing for the same income as well as because they are related through similar tastes. This latter aspect is reflected in the first term which is called the specific substitution effect. The importance of this breakdown will become apparent later, but, for the moment, it should be realised that our a priori knowledge on the degree to which goods are substitutes usually refers to the specific substitution effect and hence it is important to isolate this.

3.2.2

Eqs. (3.11)–(3.14) are a set of relations which the slopes of the demand functions must satisfy. These can be put into more convenient form as follows. Using (3.12) and (3.11),

$$\mathbf{p}'\mathbf{q}_y = \lambda_y \mathbf{p}'\mathbf{U}^{-1}\mathbf{p} = 1 \;. \tag{3.15a}$$

Also,

$$\begin{aligned} \mathbf{Q}_p'\mathbf{p} &= \lambda \mathbf{U}^{-1}\mathbf{p} - \lambda\lambda_y^{-1}\mathbf{q}_y\mathbf{q}_y'\mathbf{p} - \mathbf{q}\mathbf{q}_y'\mathbf{p} \\ &= \lambda\lambda_y^{-1}\mathbf{q}_y - \lambda\lambda_y^{-1}\mathbf{q}_y - \mathbf{q} \\ &= -\mathbf{q}\,. \end{aligned} \tag{3.16a}$$

Furthermore, since $\mathbf{U}^{-1}$ is symmetric so is $\lambda\mathbf{U}^{-1} - \lambda\lambda_y^{-1}\mathbf{q}_y\mathbf{q}_y'$ hence

$$(\mathbf{Q}_p + \mathbf{q}_y\mathbf{q}')' = (\mathbf{Q}_p + \mathbf{q}_y\mathbf{q}')\,. \tag{3.17a}$$

Notice the form of the results so far. Eq. (3.2a) reflects the demand function and (3.15a), (3.16a) and (3.17a) reflect the constraints on the parameters of the demand function stemming from the classical theory. In this particular case, i.e., case (a) the results are in terms of the slopes, i.e. $\mathbf{Q}_p$ and $\mathbf{q}_y$. In what follows the same information will be presented in terms of other concepts, e.g. in case (b) the concept will be the elasticity rather than the slope, but throughout, the numbering of the equations will be parallel.

3.2.3

To develop the analysis in terms of elasticities it is convenient to introduce these further definitions.

$$\mathbf{w} = \begin{bmatrix} w_1 \\ w_2 \\ \vdots \\ w_n \end{bmatrix} = \begin{bmatrix} \frac{p_1 q_1}{y} \\ \frac{p_2 q_2}{y} \\ \vdots \\ \frac{p_n q_n}{y} \end{bmatrix}$$

i.e. w_i is the budget share of the ith good.

$$\hat{\mathbf{q}} = \begin{bmatrix} q_1 & 0 & \dots & 0 \\ 0 & q_2 & \dots & 0 \\ \vdots & \vdots & & \vdots \\ 0 & 0 & \dots & q_n \end{bmatrix}$$

i.e. the circumflex represents the diagonal matrix corresponding to the vector concerned.

Thus

$$\hat{\mathbf{p}} = \begin{bmatrix} p_1 & 0 & \dots & 0 \\ 0 & p_2 & \dots & 0 \\ \vdots & \vdots & & \vdots \\ 0 & 0 & \dots & p_n \end{bmatrix}$$

$$\boldsymbol{\eta} = \begin{bmatrix} \eta_1 \\ \\ \eta_2 \\ \vdots \\ \eta_n \end{bmatrix} = \begin{bmatrix} \dfrac{\partial q_1}{\partial y} \cdot \dfrac{y}{q_1} \\ \\ \dfrac{\partial q_2}{\partial y} \dfrac{y}{q_2} \\ \vdots \\ \dfrac{\partial q_n}{\partial y} \dfrac{y}{q_n} \end{bmatrix} = y\hat{\mathbf{q}}^{-1}\mathbf{q}_y$$

i.e. $\boldsymbol{\eta}$ is the vector of income elasticities.

$$\mathbf{H} = \begin{bmatrix} \eta_{11} & \eta_{12} & \cdots & \eta_{1n} \\ \\ \eta_{21} & \eta_{22} & \cdots & \eta_{2n} \\ \vdots & \vdots & & \vdots \\ \eta_{n1} & \eta_{n2} & \cdots & \eta_{nn} \end{bmatrix} = \begin{bmatrix} \dfrac{\partial q_1}{\partial p_1}\dfrac{p_1}{q_1} & \dfrac{\partial q_1}{\partial p_2}\dfrac{p_2}{q_1} & \cdots & \dfrac{\partial q_1}{\partial p_n}\dfrac{p_n}{q_1} \\ \\ \dfrac{\partial q_2}{\partial p_1}\dfrac{p_1}{q_2} & \dfrac{\partial q_2}{\partial p_2}\dfrac{p_2}{p_2} & \cdots & \dfrac{\partial q_2}{\partial p_n}\dfrac{p_n}{q_2} \\ \vdots & \vdots & & \\ \dfrac{\partial q_n}{\partial p_1}\dfrac{p_1}{q_n} & \dfrac{\partial q_n}{\partial p_2}\dfrac{p_2}{q_n} & \cdots & \dfrac{\partial q_n}{\partial p_n}\dfrac{p_n}{q_n} \end{bmatrix}$$

$$= \hat{\mathbf{q}}^{-1}\mathbf{Q}_p\hat{\mathbf{p}}$$

i.e. $\mathbf{H}$ is the matrix of price elasticities.

Using these definitions and (3.2a) we find

$$\hat{\mathbf{q}}^{-1}\,\mathrm{d}\mathbf{q} = \hat{\mathbf{q}}^{-1}\mathbf{q}_y\,\mathrm{d}y + \hat{\mathbf{q}}^{-1}\mathbf{Q}_p\,\mathrm{d}\mathbf{p}$$

$$= \hat{\mathbf{q}}^{-1}\mathbf{q}_y y y^{-1}\,\mathrm{d}y + \hat{\mathbf{q}}^{-1}\mathbf{Q}_p\hat{\mathbf{p}}\hat{\mathbf{p}}^{-1}\,\mathrm{d}\mathbf{p}\,,$$

i.e.,

$$\mathrm{d}\log\mathbf{q} = \boldsymbol{\eta}\,\mathrm{d}\log y + \mathbf{H}\,\mathrm{d}\log\mathbf{p}\,. \tag{3.2b}$$

Furthermore

$$\mathbf{w}'\boldsymbol{\eta} = (y^{-1}\mathbf{p}'\hat{\mathbf{q}})y\hat{\mathbf{q}}^{-1}\mathbf{q}_y = \mathbf{p}'\mathbf{q}_y = 1 \tag{3.15b}$$

$$\mathbf{H}'\mathbf{w} = (\hat{\mathbf{p}}\mathbf{Q}_p'\hat{\mathbf{q}}^{-1})y^{-1}\hat{\mathbf{q}}\mathbf{p} = y^{-1}\hat{\mathbf{p}}\mathbf{Q}_p'\mathbf{p} = y^{-1}\hat{\mathbf{p}}(-\mathbf{q})$$

$$\therefore \quad \mathbf{H}'\mathbf{w} = -\mathbf{w} \tag{3.16b}$$

and

$$[\hat{\mathbf{w}}(\mathbf{H}+\boldsymbol{\eta}\mathbf{w}')]' = \hat{\mathbf{w}}(\mathbf{H}+\boldsymbol{\eta}\mathbf{w}') . \tag{3.17b}$$

3.2.4

The third case is a little less obvious but by premultiplying (3.2b) by $\hat{\mathbf{w}}$, i.e., $y^{-1}\hat{\mathbf{p}}\hat{\mathbf{q}}$, it is possible to derive demand functions which we shall justify later.

Thus,

$$\hat{\mathbf{w}}\,\mathrm{d}\log\mathbf{q} = \boldsymbol{\mu}\,\mathrm{d}\log y + \boldsymbol{\theta}\,\mathrm{d}\log\mathbf{p} \tag{3.2c}$$

where

$$\boldsymbol{\mu} = \hat{\mathbf{w}}\boldsymbol{\eta} = \hat{\mathbf{p}}\mathbf{q}_y$$

and

$$\boldsymbol{\theta} = \begin{bmatrix} \Theta_{11} & \Theta_{12} & \cdots & \Theta_{1n} \\ \Theta_{21} & \Theta_{22} & \cdots & \Theta_{2n} \\ \vdots & \vdots & & \vdots \\ \Theta_{n1} & \Theta_{n2} & \cdots & \Theta_{nn} \end{bmatrix} = \hat{\mathbf{w}}\mathbf{H} = y^{-1}\hat{\mathbf{p}}\mathbf{Q}_p\hat{\mathbf{p}} .$$

Thus $\boldsymbol{\mu}$ is the vector of marginal budget shares and $\boldsymbol{\theta}$ is the equivalent price response matrix. The justification for this form stems not only from the convenience of budget shares (remember that the budget shares are positive numbers between 0 and 1 which sum to unity) but also from the fact that we are often interested in the changes in budget shares per se. Budget shares will change, of course, as price and income are changed both directly, and indirectly, as the consumer adjusts the quantities that he buys.

Thus since,

$$w_i = \frac{p_i q_i}{y}$$

$$\mathrm{d}w_i = \frac{q_i}{y}\,\mathrm{d}p_i + \frac{p_i}{y}\,\mathrm{d}q_i - \frac{p_i q_i}{y^2}\,\mathrm{d}y$$

$$= \frac{p_i q_i}{y}\frac{\mathrm{d}p_i}{p_i} + \frac{p_i q_i}{y}\frac{\mathrm{d}q_i}{q_i} - \frac{p_i q_i}{y}\frac{\mathrm{d}y}{y}$$

$$= w_i\,\mathrm{d}\log p_i + w_i\,\mathrm{d}\log q_i - w_i\,\mathrm{d}\log y\ .$$

This shows that the endogenous effect on the ith budget share of a change in income and prices is $w_i\,\mathrm{d}\log q_i$. It is precisely these variables which (3.2c) explains.

If $\boldsymbol{\iota}$ is a vector of units the corresponding constraints for (3.2c) are

$$\boldsymbol{\iota}'\boldsymbol{\mu} = 1 \qquad (3.15c)$$

since $\boldsymbol{\iota}'\boldsymbol{\mu} = \boldsymbol{\iota}\hat{\mathbf{w}}\boldsymbol{\eta} = \mathbf{w}'\boldsymbol{\eta} = 1$

$$\boldsymbol{\theta}'\boldsymbol{\iota} = -\mathbf{w} \qquad (3.16c)$$

since $\boldsymbol{\theta}'\boldsymbol{\iota} = \mathbf{H}'\mathbf{w}\boldsymbol{\iota} = \mathbf{H}'\mathbf{w} = -\mathbf{w}$

$$(\boldsymbol{\theta} + \boldsymbol{\mu}\mathbf{w}')' = \boldsymbol{\theta} + \boldsymbol{\mu}\mathbf{w}' \qquad (3.17c)$$

3.2.5

So far, the utility aspect of demand analysis has been held in the background, but, in order to develop the relations between the Slutsky compensated slopes, it is necessary to introduce the direct and indirect utility functions, i.e.,

$$u = u(\mathbf{q}') = u^*(y, \mathbf{p}')$$

Thus,

$$\begin{aligned} u_y^* &= \mathbf{u}_q' \mathbf{q}_y \\ &= \lambda \mathbf{p}' \mathbf{q}_y \\ &= \lambda \end{aligned}$$

and

$$\begin{aligned} u_p^* &= \mathbf{Q}_p' \mathbf{u}_q \\ &= \lambda \mathbf{Q}_p' \mathbf{p}\,, \qquad \text{using (3.1)}\,, \\ &= -\lambda \mathbf{q}\,, \qquad \text{using (3.16a)}\;. \end{aligned}$$

Thus

$$\begin{aligned} \mathrm{d}u &= u_y^* \,\mathrm{d}y + \mathbf{u}_p^{*\prime} \,\mathrm{d}\mathbf{p} \\ &= \lambda \,\mathrm{d}y - \lambda \mathbf{q}' \,\mathrm{d}\mathbf{p} \\ &= \lambda(\mathrm{d}y - \mathbf{q}' \,\mathrm{d}\mathbf{p}) \end{aligned}$$

and

$$\mathrm{d}u = 0 \qquad \text{when } \mathrm{d}y = \mathbf{q}' \,\mathrm{d}\mathbf{p}$$

also

$$\begin{aligned} \mathrm{d}\lambda &= \lambda_y \,\mathrm{d}y + \boldsymbol{\lambda}_p' \,\mathrm{d}\mathbf{p} \\ &= \lambda_y \,\mathrm{d}y - (\lambda \mathbf{q}_y + \lambda_y \mathbf{q})' \,\mathrm{d}\mathbf{p}\,, \qquad \text{using (3.13)}\;. \end{aligned}$$

Thus

$$\begin{aligned} \mathrm{d}\lambda = 0 \qquad \text{when } \mathrm{d}y &= (\lambda \lambda_y^{-1} \mathbf{q}_y + \mathbf{q})' \,\mathrm{d}\mathbf{p} \\ &= (\phi y \mathbf{q}_y + \mathbf{q})' \,\mathrm{d}\mathbf{p} \end{aligned}$$

where $\phi = \lambda_y^{-1} \lambda y^{-1}$.

This analysis tells us what the respective changes in income must be for a consumer, faced with price changes, to maintain a constant utility and a constant marginal utility of income. The inverse of the elasticity of the marginal utility of income with respect to income, ϕ, is given a specific symbol not only because it has been suggested as an index of welfare but also because of its notational convenience (see Frisch, 1932).

Consider the case where the change in prices $\mathbf{dp}$ is accompanied by a change in income of $\mathbf{q}'\,\mathbf{dp}$ and denote the resultant quantity change by $(\mathbf{dq})^*$.

$$(\mathbf{dq})^* = \mathbf{q}_y(\mathbf{q}'\,\mathbf{dp}) + \mathbf{Q}_p\,\mathbf{dp} = (\mathbf{Q}_p + \mathbf{q}_y\mathbf{q}')\,\mathbf{dp} = \mathbf{Q}_p^*\,\mathbf{dp}$$

where $\mathbf{Q}_p^* = \boldsymbol{\lambda}\mathbf{U}^{-1} - \lambda\lambda_y^{-1}\mathbf{q}_y\mathbf{q}_y' = \lambda\mathbf{U}^{-1} - \phi y\mathbf{q}_y\mathbf{q}_y'$.

Similarly when the marginal utility of money is kept constant, the change in prices being accompanied by $(\phi y\mathbf{q}_y + \mathbf{q})'\,\mathbf{dp}$, the resultant quantity change is $(\mathbf{dq})^{**}$.

$$(\mathbf{dq})^{**} = (\mathbf{Q}_p + \mathbf{q}_y\mathbf{q}' + \phi y\mathbf{q}_y\mathbf{q}_y')\,\mathbf{dp}$$

$$= \mathbf{Q}_p^{**}\,\mathbf{dp}$$

where

$$\mathbf{Q}_p^{**} = \mathbf{Q}_p + \mathbf{q}_y\mathbf{q}' + \phi y\mathbf{q}_y\mathbf{q}_y'$$

$$= \mathbf{Q}_p^* + \phi y\mathbf{q}_y\mathbf{q}_y' = \lambda\mathbf{U}^{-1}.$$

Since $\mathbf{Q}_p = \lambda\mathbf{U}^{-1} - \phi y\mathbf{q}_y\mathbf{q}_y' - \mathbf{q}_y\mathbf{q}'$, $\mathbf{Q}_p^*$ represents the income compensated price slopes and $\mathbf{Q}_p^{**}$ represents the income and general substitution compensated slopes. With these new concepts we can rearrange the demand functions and their constraints yet again, but for ease of future reference we first collect the results achieved in terms of uncompensated parameters,

$$\mathbf{dq} = \mathbf{q}_y\,dy + \mathbf{Q}_p\,\mathbf{dp} \qquad (3.2a)$$

$$\mathbf{p}'\mathbf{q}_y = 1 \qquad (3.15a)$$

$$\mathbf{Q}_p'\mathbf{p} = -\mathbf{q} \qquad (3.16a)$$

$$(\mathbf{Q}_p + \mathbf{q}_y\mathbf{q}')' = (\mathbf{Q}_p + \mathbf{q}_y\mathbf{q}') \qquad (3.17a)$$

$$\mathrm{d}\log \mathbf{q} = \boldsymbol{\eta}\,\mathrm{d}\log y + \mathbf{H}\,\mathrm{d}\log \mathbf{p} \tag{3.2b}$$

$$\mathbf{w}'\boldsymbol{\eta} = 1 \tag{3.15b}$$

$$\mathbf{H}'\mathbf{w} = -\mathbf{w} \tag{3.16b}$$

$$[\hat{\mathbf{w}}(\mathbf{H}+\boldsymbol{\eta}\mathbf{w}')]' = \hat{\mathbf{w}}(\mathbf{H}+\boldsymbol{\eta}\mathbf{w}') \tag{3.17b}$$

$$\hat{\mathbf{w}}\,\mathrm{d}\log \mathbf{q} = \boldsymbol{\mu}\,\mathrm{d}\log y + \boldsymbol{\theta}\,\mathrm{d}\log \mathbf{p} \tag{3.2c}$$

$$\boldsymbol{\iota}'\boldsymbol{\mu} = 1 \tag{3.15c}$$

$$\boldsymbol{\theta}'\boldsymbol{\iota} = -\mathbf{w} \tag{3.16c}$$

$$(\boldsymbol{\theta} + \boldsymbol{\mu}\mathbf{w}')' = \boldsymbol{\theta} + \boldsymbol{\mu}\mathbf{w}'\,. \tag{3.17c}$$

Since

$$\mathrm{d}\mathbf{q} = \mathbf{q}_y\,\mathrm{d}y + \mathbf{Q}_p\,\mathrm{d}\mathbf{p}$$

$$\mathrm{d}\mathbf{q} = \mathbf{q}_y(\mathrm{d}y - \mathbf{q}'\,\mathrm{d}\mathbf{p}) + \mathbf{Q}_p^*\,\mathrm{d}\mathbf{p} \tag{3.2d}$$

$$\mathbf{p}'\mathbf{q}_y = 1 \tag{3.15d}$$

$$\mathbf{Q}_p^{*\prime}\mathbf{p} = (\mathbf{Q}_p + \mathbf{q}_y\mathbf{q}')'\mathbf{p} = \mathbf{Q}_p'\mathbf{p} + \mathbf{q}\mathbf{q}_y'\mathbf{p} = -\mathbf{q} + \mathbf{q} = \mathbf{0} \tag{3.16d}$$

$$\mathbf{Q}_p^{*\prime} = (\mathbf{Q}_p + \mathbf{q}_y\mathbf{q}')' = (\mathbf{Q}_p + \mathbf{q}_y\mathbf{q}') = \mathbf{Q}_p^*\,. \tag{3.17d}$$

Similarly

$$\mathrm{d}\mathbf{q} = \mathbf{q}_y(\mathrm{d}y - \mathbf{q}'\,\mathrm{d}\mathbf{p}) + \mathbf{Q}_p^{**}(\mathrm{d}\mathbf{p} - \mathbf{p}\mathbf{q}_y'\,\mathrm{d}\mathbf{p}) \tag{3.2e}$$

$$\mathbf{p}'\mathbf{q}_y = 1 \tag{3.15e}$$

$$\mathbf{Q}_p^{**\prime}\mathbf{p} = \phi y\,\mathbf{q}_y \tag{3.16e}$$

$$\mathbf{Q}_p^{**\prime} = \mathbf{Q}_p^{**}\,. \tag{3.17e}$$

Furthermore, if we introduce the concepts of compensated elasticities and compensated budget shares, four more possibilities exist. Let,

$$\mathbf{H}^* = \hat{\mathbf{q}}^{-1}\mathbf{Q}_p^*\hat{\mathbf{p}}$$

$$\mathbf{H}^{**} = \hat{\mathbf{q}}^{-1}\mathbf{Q}_p^{**}\hat{\mathbf{p}}$$

$$\mathbf{K} = [k_{ij}] = y^{-1}\hat{\mathbf{p}}\mathbf{Q}_p^*\hat{\mathbf{p}}$$

$$\mathbf{N} = [\nu_{ij}] = y^{-1}\hat{\mathbf{p}}\mathbf{Q}_p^{**}\hat{\mathbf{p}}\,.$$

Thus

$$\mathbf{H}^* = \hat{\mathbf{q}}^{-1}(\mathbf{Q}_p + \mathbf{q}_y\mathbf{q}')\hat{\mathbf{p}}$$

$$= \mathbf{H} + \boldsymbol{\eta}\,\mathbf{w}'$$

$$\mathbf{H}^{**} = \mathbf{H} + \boldsymbol{\eta}\,\mathbf{w}'(\mathbf{I} + \phi\hat{\boldsymbol{\eta}})$$

$$\mathbf{K} = \hat{\mathbf{w}}\mathbf{H}^*$$

$$= \boldsymbol{\theta} + \boldsymbol{\mu}\,\mathbf{w}'$$

$$\mathbf{N} = \hat{\mathbf{w}}\mathbf{H}^{**}$$

$$= \mathbf{K} + \phi\,\boldsymbol{\mu}\boldsymbol{\mu}'\,.$$

Hence, from (3.2b),

$$\mathrm{d}\log\mathbf{q} = \boldsymbol{\eta}\,(\mathrm{d}\log y - \mathbf{w}'\,\mathrm{d}\log\mathbf{p}) + \mathbf{H}^*\,\mathrm{d}\log\mathbf{p} \tag{3.2f}$$

$$\mathbf{w}'\boldsymbol{\eta} = 1 \tag{3.15f}$$

$$\mathbf{H}^{*\prime}\mathbf{w} = \mathbf{0} \tag{3.16f}$$

$$(\hat{\mathbf{w}}\mathbf{H}^*)' = \hat{\mathbf{w}}\mathbf{H}^* \tag{3.17f}$$

$$\mathrm{d}\log\mathbf{q} = \boldsymbol{\eta}\,(\mathrm{d}\log y - \mathbf{w}'\,\mathrm{d}\log\mathbf{p}) + \mathbf{H}^{**}\,(\mathrm{d}\log\mathbf{p} - \boldsymbol{\iota}\mathbf{w}'\hat{\boldsymbol{\eta}}\,\mathrm{d}\log\mathbf{p}) \tag{3.2g}$$

$$\mathbf{w}'\boldsymbol{\eta} = 1 \tag{3.15g}$$

$$\mathbf{H}^{**\prime}\mathbf{w} = \phi\,\hat{\mathbf{w}}\,\boldsymbol{\eta} \tag{3.16g}$$

$$(\hat{\mathbf{w}}\mathbf{H}^{**})' = \hat{\mathbf{w}}\mathbf{H}^{**}\,. \tag{3.17g}$$

And, from (3.2c)

$$\hat{\mathbf{w}} \log \mathbf{q} = \boldsymbol{\mu} (\mathrm{d} \log y - \mathbf{w}' \,\mathrm{d} \log \mathbf{p}) + \mathbf{K} \,\mathrm{d} \log \mathbf{p} \tag{3.2h}$$

$$\boldsymbol{\iota}'\boldsymbol{\mu} = 1 \tag{3.15h}$$

$$\mathbf{K}'\boldsymbol{\iota} = \mathbf{0} \tag{3.16h}$$

$$\mathbf{K}' = \mathbf{K} \tag{3.17h}$$

$$\hat{\mathbf{w}} \,\mathrm{d} \log \mathbf{q} = \boldsymbol{\mu} (\mathrm{d} \log y - \mathbf{w}' \,\mathrm{d} \log \mathbf{p}) + \mathbf{N}(\mathrm{d} \log \mathbf{p} - \boldsymbol{\iota} \boldsymbol{\mu}' \,\mathrm{d} \log \mathbf{p}) \tag{3.2i}$$

$$\boldsymbol{\iota}'\boldsymbol{\mu} = 1 \tag{3.15i}$$

$$\mathbf{N}'\boldsymbol{\iota} = \phi \boldsymbol{\mu} \tag{3.16i}$$

$$\mathbf{N}' = \mathbf{N}\,. \tag{3.17i}$$

This completes the review of the forms stemming from the classical consumer theory. These sets of equations present the form of the demand functions and the constraints in terms of nine different concepts. This enables us to choose the respective form for whichever concept we wish to take as a constant. For example, if we wish to consider the uncompensated elasticities as constants then (3.2b) is the relevant demand function not the log linear form which is often used.

3.2.6

The theory expounded above is really too general to allow econometric analysis. One way of reducing this generality is by assumptions on the form of the utility function. One assumption that has been found useful especially when goods are broadly defined is that of additivity, i.e., there are no substitutes or complements with regard to taste. Formally,

$$u = u(q_1, q_2 \dots q_n) = \sum_{i=1}^{n} u^i(q_i)\,,$$

which implies that $\mathbf{U}$ and $\mathbf{U}^{-1}$ are diagonal. The impact of this and the usefulness of the final set of equations, i.e., (3.2i)–(3.17i) can both be seen from the following,

$$\mathbf{N} = \lambda y^{-1}\hat{\mathbf{p}}\mathbf{U}^{-1}\hat{\mathbf{p}} \tag{3.18}$$

thus, under additivity, $\mathbf{N}$ is diagonal but since,

$$\mathbf{N}\boldsymbol{\iota} = \phi\boldsymbol{\mu}$$

$$\mathbf{N} = \phi\hat{\boldsymbol{\mu}} \tag{3.19}$$

i.e.,

$$\nu_{ij} = \begin{cases} \phi\mu_i & i = j \\ 0 & i \neq j \end{cases}$$

This implies that the interaction effects can be written in terms of ϕ and the income effects †.

The assumption of additivity enables considerable economy in parameters because, since y, p_i, q_i and w_i are observable, only the estimation of ϕ and the μ_i is necessary. It will be realised, however, that the assumption involves certain drawbacks. Obviously no specific substitutes are possible, but neither are inferior goods or complementary goods ‡.

Additivity is still a rather general condition for a utility function to satisfy. If we go further and completely specify the form of the utility function it is possible to derive the exact demand functions. Often these demand functions are not very convenient and some researchers prefer to specify demand functions without reference to the form of the utility functions. These pragmatic functions which do not fit the classical consumer theory constraints exactly have been used a great deal. Before reviewing them let us consider those forms which do satisfy the classical theory.

† Perhaps this aspect is clearer when one considers the cross elasticities, i.e., η_{ij}. Under additivity,

$$\eta_{ij} = \begin{cases} \phi\eta_i - \eta_i w_i(1+\phi\eta_i) & i=j \\ \quad - \eta_i w_i(1+\phi\eta_j) & i\neq j \end{cases}$$

Thus the cross elasticity can be expressed in terms of the income elasticities η_i, η_j, the budget share, w_i, and ϕ.

‡ This can be seen as follows. Since $\mu_i = \nu_{ii}/\phi$ and $\nu_{ii} < 0$ and $\phi < 0$, $\mu_i = w_i\eta_i > 0 \therefore \eta_i > 0$ $\therefore \partial q_i/\partial y > 0$. Also since $\mathbf{N} = \mathbf{K} + \phi\boldsymbol{\mu}'$, $k_{ij} = -\phi\mu_i\mu_j$ but $\phi < 0$, $\mu_j > 0 \therefore k_{ij} > 0$ and $\eta^*_{ij} > 0 \therefore \partial q^*_i/\partial p_j > 0$.

3.3. Time series studies

3.3.1. *Models which exactly satisfy the static theory*

3.3.1.a. The linear expenditure system (Stone, 1954b)

This system is derived from a Stone–Geary utility function and has many convenient features. The Stone–Geary utility function is as follows,

$$u = \sum_{i=1}^{n} \beta_i \log (q_i - \gamma_i) \qquad 0 < \beta_i < 1 \qquad 0 \leqslant \gamma_i$$

$$\sum_{i=1}^{n} \beta_i = 1 \qquad 0 < (q_i - \gamma_i)$$

and the corresponding demand functions are

$$q_i = \gamma_i + \beta_i p_i^{-1}(y - \sum_{i=1}^{n} p_j \gamma_j) \qquad (i = 1, 2, ..., n) .$$

The γ_i of the utility function can be interpreted as the subsistence quantity of each good. Obviously the utility function is additive and so embodies all the simplifications which accompany that assumption. Rewriting the utility function in matrix terms,

$$u = \boldsymbol{\beta}' \log (\mathbf{q} - \boldsymbol{\gamma})$$

where $\boldsymbol{\beta}$, $\mathbf{q}$ and $\boldsymbol{\gamma}$ are n dimensional vectors.

$$\boldsymbol{\iota}'\boldsymbol{\beta} = 1$$

$$0 < (\mathbf{q} - \boldsymbol{\gamma})$$

thus

$$\mathbf{u}_q = (\hat{\mathbf{q}} - \hat{\boldsymbol{\gamma}})^{-1} \boldsymbol{\beta} \cdot$$

Putting

$$\mathbf{u}_q = \lambda \mathbf{p},$$

$$(\hat{\mathbf{q}} - \hat{\boldsymbol{\gamma}})^{-1} \boldsymbol{\beta} = \lambda \mathbf{p}$$

$$\therefore \quad \boldsymbol{\beta} = \lambda (\hat{\mathbf{q}} - \hat{\boldsymbol{\gamma}}) \mathbf{p} = \lambda \hat{\mathbf{p}} (\mathbf{q} - \boldsymbol{\gamma}) \quad .$$

Since

$$1 = \boldsymbol{\iota}' \boldsymbol{\beta} = \lambda \boldsymbol{\iota}' \hat{\mathbf{p}} (\mathbf{q} - \boldsymbol{\gamma}) = \lambda (y - \mathbf{p}' \boldsymbol{\gamma}),$$

$$\lambda = (y - \mathbf{p}' \boldsymbol{\gamma})^{-1}$$

$$\therefore \quad \boldsymbol{\beta} = (y - \mathbf{p}' \boldsymbol{\gamma})^{-1} \hat{\mathbf{p}} (\mathbf{q} - \boldsymbol{\gamma}),$$

i.e.,

$$\hat{\mathbf{p}} (\mathbf{q} - \boldsymbol{\gamma}) = (y - \mathbf{p}' \boldsymbol{\gamma}) \boldsymbol{\beta} .$$

$$\therefore \quad \hat{\mathbf{p}} \mathbf{q} = \hat{\mathbf{p}} \boldsymbol{\gamma} + (y - \mathbf{p}' \boldsymbol{\gamma}) \boldsymbol{\beta}$$

and

$$\mathbf{q} = \boldsymbol{\gamma} + (y - \mathbf{p}' \boldsymbol{\gamma}) \hat{\mathbf{p}}^{-1} \boldsymbol{\beta} .$$

These demand functions have a number of advantages. They involve very few parameters. These parameters have easy interpretation which is best seen with regard to the expenditure functions. Here the consumer is seen to have to purchase γ_i of each quantity and hence spend $p_i \gamma_i$ on each good at least. The sum of these expenditures, i.e., $\mathbf{p}'\boldsymbol{\gamma}$ can be called subsistence income. The residual, or supernumerary, income is then distributed among all goods according to the proportions β_i. Because the utility function is specific it is possible to derive an exact index number for price changes which Stone (1962a) uses in his growth model.

The system, though not linear in parameters, is linear in variables which makes it quite convenient. Furthermore a number of extensions are feasible including one which allows $\boldsymbol{\beta}$ and $\boldsymbol{\gamma}$ to change slowly through time. Naturally enough the system has disadvantages too. Because of its additive utility form it is less likely to be of value when goods are finely divided. Also the Engel curves derived from this system are linear which is likely to conflict with the data if income varies much, for this reason the linear expenditure system is not so useful for explaining cross-section data. However, the usefulness of cross-section data itself, in this context, is also open to doubt. The non-linearity of the parameters makes estimation a little less straight forward than some of the earlier studies, but Stone suggests a procedure which is based on using ordinary least squares iteratively.

If **c** and **b** are estimates of $\boldsymbol{\gamma}$ and $\boldsymbol{\beta}$, then

$$\hat{\mathbf{p}}_t\mathbf{q}_t = \hat{\mathbf{p}}_t c + (y_t - \mathbf{p}_t'\mathbf{c})\mathbf{b} + \mathbf{e}_t$$

where $\mathbf{e}_t = \begin{bmatrix} e_{1t} \\ e_{2t} \\ \vdots \\ e_{nt} \end{bmatrix}$

Stone suggests minimising $\sum_{i=1}^{n} \sum_{t=1}^{T} e_{it}^2$ as a criterion for choosing **c** and **b**. Furthermore letting

$$\mathbf{v}_t = \hat{\mathbf{p}}_t\mathbf{q}_t = y_t\mathbf{b} + (\mathbf{I} - \mathbf{b}\boldsymbol{\iota}')\hat{\mathbf{p}}_t\mathbf{c} + \mathbf{e}_t\ ,$$

$$(\mathbf{v}_t - \mathbf{y}_t\mathbf{b}) = (\mathbf{I} - \mathbf{b}\boldsymbol{\iota}')\hat{\mathbf{p}}_t\mathbf{c} + \mathbf{e}_t\ .$$

Hence, given **b**, the value of **c** which minimises $\sum_{t=1}^{T} \sum_{i=1}^{n} e_{it}$ is

$$\mathbf{c} = (\mathbf{X}'\mathbf{X})^{-1}\ \mathbf{X}'\mathbf{Y} \tag{3.20}$$

where

$$\mathbf{Y} = \begin{bmatrix} \mathbf{v}_1 - y_1\mathbf{b} \\ \mathbf{v}_2 - y_2\mathbf{b} \\ \vdots \\ \mathbf{v}_T - y_T\mathbf{b} \end{bmatrix}$$

and

$$\mathbf{X} = \begin{bmatrix} (\mathbf{I} - \mathbf{b}\boldsymbol{\iota}')\hat{\mathbf{p}}_1 \\ (\mathbf{I} - \mathbf{b}\boldsymbol{\iota}')\hat{\mathbf{p}}_2 \\ \vdots \\ (\mathbf{I} - \mathbf{b}\boldsymbol{\iota}')\hat{\mathbf{p}}_T \end{bmatrix}$$

Furthermore,

$$[\mathbf{v}_t - \hat{\mathbf{p}}_t\mathbf{c}] = (y_t - \boldsymbol{\iota}'\hat{\mathbf{p}}_t\mathbf{c})\mathbf{b} + \mathbf{e}_t$$

i.e.,

$$(v_{1t} - p_{1t}c_1) = (y_t - \sum_{j=1}^{n} p_{jt}c_j)b_1 + e_{1t} \qquad (t = 1, 2, ..., T)$$

$$(v_{2t} - p_{2t}c_2) = (y_t - \sum_{j=1}^{n} p_{jt}c_j)b_2 + e_{2t} \qquad (t = 1, 2, ..., T)$$

$$(v_{nt} - p_{nt}c_n) = (y_t - \sum_{j=1}^{n} p_{jt}c_j)b_n + e_{nt} \qquad (t = 1, 2, ..., T)$$

Hence, $b_i = (\mathbf{W}'\mathbf{W})^{-1}\mathbf{W}'\mathbf{Z}_i$, where

$$\mathbf{W} = \begin{bmatrix} y_i - \sum p_{ji}c_j \\ y_2 - \sum p_{j2}c_j \\ \vdots \\ y_T - \sum p_{jT}c_j \end{bmatrix}$$

$$\mathbf{Z}_i = \begin{bmatrix} v_{i1} - p_{i1} c_i \\ v_{i2} - p_{i2} c_i \\ \vdots \\ v_{iT} - p_{iT} c_i \end{bmatrix} \qquad (i = 1, 2, ..., n)$$

minimises $\sum_{t=1}^{T} \sum_{i=1}^{n} e_{it}^2$ for a given set of c_i.

Using annual time series data for the U.K., 1900–1938 Stone produces a number of estimated expenditure systems for the following six commodity groups:

1. meat, fish, dairy products and fats;
2. fruit and vegetables;
3. drink and tobacco;
4. household running expenses;
5. durable goods;
6. all other consumer goods and services.

Setting $c_i = 0$ $(i = 1, 2, ..., n)$ in (3.21) produces a naive model of consumer expenditures in which a consumer allocates his expenditure between the six groups in the same proportion each period. Table 3.1 shows the results for this naive model and for the more sophisticated model where c_i and b_i are derived by using (3.21) and (3.20) iteratively. On the basis of goodness of fit it would appear that the naive model is better for group 3 and 6 but for 5 and 6 there is very little to choose between the two models. Using combinations of the simple and sophisticated model it is possible to produce further models. Here we report only one although Stone produces three such systems. Using the simple system for 3 and 6 and adjusting the values of b_i such that they sum to unity gives us a mixed system (table 3.2).

As a test of his alternate systems, Stone applies them to data for 1900. The percentage errors of the different models appear in table 3.3. That group 3 and 5 have the largest errors is hardly surprising, group 3 is drink and tobacco and group 5 is durables. The desire for durables increased considerably in the interwar period and the taste for drink declined. These results do suggest that it is necessary to take into account changing taste if such long period forecasts are to be attempted. However, given the long period of the forecast the results are quite encouraging.

Stone goes on to use his model to look at what the pattern of expenditures

Table 3.1
Stone's linear expenditure system with six commodities – U.K.

Group	Naive model			More sophisticated model		
	b	*c*	*r*	*b*	*c*	*r*
1	0.18	–	0.88	0.12	14	0.97
2	0.05	–	0.88	0.04	3	0.97
3	0.11	–	0.95	0.06	10	0.57
4	0.19	–	0.23	0.23	11	0.81
5	0.23	–	0.95	0.30	12	0.97
6	0.24	–	0.98	0.25	15	0.97

r represents the sample correlations between actual and calculated expenditures.

Table 3.2
Mixed system for six-commodity groups.

Group	*b*	*c*	*r*
1	0.13	17	0.98
2	0.05	4	0.95
3	0.11	–	0.95
4	0.17	17	0.93
5	0.30	19	0.99
6	0.24	–	0.98

Table 3.3
Percentage errors of 1900 forecast.

Group	Naive	Sophisticated	Mixed
1	–3	4	–2
2	4	10	0
3	–15	–35	–15
4	–7	–2	–3
5	30	35	25
6	–6	–9	–6

Table 3.4
Percentage excess of projected over actual expenditures in 1952.

Group	Naive	Sophisticated	Mixed
1	16	8	16
2	–15	–17	–7
3	–28	1	–28
4	41	20	15
5	4	5	17
6	–13	–16	–13

Table 3.5
Percentage excess of projected over actual expenditures in 1952.

Group	Naive	Sophisticated	Mixed
1	16	27	52
2	–15	–38	–46
3	–28	3	–28
4	41	35	5
5	4	6	9
6	–13	–31	–13

would have been in 1952 if there had not been any rationing and if the prices and incomes were those which did in fact occur. Again these results are expressed as percentage errors in table 3.4.

Although these results are different they all tend to reflect the fact that consumers would want more meat, dairy and fat products, and household running expenses, e.g. fuel and rent, counter-balanced by less fruit and vegetables and other expenses. Of course, if a free market were to have reigned in 1952 then prices would probably not have been the same since supplies were not infinitely elastic. One further use to which Stone puts his model is to give an indication of how prices would have had to differ from what actually occurred in 1952 if the quantities emanating from the demand functions were the same as the actual. The results in terms of expenditures are given in table 3.5.

These calculations can only be called suggestive, but Stone's article as a whole, does indicate that the linear expenditure system is a useful tool for studies of the allocation of consumers expenditure provided the commodity groups are broadly defined.

3.3.1.b. Other utility function based approaches

The quadratic utility function has been used in many decision theory situations, but its impact in the consumer demand field has been negligible probably because the demand functions which result are rather awkward. Houthakker (1960) deduced the implications for demand curves of the following utility function

$$u = \sum_{i=1}^{n} \alpha_i q_i^{\beta_i} \qquad \alpha_i > 0$$

Unfortunately, explicit demand functions are not forthcoming unless one assumes all β_i to be equal, in which case it can be shown that

$$q_i = \frac{(p_i/\alpha_i)^{(\beta-1)^{-1}}}{\sum_j p_j (p_j/\alpha_j)^{(\beta-1)^{-1}}}\, y\,.$$

If, however, the utility function is assumed to be,

$$u = \sum_{i=1}^{n} \alpha_i (y/p_i)^{\beta_i}$$

the demand functions are

$$q_i = \frac{\alpha_i \beta_i (y/p_i)^{1+\beta_i}}{\sum_{k=1}^{n} \alpha_k \beta_k (y/p_k)^{\beta_k}} \qquad (i = 1, 2, ..., n)\,.$$

This form has been used empirically but the results are not widely available. Furthermore, the utility function has little intuitive appeal.

3.3.2. *Models which approximately satisfy the static theory*

The previous sections have involved functional forms which were derived from a utility function and which automatically satisfied the constraints of the classical theory. Another approach is to start with demand functions and attempt to impose these constraints on the coefficients. Indeed it has been pointed out that Stone's linear expenditure system is the only linear expenditure system with coefficients which satisfy all the constraints of the classical theory exactly (see Goldberger, 1967). The more pragmatic approaches of this section will satisfy the classical constraints only approximately.

3.3.2.a. Powell's linear expenditure system

Powell (1966) starts with a linear expenditure system of the following form:

$$\hat{\mathbf{p}}\mathbf{q} = y\boldsymbol{\beta} + \mathbf{A}\mathbf{p},$$

where $\mathbf{A}$ is an arbitrary $n \times n$ matrix, i.e.,

$$\mathbf{q} = \hat{\mathbf{p}}^{-1}(y\boldsymbol{\beta} + \mathbf{A}\mathbf{p})$$

$$\therefore \quad \mathbf{q}_y = \hat{\mathbf{p}}^{-1}\boldsymbol{\beta}$$

and

$$\mathbf{Q}_p = \hat{\mathbf{p}}^{-1}[\mathbf{A} - (y\hat{\boldsymbol{\beta}} + \widehat{\mathbf{A}\mathbf{p}})\hat{\mathbf{p}}^{-1}]$$

$$= \hat{\mathbf{p}}^{-1}(\mathbf{A} - \hat{\mathbf{q}})$$

$$\therefore \quad \mathbf{A} = \hat{\mathbf{p}}\mathbf{Q}_p + \hat{\mathbf{q}}.$$

Assuming additive utility (3.19), (3.18), (3.12) and (3.14), imply the following constraint,

$$\mathbf{Q}_p = \phi y \hat{\mathbf{q}}_y(\hat{\mathbf{p}}^{-1} - \boldsymbol{\iota}\mathbf{q}_y') - \mathbf{q}_y\mathbf{q}'$$

i.e.,

$$\mathbf{A} = \phi y \hat{\mathbf{q}}_y(\mathbf{I} - \mathbf{p}\mathbf{q}_y') - \hat{\mathbf{p}}\mathbf{q}_y\mathbf{q}' + \hat{\mathbf{q}}$$

$$= (\mathbf{I} - \boldsymbol{\beta}\boldsymbol{\iota}')(\hat{\mathbf{q}} + \phi y \hat{\boldsymbol{\beta}}\hat{\mathbf{p}}^{-1})$$

Since $\mathbf{A}$ and $\boldsymbol{\beta}$ are constant, $\hat{\mathbf{q}} + \phi y \hat{\boldsymbol{\beta}}\hat{\mathbf{p}}^{-1}$ must be constant. If, however, instead of $\mathbf{A} = (\mathbf{I} - \boldsymbol{\beta}\boldsymbol{\iota}')(\mathbf{q} + \phi y \hat{\boldsymbol{\beta}}\hat{\mathbf{p}}^{-1})$, we impose the constraint,

$$\mathbf{A} = (\mathbf{I} - \boldsymbol{\beta}\boldsymbol{\iota}')(\hat{\bar{\mathbf{q}}} + \phi y \hat{\boldsymbol{\beta}}\hat{\bar{\mathbf{p}}}^{-1})$$

where $\bar{\mathbf{q}}$ and $\bar{\mathbf{p}}$ represent the vectors of sample means; then,

$$\hat{\mathbf{p}}\mathbf{q} = \hat{\mathbf{p}}\bar{\mathbf{q}} + (y - \mathbf{p}'\bar{\mathbf{q}})\boldsymbol{\beta} - \sigma\hat{\boldsymbol{\beta}}(\mathbf{I} - \boldsymbol{\iota}\boldsymbol{\beta}')\dot{\mathbf{p}}$$

where $\sigma = -\phi y$, and

$$\dot{\mathbf{p}} = \begin{bmatrix} \dfrac{p_1}{\bar{p}_2} \\ \\ \dfrac{p_2}{\bar{p}_2} \\ \vdots \\ \dfrac{p_n}{\bar{p}_n} \end{bmatrix}$$

i.e.

$$p_i q_i = p_i \bar{q}_i + \beta_i (y - \sum_j p_j \bar{q}_j) - \sigma \beta_i \left[\frac{p_i}{\bar{p}_i} - \sum_j \beta_j \frac{p_j}{\bar{p}_j} \right]$$

$$(i = 1, 2, ..., n) .$$

These equations can be compared to Stone's linear expenditure system showing the influence of the consumers typical quantity $\bar{q}_i$, the supernumary income and a substitution term. The number of parameters is $n - 1$ less than that of Stone's linear expenditure system.

The actual forms that Powell estimates involve a linear trend term too, i.e.,

$$p_i q_i = p_i \bar{q}_i + b_i (y - \sum_j p_j \bar{q}_j) - \sigma b_i \left[\frac{p_i}{\bar{p}_i} - \sum_j b_j \frac{p_j}{\bar{p}_j} \right] + c_i t + e_i .$$

The coefficients b_i and c_i are chosen so as to minimise the grand total sum of squared residuals, i.e. $\sum_{i=1}^{n} \sum_{t=1}^{T} e_{it}^2$, which is achieved by an iterative procedure in which the estimated coefficients seem to converge after four or five iterations.

The data Powell uses are taken from the Australian National Accounts and provide a breakdown of the categories of consumers expenditure. Unfortunately, only five price indices are available and so the 'miscellaneous' price

Table 3.6
Powell's linear expenditures system for 10 commodities – Australia 1949–1950 to 1961–1962.

Commodity group	b_i	c_i	η_i^*	η_{ii}^{**} (–)	R^2	$\frac{\sum e_t e_{t-1}}{\sum e_t^2}$
Food	0.1227	–0.4935	0.484	0.303	0.998	–0.169
Clothing	0.1840	–1.1237	1.452	0.687	0.987	–0.242
Housing	0.0941	0.6287	1.167	0.543	0.991	0.025
Gas and electricity	0.0084	0.3791	0.319	0.143	0.997	–0.101
Durable household goods	0.1519	–0.1072	1.884	0.830	0.968	0.384
Other goods	0.0903	0.1116	1.235	0.567	0.989	0.515
Fares	0.0062	–0.1733	0.161	0.074	0.972	0.679
Tobacco and drink	0.0324	0.1201	0.308	0.159	0.993	0.473
Services	0.1156	0.3420	0.839	0.431	0.996	0.370
Motor vehicles and running expenses	0.1944	0.3162	2.503	1.051	0.996	–0.259

* Calculated at mean sample values.

index is used for 'fares', 'tobacco and drink', 'services', and 'motor vehicles and running expenses'. Similarly 'household supplies and appliances' is used for 'durable household goods', 'other goods' and 'gas and electricity'. Using annual time series for 1949–1950 to 1961–1962 produces the results reported in table 3.6. These results look quite reasonable suggesting that the Powell linear expenditure system could be a useful pragmatic approach to demand study.

3.3.2.b. The constant elasticity models

One of the forms which has been very popular in empirical demand studies is the constant elasticity function, i.e.

$$\log \mathbf{q} = \boldsymbol{\alpha} + {}_1\boldsymbol{\eta} \log y + {}_1\mathbf{H} \log \mathbf{p}$$

where ${}_1\boldsymbol{\eta}$ and ${}_1\mathbf{H}$ are supposed to be the income and price elasticities.

This form does not satisfy the classical theory – a fact which can be shown as follows. If goods do have constant income elasticities, as income increases the consumer will devote more of his total expenditure to those goods with high income elasticities and $\sum_{i=1}^{n} w_i \, {}_1\eta_i$ will increase. This is impossible since we have shown that $\sum_{i=1}^{n} w_i \eta_i$ is always unity. However, ease of estimation is an attractive feature of this system and although it does not satisfy exactly the classical theory it may still be useful. It does, however, involve a considerable number of parameters but these can be reduced. Defining,

$$\log \pi = \mathbf{w}' \log \mathbf{p}$$

then

$$\log \mathbf{q} = \boldsymbol{\alpha} + {}_1\boldsymbol{\eta} (\log y - \log \pi) + ({}_1\mathbf{H} + {}_1\boldsymbol{\eta}\mathbf{w}') \log \mathbf{p} .$$

From Section 3.2.5

$$\mathbf{H} + \boldsymbol{\eta}\mathbf{w}' = \mathbf{H}^* .$$

By analogy, defining,

$${}_1\mathbf{H}^* = {}_1\mathbf{H} + {}_1\boldsymbol{\eta}\mathbf{w}' ,$$

$$\log \mathbf{q} = \boldsymbol{\alpha} + {}_1\boldsymbol{\eta} \log y/\pi + {}_1\mathbf{H}^* \log \mathbf{p} .$$

Again by analogy with the classical theory if we impose the constraint ${}_1\mathbf{H}\boldsymbol{\iota}^* = \mathbf{0}$†, then

$$\log q_i = \alpha_i + {}_1\eta_i \log \frac{y}{\pi} + \sum_{j \neq k} {}_1\eta_{ij}^* \log \frac{p_j}{p_k} \qquad (i = 1, 2, ..., n)\,.$$

However, this form still has many parameters to be estimated. An alternative approach is as follows: since

$${}_1\eta_{ii}^* \log \pi^* = -\sum_{j \neq k}^{n} {}_1\eta_{ij}^* \log \pi^*$$

$$\log q_i = \alpha_i + {}_1\eta_i \log \frac{y}{\pi} + {}_1\eta_{ii}^* \log \frac{p_i}{\pi^*} + \sum_{j \neq i} {}_1\eta_{ij}^* \log \frac{p_j}{\pi^*}$$

where π^* is any conventional price index.

Thus if we assume π is approximately equal to π^* we can write

$$\log q_i \approx \alpha_i + {}_1\eta_i \log \frac{y}{\pi^*} + {}_1\eta_{ii}^* \log \frac{p_i}{\pi^*} + \sum_{j \neq i} {}_1\eta_{ij} \log \frac{p_j}{\pi^*}\,.$$

Houthakker (1965) takes $\sum_{j \neq i} {}_1\eta_{ij}^* \log (p_j/\pi^*) \approx 0$ and thus the form he uses reduces to $\log q_i = \alpha_i + {}_1\eta_i \log (y/\pi^*) + {}_1\eta_{ii}^* \log (p_i/\pi^*)$. Stone (1954) (see Section 3.5.1) prefers to introduce elements of this expression depending on whether he considers the goods are close substitutes or complements. In fact both Stone and Houthakker fitted their models in first difference form which make the results perhaps closer to the classical theory than the above

† $$\begin{aligned} \mathbf{H}\boldsymbol{\iota}^* &= (\mathbf{H} + \boldsymbol{\eta}\mathbf{w}')\boldsymbol{\iota} = \hat{\mathbf{w}}^{-1}\, \hat{\mathbf{w}}(\mathbf{H} + \boldsymbol{\eta}\mathbf{w}')\,\boldsymbol{\iota} \\ &= \hat{\mathbf{w}}^{-1}\, [\hat{\mathbf{w}}(\mathbf{H} + \boldsymbol{\eta}\mathbf{w}')]'\boldsymbol{\iota} \\ &= \hat{\mathbf{w}}^{-1}\, (\mathbf{H}'\mathbf{w} + \mathbf{w}\boldsymbol{\eta}'\mathbf{w}) \\ &= \hat{\mathbf{w}}^{-1}\, (-\mathbf{w} + \mathbf{w}) \\ &= \mathbf{0}\,. \end{aligned}$$

discussion suggests, see (3.2b). These works of Stone and Houthakker are interesting from another point of view. Both authors are concerned that annual time series do not provide enough degrees of freedom for much faith to be placed in the estimates derived from them. Stone's approach is to use estimates of the income elasticity derived from cross section studies. Houthakker, on the other hand, attempts to use time series from different countries and it is his study that we report in this section.

Houthakker (1965)

Houthakker's aim is to show that although parameters vary significantly between countries, this variation is not so great as to make certain typical values wholly unrealistic or useless. The data used are taken from O.E.C.D. *General Statistics* and relate to five categories of consumer expenditure – food, clothing, rent durables and miscellaneous. The figures, in local currencies, are given in current and constant (1954) prices. The sample, involving 13 countries, contains 140 observations from the period 1948–1950, (some incomplete or non-standard observations being excluded). Throughout, all aggregates are converted to a per capita basis.

We have already indicated that the form used in this study is

$$\Delta \log q_i = a_i + b_i \Delta \log \frac{y}{\pi^*} + c_i \Delta \log \frac{p_i}{\pi^*}$$

where

q_i is per capita expenditure on the ith good in 1954 prices;
y is per capita total expenditure in 1954 prices;
π^* is the implicit deflator of total expenditure.

This form has the advantage that no account need be taken of the fact that observations are in different currencies since the first difference of the logarithm transformation implies variables in rate of growth form. The existence of a constant term reflects a linear trend term in the original demand function.

Houthakker distinguishes two sets of regression results – the 'within' and 'between' country regressions. The 'within' results stem from using 127 annual deviations from country means to estimate

$$\Delta \log q_i - \overline{\Delta \log q_i} = b_{iw}\left(\Delta \log \frac{y}{\pi^*} - \overline{\Delta \log \frac{y}{\pi^*}}\right) + c_{iw}\left(\Delta \log \frac{p_i}{\pi^*} - \overline{\Delta \log \frac{p_i}{\pi^*}}\right)$$

Table 3.7
International demand elasticities of total expenditure and price for 5 commodities.

	Within		Between	
	b_{iw}	c_{iw}	b_{ib}	c_{ib}
Food	0.351 (0.070)	−0.161 (0.075)	0.744 (0.071)	0.234 (0.183)
Clothing	1.574 (0.132)	−0.282 (0.085)	0.713 (0.177)	−0.052 (0.284)
Rent	0.029 (0.067)	−0.114 (0.106)	1.545 (0.221)	−0.362 (0.102)
Durables	3.919 (0.266)	−0.502 (0.236)	1.946 (0.371)	−1.371 (0.766)
Miscellaneous	−0.755 (0.053)	−0.388 (0.086)	0.934 (0.060)	0.455 (0.181)

where the barred terms represent country means. The 'between' results stem from using the 13 observations, i.e., one for each country, to estimate

$$\overline{\Delta \log q_i} = a_{ib} + b_{ib}\, \overline{\Delta \log \frac{y}{\pi^*}} + c_{ib}\, \overline{\Delta \log \frac{p_i}{\pi^*}}\,.$$

However, in the sample period total expenditure is correlated with the trend term and Houthakker feels that the more relevant results for comparison are those where the trend term, i.e., the intercept, is suppressed (table 3.7). In deriving these results each country's observations are weighted by that country's population. Casual perusal of these results suggests that the 'within' and 'between' regressions are different, and an analysis of covariance confirms the significance of this difference.

In order to help interpret these results Houthakker develops a dynamic model in which a stock variable also influences demand. Thus,

$$q_i = a_i + b_i y + k_i s_i$$

where s_i represents inventories or force of habit. Adding the identity

$$\frac{\mathrm{d}s_i}{\mathrm{d}t} = q_i + w_i s_i$$

where w_i is the depreciation rate and usually negative. In the long run equilibrium, $ds/dt = 0$

$$\therefore \qquad -w_i\tilde{s}_i = a_i + b_i y + k_i\tilde{s}_i$$

where the tilde represents long run values. Then,

$$\tilde{q}_i = \frac{a_i \; w_i}{k_i+w_i} + \frac{b_i \; w_i}{k_i+w_i}\, y$$

$$= \tilde{a}_i + \tilde{b}_i y \; .$$

Assuming that both $\tilde{b}_i$ and b_i are positive, then $b_i > \tilde{b}_i$ if $k_i < 0$ and $\tilde{b}_i > b$ if $k_i > 0$. We would expect that in the case of durable goods k would be negative whereas in the non-durable case where habit is important then k should be positive. Thus the results obtained suggest that the 'between' elasticities should be thought of as long run elasticities and the 'within' as the short run elasticities. Estimates for individual countries are also provided but in this case the model is used in its original form, i.e. first differences are not used, see table 3.8. These results show considerable variety in the value of the elasticities especially the price elasticities. Although these differences are significant Houthakker believes that data from different countries should be used together to guard against the risk of arriving at nonsensical results. Although Houthakker's numerical results are inconclusive his paper highlights important points that we shall consider. These relate to the form of the relationship, the role of cross-section data and the dynamic element in demand studies.

Houthakker's claim, in 1965, that the constant elasticity model is "without serious rivals in respect of goodness of fit, ease of estimation and immediacy of interpretation" has been questioned by Goldberger and Gamaletsos (1967) who propose the linear expenditure system as a serious rival. It may be that the more recent formulation of the Rotterdam school may also be a serious contender. The Rotterdam model is also a pragmatic function with the classical constraints only approximately satisfied. We shall return to this model later but first we shall present some of Goldberger and Gamaletsos's arguments and results.

Table 3.8
Parameter estimates: CEDS model (1948–1959).

	Income elasticity (η_i)					Price elasticity (δ_i)				
	F	C	R	D	O	F	C	R	D	O
Austria	0.74	0.64	0.45	2.43	1.11	−0.54	0.02	−0.2	−0.94	−0.58
Belgium	0.92	0.06	0.33	2.23	1.13	−0.69	0.32	0.05	0.44	−0.11
Canada	0.69	−0.09	1.27	3.44	0.90	−0.29	−0.38	−0.09	0.96	−0.36
Denmark	0.48	0.35	0.85	3.68	0.87	−0.53	0.03	0.52	0.35	−0.08
France	0.68	1.47	0.87	2.53	1.04	−0.16	0.53	−0.17	−0.15	−0.06
Greece	0.73	1.17	1.67	1.80	−1.28	−0.34	−0.88	−0.12	−1.13	−0.94
Italy	0.78	0.59	0.70	2.72	1.34	−0.26	−0.19	−0.10	0.41	−0.32
Luxemberg	1.15	0.15	0.59	1.81	1.06	−1.02	−0.11	5.69	−0.81	−0.29
Netherlands	0.57	1.81	0.32	1.99	0.85	0.60	0.47	0.36	−2.19	−0.29
Norway	0.78	1.38	1.99	0.80	0.56	−0.20	−0.17	−0.28	−2.20	0.44
Sweden	0.38	−0.94	1.58	2.87	1.28	0.06	−1.81	−0.33	0.52	−0.86
U.K.	0.73	1.04	0.66	3.00	0.81	0.12	−0.09	−0.19	−1.46	0.24
U.S.A.	0.32	0.78	1.67	2.03	1.11	−0.34	0.42	0.08	1.09	−0.06

F = food; C = clothing; R = rent; D = durables; O = other.

3.3.2.c. Digression: a comparison of the linear expenditure and the constant elasticity systems.

Goldberger and Gamaletsos indicate that the price coefficients estimated by Houthakker cannot be interpreted as either the Slutsky compensated or the "uncompensated price elasticities because of the use of a general price deflator for both income and price terms. In fact given Houthakker's model, i.e.,

$$\log q_i = a_i + b_i \log \frac{y}{\pi^*} + c_i \log \frac{p_i}{\pi^*} + d_i t$$

and letting $\pi^* \approx \pi$, where $\log \pi = \sum_{i=1}^{n} w_i \log p_i$, then

$$\mathrm{d} \log \frac{y}{\pi^*} \approx \mathrm{d} \log y - \sum w_i \, \mathrm{d} \log p_i \, .$$

If $\mathrm{d} \log p_i = 1$ and all other prices and money income are kept constant then $\mathrm{d} \log (y/\pi^*) \approx w_i$ and $\mathrm{d} \log (p_i/\pi^*) \approx 1 - w_i$. Hence, if p_i changes such that $\mathrm{d} \log p_i = 1$ then,

$$\begin{aligned} \mathrm{d} \log q_i &= b_i \, \mathrm{d} \log \frac{y}{\pi^*} + c_i \, \mathrm{d} \log \frac{p_i}{\pi^*} \\ &= -w_i b_i + (1 - w_i) c_i \\ &= c_i - (b_i + c_i) w_i \, . \end{aligned}$$

Thus, the uncompensated price elasticity is not c_i but $c_i - (b_i + c_i) w_i$. Similarly it can be shown that the Slutsky compensated price elasticity is $(1 - w_i) c_i$. According to the theory, all Slutsky compensated price elasticities should be negative but Houthakker's results include many positive values. There are even 3 negative income elasticities. These results, plus the difficulties of obtaining cross elasticities from this type of model lead the authors to consider how well the linear expenditure system fits the same data that Houthakker used. In fact the data used in this study is updated a little (to 1961) and Ireland is substituted for Austria. The changes in relative prices during the sample period seem quite substantial which is desirable, but unfortunately, there also seems to be a fair amount of multicollinearity.

The results of the linear expenditure model are reproduced in table 3.9. These results were derived using Stone's method (see Section 3.3.1.a). This would be appropriate if the stochastic terms $\epsilon_i(t)$ $(i = 1, 2, ..., n)$ were such

Table 3.9
Parameter estimates: LES model.

	Marginal budget share (β_i)					Minimum required quantity (γ_i)				
	F	C	R	D	O	F	C	R	D	O
Belgium	0.178	0.098	0.028	0.240	0.456	11.00	3.98	4.54	4.17	15.15
Canada	0.177	0.029	0.279	0.133	0.382	0.20	0.10	0.06	0.07	0.32
Denmark	0.110	0.003	0.137	0.366	0.384	0.97	0.46	0.05	−0.19	1.09
France	0.237	0.144	0.030	0.174	0.415	0.93	0.36	0.10	0.20	1.06
Greece	0.314	0.141	0.126	0.082	0.337	2.02	0.59	0.10	0.13	0.79
Ireland	0.267	0.083	0.052	0.180	0.418	48.1	14.9	6.4	5.5	44.2
Italy	0.393	0.076	0.054	0.081	0.396	0.074	0.019	0.006	0.004	0.051
Luxemberg	0.393	0.038	0.059	0.175	0.335	3.01	4.03	1.86	−0.67	3.51
Netherlands	0.193	0.250	0.043	0.248	0.266	0.52	0.30	0.10	0.17	0.54
Norway	0.207	0.134	0.077	0.247	0.335	1.09	0.63	0.21	0.23	1.32
Sweden	0.114	0.110	0.155	0.217	0.404	0.94	0.36	0.09	0.04	0.75
U.K.	0.172	0.130	0.052	0.269	0.377	0.074	0.27	0.020	0.022	0.106
U.S.A.	0.081	0.055	0.190	0.096	0.578	0.33	0.14	0.14	0.15	0.52

Underlined coefficients are less, in absolute value, than twice their standard errors.

F = food; C = clothing; R = rent; D = durables; 0 = other.

that

$$E\boldsymbol{\varepsilon}(t)\boldsymbol{\varepsilon}'(s) = \begin{cases} \sigma^2 \mathbf{I} & t = s \\ \mathbf{0} & t \neq s \end{cases}$$

where σ^2 is a scalar and $\boldsymbol{\varepsilon}$

$$\boldsymbol{\varepsilon}(t) = \begin{bmatrix} \epsilon_1(t) \\ \epsilon_2(t) \\ \vdots \\ \epsilon_n(t) \end{bmatrix}$$

However, since goods differ in average and marginal budget shares the assumption of constant variance over goods is unlikely to be valid. Also since all disturbances must sum to zero across all goods in each period, contemporaneous correlation is inherent, i.e., all off diagonal terms cannot be zero. Goldberger and Gamaletsos suggest that

$$E\boldsymbol{\varepsilon}(t)\boldsymbol{\varepsilon}'(s) = \begin{cases} \boldsymbol{\Sigma} & t = s \\ \mathbf{0} & t \neq s \end{cases}$$

where $\boldsymbol{\Sigma}\ \iota = 0$, is a more adequate specification †. The expected values of the Stone estimators should not be affected but there will be a loss of efficiency.

The results of fitting the constant elasticity model are reproduced in table 3.10. These elasticities have not been estimated on a first difference basis (cf. Houthakker) but on a straight forward regression basis. In order to compare these results with those of the LES Goldberger and Gamaletsos derive the mean elasticities for each model (see tables 3.11 and 3.12). A comparison of these elasticities shows that the income elasticities are quite similar but the price elasticities are not. Twenty out of sixty-five compensated own price elasticities are positive for linear expenditure system (LES) model and twenty-four for the constant elasticity (CEDS) model. The LES elasticities

† Barten developes this type of specification from a stochastic model of classical consumer theory, see Section 3.3.2.d.

Table 3.10
Parameter estimates: CEDS model.

	Income elasticity (η_i)					Price elasticity (δ_i)				
	F	C	R	D	O	F	C	R	D	O
Belgium	0.52	0.87	0.11	1.91	1.00	−0.59	−1.41	0.25	−0.98	0.09
Canada	0.78	0.58	1.93	1.24	1.13	−0.25	0.22	−0.46	−0.66	−0.99
Denmark	0.39	0.24	0.32	3.58	0.91	−0.38	0.38	0.78	1.54	−0.26
France	0.53	1.53	1.19	2.55	1.03	−0.51	0.65	−0.29	−0.13	0.01
Greece	0.70	0.94	1.82	1.52	1.24	−0.58	−0.03	−0.01	0.23	−0.27
Ireland	0.72	1.06	0.91	2.62	1.05	−0.42	0.55	0.11	−0.59	−0.09
Italy	0.78	0.59	0.27	2.78	1.22	−0.65	−0.20	0.10	0.32	0.11
Luxemberg	1.12	0.23	0.63	1.74	1.04	−0.98	−0.11	6.73	−0.84	−0.25
Netherlands	0.60	1.75	0.46	2.23	0.81	0.04	0.38	0.16	−1.10	−0.05
Norway	0.73	1.07	0.19	2.36	0.86	−0.39	0.18	0.33	−0.84	−0.14
Sweden	0.37	1.01	1.54	1.17	1.18	−0.12	0.04	−0.40	−2.44	−0.91
U.K.	0.57	1.17	0.70	1.16	0.87	0.13	−0.08	−0.08	−3.08	0.23
U.S.A.	0.12	0.57	1.63	1.37	1.75	−0.59	−0.06	−0.24	0.80	−1.23

Underlined coefficients are less, in absolute value, than twice their standard errors.

F = food; C = clothing; R = rent; D = durables; O = other.

Table 3.11
Mean elasticities: LES model.

	Income elasticity (η_i)					Own price elasticity (uncompensated) (η_{ii})					Own-price elasticity (compensated) (η_{ii}^*)				
	F	C	R	D	O	F	C	R	D	O	F	C	R	D	O
Belgium	0.63	0.99	0.21	2.45	1.17	−0.16	−0.06	−0.02	−0.17	−0.43	0.02	0.04	0.01	0.07	0.03
Canada	0.75	0.29	1.93	1.26	0.92	−0.37	−0.12	−0.72	−0.48	−0.56	−0.19	−0.10	−0.44	−0.35	−0.18
Denmark	0.42	0.03	1.82	2.78	0.90	−0.28	−0.02	−0.88	−1.19	−0.64	−0.17	−0.02	−0.74	−0.82	−0.28
France	0.68	1.09	0.69	2.55	1.02	−0.22	−0.11	−0.00	−0.09	−0.39	0.02	0.03	0.03	0.08	0.03
Greece	0.67	0.94	1.95	1.52	1.27	−0.49	−0.46	−0.79	−0.62	−0.66	−0.18	−0.32	−0.63	−0.54	−0.32
Ireland	0.70	0.74	0.93	2.80	1.08	−0.34	−0.18	−0.18	−0.52	−0.51	−0.07	−0.10	−0.13	−0.34	−0.09
Italy	0.85	0.67	0.96	2.27	1.19	−0.49	−0.19	−0.21	−0.46	−0.53	−0.10	−0.11	−0.16	−0.38	−0.13
Luxemberg	1.13	0.28	0.64	1.77	1.04	−0.86	−0.22	−0.47	−1.16	−0.80	−0.47	−0.18	−0.41	−0.98	−0.46
Netherlands	0.60	1.48	0.61	2.59	0.78	−0.18	−0.21	−0.02	−0.18	−0.25	0.01	0.04	0.02	0.07	0.02
Norway	0.68	0.82	1.07	2.76	0.90	−0.28	−0.23	−0.21	−0.53	−0.42	−0.08	−0.10	−0.13	−0.28	−0.08
Sweden	0.39	0.80	1.71	2.13	1.08	−0.26	−0.41	−0.77	−0.93	−0.68	−0.15	−0.30	−0.61	−0.71	−0.28
U.K.	0.57	1.28	0.60	3.33	0.88	−0.16	−0.10	−0.03	−0.20	−0.36	0.01	0.03	0.02	0.07	0.02
U.S.A.	0.35	0.56	1.54	0.85	1.34	−0.13	−0.13	−0.37	−0.20	−0.66	−0.05	−0.07	−0.18	−0.10	−0.08

F = food; C = clothing; R = rent; D = durables; O = other.

Table 3.12
Mean elasticities: CEDS model.

	Income elasticity (η_i)					Own-price elasticity (uncompensated) (η_{ii})					Own-price elasticity (compensated) (η_{ii}^*)				
	F	C	R	D	O	F	C	R	D	O	F	C	R	D	O
Belgium	0.52	0.87	0.11	1.91	1.00	−0.67	−1.36	0.21	−1.07	−0.34	−0.42	−1.27	0.22	−0.88	0.05
Canada	0.78	0.58	1.93	1.24	1.13	−0.37	0.14	−0.67	−0.72	−1.05	−0.19	0.20	−0.39	−0.59	−0.58
Denmark	0.39	0.24	0.32	3.58	0.91	−0.38	0.31	0.70	0.88	−0.54	−0.28	0.34	0.72	1.34	−0.15
France	0.53	1.53	1.19	2.55	1.03	−0.52	0.35	−0.33	−0.29	−0.41	−0.33	0.56	−0.28	−0.12	0.01
Greece	0.70	0.94	1.82	1.52	1.24	−0.64	−0.17	−0.12	0.14	−0.52	−0.31	−0.03	−0.01	0.22	−0.20
Ireland	0.72	1.06	0.91	2.62	1.05	−0.54	0.37	0.05	−0.72	−0.47	−0.26	0.49	0.10	−0.55	−0.06
Italy	0.78	0.59	0.27	2.78	1.22	−0.71	−0.25	0.08	0.21	−0.33	−0.35	−0.18	0.09	0.31	0.07
Luxemberg	1.12	0.23	0.63	1.74	1.04	−1.03	−0.12	6.05	−0.93	−0.51	−0.64	−0.09	6.11	−0.76	−0.17
Netherlands	0.60	1.75	0.46	2.23	0.81	−0.17	0.02	0.12	−1.21	−0.31	0.03	0.32	0.15	−1.00	−0.03
Norway	0.73	1.07	0.19	2.36	0.86	−0.49	−0.03	0.30	−0.98	−0.41	−0.27	0.15	0.31	−0.77	−0.09
Sweden	0.37	1.01	1.54	1.17	1.18	−0.19	−0.11	−0.50	−2.32	−1.01	−0.08	0.03	−0.36	−2.20	−0.57
U.K.	0.57	1.17	0.70	1.16	0.87	−0.08	−0.19	−0.13	−2.93	−0.25	0.09	−0.07	−0.07	−2.84	0.13
U.S.A.	0.12	0.57	1.63	1.37	1.75	−0.48	−0.11	−0.41	0.56	−1.45	−0.45	−0.05	−0.21	0.71	−0.70

F = food; C = clothing; R = rent; D = durables; O = other.

are evaluated at the sample means but if the terminal values are used then there are no positive elasticities. However, of the twenty-four 'wrong' signs in the CEDS model only five are significantly different from zero.

When the goodness of fit of the two models are compared it appears that the LES model does better than the CEDS. However, the LES is explaining expenditures and the CEDS logarithms of quantities. The authors suggest a comparison on the neutral ground of how well the two models account for the variation in average budget shares over the sample. For the LES this is straight forward since $\hat{v}_i(t)$, the calculated expenditure on the ith good is obtained directly from the estimated equations and $w_i(t) = \hat{v}_i(t)/y(t)$. For the CEDS $\log q_i(t)$, the calculated value of $\widetilde{\log}\, q_i(t)$, is transformed to obtain $\tilde{q}_i(t)$ (i.e. antilog $[\widetilde{\log}\, q_i(t)]$). Then $\tilde{v}_i(t) = p_i(t)\tilde{q}_i(t)$ and $\tilde{w}_i(t) = \tilde{v}_i(t)/\sum_{i=1}^{n} \tilde{v}_i(t)$ and

$$\hat{R}_i^2 = 1 - \frac{\sum_{t=1}^{T} (w_i(t) - \hat{w}_i(t))^2}{\sum_{t=1}^{T} (w_i(t) - \bar{w}_i)^2}$$

$$\tilde{R}_i^2 = 1 - \frac{\sum_{t=1}^{T} (w_i(t) - \tilde{w}_i(t))^2}{\sum_{t=1}^{T} (w_i(t) - \bar{w}_i)^2}$$

where $\bar{w}_i$ is the sample average budget share of the ith good. These goodness of fit statistics are calculated for each good and each country and appear in table 3.13.

Only in 7 out of 65 cases does the LES have a better fit than the CEDS. It should be remembered, however, that the former system does involve fewer parameters ($2n - 1$, i.e., 9) than the latter ($3n$, i.e., 15). Of course the fits for individual goods are not independent since an over-estimate of the budget share of one good will imply an under-estimate in one or more other goods. As a single measure of the accuracy of the predictions for all goods for each country the authors use Theil's information inaccuracy index (see Theil, 1967), i.e.

Table 3.13
Goodness of fit for average budget shares: linear expenditure system and constant elasticity demand system.

	LES	CEDS	LES	CEDS	LES	CEDS	LES	CEDS	LES	CEDS
Belgium	0.944	0.953	−0.529	−0.156	0.975	0.986	0.788	0.783	0.835	0.861
Canada	0.967	0.959	0.976	0.978	0.938	0.948	−0.033	−0.002	0.339	0.572
Denmark	0.911	0.922	0.893	0.917	0.816	0.956	0.889	0.905	0.366	0.122
France	0.950	0.976	0.947	0.986	0.935	0.971	0.934	0.977	0.951	0.964
Greece	0.782	0.856	0.750	0.824	0.934	0.972	0.711	0.862	0.681	0.728
Ireland	0.686	0.793	0.806	0.886	0.227	0.297	0.653	0.678	0.886	0.810
Italy	0.928	0.970	0.916	0.922	0.990	0.999	0.765	0.886	0.789	0.842
Luxemberg	0.862	0.914	0.866	0.866	0.545	0.725	0.927	0.939	0.459	0.737
Netherlands	0.849	0.852	0.836	0.872	0.972	0.982	0.926	0.942	0.830	0.836
Norway	0.569	0.741	0.908	0.929	0.974	0.990	0.823	0.851	0.553	0.490
Sweden	0.975	0.972	0.803	0.816	0.952	0.972	0.849	0.890	0.371	0.540
U.K.	0.973	0.974	0.726	0.744	0.993	0.993	0.805	0.866	0.851	0.900
U.S.A.	0.934	0.948	0.960	0.941	0.826	0.852	0.202	0.240	0.828	0.884

LES = linear expenditure system; CEDS = constant elasticity demand system.

F = food; C = clothing; R = rent; D = durables; O = other.

$$\hat{I}(t) = \sum_{i=1}^{n} w_i(t) \log [w_i(t)/\hat{w}_i(t)]$$

and

$$\tilde{I}(t) = \sum_{i=1}^{n} w_i(t) \log [w_i(t)/\tilde{w}_i(t)] \ .$$

Perfect prediction will be reflected by zero value in the index, and poor prediction by high values. The indices for the two models are reported in table 3.14. It would appear, then, that in terms of fit of the average budget shares, the CEDS is better than the LES. However, this is achieved at the cost of the introduction of more parameters and the abandonment of a tight theoretical framework.

In addition to this conclusion Goldberger and Gamaletsos draw our attention to some further points in this section of their paper. Firstly, the parameters vary between countries. Secondly, a model which predicts expenditures

Table 3.14
Average information inaccuracy: linear expenditure system and constant elasticity demand system.
(All entries should be multiplied by 10^{-6}.)

	LES	CEDS
Belgium	102	151
Canada	240	214
Denmark	539	417
France	155	62
Greece	641	412
Ireland	248	216
Italy	191	116
Luxemberg	114	89
Netherlands	241	185
Norway	224	178
Sweden	218	177
U.K.	208	151
U.S.A.	376	333

Unit of measurement is 10^{-6} *nit*.
LES = linear expenditure system;
CEDS = constant elasticity demand system.

may not predict average budget shares accurately. Finally, if we are interested in changes in the composition of consumption then perhaps the predictions of changes in budget shares ought to be our concern. It is reasoning such as this that has led to the Rotterdam models in which the demand functions are formulated directly in terms of changes in the budget shares.

3.3.2.d. The Rotterdam school: Barten (1968)

In Section 3.2.4 we showed how demand functions could be set up in terms of average budget shares. The Rotterdam school uses this approach but their models are approximate because they use first differences in the place of differentials. Barten's study is interesting since it introduces stochastic factors into the utility function. This enables the form of the variance–covariance matrix of the disturbance terms to be derived. Barten also shows that aggregation across commodities, which are utility interdependent, is possible, provided the aggregates are defined in a certain way. To estimate the system an estimator suggested by Theil which is "not too different from" a best linear unbiased estimator is used with Netherlands data for four commodity groups.

It will be recalled from Section 3.2.5 that

$$\hat{\mathbf{w}}\,\mathrm{d}\log q = \boldsymbol{\mu}(\mathrm{d}\log y - \mathbf{w}'\,\mathrm{d}\log\mathbf{p}) + \mathbf{N}(\mathrm{d}\log\mathbf{p} - \boldsymbol{\iota}\boldsymbol{\mu}'\,\mathrm{d}\log\mathbf{p}) \qquad (3.2\mathrm{i})$$

$$\boldsymbol{\iota}'\boldsymbol{\mu} = 1 \qquad (3.15\mathrm{i})$$

$$\mathbf{N}\boldsymbol{\iota} = \phi\boldsymbol{\mu} \qquad (3.16\mathrm{i})$$

$$\mathbf{N}' = \mathbf{N} \qquad (3.17\mathrm{i})$$

i.e.,

$$w_i\,\mathrm{d}\log q_i = \mu_i(\mathrm{d}\log y - \sum_{k=1}^{n} w_k\,\mathrm{d}\log p_k)$$

$$+ \sum_{j=1}^{n} \nu_{ij}(\mathrm{d}\log p_j - \sum_{k=1}^{n} \mu_k\,\mathrm{d}\log p_k) \qquad (i = 1, 2, ..., n) \qquad (3.22)$$

This is approximated by

$$\frac{w_{it}+w_{it-1}}{2}\,\Delta\log q_{it}=\mu_i[\Delta\log y_t-\sum_{k=1}^{n}\frac{w_{kt}+w_{kt-1}}{2}\,\Delta\log p_{kt}]$$

$$+\sum_{j=1}^{n}\nu_{ij}\,[\Delta\log p_{jt}-\sum_{k=1}^{n}\mu_k\,\Delta\log p_{kt}]\qquad (i=1,2,\ldots,n)\,. \tag{3.23}$$

Letting

$$w_i^*=\frac{w_{it}+w_{it-1}}{2}\qquad (i=1,2,\ldots,n)$$

and since

$$\mathrm{d}w_i=w_i\,\mathrm{d}\log q_i+w_i\,\mathrm{d}\log p_i-w_i\,\mathrm{d}\log y\qquad (i=1,2,\ldots,n)$$

$$\Delta w_i\approx w_i^*\,\Delta\log q_i+w_i^*\,\Delta\log p_i-w_i^*\,\Delta\log y\,. \tag{3.24}$$

Since

$$\sum_{i=1}^{n}w_i=1\,,\qquad \sum_{i=1}^{n}\Delta w_i=0$$

by summing (3.24),

$$\Delta\log y-\sum_{i=1}^{n}w_i^*\,\Delta\log p_i=\sum_{i=1}^{n}w_i^*\,\Delta\log q_i\,.$$

Letting

$$\sum_{i=1}^{n}w_i^*\,\Delta\log q_i=\Delta\log q$$

and

$$\Delta \log p_j - \sum_{k=1}^{n} \mu_k \Delta \log p_k = \Delta \log \bar{p}_j'$$

then (3.23) becomes

$$w_i^* \Delta \log q_i = \mu_i \Delta \log q + \sum_{j=1}^{n} \nu_{ij} [\Delta \log \bar{p}_j'] \qquad (i = 1, 2, ..., n) \; . \tag{3.25}$$

Introducing the notation that D represents the first difference of the logarithm, (3.25) can be rewritten as

$$w_i^* \mathrm{D}\, q_i = \mu_i \mathrm{D}\, q + \sum_{j=1}^{n} \nu_{ij} \mathrm{D}\, \bar{p}_j' \qquad (i = 1, 2, ..., n) \tag{3.26}$$

This set of equations, i.e. (3.26) explains the reaction of a consumer to changes in prices and income. If the consumer's tastes are influenced by random elements these would cause him to alter his pattern of expenditure even if prices and income are held constant. These effects can be introduced by incorporating a stochastic term into the utility function. Thus we assume that the utility function is approximated by

$$u(\mathbf{q}) = \mathbf{a}'\mathbf{q} + \tfrac{1}{2}\mathbf{q}'\mathbf{U}\mathbf{q}$$

where $\mathbf{a}$ is an n element vector of stochastic terms, independent of $\mathbf{q}$, and $\mathbf{U}$ is the matrix of second order partials, which are non-stochastic.

Hence

$$\mathbf{u}_q = \mathbf{a} + \mathbf{U}\mathbf{q} \tag{3.28}$$

and

$$\mathbf{a} + \mathbf{U}\mathbf{q} = \lambda \mathbf{p} \; . \tag{3.29}$$

It will be recalled, from Section 3.2.6, that

$$\mathbf{N} = \frac{\lambda}{y} \hat{\mathbf{p}} \mathbf{U}^{-1} \hat{\mathbf{p}} , \tag{3.30}$$

however, λ is stochastic and so, strictly speaking, is **N**. However, because of the inconvenience of having stochastic parameters λ is replaced by $E(\lambda)$ in the definition of **N**. It follows that

$$\mathbf{U} = \frac{E(\lambda)}{y}\,\hat{\mathbf{p}}\mathbf{N}^{-1}\hat{\mathbf{p}}$$

and

$$\mathbf{a} + \frac{E(\lambda)}{y}\,\hat{\mathbf{p}}\mathbf{N}^{-1}\hat{\mathbf{p}}\mathbf{q} = \lambda\mathbf{p}\,.$$

Hence

$$\frac{1}{E(\lambda)}\,\hat{\mathbf{p}}^{-1}\mathbf{a} + \mathbf{N}^{-1}\mathbf{w} = \frac{\lambda}{E(\lambda)}\,\boldsymbol{\iota}$$

and

$$\frac{1}{E(\lambda)}\,\hat{\mathbf{p}}^{-1}\Delta\mathbf{a} + \mathbf{N}^{-1}\Delta\mathbf{w} = \frac{\Delta\lambda}{E(\lambda)}\,\boldsymbol{\iota}$$

$$\therefore \qquad \Delta\mathbf{w} = \frac{\Delta\lambda}{E(\lambda)}\,\mathbf{N}\boldsymbol{\iota} - \mathbf{N}\mathbf{s}$$

where $\mathbf{s} = [1/E(\lambda)]\,\hat{\mathbf{p}}^{-1}\,\Delta\mathbf{a}$

i.e., the effect of the change in the stochastic variable.

But

$$\boldsymbol{\iota}'\Delta\mathbf{w} = 0$$

$$\therefore \qquad \frac{\Delta\lambda}{E(\lambda)}\,\boldsymbol{\iota}'\mathbf{N}\boldsymbol{\iota} = \boldsymbol{\iota}'\mathbf{N}\mathbf{s}$$

i.e.,

$$\frac{\Delta\lambda}{E(\lambda)}\,\boldsymbol{\iota}'\phi\boldsymbol{\mu} = \boldsymbol{\mu}'\phi\mathbf{s} \qquad \text{from (3.20)}$$

$$\frac{\Delta\lambda}{E(\lambda)} = \boldsymbol{\mu}'\mathbf{s} \qquad \text{from (3.19)}$$

$$\therefore \qquad \Delta\mathbf{w} = (\mathbf{N} - \phi\,\boldsymbol{\mu}\boldsymbol{\mu}')\mathbf{s}\,.$$

Thus, we have derived the effect of $\mathbf{s}$ (i.e., a function of a change in the stochastic term) on $\Delta\mathbf{w}$ when prices and income are constant, namely,

$$\Delta w_i = -\sum_j (\nu_{ij} - \phi\mu_i\mu_j)s_j \qquad (i = 1, 2, ..., n)\,.$$

Thus, from (3.24),

$$w_i^* \,\Delta \log q_i = -\sum_j (\nu_{ij} - \phi\mu_i\mu_j)s_j \qquad (i = 1, 2, ..., n)\,. \quad (3.31)$$

If we allow prices and incomes to change and assume that these are not correlated with changes in the random term then,

$$w_i^* \,\Delta \log q_i = \mu_i \mathrm{D}\,q + \sum_{j=1}^{n} \nu_{ij}\,\mathrm{D}\,\bar{p}_j' - \sum_j (\nu_{ij} - \phi\mu_i\mu_j)s_j \qquad (i = 1, 2, ..., n)\,.$$

This set of equations is a set of demand functions with distinct disturbance terms. Since $\sum\sum(\nu_{ij} - \phi\mu_i\mu_j) = 0$, the variance–covariance matrix of the disturbances at a single point of time is singular.

Let

$$\upsilon_{it} = -\sum_j (\nu_{ij} - \phi\mu_i\mu_j)s_{jt}$$

then if

$$E(s_{it}) = 0 \qquad \text{all } i \text{ and } t\,,$$

$$E(\upsilon_{it}) = 0 \qquad \text{all } i \text{ and } t\,.$$

Similarly if

$$E(s_{it}s_{jt'}) = 0 \qquad t \neq t', \text{ for all } i \text{ and } j\,,$$

i.e. no serial correlation of any kind in the stochastic terms, then,

$$E(v_{it}v_{jt'}) = 0 \qquad t \neq t', \text{ for all } i \text{ and } j\,.$$

In any one period Barten assumes that the correlation between the random terms is as follows

$$E(\mathbf{s}_t\mathbf{s}_t') = \frac{\sigma^2}{\phi}\,\mathbf{N}^{-1} \tag{3.33}$$

where σ^2 is a positive scalar.

This assumption implies that

$$E(\mathbf{v}_t\mathbf{v}_t') = \frac{\sigma^2}{\phi}\,(\mathbf{N} - \phi\,\boldsymbol{\mu}\boldsymbol{\mu}')^{\dagger}\,. \tag{3.34}$$

It will be recalled from (3.2i) and (3.16i) that the demand functions can be written

$$\hat{\mathbf{w}}\,\mathrm{d}\log\mathbf{q} = \boldsymbol{\mu}(\mathrm{d}\log y - \mathbf{w}'\,\mathrm{d}\log\mathbf{p}) + (\mathbf{N} - \phi\,\boldsymbol{\mu}\boldsymbol{\mu}')\,\mathrm{d}\log\mathbf{p}\,. \tag{3.35}$$

Thus, the variance covariance matrix of disturbances is the same as the matrix of the substitution effects of prices. When additivity of the utility function is assumed (3.34) takes the following simple form,

$$\mathrm{var}\; v_{it} = \sigma^2\mu_i(1 - \mu_i)$$

$$\mathrm{cov}\,(v_{it}v_{jt}) = -\sigma^2\mu_i\mu_j \qquad i \neq j \;\; (i, j = 1, 2, \ldots, n)\,. \tag{3.36}$$

The justification for using (3.33) is that it implies that

† Since

$$\mathbf{v}_t = -(\mathbf{N} - \phi\boldsymbol{\mu}\boldsymbol{\mu}')\,,$$

$$E(\mathbf{v}_t\mathbf{v}_t') = \sigma^2/\phi\,(\mathbf{N} - \boldsymbol{\mu}\boldsymbol{\mu}'\phi - \boldsymbol{\mu}\boldsymbol{\mu}'\phi + \phi\boldsymbol{\mu}\boldsymbol{\mu}'\mathbf{N}^{-1}\boldsymbol{\mu}\boldsymbol{\mu}'\phi)$$

and

$$\phi\boldsymbol{\mu}'\mathbf{N}^{-1}\boldsymbol{\mu} = \boldsymbol{\mu}'\mathbf{N}^{-1}\mathbf{N}\boldsymbol{\iota} = \boldsymbol{\mu}'\boldsymbol{\iota} = 1\,.$$

$$E[(\Delta\mathbf{a})(\Delta\mathbf{a})'] = \phi^{-1}\sigma^2 E(\lambda) y \mathbf{U},$$

and this can be interpreted in the following way. If a commodity, i, is such that for a change in q_i its marginal utility changes little, i.e., $\partial^2 u/\partial q_i \partial q_i$ is small then its random shock term will have a small variance. Similarly if the impact on the marginal utility of the ith good of a change in the jth good is small, the correlation between random shocks of the two variables will be low.

We now have the complete model but because of the nature of the data, we are usually estimating demand functions for a group of goods rather than for individual goods. Barten shows that if we can group goods such that each good is only utility related to goods in its own group, i.e., block additivity of $\mathbf{U}$, then it is possible to aggregate such that the essential structure of the theory holds for the composite good.

This can be shown by considering the gth group which, let us say, contains two goods. The individual demand functions for these two goods will be (see 3.26)

$$w_1^* \, \mathrm{D}\, q_1 = \mu_1 \, \mathrm{D}\, q + \nu_{11} \, \mathrm{D}\, \bar{p}_1' + \nu_{12} \, \mathrm{D}\, \bar{p}_2' + v_{1t}$$

$$w_2^* \, \mathrm{D}\, q_2 = \mu_2 \, \mathrm{D}\, q + \nu_{21} \, \mathrm{D}\, \bar{p}_1' + \nu_{22} \, \mathrm{D}\, \bar{p}_2' + v_{2t} \, .$$

Using (3.16i) and (3.17i),

$$\nu_{12} = \nu_{21}$$

$$\nu_{11} + \nu_{12} = \phi\mu_1$$

$$\nu_{21} + \nu_{22} = \phi\mu_2$$

Thus

$$w_1^* \, \mathrm{D}\, q_1 + w_2^* \, \mathrm{D}\, q_2 = (\mu_1 + \mu_2) \, \mathrm{D}\, q + \phi(\mu_1 \, \mathrm{D}\, \bar{p}_1' + \mu_2 \, \mathrm{D}\, \bar{p}_2') + v_{1t} + v_{2t} \, .$$

For any block additive group, g, containing m of the n goods we can write,

$$W_g^* \, \mathrm{D}\, Q_g = M_g \, \mathrm{D}\, q + \phi M_g \, \mathrm{D}\, \bar{P}_g' + V_{gt} \qquad (3.37)$$

where

$$W_g^* = \sum_{i=1}^{m} w_i^*$$

$$\mathrm{D}\,Q_g = \sum_{i=1}^{m} \frac{w_i^*}{W_g^*}\,\mathrm{D}\,q_i$$

$$M = \sum_{i=1}^{m} \mu_i$$

$$V_{gt} = \sum_{i=1}^{m} v_{it}$$

$$\mathrm{D}\,\bar{P}_g' = \sum_{i=1}^{m} \frac{\mu_i}{M_g}\,\mathrm{D}\,p_i - \sum_{i=1}^{m} \frac{\mu_i}{M_g} \sum_{k=1}^{n} \mu_k\,\mathrm{D}\,p_k$$

$$= \sum_{i=1}^{m} \frac{\mu_i}{M_g}\,\mathrm{D}\,p_i - \sum_{h=1}^{n} M_h \sum_{k=1}^{h} \frac{\mu_k}{M_h}\,\mathrm{D}\,p_k\,.$$

Using (3.26) and recalling that, with additivity assumed,

$$\nu_{ij} = 0 \quad \text{and} \quad \nu_{ii} = \phi\mu_i$$

$$w_i^*\,\mathrm{D}\,q_i = \mu_i\,\mathrm{D}\,q + \phi\mu_i\,\mathrm{D}\,\bar{p}_t' + v_{it}\,. \tag{3.38}$$

Thus, comparing (3.37) and (3.38), provided we aggregate the variables in the prescribed way a composite good can be treated exactly like an individual good under additivity. Unfortunately, in order to derive the aggregate price variables we need to know μ_i/M_g. These can be derived from budget studies but if we can assume that within a commodity group the income elasticities of the elementary goods are equal, we can take

$$\frac{\mu_i}{M_g} = \frac{\eta_i w_i^*}{\sum_{i=1}^{n} \eta_i w_i^*} = \frac{w_i^*}{W_g^*}$$

since $\mu_i = w_i \eta_i$. In his empirical section Barten uses this assumption to construct the price variables for sixteen composite goods and then uses budget weights to aggregate the sixteen into four composite goods price indices.

The estimation of (3.38) is not straightforward because of the non-linearity in the parameters. This can be seen more easily when (3.38) is rewritten as

$$w_i^* \, \mathrm{D}\, q_i = \frac{\nu_{ii}}{\sum_{j=1}^{n} \nu_{jj}} \mathrm{D}\, q + \nu_{ii} \, \mathrm{D}\, p_i - \frac{\nu_{ii}}{\sum_{j=1}^{n} \nu_{jj}} \sum_{k=1}^{n} \nu_{kk} \, \mathrm{D}\, p_k + \upsilon_i \, . \tag{3.39}$$

However, the parameters can be linearised using the following approximation for a function of n variables,

$$f(x_1, x_2, ..., x_n) \approx f(x_1^0, ..., x_2^0, ..., x_n^0) + (x_1 - x^0) f_{x_1}$$
$$+ (x_2 - x^0) f_{x_2} + ... + (x_n - x_n^0) f_{x_n}$$

where x_1^0 are fixed values and f_{x_i} are partial derivations evaluated at these fixed values. Thus, letting $\nu_{ii}/\sum_j \nu_{jj} = f(\nu_{11}, \nu_{22}, ..., \nu_{nn})$,

$$\frac{\nu_{ii}}{\sum_j \nu_{jj}} \approx \frac{\nu_{ii}^0}{\phi^0} - (\nu_{11} - \nu_{11}^0) \frac{\nu_{ii}^0}{(\sum \nu_{jj}^0)^2} - (\nu_{22} - \nu_{22}^0) \frac{\nu_{ii}^0}{(\sum \nu_{jj}^0)^2}$$
$$+ ... + (\nu_{ii} - \nu_{ii}^0) \left[\frac{-\nu_{ii}^0}{(\sum \nu_{jj}^0)^2} + \frac{1}{\sum \nu_{jj}^0} \right]$$
$$- (\nu_{i+1\, i+1} - \nu_{i+1\, i+1}^0) \frac{\nu_{ii}^0}{(\sum \nu_{jj}^0)^2} + ... - (\nu_n - \nu_n^0) \frac{\nu_{ii}^0}{(\sum \nu_{jj})^2}$$
$$= \frac{\nu_{ii}^0}{\phi^0} + \frac{\nu_{ii} - \nu_{ii}^0}{\phi^0} - \frac{\nu_{ii}^0 \sum_{j=1}^{n} (\nu_{jj} - \nu_{jj}^0)}{\phi^{02}}$$
$$= \mu_i^0 + \frac{\nu_{ii}}{\phi^0} - \frac{\mu_i^0}{\phi^0} \sum_{j=1}^{n} \nu_{jj}$$

where ν_{ii}^0 are an initial set of ν_{ii}.

$$\nu_{ii}^0 = \phi^0 \mu_i^0$$

$$\phi^0 = \sum_{j=1}^{n} \nu_{jj}^0 .$$

Similarly setting

$$\frac{\nu_{ii}}{\sum_{j=1}^{n} \nu_{jj}} \nu_{kk} = f(\nu_{11}, \nu_{22}, ..., \nu_{nn}) ,$$

and then summing the approximation over k, we find

$$\frac{\nu_{ii}}{\sum_{j=1}^{n} \nu_{jj}} \sum_{k=1}^{n} \nu_{kk} \approx \nu_{ii} \sum_{k=1}^{n} \mu_k^0 + \mu_i^0 \sum_{k=1}^{n} \nu_{kk} - \mu_i^0 \sum_{k=1}^{n} \mu_k \sum_{j=1}^{n} \nu_{jj} .$$

Substituting these approximations in (3.39) and rearranging, we obtain

$$w_i^* \,\mathrm{D}\, q_i - \mu_i^0 \,\mathrm{D}\, q = \nu_{ii} (\mathrm{D}\, p_i + \frac{1}{\phi^0} \mathrm{D}\, q - \sum_{k=1}^{n} \mu_k^0 \,\mathrm{D}\, p_k)$$

$$- \mu_i^0 \sum_{j=1}^{n} \nu_{jj} (\mathrm{D}\, p_j + \frac{1}{\phi^0} \mathrm{D}\, q - \sum_{k=1}^{n} \mu_k^0 \,\mathrm{D}\, p_k) + \upsilon_{it} \qquad (i = 1, 2, ..., n) . \tag{3.40}$$

The terms in brackets are now observable quantities yet further simplification of notation is possible. It will be recalled that

$$\mathrm{d}\lambda = \lambda_y \,\mathrm{d}y - (\lambda \mathbf{q}_y + \lambda_y \mathbf{q})' \,\mathrm{d}\mathbf{p}$$

$$\therefore \qquad \frac{\mathrm{d}\lambda}{y} = \frac{y\lambda_y}{y} \frac{\mathrm{d}y}{y} - (\mathbf{q}_y + \frac{\lambda_y}{\lambda} \mathbf{q})' \hat{\mathbf{p}} \hat{\mathbf{p}}^{-1} \,\mathrm{d}\mathbf{p}$$

$$\therefore \qquad \mathrm{d} \log \lambda = \frac{1}{\phi} [\mathrm{d} \log y - \mathbf{w}' \,\mathrm{d} \log \mathbf{p}] - \mathbf{q}_y' \hat{\mathbf{p}} \,\mathrm{d} \log \mathbf{p} .$$

Thus we can consider

$$\mathbf{D}\lambda^0 = \frac{1}{\phi^0} \mathrm{D}\, q - \sum_{k=1}^{n} \mu_k^0 \,\mathrm{D}\, p_k \ .$$

Furthermore, since

$$u_i = \lambda p_i$$

$$\log u_i = \log \lambda + \log p_i$$

$$\mathrm{d} \log u_i = \mathrm{d} \log \lambda + \mathrm{d} \log p_i$$

$$\therefore \qquad \mathrm{D}\, u_i^0 = \mathrm{D}\, p_i + \mathrm{D}\, \lambda^0 \ .$$

Hence (3.40) becomes

$$w_i^* \,\mathrm{D}\, q_i - \mu_i^0 \,\mathrm{D}\, q = \nu_{ii} \,\mathrm{D}\, u_i^0 - \mu_i^0 \sum_{k=1}^{n} \nu_{kk} \,\mathrm{D}\, u_k^0 + v_i \qquad (i = 1, 2, ..., n)\ . \ (3.41)$$

Since each equation involves all ν_{ii} the estimation should be performed simultaneously to obtain a unique set of coefficients. To perform the estimation Barten defines the following vectors,

$$\mathbf{y}_t = \begin{bmatrix} w_{1t}^* \,\mathrm{D}\, q_{1t} - \mu_1^0 \,\mathrm{D}\, q_t \\ w_{2t}^* \,\mathrm{D}\, q_{2t} - \mu_2^0 \,\mathrm{D}\, q_t \\ \vdots \\ w_{nt}^* \,\mathrm{D}\, q_{nt} - \mu_n^0 \,\mathrm{D}\, q_t \end{bmatrix} \qquad \mathbf{z}_t = \begin{bmatrix} \mathrm{D}\, u_{1t}^0 \\ \mathrm{D}\, u_{2t}^0 \\ \vdots \\ \mathrm{D}\, u_{nt}^0 \end{bmatrix}$$

$$\boldsymbol{\mu}_0 = \begin{bmatrix} \mu_1^0 \\ \mu_2^0 \\ \vdots \\ \mu_n^0 \end{bmatrix} \qquad \boldsymbol{\nu} = \begin{bmatrix} \nu_{11} \\ \nu_{22} \\ \vdots \\ \nu_{nn} \end{bmatrix}$$

Then (3.41) becomes

$$\begin{aligned} \mathbf{y}_t &= \hat{\mathbf{z}}_t \boldsymbol{\nu} - \boldsymbol{\mu}_0 \mathbf{z}_t' \boldsymbol{\nu} + \mathbf{v}_t \\ &= (\mathbf{I} - \boldsymbol{\mu}_0 \boldsymbol{\iota}') \hat{\mathbf{z}}_t \boldsymbol{\nu} + \mathbf{v}_t \\ &= \mathbf{X}_t \boldsymbol{\nu} + \mathbf{v}_t \end{aligned}$$

where $\mathbf{X}_t = (\mathbf{I} - \boldsymbol{\mu}_0 \boldsymbol{\iota}') \hat{\mathbf{z}}_t = \hat{\mathbf{z}}_t - \boldsymbol{\mu}_0 \mathbf{z}_t'$. Let

$$\mathbf{y} = \begin{bmatrix} \mathbf{y}_1 \\ \mathbf{y}_2 \\ \vdots \\ \mathbf{y}_T \end{bmatrix} \qquad \mathbf{X} = \begin{bmatrix} \mathbf{X}_1 \\ \mathbf{X}_2 \\ \vdots \\ \mathbf{X}_T \end{bmatrix} \qquad \mathbf{v} = \begin{bmatrix} \mathbf{v}_1 \\ \mathbf{v}_2 \\ \vdots \\ \mathbf{v}_T \end{bmatrix}$$

Hence,

$$\mathbf{y} = \mathbf{X} \boldsymbol{\nu} + \mathbf{v}$$

Barten assumes that $\mathbf{X}$ has rank n and that ϕ^0 and μ_i^0 are selected independently of the disturbance terms, which implies that $\mathbf{X}$ is independent of $\mathbf{v}$. ($\mathrm{D}\,p_{it}$ and $\mathrm{D}\,q_{it}$ have already been assumed to be independent of v_{it}.)

From the earlier discussion of the stochastic term

$$E(\mathbf{v}) = \mathbf{0}$$

$$E(\mathbf{v}\mathbf{v}') = \Sigma$$

$$\text{where} \quad = \begin{bmatrix} \boldsymbol{\Omega} & 0 & \dots & 0 \\ 0 & \boldsymbol{\Omega} & \dots & 0 \\ \vdots & \vdots & & \vdots \\ 0 & 0 & \dots & \boldsymbol{\Omega} \end{bmatrix}$$

and from (3.36) it can be seen that

$$\boldsymbol{\Omega} = \sigma^2 (\hat{\boldsymbol{\mu}} - \boldsymbol{\mu}\boldsymbol{\mu}') .$$

The estimator that Barten uses to estimate $\mathbf{v}$ is

$$\mathbf{b} = (\mathbf{X}'\mathbf{H}\mathbf{X})^{-1}\mathbf{X}'\mathbf{H}\mathbf{y} \tag{3.42}$$

$$\text{where } \mathbf{H} = \begin{bmatrix} \hat{\boldsymbol{\mu}}_0^{-1} & 0 & \dots & 0 \\ 0 & \hat{\boldsymbol{\mu}}_0^{-1} & \dots & 0 \\ \vdots & \vdots & & \vdots \\ 0 & 0 & \dots & \hat{\boldsymbol{\mu}}_0^{-1} \end{bmatrix}$$

Barten shows that if $\boldsymbol{\Omega} = \sigma^2(\hat{\boldsymbol{\mu}} - \boldsymbol{\mu}\boldsymbol{\mu}')$ and $\boldsymbol{\mu}_0 = \boldsymbol{\mu}$, (3.42) are best linear unbiased estimates. Although we do not know $\boldsymbol{\mu}$, hopefully it will be fairly close to $\boldsymbol{\mu}_0$ and thus $\mathbf{b}$ will be almost best linear unbiased estimates. Barten also derives an estimated variance–covariance matrix of disturbances but we will omit this. The empirical data that Barten uses are Dutch data for four composite goods. Annual time series from 1922 to 1963 are available but in fact only 29 sets of observations are used in the estimation, the war years and 1922, 1949, 1962 and 1963 being excluded. The numerical results and the initial values they are based on appear in table 3.15, the corresponding elasticities for four particular years appear in table 3.16. Although Barten in this article is dealing with very aggregative goods the statistical significance of the coefficients and the absence of any wrong signs is quite satisfying.

Because four years were omitted from the sample during estimation it is possible to use these to see how the model performs outside of the sample. Barten maintains that 1922 and 1949 were abnormal years (rationing was abolished in 1948–1949) so that only for 1962 and 1963 would he expect reasonable results. The errors for all four years and the standard deviations of sample residuals are given in table 3.17. These forecasts are encouraging but Barten stresses that in order for his system to be valuable for forecasting further work on the explanation of the 'random' fluctuations in preferences is necessary.

In this study we see how stochastic elements are incorporated into the consumers decision model and how this leads to restrictions on the variance–covariance matrix of the disturbances. One further aspect is the use of values from other studies in the estimation techniques. These are called extraneous

Table 3.15
Parameter estimates of Rotterdam school demand functions for four commodities.

	ν_{ii}	μ_i	$\mu_i^{0\,\dagger}$
Food	−0.0660 (0.0243)	0.2061 (0.0488)	0.21
Pleasure goods	−0.0307 (0.0080)	0.0959 (0.0179)	0.08
Durables	−0.1619 (0.0342)	0.5058 (0.0680)	0.36
Remainder	−0.0615 (0.0382)	0.1922 (0.0752)	0.35
ϕ	−0.3201 (0.0909)	ϕ^0	−0.5

† These values are taken from Houthakker (1965).

Table 3.16
Elasticities for four years derived from Rotterdam school demand functions.

	1928	1938	1951	1961
		Income elasticities estimates		
Food	0.66	0.70	0.71	0.77
Pleasure goods	1.06	1.11	0.94	0.95
Durables	2.14	2.46	1.83	1.87
Remainder	0.54	0.46	0.58	0.53
		Own price elasticities		
Food	−0.37	−0.38	−0.39	−0.40
Pleasure goods	−0.40	−0.42	−0.37	−0.37
Durables	−0.84	−0.89	−0.80	−0.80
Remainder	−0.33	−0.31	−0.34	−0.33

estimators and their use with time series is a form of mixed estimation. In this particular study the initial estimates which are necessary to begin the estimation process are of a non-stochastic nature, i.e., they are treated as fixed numbers. Similarly, the values taken from budget studies in order to perform the aggregation of the price series are also considered fixed. There are techniques available (see Theil and Goldberger, 1960) which use stochastic extraneous

Table 3.17
Residuals for four non-sample years †.

Years	F	P	D	R
1922	117	−55	35	− 98
1949	90	− 6	138	−222
1962	4	− 2	−31	28
1963	−16	− 2	17	1
Standard deviations estimation period	57	20	58	50

† All entries are to be multiplied by 10^{-4}.

estimates, and in Section 3.5.2 we shall return to another Barten study where he uses such a technique. Before doing this it will be necessary to consider demand studies using cross section data.

3.4. Cross section studies

We have already considered the use of cross section data in analysing the savings decision and in Houthakker's article where the 'between' country regressions were based on international cross section data. In this section we shall be concerned with the use of budget studies or family expenditure surveys, to explore the allocation decision. The reasons for wanting to use this data stems from the apparent richness of the statistical information. The sample size is usually large and often many factors such as social class are identified. With reference to demand functions which aim to measure the effects of price and income changes on quantities bought, we have seen that the estimates of price effects have not been too successful. This, it has been claimed, stems from the correlation between income and prices which usually occurs in time series data. With cross-section data prices are usually considered fixed and thus it may be that the income effect can be measured best by using this kind of data.

Expenditure surveys often enable us to do much more than just measure income effects, because observations on the so-called 'nuisance' factors can provide estimates which allow us to assess the effects on demand of demographic changes. Even more interestingly, expenditure surveys can provide the data to measure the economies of scale in consumption, and derive equivalent adult scales. Most of these things are done in Prais and Houthakker (1955) where two British surveys are analysed. Similar work has been performed in the U.S. but we shall concentrate on this study.

3.4.1. Prais and Houthakker (1955)

This study begins with a consideration of the difficulties of using cross-section data to quantify the concepts of theoretical demand analysis. The basic assumption is that "... by observing consumers in different circumstances at the same time, information may be obtained which is relevant in forecasting the behaviour of any particular consumer when his circumstances change through time". This means that budget studies may not be useful if dynamic factors or consumer interdependence are present. Dynamic factors stem from habit formation, durability or decisions being based on expectations. This last factor is probably much more important in the savings decision than in the allocation decision but habit and durability do limit the usefulness of budget studies and we shall return to these topics later. Even assuming no difficulties arise from these quarters there are other problems that Prais and Houthakker indicate.

Because their data are presented in the form of average expenditure for groups of households it is necessary to consider the aggregation problem. If v_{ir} and v_{0r} represent the expenditure of consumer r on good i and all goods, respectively, and V_i and V_0 the corresponding total expenditures, i.e.,

$$\sum_r v_{ir} = V_i$$

- all consumers - good i

$$\sum_r v_{0r} = V_0$$

- all consumers - all goods

then the aggregate elasticity is

$$\frac{V_0}{V_i} \cdot \frac{\partial V_i}{\partial V_0} = \frac{1}{V_i} \sum_r \left\{ v_{ir} \left(\frac{v_{0r}}{v_{ir}} \frac{\partial v_{ir}}{\partial v_{0r}} \right) \left(\frac{V_0}{V_{0r}} \frac{\partial v_{0r}}{\partial V_0} \right) \right\} .$$

If all incomes change in the same proportion then

$$\frac{V_0}{v_{0r}} \frac{\partial v_{0r}}{\partial V_0} = 1$$

and

$$\frac{V_0}{V_i}\frac{\partial V_i}{\partial V_0} = \frac{1}{V_i}\sum_r v_{ir}\left(\frac{v_{0r}}{v_{ir}}\frac{\partial v_{ir}}{\partial v_{0r}}\right) .$$

Thus, the group elasticity is a weighted average of the individual elasticities, unless income redistribution occurs.

Aggregation over commodities is a more troublesome problem. In the pure theory of the consumer there are n 'goods'. The statistical definition of a 'good' may include a number of qualities or varieties of the good which in theory should be separate goods. Furthermore new goods are introduced to the consumer whereas the theory assumes the number of goods are fixed. When a new good is introduced expenditure on substitute goods is discouraged. Since substitutes must predominate in a consumer's budget and since more new goods are introduced as a consumer becomes wealthier we should expect the typical Engel curve (i.e., the relation between expenditure on good i and income) to approach an asymptote. This suggests a characteristic that the form of the function used should possess, but before reporting the considerations that lead to their particular form let us consider the form of the data.

Two budget surveys are used. Both were carried out between 1937 and 1939. The working class survey was based on a sample taken from the register of persons insured against unemployment which covered all manual workers and non-manual workers earning less than or equal to £250 per year., though some allowance was made for occupations which historically were not covered by this insurance scheme. The middle class survey was drawn from the lists of three professional bodies: civil servants, local government officials and teachers. It was estimated that the working households could be taken as representative of 74% of the total number of households in the country and the middle class one 8%. The information from each household related to a week's expenditure in each quarter of the year. A special survey covering the whole year was carried out for clothing expenditure because of the infrequency of purchase. Households recorded their expenditure on the different items of consumption and hence their total expenditure. For the middle class group, income figures are available but Prais and Houthakker prefer to use total expenditure rather than income. For the working class, data on quantities were also provided which enables the authors to analyse quality variations. Prais and Houthakker present a detailed discussion of the probable biases in the data they use, but we do not attempt to reproduce their discussion, preferring to pass on to their econometric work.

Their first aim is to derive the expenditure elasticities for over a 100 categories of expenditure. We shall only concern ourselves here with six food aggregates. The first step in the analysis is to decide on a functional form. Two a priori considerations are taken into account namely (1) in general there will be a level of income below which the consumer purchases none of the good and (2) there will usually be a saturation level unless the consumer switches to a better quality in which case the expenditure will continue to rise but more slowly. Thus the function should have the shape illustrated in fig. 3.1.

In fact Prais and Houthakker consider five functions.

$$v_i = \alpha - \beta/v_0 \tag{3.43}$$

$$v_i = \alpha + \beta v_0 \tag{3.44}$$

$$\log v_i = \alpha + \beta \log v_0 \tag{3.45}$$

$$\log v_i = \alpha - \beta/v_0 \tag{3.46}$$

$$v_i = \alpha + \beta \log v_0 \,. \tag{3.47}$$

The first function is included to allow for the possibility of a saturation point, the next two have been used by previous researchers, the fourth passes

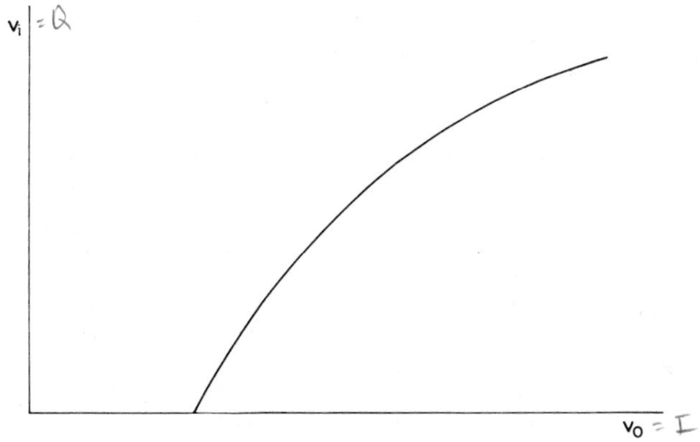

Fig. 3.1. Typical shape of an Engel curve.

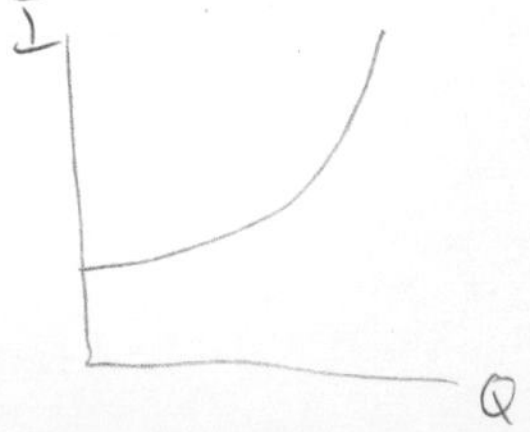

through the origin and has an asymptote, and the last is similar to the hyperbolic but with no assymptotic value and has the added advantage of always giving a positive income value. Although the authors tend to favour (3.45) and (3.47) they do not wish to exclude the others on a priori grounds but rather to allow the data to discriminate. The forms are fitted not to the actual expenditures but to expenditure per head. This assumes no economies of scale in consumption which is a rather crude assumption and which is investigated later. Furthermore, using expenditure per head does not distinguish between households of say 4 adults from those of 2 adults and 2 children. This aspect will also be investigated later.

All five forms are fitted for the six categories of food, (a) farinaceous foods, (b) dairy products, (c) vegetables, (d) fruit, (e) fish, and (f) meat. The elasticities at mean values are given in table 3.18. Some of these estimates, especially fruit, vary considerably and at non mean values the differences are likely to be greater, thus the choice of functional form is important. The criteria of choice that the authors use are the closeness and linearity of fit. The correlation coefficient is used for the first criterion and a non-parametric test based on the number of runs of the same sign in the residuals for the linearity criterion. This latter test is similar to the Durbin–Watson test for serial correlation †.

The results are set out in table 3.19. Perfect linearity of fit is indicated by the value of λ being zero, and significant non linearity of fit is indicated by a value of λ greater than 3. Both the hyperbolic, (3.43), and the linear, (3.44), forms have poorer fits than the other three although the differences are not very big. Using the criterion of linearity the semi-log (3.47) version and the double-log (3.45) come out best, especially if fruit (poor in all cases) is ig-

† see Griliches et al. (1962) for more recent discussion of a similar test.

Table 3.18

Cross-section income elasticities based on alternative regression forms U.K. (Calculated at means of the data.)

Form	(3.43)	(3.44)	(3.45)	(3.46)	(3.47)
Farinaceous	0.25	0.30	0.36	0.27	0.35
Dairy	0.35	0.41	0.53	0.41	0.48
Vegetables	0.40	0.50	0.62	0.46	0.58
Fruit	0.66	0.98	1.20	0.90	1.03
Fish	0.51	0.66	0.84	0.62	0.76
Meat	0.44	0.51	0.69	0.53	0.62

Table 3.19
Closeness and linearity of fit for alternative forms.

	(3.43)		(3.44)		(3.45)		(3.46)		(3.47)	
	r	λ	r	λ	r	λ	r	λ	r	λ
Farinaceous	−0.80	3.0	0.74	2.0	0.82	0.3	−0.82	2.4	0.82	0.5
Dairy	−0.90	2.3	0.83	3.2	0.94	2.9	−0.98	0.6	0.92	0.1
Vegetable	−0.86	1.5	0.84	1.2	0.92	0.2	−0.93	1.5	0.91	−0.4
Fruit	−0.83	5.7	0.96	2.5	0.96	2.7	−0.98	1.9	0.94	3.0
Fish	−0.84	2.9	0.84	0.3	0.94	−0.8	−0.94	2.4	0.92	2.0
Meat	−0.90	3.0	0.81	3.2	0.92	2.9	−0.96	1.4	0.92	0.9

nored. Prais and Houthakker reject all but these two forms and make use of the existence of two samples to discriminate between them. The double-log form implies a constant elasticity regardless of the level of income. Thus if the elasticities of working and middle class families are significantly different we have reason to reject the double-log form. In fact the authors perform something similar to a Chow (1960) test to see if the same form fits both samples. On the basis of this they decide to adopt the semi-log form for their food analysis.

For non-food items the results are not so satisfactory. In this case the authors only consider the semi- and double-log forms for the separate and combined samples. The correlation coefficients of the double-log function are significantly higher than those of the semi-log but it is obvious that for non-food items more complicated formulations are necessary.

Although the elasticities presented are based on a fine classification is it still likely that for each good there will be a number of different qualities available. Thus, as income increases consumers may switch to the higher quaiity. Because the working class survey gives information on both quantity and expenditure it is possible to derive the average price. If we are assuming that all consumers are faced with the same price for an equivalent good, i.e., no regional differences or monopoly discrimination, then a higher average price should reflect a higher quality. Prais and Houthakker regress the average price, i.e., the quality variable, on total expenditure to estimate quality elasticities. Again allowance has to be made for the number of people in the household. After consideration of the scatter diagrams the authors decide on the following function,

$$p_j = \alpha + \beta \log \frac{v_{0j}}{N_j}$$

where N_j is the number in the jth household. As a check as to whether this form is useful it is fitted for total food expenditure. The price (quality) variable is

$$P_j = \frac{\sum_{i=1}^{n} q_{0i} p_{ij}}{\sum_{i=1}^{n} q_{0i} p_{0i}}$$

where q_{0i} and p_{0i} are the mean quantity and price for all households of good i, and p_{ij} is the price that household j pays for good i.

The results of this regression are

$$P_j = 0.54 + \underset{(0.01)}{0.26} \log \frac{v_{0j}}{N_j} \qquad R^2 = 0.85$$

and the quality elasticity, evaluated at mean values, is 0.11. The scatter diagram suggests that the linearity of the fit is reasonable. One further test stems from the availability of data for different size households. The quality function can be rewritten

$$p_j = \alpha - \beta \log N_j + \beta \log v_{0j} \,.$$

Thus, for each size of household a regression can be obtained and these should have the same slope but varying intercepts. This can be tested by covariance analysis. Prais and Houthakker illustrate this test using expenditures on tea (not reported here).

By dividing the expenditure equation by the quality equation it is possible to derive a quantity equation. This is done for total food expenditure for working class families and presented diagramatically in fig. 3.2. This illustrates the shift to quality as income rises. A finer break down of food expenditure is possible and quality elasticities for 32 commodities are reported. However, it should be noted that for computational convenience these are calculated using the double-log form. The results are very much in keeping with what

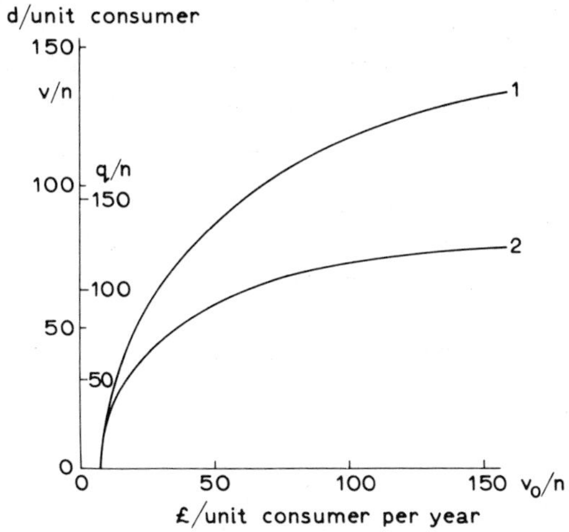

Fig. 3.2. Total expenditure and derived quantity Engel curves for total food. Curve 1: $v/N = 101 \log (v_0/N) - 0.82$; curve 2: $q/N = 328(\log (v_0/N) - 0.82)/(\log (v_0/N) + 1.53)$.

one would expect namely that meat, fish, cake mixtures and biscuits have higher quality elasticities than other commodities but that none of the food elasticities are particularly high.

So far the only differences between households that have been taken account of are differences in size. Composition of households also varies, and from the point of view of demand the important elements are the number, sex and age of the individuals of the household. The surveys do report these characteristics and Prais and Houthakker use this information to produce unit consumer scales. These scales indicate the relative importance in the household's consumption of a good that each category of person has. For instance, they found that for farinaceous products, if the adult male's consumption is given the value of 1, then the adult female's is 0.85 and the male 14–17 years value is 1.01, indicating that for foods like bread the younger male eats more than his father. It is also possible to derive a scale of total expenditure which is called an 'income scale', as opposed to the 'specific scales' for particular goods. These unit scales reflect the cost to the household in total expenditure or specific item expenditures of each category of persons. Such knowledge is important in such policy matters as the extent and structure of taxation allowances, family allowances and social security payments.

The method of calculation for these scales involves assuming that we know the form of the Engel curve and the income scale. The latter is not restrictive because once the specific scales are known it is possible to derive the corresponding income scale, hence an iterative procedure is possible. In fact Prais and Houthakker do not bother with this refinement. They do, however, work out the specific scales for both the semi-log and the double-log form but the results are quite similar. Here we shall consider only the semilog form.

Let

N_t be the number of people of type t;
k_{it} be the value of type t on ith specific scale;
k_{0t} be the value of type t on the income scale.

Thus the adjusted Engel curve for good i is,

$$\frac{v_i}{\sum_{t=1}^{T} N_t k_{it}} = \alpha_i + \beta_i \log \frac{v_0}{\sum_{t=1}^{T} N_t k_{0t}} .$$

Let

$$\frac{v_0}{\sum_{t=1}^{T} N_t k_{0t}} = m$$

then

$$\frac{v_i}{\alpha_i + \beta_i \log m} = N_1 k_{i1} + N_2 k_{i2} + \ldots + N_T k_{iT} .$$

i.e.

$$\frac{v_i}{(\gamma_i + \log m)} = \beta_i k_{i1} N_1 + \beta_i k_{i2} N_2 + \ldots + \beta_i k_{iT} N_T .$$

If we assume that we know the income scale we can calculate m. Since v_i and N_t are known, for a given value γ_i we can calculate regression values for $\beta_i k_{it}$ ($t = 1, 2, \ldots, T$) and the corresponding R^2. Searching over different values of γ_i we can find the set of $\beta_i k_{it}$ corresponding to the highest R^2 and these, when normalised to give the adult male value equal to unity, form the specific scale for this particular good. Prais and Houthakker distinguish eight categories of persons and assume that the income scale is unity for all types. Their results for the semi-log version appear in table 3.20.

Because these scales are derived from behaviour, the values do not necessarily relate the consumption to the actual individual. For instance, if the

Table 3.20
Specific scales for foodstuffs based on semi-log Engel curves.

	Farinaceous	Dairy	Vegetables	Fruit	Fish	Meat
Adult male	1	1	1	1	1	1
Adult female	0.85	0.97	0.91	1.22	0.91	0.70
Male 14–17	1.01	0.87	1.03	0.65	0.68	0.55
Female 14–17	0.73	0.71	0.72	0.68	0.59	0.48
10–13	0.89	0.75	0.87	0.66	0.84	0.54
5–9	0.65	0.58	0.78	0.65	0.41	0.35
1–4	0.55	0.63	0.75	0.59	0.43	0.30
<1	0.39	0.83	0.36	−0.36	0	0.09
R^2	0.93	0.95	0.87	0.77	0.70	0.93
Elasticity	0.27	0.40	0.48	0.68	0.53	0.47

addition of a new child causes the mother to buy some new aprons, these aprons will appear in the child's value not the mother's. However, such items are not going to be too numerous. The results, which are based on the working class survey, give the greatest weight to the adult males. The effect of taking account of the household composition on the estimates of the income elasticities can be seen by comparing the final column of table 3.18 with the last line of table 3.20.

One further question which is analysed in this study is the existence of economies of scale in consumption. One possible formulation for this, if we abstract from the household composition problem, is,

$$\frac{v_i}{N^{\theta_i}} = f_i\left(\frac{v_0}{N^{\theta_0}}\right) . \tag{3.48}$$

If there are no economies of scale in the consumption of good i then $\theta_i = 1$ and if no economies in any good then $\theta_0 = 1$. If the double-log form is used for f_i then,

$$\frac{v_i}{N} = A\left(\frac{v_0}{N}\right)^{\beta} N^{\gamma} \tag{3.49}$$

where $\gamma = \beta(1-\theta_0) - (1-\theta_i)$. Thus, if θ_0 is known we can derive θ_i. An estimate of θ_0 can be obtained from the quality equation for all food since it seems reasonable that quality variation should only be affected by total economies of scale. Thus

$$p = \alpha + \beta \log \frac{v_0}{N^{\theta_0}}$$

i.e.

$$p = \alpha + \beta \log \left(\frac{v_0}{N}\right) + \gamma \log N$$

where $\gamma = \beta(1 - \theta_0)$. The estimate of θ_0 which the authors obtain is 0.87 and this implies a value of 0.13 for the economies of scale (income effects). Given this value, an estimate for θ_i can be derived by fitting (3.49) or the equivalent semi-log form.

The results, which appear in table 3.21, with the exception of 'durables' and perhaps 'clothes' are more or less what one would expect. Fruit is low because many of the economies come in the cooking and preparing stage and fruit tends to be eaten raw. 'Rent' and 'fuel' are the two items one would expect to have the largest economies. The 'clothes' and 'durables' figures are suspect because of the general problem of durable items in a static model. In fact, the authors make no great claims for these estimates since no account has been taken of the differing composition between households. The effect of taking account of economies of scale on the elasticity estimates is similar to that of household composition, namely, a slight decline for the estimates of all commodities.

Table 3.21
Economies of scale.

Commodity	Elasticity	$1 - \theta_i$
† Farinaceous	0.25	0.22
† Dairy	0.43	0.16
† Vegetables	0.52	0.15
† Fruit	1.04	0.08
† Fish	0.70	0.17
† Meat	0.53	0.21
Rent	0.56	0.67
Fuel	0.52	0.50
Clothes	1.01	−0.01
Durables	1.98	−0.18

† Semi-log form used.

In later chapters the authors discuss differences in consumption stemming from differences in social class, occupation and location, concluding that these are complicated matters and that the mere use of dummy variables is not likely to be very satisfactory. The general conclusions from their work are that for food items a model using a semi log form which allows for household composition and economics of scale, is useful for analysing consumer budgets, but for non-food items this is not so.

3.5. **Mixed data studies**

Before the discussion of the cross-section studies we referred to the estimation of demand functions using two types of data. When the collinearity of the explanatory variable is strong we have difficulty in estimating the individual influence of each variable. This has been true in demand studies and because of this cross-section data have been used to estimate the income coefficient before estimating the price coefficients from time series data.

The simplest way of using the two types of data can be illustrated by a simple example. Consider the model

$$y = \alpha + \beta_1 x_1 + \beta_2 x_2 + u$$

i.e.

$$y - \beta_1 x_1 = \alpha + \beta_2 x_2 + u \, .$$

If in cross-section data x_2 is constant, by regressing y on x, b_1, the least squares estimate of β_1, can be obtained. Then, using the time series, $(y - b_1 x_1)$ regressed on x_2 will produce an estimate of β_2. This estimation approach disregards the fact that b_1 is a stochastic variable. More recently however, techniques of mixed estimation have been developed, which allow for the use of stochastic information. Barten (1964), using these more recent developments, introduces extraneous estimates of means and variances of coefficients into his estimation procedure. Unfortunately there are problems involved in the combined use of time series and cross section data. For simplicity we shall discuss these problems in terms of estimating price and income elasticities.

Cross-section data usually refers to expenditures rather than quantities. We have seen how Prais and Houthakker were able to adjust their income or rather total expenditure elasticities to take account of quality changes. In most budget studies this is impossible hence the measured elasticities from budget studies are conceptually different from those based on a time series approach. Similarly a conceptual difference occurs if the budget studies use total expenditure as opposed to the income concept often used with time series. Usually the coverage of the data differ too. Cross-section data very often relate only to certain sections of the population, for instance in Prais and Houthakker only the working class and certain professions are represented. Time series data usually cover the whole population. These factors help to explain why 'income' elasticities derived from cross-section data tend to be higher than those derived from time series. However, it may be that these differences stem from the fact that consumers take time to adjust their consumption after income changes and that the cross section estimates reflect the long run adjustment whereas the time series estimates reflect the short adjustment. It is easy to see this by artificially generating the data. Consider a slowly adjusting individual and move him one period further on and change his income in this new period (the short run). His consumption will change only a little. If we repeat this process we would generate the time series for an individual and the current consumption will only change a little relative to income. Now consider moving an individual up the income scale but where time is held constant. In this case we will not generate data similar to cross-section data because the individual will not adjust his social class or habits. In the cross section studies the average person in the income group will also have the average tastes associated with that level of income. Hence cross-section data reflect the process of moving a man up the income scale and changing his tastes accordingly. It follows that cross-section estimates will tend to reflect long run elasticities. Bearing in mind these problems let us explore the studies which, in different ways, combine information of different sorts to produce demand elasticities.

3.5.1. Stone (1954a)

This monumental work has two aims – the first, to produce time series of detailed items of consumption for the years 1920–1938, and the second, to estimate the price and income elasticities of the detailed commodities. The form of relation that Stone adopts is the double log form † with the relative prices of substitutes and complements introduced explicitly.

This form is used both for his estimation of the income elasticities and for the price elasticities. However, the cross-section form incorporates the use of an equivalent adult scale, borrowed from a Dutch study, and also a dummy variable introduced to take account of the differences between the working class and the professional class. Originally he included a term to take account

† See Section 3.3.2.b.

of economies of scale but because of multicollinearity decided to exclude it. The income elasticities are based on the same data that Prais and Houthakker use but predate their results. It will be recalled that these authors found that the semi-log form was more useful for food items.

The form for the time series estimation includes a linear trend but since, in an attempt to reduce the serial correlation, he uses a first difference transformation, the trend coefficient appears as a constant. The income and quantity variables are measured in per capita terms. The price terms include the price of the commodity to be explained plus, where possible, the prices of important substitutes and complements. All prices are deflated by a price index of all other prices. Before incorporating the income elasticities estimated from the budget data Stone reduces them all by 10%. This is to take account of the problem that total expenditure is used in the budget studies. This seemingly arbitrary adjustment does have some empirical justification. The middle class survey that Prais and Houthakker used did report incomes as well as total expenditures. Because of this they were able to compare the total expenditure elasticities with the income elasticities. Furthermore, for 1905 households including only one earner they obtained the following regression

$$\log v_0 = \underset{}{0.35} + \underset{(0.04)}{0.89} \log Y \qquad R^2 = 0.88$$

which supports Stone's adjustment factor.

Stone presents the different regressions that he experimented with and his belief as to the best equation for each commodity and certain combined commodities. He also presents measures of fit and serial correlation. There are over thirty individual food commodities but his food results can be summarised by a frequency table (see table 3.22). These results include all those equations which have a significant R^2. The values of the DW statistic suggest that on the whole using first differences reduces the serial correlation problem considerably. The values of the estimates seem reasonable. On the basis of numbers alone substitution is more important than complementarity, which is consistent with theory (see Hicks, 1946, pp. 42–52).

It will be recalled from Section 3.3.2.b that Stone's form involves the constraint that the price elasticities sum to zero. Stone tests this by performing the regressions without the constraint. In all but two cases the sum of the substitution elasticities is not significantly different from zero. One feature of Stone's results is the number of significant price coefficients, which seems to justify the use of extraneous estimators. It should be remembered, however, that in other studies, we have been concerned with more aggregated commo-

Table 3.22
Frequency table of elasticities for food commodities, U.K. 1920–1938.

Range	Income		Own price		Other specific prices	
−2 to −1½			2	(2)	1	(0)
−1½ to −1			5	(4)	4	(4)
−1 to −½	1	(1)	16	(11)	5	(4)
−½ to 0	4	(0)	10	(6)	7	(3)
0 to ½	10½	(7½)	3	(0)	15½	(7½)
½ to 1	12½	(12½)			13½	(10½)
1 to 1½	2	(2)			7	(7)
1½ to 2	2	(2)			5	(5)
2 to 2½					2	(2)
2½ to 3					1	(1)
3 to 3½					1	(1)
	32	(25)	36	(23)	62	(45)

Figures in brackets represent the number of estimates significantly different from zero.

dities and thus substitution is likely to be less strong. Indeed many of the other studies have used the assumption of additivity. Barten (1964) attempts a method of estimating demand functions where preferences are almost additive and where the investigator is prepared to specify a priori the approximate strength of the interdependence.

3.5.2. Barten (1964)

Barten's aim is to derive consumer demand functions for the Netherlands for a commodity breakdown which prevents full additivity being assumed. In addition to his concept of almost additive preferences the article is interesting from the point of view that he incorporates stochastic extraneous estimates. Furthermore, these estimates are taken from the works of Stone and Prais and Houthakker which relate the United Kingdom data whereas Barten's functions relate to the Netherlands.

The data are annual time series for fourteen (originally sixteen but two groups are excluded) groups of commodities for the periods 1921–1939 and 1948–1958. Per capita volume figures are derived from figures on the value of expenditures, price index numbers and population figures.

The form of Barten's equation can best be appreciated by recalling from Section 3.2 that,

$$\text{d} \log \mathbf{q} = \boldsymbol{\eta} \,\text{d} \log y + \mathbf{H} \,\text{d} \log \mathbf{p}$$

and

$$\mathbf{H}^{**} = \mathbf{H} + \boldsymbol{\eta}\mathbf{w}'(\mathbf{I} + \phi\hat{\boldsymbol{\eta}})$$

$$= \hat{\mathbf{q}}^{-1}\lambda\mathbf{U}^{-1}\hat{\mathbf{p}}$$

$$\therefore \quad \mathbf{H} = \mathbf{H}^{**} - \boldsymbol{\eta}\mathbf{w}' - \boldsymbol{\eta}\mathbf{w}'\phi\hat{\boldsymbol{\eta}}$$

hence

$$\text{d} \log \mathbf{q} = \boldsymbol{\eta} \,\text{d} \log y + (\mathbf{H}^{**} - \boldsymbol{\eta}\mathbf{w}' - \boldsymbol{\eta}\mathbf{w}'\phi\hat{\boldsymbol{\eta}}) \,\text{d} \log \mathbf{p}$$

i.e.

$$\text{d} \log q_i = \eta_i \,\text{d} \log y + \sum_{j=1}^{n} (\eta_{ij}^{**} - \phi\eta_i\eta_j w_j - \eta_i w_j) \,\text{d} \log p_j \qquad (i = 1, 2, ..., n)\,.$$

Barten's form is

$$\Delta \log q_i = \alpha_i + \sum_{j=1}^{n} (\eta_{ij}^{**} - \phi\eta_i\eta_j w_j - \eta_i w_j) \,\Delta \log p_j + \eta_i \,\Delta \log y + u_i\,. \tag{3.50}$$

He imposes the constraints of classical theory on the estimated coefficients of (3.50). His particular form of these constraints can be derived as follows, from Section 3.2.

$$\mathbf{w}'\boldsymbol{\eta} = 1 \tag{3.15g}$$

$$\mathbf{H}^{**\prime}\mathbf{w} = \phi\hat{\mathbf{w}}\boldsymbol{\eta} \tag{3.16g}$$

$$(\hat{\mathbf{w}}\mathbf{H}^{**})' = \hat{\mathbf{w}}\mathbf{H}^{**}\,. \tag{3.17g}$$

Premultiplying (3.16g) by $\hat{\mathbf{w}}^{-1}$ gives,

$$\hat{\mathbf{w}}^{-1}\mathbf{H}^{**\prime}\mathbf{w} = \hat{\mathbf{w}}^{-1}\mathbf{H}^{**\prime}\hat{\mathbf{w}}\boldsymbol{\iota} = \hat{\mathbf{w}}^{-1}(\hat{\mathbf{w}}\mathbf{H}^{**})'\boldsymbol{\iota} = \hat{\mathbf{w}}^{-1}\hat{\mathbf{w}}\mathbf{H}^{**}\boldsymbol{\iota} = \hat{\mathbf{w}}^{-1}\phi\hat{\mathbf{w}}\boldsymbol{\eta}$$

i.e.

$$\mathbf{H}^{**}\boldsymbol{\iota} = \phi\boldsymbol{\eta}$$

Thus Barten's constraints are

$$\sum_{i=1}^{n} w_i\eta_i = 1 \tag{3.51}$$

$$\sum_{j=1}^{n} \eta_{ij}^{**} = \phi\eta_i \qquad (i = 1, 2, ..., n) \tag{3.52}$$

$$w_i\eta_{ij}^{**} = w_j\eta_{ji}^{**} \qquad (i, j = 1, 2, ..., n)\ . \tag{3.53}$$

The concept of additivity is reflected in the diagonality of the matrix **U** and, as one would expect, the concept of almost additivity is also reflected in the shape of **U**. **U** can be written without lack generality in the following way

$$\mathbf{U} = -\begin{bmatrix} {}_1u^2 & \theta_{12}\ {}_1u_2u & \cdots & \theta_{1n}\ {}_1u_nu \\ \theta_{21}\ {}_2u_1u & {}_2u^2 & \cdots & \theta_{2n}\ {}_2u_nu \\ \vdots & \vdots & & \vdots \\ \theta_{n1}\ {}_nu_1u & \theta_{n2}\ {}_nu_2u & \cdots & {}_nu^2 \end{bmatrix}$$

where $-{}_iu^2 = \partial^2 u/\partial q_i^2$, i.e.,

$$\mathbf{U} = -\begin{bmatrix} {}_1u & 0 & \cdots & 0 \\ 0 & {}_2u & \cdots & 0 \\ \vdots & \vdots & & \vdots \\ 0 & 0 & \cdots & {}_nu \end{bmatrix} \begin{bmatrix} 1 & \theta_{12} & \cdots & \theta_{1n} \\ \theta_{21} & 1 & \cdots & \theta_{2n} \\ \vdots & \vdots & & \vdots \\ \theta_{n1} & \theta_{n2} & \cdots & 1 \end{bmatrix} \begin{bmatrix} {}_1u & 0 & \cdots & 0 \\ 0 & {}_2u & \cdots & 0 \\ \vdots & \vdots & & \vdots \\ 0 & 0 & \cdots & {}_nu \end{bmatrix}$$

$$= -\,\hat{\mathbf{u}}\,[\mathbf{I}+\boldsymbol{\theta}]\,\hat{\mathbf{u}}$$

where $\mathbf{u} = \begin{bmatrix} {}_1u \\ {}_2u \\ \vdots \\ {}_nu \end{bmatrix}$,

and $\boldsymbol{\theta} = \begin{bmatrix} 0 & \theta_{12} & \dots & \theta_{1n} \\ \theta_{21} & 0 & \dots & \theta_{2n} \\ \vdots & \vdots & & \vdots \\ \theta_{n1} & \theta_{n2} & \dots & 0 \end{bmatrix}$

and is symmetric (**U** is symmetric).

Assuming that the elements of $\boldsymbol{\theta}$ are sufficiently close to zero

$$\mathbf{U}^{-1} \approx -\,\hat{\mathbf{u}}^{-1}(\mathbf{I}-\boldsymbol{\theta})\hat{\mathbf{u}}^{-1} .$$

This is why preferences are called almost additive, i.e., θ_{ij} should be close to zero. We can now derive formulae for η_{ij}^{**} from η_{ii}^{**} and η_{jj}^{**}, since,

$$\mathbf{H}^{**} = \hat{\mathbf{q}}^{-1}\lambda\mathbf{U}^{-1}\hat{\mathbf{p}}$$

$$\approx \lambda \begin{bmatrix} \dfrac{-p_1}{{}_1u^2\, q_1} & \dfrac{p_2\ \theta_{12}}{{}_1u_2uq_1} & \dots & \dfrac{p_n\ \theta_{1n}}{{}_1u_nuq_1} \\ \dfrac{p_1\ \theta_{12}}{{}_1u_2uq_2} & \dfrac{-p_2}{{}_2u^2\, q_2} & \dots & \dfrac{p_n\ \theta_{2n}}{{}_2u_nuq_2} \\ \vdots & \vdots & & \vdots \\ \dfrac{p_1\ \theta_{1n}}{{}_1u_nuq_n} & \dfrac{p_2\ \theta_{2n}}{{}_2u_nuq_n} & \dots & \dfrac{-p_n}{{}_nu^2\, q_n} \end{bmatrix}$$

Hence

$$\eta_{ii}^{**} = \frac{-\lambda p_i}{{}_iu^2 q_i}$$

and

$$\eta_{ii}^{**}\eta_{jj}^{**} = \frac{\lambda^2 p_i p_j}{{}_iu^2 {}_ju^2 q_i q_j}$$

and

$$\eta_{ij}^{**} = \frac{\lambda p_j \theta_{ij}}{{}_iu_j u q_i}$$

$$\therefore \quad \eta_{ij}^{**} = \theta_{ij}\sqrt{\frac{w_j}{w_i}\eta_{ii}^{**}\eta_{jj}^{**}} \qquad j \neq i$$

$$\approx -\tfrac{1}{2}(\eta_{ii}^{**} + \eta_{jj}^{**})\theta_{ij}\sqrt{w_j/w_i}\,. \tag{3.54}$$

Thus if we have estimates of the η_{ii}^{**} and we are prepared to state the value of θ_{ij} a priori, we can derive values for η_{ij}^{**} and thus we know $\mathbf{H}^{**}$ †. Barten assumes that θ_{ij} is either 0.2 or 0.1 (the one exception is 'textile and clothing' and 'footwear' where $\theta_{ij} = -0.1$) and that they have standard errors of 0.1 and 0.15, respectively. For his prior estimates of η_{ii}^{**} he uses figures based partly on Stone's own price elasticities and partly on introspection. The standard errors of these prior estimates are taken to be 0.25 except where the value of the elasticity is greater than -0.5 in which case the standard error is taken to be a half of the estimate. From (3.54) formulae for the variance and covariances of η_{ij}^{**} in terms of the θ_{ij}, w_i, and η_{ii}^{**} are derived. The prior estimates of the income elasticities η_i are chosen partly from Prais and Houthakker and partly by introspection. Let us summarise the a priori information we have described so far. The pure theory provided a set of exact constraints on the coefficients, the assumption of almost additivity showed how all prior price estimates could be related to stochastic prior estimates of θ_{ij} and η_{ii}^{**} and finally stochastic prior estimates of the income elasticities were specified.

The specification of the stochastic term, to which we now turn, also introduces an unusual element. Barten assumes that

$$Eu_i(t) = 0 \qquad \text{for all } i \text{ and } t$$

† The budget shares are assumed by Barten to remain at the average sample value.

$$E[u_i(t)u_j(t')] = 0 \qquad \text{if } t \neq t'$$
$$= \sigma_{ij} \qquad \text{if } t = t' \leq 1939$$
$$= \tfrac{1}{2}\sigma_{ij} \qquad \text{if } t = t' \geq 1948\,. \tag{3.55}$$

This specification allows interequation correlation but not intertemporal correlation. Furthermore, because Barten feels that the post-war data are superior to the pre-war ones, the variance of the stochastic term of the pre-war years has been assumed to be twice that of the post-war. The practical significance of this assumption is that weighted regression is used where we would normally use unweighted regression.

Since the estimation technique which takes account of all this prior information is rather involved we will leave the interested reader to consult the article for the details and only report the results here. It produces two estimates, i.e., the sample and the posterior estimates, for each coefficient. The

Table 3.23
Income elasticities η_i.

	Prior	Sample	Posterior
Groceries	0.50 (0.25)	0.917 (0.226)	0.672 (0.155)
Dairy products	1.0 (0.30)	0.465 (0.150)	0.565 (0.126)
Vegetables and fruit	1.0 (0.30)	0.724 (0.243)	0.840 (0.172)
Meat and meat products	1.0 (0.30)	1.110 (0.252)	0.923 (0.190)
Fish	1.0 (0.30)	0.107 (0.695)	0.878 (0.407)
Confectionary	0.75 (0.25)	0.458 (0.217)	0.624 (0.150)
Tobacco products	0.50 (0.25)	0.720 (0.230)	0.620 (0.153)
Drinks	1.50 (0.35)	0.536 (0.297)	0.891 (0.192)
Bread	0.30 (0.15)	−0.081 (0.117)	0.122 (0.064)

Table 3.24
Direct price elasticities η_{ii}^{**} †.

	Prior	Sample	Posterior
Groceries	−0.500 (0.250)	−0.554 (0.148)	−0.519 (0.100)
Dairy	−0.490 (0.245)	−0.341 (0.115)	−0.378 (0.085)
Vegetable and fruit	−0.700 (0.250)	−0.318 (0.107)	−0.424 (0.086)
Meat and meat products	−0.550 (0.250)	−0.279 (0.140)	−0.421 (0.099)
Fish	−0.740 (0.250)	−0.540 (0.289)	−0.716 (0.170)
Confectionary	−0.660 (0.250)	−0.413 (0.182)	−0.487 (0.108)
Tobacco products	−0.410 (0.205)	−0.533 (0.172)	−0.400 (0.090)
Drinks	−0.700 (0.250)	−0.442 (0.202)	−0.586 (0.111)
Bread	−0.080 (0.040)	0.039 (0.055)	−0.053 (0.029)

† These are not the total price elasticities $\eta_{ij} = \eta_{ij}^{**} - \phi\eta_i\eta_j w_j - \eta_i w_j$ Barten estimates $\phi = -0.463$.

posterior estimates reflect the impact of the prior beliefs that have been incorporated. In tables (3.23), (3.24) and (3.25) we report direct price, income, and price interaction elasticities of the food items, and for each, we give the prior, sample, and posterior estimates and their standard errors.

All the results reflect the efficiency gain from using the prior information. The mean values of the estimates for the income elasticities are changed more than the price elasticities through the prior information influence. All food items are income inelastic if the posterior estimates are accepted. The posterior estimates of the own price elasticities (compensated) are significantly negative with the exception of bread. The interaction elasticities are insignificant with one exception, 'groceries'–'dairy', and leads one to the conclusion that additivity is a reasonable assumption even at this level of disaggregation.

Although we have not reported them, Barten produces estimates for five durable commodity groups. These results, rather surprisingly, seem to be as

Table 3.25
Interaction elasticities η_{ij}^{**} †.

	Prior	Sample	Posterior
Groceries– dairy produce	0.113 (0.094)	0.282 (0.118)	0.169 (0.070)
Groceries– vegetables and fruit	0.053 (0.055)	−0.031 (0.074)	0.022 (0.042)
Groceries– meat and meat products	0.061 (0.064)	−0.124 (0.113)	0.018 (0.054)
Dairy–meat	0.105 (0.086)	−0.152 (0.079)	−0.038 (0.056)
Dairy–fish	0.019 (0.020)	0.054 (0.038)	0.021 (0.016)
Meat–fish	0.040 (0.032)	−0.005 (0.033)	0.011 (0.018)
Confectionary– tobacco	0.057 (0.060)	0.119 (0.140)	0.076 (0.052)
Confectionary– drinks	0.133 (0.105)	0.078 (0.155)	0.123 (0.079)
Tobacco–drinks	0.048 (0.050)	0.094 (0.134)	0.048 (0.044)

† These results refer to η_{ij}^{**} not η_{ji}^{**} which we have not reported.

successful as the food equations. Surprisingly, because we have seen that Stone's linear expenditure system was less useful for explaining durables and drink and tobacco than food. Also in his earlier work using the constant elasticity model, the non-food items (which we have not reported) were similarly less successful than the food items. Indeed in most studies authors have been at pains to suggest a dynamic formulation is necessary for durables. Houthakker, as we have seen, developed a dynamic model in order to interprete his results. The differences between budget income elasticity estimates and time series estimates can be partly explained by appeal to a dynamic form for the demand relations. In fact Barten's form is dynamic, in as much as his constant terms reflect the existence of trends. In five cases, 'tobacco', 'drinks', 'textile and clothing', 'household articles and furniture', and 'fuel additivities', he allows for trend influences. Similar methods have been incorporated by others using the basic static form. There have, however, been more fundamental changes to the basic system and it is these to which we now turn our attention.

3.6. Dynamic studies

In recent times expenditure on durable goods has grown considerably and some governments have concentrated their attempts to control consumption on durable expenditure. The important aspect of a durable good is that although its consumption is more or less evenly spread over its life the impact on the production sector of the economy is concentrated on the actual moment of purchase. From the point of view of a government policy maker this means that it may be important to persuade consumers to delay or hasten their purchases from time to time. From the point of view of the individual consumer the static model collapses since the utility of the good extends beyond the purchase period. In a similar way, habit causes the classical theory to be less useful than we have suggested for even non-durable commodities. A dynamic theory convenient for econometric functions has yet to be developed but the problems that arise can be indicated by analysing how the static theory is deficient.

Dynamic elements need to be introduced into the utility function. As we have seen the utility of durable goods should be related to the quantities purchased in a previous period. However, perhaps the difficulties can be reduced by assuming that the utility function arises from the quantity held, i.e., a stock concept. This of course then leads to the problem of relating the level of purchases in any one period to the stocks held. We shall see that this approach is adopted in most econometric studies. Habit implies that the consumers utility function is influenced by previous purchases which will thus influence present purchases. We cannot assume that the income constraint will remain unchanged in a truly dynamic theory. A truly dynamic consumer will avail himself of the possibilities of borrowing. This leads back to a concept of permanent income. It will be recalled, however, that in our discussion of the savings decision durable items were excluded from the definition of consumption. Thus a combination of the theory of the savings decision and the allocation decision seems to be consistent and useful (if we exclude the influence of habit). However, this leaves the purchases of durable commodities unexplained. Since durables can be thought of as assets we need a theory of portfolio decisions for the consumer but this is as yet undeveloped and even if it were durables would present further difficutlies since in many cases facilities for borrowing are specifically tied to durable items.

A further complication that a truly dynamic theory might involve is a speculative effect. If a consumer feels that prices are likely to rise he may speed up his purchase of a commodity. Many observers believe this behaviour occurs whenever rumours of changes in purchase tax are strong. In econometric work involving annual data such influences are less likely to be important.

The empirical studies of dynamic demand reflect these difficulties by incorporation of ad hoc devices into the demand function. A few lines of approach have been suggested, aimed at incorporating dynamic elements directly into the utility function, for instance, Barten (1968) indicates how it may be possible to incorporate habit formation into his scheme. In a different context Tsujimura and Sato (1964) actually incorporate habit formation into their empirical study which is concerned with measuring consumer preference fields for Japan. If we keep to our original theme of explaining the breakdown of consumer expenditure including durable and habit goods, three approaches have been used. The first is to add trend terms to the demand equations derived from classical theory. These have been reported in our earlier section. The second involves introducing trends into the parameters of models derived from classical theory. The third is to develop a model of essentially market demand where quantities purchased depend on actual stocks existing. To illustrate the second approach we shall use Stone's dynamic form of the linear expenditure system, and Houthakker and Taylor's study of consumer demand in the U.S. to illustrate the third approach, although Stone himself has been associated with a very similar model (see Stone and Rowe, 1957).

Stone (1966)

The purpose of this study is to show how to allow for changes in the coefficients of the linear expenditure system. It will be recalled that the linear expenditure system is

$$\hat{\mathbf{p}}\mathbf{q} = \hat{\mathbf{p}}\boldsymbol{\gamma} + (y - \mathbf{p}'\boldsymbol{\gamma})\boldsymbol{\beta}\,.$$

Stone shows how the following modifications can be accommodated.

(i) $\boldsymbol{\beta}_t = \boldsymbol{\beta}^* + \boldsymbol{\beta}^{**}t$ $\qquad \boldsymbol{\gamma}_t = \boldsymbol{\gamma}^* + \boldsymbol{\gamma}^{**}t$

(ii) $\boldsymbol{\beta}_t = \boldsymbol{\beta}^* + \boldsymbol{\beta}^{**}t + \boldsymbol{\beta}^{***}t^2$ $\qquad \boldsymbol{\gamma}_t = \boldsymbol{\gamma}^* + \boldsymbol{\gamma}^{**}t + \boldsymbol{\gamma}^{**}t^2$

(iii) $\boldsymbol{\beta}_t = \boldsymbol{\beta}^* + \mathbf{i}'\mathbf{e}_t^*\boldsymbol{\beta}^{**}$ $\qquad \boldsymbol{\gamma}_t = \boldsymbol{\gamma}^* + \hat{\mathbf{e}}_t^*\boldsymbol{\gamma}^{**}$

where $\mathbf{e}_t^*$ represents a vector of moving averages ending in period t–1 of the components of demand.

In fact the results that are available only relate to the linear and quadratic trend models, i.e. (i) and (ii). The data used to estimate these models are annual time series for the U.K. 1900–1960 (excluding 1914–1919 and 1940–1947) of expenditure per head and the corresponding price index numbers. These are 30 independent parameters if the linear model is used, as opposed to 45 for the quadratic. However, there are 376 observations with which to determine the parameters. The results are given in tables 3.26 and 3.27. In these tables $t = 0$ for 1960 and the values of the c_i are in terms of pounds at 1938 prices. For instance, table 3.27 tells us that if the linear form is used, the committed food expenditure in 1938 prices rose £0.332 per annum until in 1960 it reached £33.73. Similarly from table 3.26 the proportion of uncommitted income spent on food fell by 0.39% per year to 8.05% in 1960. Approximately $\frac{2}{3}$ of committed expenditure went on food, clothing and household in 1960 and about half of uncommitted expenditure went on household and transport. These results seem reasonable.

The fits of the different functions are presented in the form of graphs which makes them difficult to judge. However, Stone maintains that there is very little to choose between the linear and the quadratic models on this account.

The values of the elasticities for 1938 and 1960 can be compared to those derived from budget studies. Only those for food and clothing are given and we reproduce them in table 3.28. On this basis the linear model looks superior

Table 3.26
Estimates of the b coefficients in the dynamic linear expenditure system.

	b^*		b^{**}		b^{***}	
	L	Q	L	Q	L	Q
Food	0.0805	0.0948	–0.00390	0.00039	–	0.000086
Clothing	0.1569	0.1813	0.00210	–0.00008	–	–0.000035
Household	0.2263	0.1724	0.00210	–0.00961	–	–0.000137
Communications	0.0023	–0.0018	–0.00040	0.00010	–	0.000002
Transport	0.2342	0.2588	0.00160	0.01080	–	0.000117
Drink and tobacco	0.0956	0.0618	–0.00190	–0.00161	–	–0.000038
Entertainment	–0.0143	–0.0018	–0.00080	0.00236	–	0.000035
Other	0.2186	0.2346	0.00120	–0.00236	–	–0.000029
Total	1.0001	1.0001	0.00000	–0.00001	–	0.000001

Table 3.27
Estimates of the c coefficients in the dynamic linear expenditure system. (£ in 1938 prices.)

	c^*		c^{**}		c^{***}	
	L	Q	L	Q	L	Q
Food	33.73	35.06	0.3320	0.2575	–	−0.000518
Clothing	9.26	12.25	0.0430	0.0557	–	−0.000544
Household	24.59	28.63	0.0540	−0.0383	–	−0.004702
Communications	1.13	1.15	0.0260	0.0358	–	0.000366
Transport	8.97	14.62	0.1650	0.3979	–	0.003135
Drink and tobacco	10.20	11.56	0.0580	0.1572	–	0.003829
Entertainment	5.05	4.86	0.0750	0.1035	–	0.000778
Other	9.99	14.15	0.0640	−0.0229	–	−0.002401
Total	102.92	122.28	0.9170	0.9464	–	−0.000057

Table 3.28
Income elasticities from the dynamic LES and budget studies.

	Linear	Quadratic	Budget
		Food	
1938	0.6	0.4	0.6
1960	0.3	0.3	0.3
		Clothing	
1938	1.1	1.6	1.1
1953	1.4	1.7	1.4

to the quadratic but the difficulties involved in interpreting budget elasticities should be recalled, see Section 3.5.

The quadratic model also produces the strange phenomenon of uncommitted expenditure always being negative. It will be recalled (Section 3.3.1.a) that the utility foundations of the linear expenditure system do not allow this. If the classical theory is considered to be an equilibrium theory only temporary aberrations can be allowed, these in fact occur with the linear model since negative uncommitted expenditure only occurs during the war and immediate post-war years.

In this study Stone does allow for the habits effect but not for the durability effect although he states this can be incorporated. Houthakker and Taylor's model does allow for both effects but only by discarding the classical theoretical base.

Houthakker and Taylor (1966)

This monograph attempts to forecast all items of U.S. private consumption in 1970, i.e., six years ahead of its completion. The work was the result of a request from a government department and was undertaken as a practical project rather than an academic exercise. The authors acknowledge a long process of experimentation and elimination, their criterion of satisfaction being a mixture of statistical tests, economic meaningfulness and the plausibility of the projections. Although for most items of expenditure they use a linear dynamic model, they do not restrict themselves to this and occasionally use a linear or log linear static form.

The data that they use are the U.S. Department of Commerce annual series of consumer expenditure 1929–1961 excluding 1942–1945. All relevant variables are expressed in 1950 dollars and where necessary these were made available by the Office of Business Economics. The analyses are performed on per capita variables. The availability of pre-war and post-war data is welcomed since the model allows for some changes in tastes. Where necessary a dummy variable is introduced in an attempt to take account of extra model changes.

The dynamic model that they develop takes account of both durable and habit goods. It will be easier to explain it in terms of a durable good and then indicate how the habit goods are accommodated. The theoretical model is developed in continuous time and then finite approximations are made to obtain an estimating equation. It is assumed that the quantity bought is determined by the quantity in existence and other factors which for the moment we shall consider to consist only of income (in fact total expenditure). Thus,

$$q(t) = \alpha + \beta s(t) + \gamma x(t) \tag{3.56}$$

where

$q(t)$ is the rate of demand at time t;
$x(t)$ is the rate of income at time t;
$s(t)$ is the stock of good at time t.

The rate of change of the stock depends on the rate of purchase and the wearing out of the stock, namely

$$\dot{s}(t) = q(t) - \delta s(t) \tag{3.57}$$

where δ is a constant depreciation rate; and the period represents the rate of change through time.

From (3.56)

$$s(t) = \frac{1}{\beta}[q(t) - \alpha - \gamma x(t)]$$

$$\therefore \quad \dot{s}(t) = q(t) - \frac{\delta}{\beta}[q(t) - \alpha - \gamma x(t)] \,. \tag{3.58}$$

Also from (3.56)

$$\dot{q}(t) = \beta \dot{s}(t) + \gamma \dot{x}(t) \,,$$

i.e.,

$$\dot{s}(t) = \frac{1}{\beta}[\dot{q}(t) - \gamma \dot{x}(t)] \tag{3.59}$$

$\therefore$ substituting (3.59) into (3.58) and rearranging we get

$$\dot{q}(t) = \alpha\delta + (\beta - \delta) q(t) + \delta\gamma x(t) + \gamma \dot{x}(t) \,. \tag{3.60}$$

We have thus eliminated the stock variable. In order to use this model for habit goods we can think of $s(t)$ as representing psychological influences which cause one to buy goods which one has grown accustomed to. Whereas for durable goods one would expect β to be negative, with habit goods it should be positive.

The model is not yet in estimable form and thus necessitates approximation. Houthakker and Taylor develop this in detail but what results is that first differences are used in place of rates of change and two period backward moving averages are used for actual rates, e.g.

$$\dot{q}(t) \approx q_t - q_{t-1} \,, \qquad q(t) \approx \tfrac{1}{2}(q_t + q_{t-1}) \,.$$

Using these approximations and rearranging, the following equation can be obtained,

$$q_t = \frac{\alpha\delta}{1-\frac{1}{2}(\beta-\delta)} + \frac{1+\frac{1}{2}(\beta-\delta)}{1-\frac{1}{2}(\beta-\delta)} q_{t-1} + \frac{\gamma(1+\frac{1}{2}\delta)}{1-\frac{1}{2}(\beta-\delta)} \Delta x_t + \frac{\gamma\delta}{1-\frac{1}{2}(\beta-\delta)} x_{t-1} \tag{3.61}$$

or

$$q_t = A_0 + A_1 q_{t-1} + A_2 \Delta x_t + A_3 x_{t-1} \tag{3.62}$$

where

$$\alpha = \frac{2A_0(A_2 - \frac{1}{2}A_3)}{A_3(A_1+1)};$$

$$\beta = \frac{2(A_1-1)}{A_1+1} + \frac{A_3}{A_2 - \frac{1}{2}A_3};$$

$$\gamma = \frac{2(A_2 - \frac{1}{2}A_3)}{A_1+1};$$

$$\delta = \frac{A_3}{A_2 - \frac{1}{2}A_3}.$$

This implies that from the estimates of the fitted equation the original parameters can be deduced.

If we wish to include prices and a stochastic term as well as income, i.e.,

$$q(t) = \alpha + \beta s(t) + \gamma x(t) + \eta p(t) + u(t)$$

the estimating equation becomes

$$q_t = A_0 + A_1 q_{t-1} + A_2 \Delta x_t + A_3 x_{t-1} + A_4 \Delta p_t + A_5 p_{t-1} + V_t \tag{3.63}$$

where

$$A_4 = \frac{\eta(1+\frac{1}{2}\delta)}{1-\frac{1}{2}(\beta-\delta)};$$

$$A_5 = \frac{\eta\delta}{1-\frac{1}{2}(\beta-\delta)};$$

$$V_t = \frac{(1+\frac{1}{2}\delta)u_t - (1-\frac{1}{2}\delta)u_{t-1}}{1-\frac{1}{2}(\beta-\delta)}.$$

It follows that

$$\delta = \frac{A_5}{A_4 - \frac{1}{2}A_5} .$$

This means that we have two estimates of δ, i.e., δ is overidentified. These two estimates of δ will be the same if

$$A_2 A_5 = A_3 A_4 \quad . \tag{3.64}$$

Thus it is necessary to estimate (3.63) subject to (3.64). The authors show how this can be achieved by an iterative procedure. In fact twenty-three out of seventy-two equations are estimated this way.

The introduction of a stochastic term into the model produces, as is well known, a serially correlated stochastic term in the estimating equation. Given the presence of lagged variables this is a considerable problem. After consideration of some Monte Carlo experiments they decide to use three pass least squares † in such cases.

The results tend to justify the use of the dynamic model for 72 of the 83 ‡ items are best explained by it. The authors also maintain that its use helps them to avoid to some extent the problem of serial correlation. This is based on an inspection of the DW statistic although when lagged values are present this statistic is biased towards 2. The fits of their equations are satisfactory, 55 have R^2 greater than 0.95 and 70 are greater than 0.90. The lagged variable and the income variable are statistically significant although many price coefficients are only just bordering on significance.

The most important variable in explaining the pattern of expenditure is total expenditure, in 80 out of 83 it is included. Prices are much less important appearing in only 45 cases, and then, in many cases are only just significant. This is consistent with the strong influence of habit, which can be ascertained from the fact that 50 out of 69 stock coefficients are positive. The inventory influence, i.e., negative stock coefficient, is much less important as there are only 18 such cases. In terms of percentages of total expenditure, 58.4% is subject to the habit influence and 28.2% to the inventory influence.

The availability of post sample data for the two years 1962 and 1963 enables the authors to assess somewhat the value of their results for predic-

† Taylor and Wilson (1964).

‡ In fact there are 84 items of expenditure but no equation was produced for "clothing issued to military personnel".

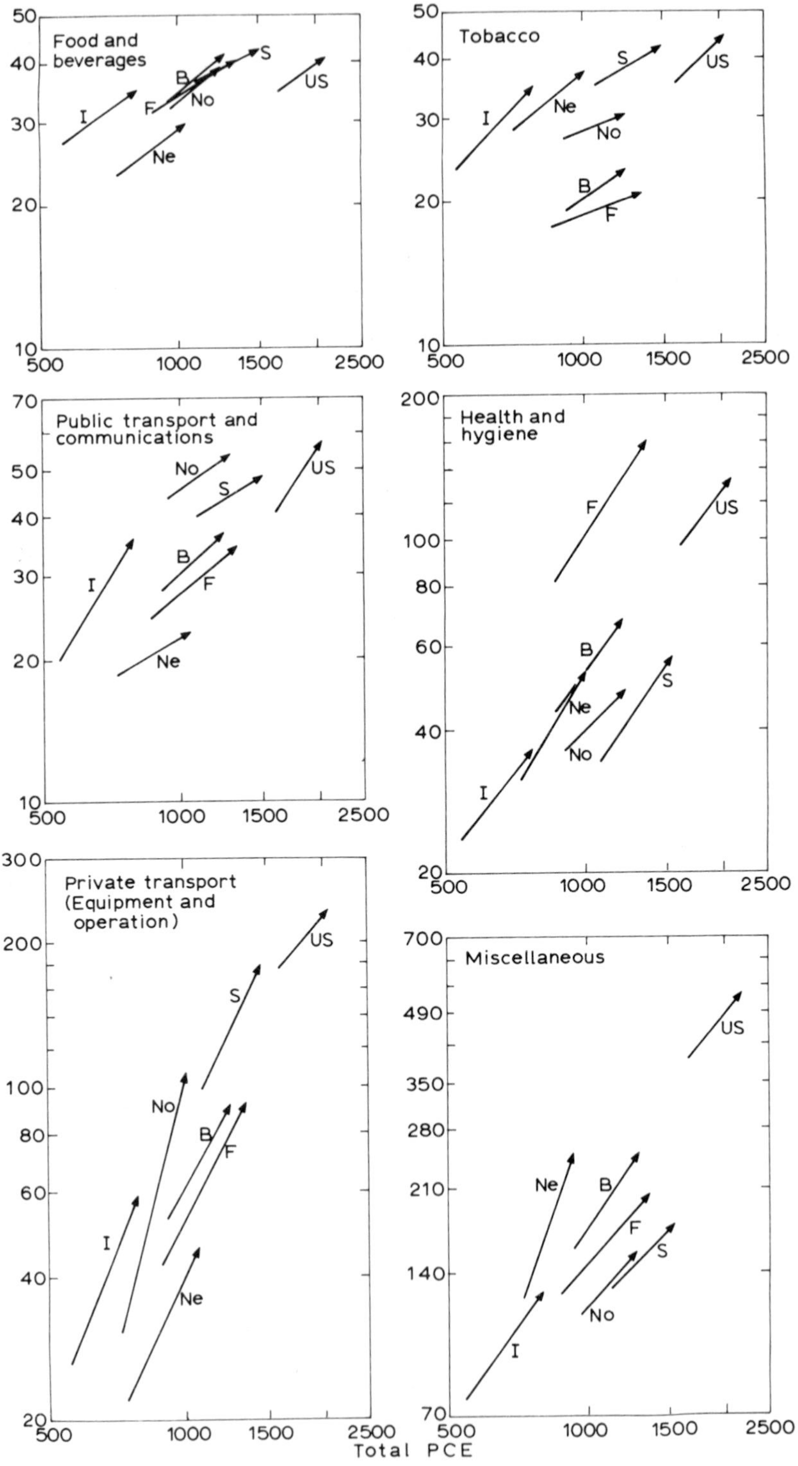

Food and beverages
I
B
F
No
S
Ne
US
Tobacco
S
US
I
Ne
No
B
F
Public transport and communications
No
S
US
B
I
F
Ne
Health and hygiene
F
US
B
Ne
S
No
I
Private transport (Equipment and operation)
US
S
No
B
F
I
Ne
Miscellaneous
US
Ne
B
F
S
No
I
Total PCE

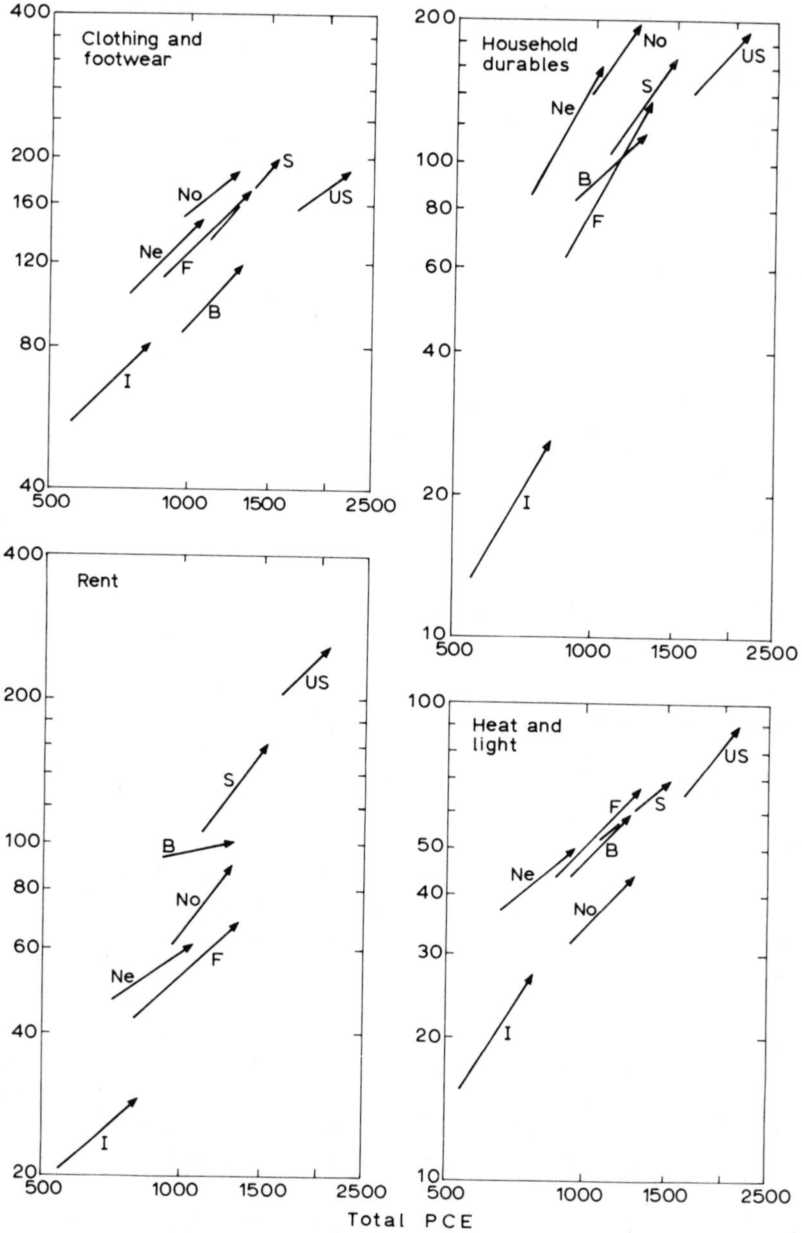

Fig. 3.3. Forecasts for 1970 for six European countries and the U.S.

tion. Unfortunately there was a definitional change in the data but the authors do not think it worthwhile to re-estimate the equations. The forecasts for 1962 are quite good. The weighted correlation (R^2) between the actual and predicted values is 0.86. Sixty-two of the forecasts are in the right direction and there is no systematic tendency to over- or under-estimate. The forecasts for 1963 are less successful although Houthakker and Taylor claim that one or two large errors have a disproportionate effect on the summary statistics. The R^2 for 1963 when actual values for q_{t-1} are used is 0.03, and 0.01 when forecast values for q_{t-1} are used.

The object of the study was to produce forecasts for 1970. These duly appear based on 4% and 5% growth rates of the explanatory variables, except relative prices, from their 1961 base. Two different sets of relative prices for 1970 are used, one is based on trends during the five years prior to 1961 and the other is based on the relative prices of 1961. Both projected actual quantities and budget share are produced. The general results are that actual values tend to be insensitive to relative prices in 1970 and that the budget shares are insensitive to the rate of growth of total expenditure.

3.7. Conclusion

From all the studies we have considered it is possible to pick out some general points that have emerged. The importance of prices in econometric demand studies seem to be less than economic theory would suggest. Indeed the extent to which prices are important seems to depend on the degree of which we restrict our models by classical theory. The degree of taste interdependence of goods seems to be low and only important if a fine definition of commodities is used. The practical implications of this apparent lack of sensitivity to prices is that considerable alterations to purchase and excise taxes are necessary if a government wishes to change the distribution of consumers' expenditure more than marginally for a given income. Indeed it could be that the changes would need to be so great that the estimated functions themselves would lose their value.

When we consider forecasting with estimated demand functions this price insensitivity makes the task easier since unforseen changes in relative prices are unlikely to affect the forecasts much. The success of econometric forecasts of demand, we have not considered. We did, in passing, look at a few forecasts but these appeared in published studies which would probably not have been published if the forecasts had not been reasonable. Houthakker and Taylor have forecast 1970 consumption for the U.S. Similar forecasts for

European countries are available in Sandee (1964). Perhaps when the time comes someone will analyse the forecasts in detail.

The forecasts for 1970 which reflect econometric studies in different countries highlight one element of demand analysis that we have touched on from time to time, namely international comparisons. Houthakker (1957) studied income elasticities derived from budget studies concluding that these were similar between countries. In Houthakker (1965) (see Section 3.3.2.b) he maintains this belief for income elasticities even though price elasticities seem to differ. Barten, by his willingness to use Stone's results, also seems to accept this view. Sandee constructs a set of diagrams which reflect the similarity. Later Houthakker and Taylor refined Sandee's idea by using purchasing power parities rather than offical exchange rates so we shall reproduce their diagrams which include the U.S. In fig. 3.3 the diagrams involve an arrow for each country; the point of the arrow represents the forecast values of total expenditure and expenditure on the particular good in 1960 prices for 1970, whereas the other end represents the actual values for 1960. The diagrams do present very similar pictures of consumption for the different countries.

3.8. **Summary**

Using the theory of consumer behaviour exact constraints for complete sets of demand functions were derived. Then we reviewed those studies which satisfied these constraints exactly. Later more pragmatic forms were considered including the constant elasticity form. At first only time series studies were reported but later cross section and mixed studies were reviewed. After a short discussion of the problems involved in a dynamic theory of the consumer we considered two studies that have faced some of the problems.

Looking back it seems that much has been ignored. We have concentrated on complete systems excluding the many studies of individual commodities. The demand for durables and the interesting aspects of financing durable expenditure have hardly been touched. The geographical coverage of the studies we have reported has been strongly biased to U.K., U.S. and Dutch studies though many studies are available for other countries. Methodologically we have tended to concentrate the reader's attention on the use of a priori and extraneous information in estimation and ignored many other aspects of estimation. This stems mainly from the nature of the topic but we could have for instance explained Houthakker and Taylor's use of principle components as an indicator of the extent of multicollinearity or their estimation method designed to cope with serial correlation and lagged variables. Aggregation has probably not received enough attention though we have reported its discussion in the studies we have considered. Two methodological points that have been totally ignored are the problems of identification and simultaneous bias. The reason for this is the belief that these problems are not likely to be particularly great in the type of study we have reported, which also seems to be the view of the authors of such studies. Stone (1954a) for example, realises his estimates may be biased and inconsistent but not strongly and that alternative estimation procedures involve consideration beyond the scope of his study. They are also beyond the scope of this chapter.

CHAPTER 4

INVESTMENT

4.1. Introduction

Macro economists have long been concerned with the determinants of aggregate investment mainly because of its apparently destabilising effect on national product but also because of its importance with regard to growth. Most of the econometric work has been geared to the first aspect, namely, the discovery of policy instruments that can help control investment in a stabilisation policy. Most particularly, much of the earlier work tended to discuss whether profits or the accelerator was the main determinant of investment. Another issue revolved around whether the rate of interest, and hence monetary policy, had any effect. Although early studies took an "either-or" view of the determinants, it is by no means clear that any of the variables mentioned so far should be excluded from an investment function. One could also make a case for the inclusion of undistributed profits, the stock of liquid assets, the stock exchange valuation of the company, the capital stock as well as the relative price of investment goods to wages. However, the poverty of the data limits the number of variables that can be included. Few aggregate time series are available for much more than about twenty years and the position was worse when most of the early studies were begun. Furthermore, many econometricians would doubt the validity of using any long time series that are available, because of the possibility of structural change (see Fisher, 1962, p. 5). In addition to this problem, the probability that the aggregate variables we have mentioned are collinear is very great. Thus any straightforward attempt to apply regression techniques to carelessly specified equations is likely to be unrewarding.

Considering these problems it is hardly surprising that more recent econometric research has involved more disaggregated studies using quarterly time series and cross section data. Another development has been the more careful specification of the model using as much a priori knowledge from economic theory as possible. Unfortunately, the economic theory of investment is in a rather confused state. When certainty and perfect money markets are assumed it is easy enough to derive the demand for capital from the assumption of maximisation of net worth. Unfortunately, the instantaneous adjustment of a firm's capital stock is not usually feasible and theory gives little guide to the speed of adjustment, although some attempt has been made to incorporate this aspect by allowing for adjustment costs (see Eisner and Strotz, 1963). If the investigator is not prepared to accept the certainty model as an approximation of the investment process, explicit and simple formulations are not available. One approach to uncertainty is to develop a model in which some variables, e.g. sales, are stochastic and which assumes that firms maximise expected net worth. Unfortunately, this approach is usually very unwieldy. The studies that have tried to incorporate uncertainty have done so by developing models at a lower level of abstraction incorporating institutional phenomena. The starting point of these models has been the corporate form of modern enterprise and their emphasis has been on the financing of investment. This is not surprising since it will be easier and cheaper to get finance if the financing public has sanguine expectations about a company's prospects, usually thought of as being represented by the Stock Market valuation of the company. However, the problem then revolves around exploring how these expectations are formed and about this there exists considerable disagreement. Thus the problem of uncertainty complicates not only the evaluation of projects but also the financial considerations, especially since once the model is set up in terms of the corporate firm, a number of methods of financing are available, especially debt, equity, and retentions. However, decisions on these will reflect on the market value and other factors. Thus, what emerges is a model of interdependent decisions, one of which is the level of investment. At the moment no generally accepted theoretical framework is available for investment decisions under uncertainty and usually the linkage of theoretical and empirical results is rather tenuous. In contrast, Jorgenson's (1965) certainty model presents a simple and seemingly successful framework for empirical studies. We shall use this model as a basis from which to explore a few ideas of those who would incorporate financial considerations.

4.2. Survey of the theory: certainty

Jorgenson assumes that a firm combines labour and capital to produce output, in situations where prices of factors and goods are given, in such a way as to maximise its net worth. Two constraints restrict the firm's behaviour: the Cobb–Douglas production function and an identity relating capital, investment and depreciation. For convenience he uses continuous time and as a consequence the model can be set out as

$$\max \mathrm{NW} = \max \int_0^\infty e^{-rt} [pX - sL - qI - u(t)$$

$$\times \{pX - sL - q[v(t)\delta + w(t)r - x(t)\frac{\dot{q}}{q}]K\}] \, dt \qquad (4.1)$$

subject to

$$X = AK^\alpha L^\beta \qquad (4.2)$$

$$\dot{K} = I - \delta K \qquad (4.3)$$

where,

δ	= depreciation rate;	K	= stock of capital;
$u(t)$	= tax rate of net income;	X	= output;
$v(t)$	= tax allowance on depreciation;	L	= labour;
$w(t)$	= tax allowance for debt finance;	I	= investment;
$x(t)$	= tax allowance for capital loss;	r	= cost of capital;
A	= constant;	p	= price of unit output;
$\dot{K}$	= rate of change of K;	q	= price of capital good;
$\dot{q}$	= rate of change of q;	s	= wage rate.

This is a calculus of variations problem and can be solved (see Allen, 1937; Jorgenson, 1965), to show that,

$$K = \alpha \frac{pX}{c} \qquad (4.4)$$

where

$$c = q\left[\left(\frac{1-uv}{1-u}\right)\delta + \left(\frac{1-uw}{1-u}\right)r - \left(\frac{1-ux}{1-u}\right)\frac{\dot{q}}{q}\right]. \qquad (4.5)$$

(The variable, c, can be interpreted as the cost of using a unit of capital.) This gives us the equilibrium capital stock in any period related to the equilibrium output level. The equilibrium capital stock may not be that actually in existence, therefore measures are set about to correct the situation, i.e., projects are started, but since these cannot be completed instantaneously, the actual and desired capital stocks are seldom equal. This implies some inconsistencies in the model since the constraints really relate to actual capital stock. In spite of this Jorgenson uses the relation between the equilibrium capital stock, equilibrium output and relative prices to explain the desired capital stock, i.e., he relates desired capital to actual output. The difference between desired and actual capital stock is then used to explain investment. For ease of estimation his model is translated into discrete time and the result is called a capital stock adjustment model. Similar models have been used by other authors.

One feature which has distinguished investment studies is the supply reponse. This determines the number of periods over which the desired actual discrepancy is made good. Most studies have ignored the details of the supply response and simply assumed a fixed speed of adjustment. Jorgenson does likewise but his adjustment process is one of the more sophisticated. He assumes that investment orders are placed to the extent of the discrepancy, unless the firm has previous orders not yet fulfilled. In this case it will order only that equipment necessary to bring the capital stock to the desired level when all orders are completed. Thus

$$\mathrm{IN}_t + \text{orders outstanding} = K_t^{\mathrm{E}} - K_{t-1}$$

where

IN_t = new projects initiated in period t;
K_t^{E}, K_t = the desired and actual capital stocks at the end of period t.

At the end of period $t-1$ the firm will have on hand or on order a total capital stock of K_{t-1}^{E}, thus during the next period (i.e., period t) it will need to order $K_t^{\mathrm{E}} - K_{t-1}^{\mathrm{E}}$, i.e.,

$$\mathrm{IN}_t = K_t^{\mathrm{E}} - K_{t-1}^{\mathrm{E}} \,. \tag{4.6}$$

Turning to investment actually completed, if the completion of projects ordered in period t is distributed in the following proportions, μ_0 in the current period, μ_1 in the period $t + 1$, μ_2 in period $t + 2$, etc., then

$$\mathrm{IE}_t = \mu_0 \mathrm{IN}_t + \mu_1 \mathrm{IN}_{t-1} + \mu_2 \mathrm{IN}_{t-2} + \ldots \tag{4.7}$$

where IE_t = the level of investment completions in period t. For convenience Jorgenson introduces the lag operator θ, such that $\theta a_t = a_{t-1}$, and the notation $\mu(\theta) = \mu_0 + \mu_1\theta + \mu_2\theta^2 + \ldots$.

Hence

$$\mathrm{IE}_t = \mu(\theta)\mathrm{IN}_t \,. \tag{4.8}$$

Substituting (4.6) into (4.8),

$$\mathrm{IE}_t = \mu(\theta)[K_t^{\mathrm{E}} - K_{t-1}^{\mathrm{E}}] \tag{4.9}$$

and from (4.4)

$$\mathrm{IE}_t = \mu(\theta)\left[\left(\frac{\alpha pX}{c}\right)_t - \left(\frac{\alpha pX}{c}\right)_{t-1}\right]. \tag{4.10}$$

This equation represents the determinants of investment for expansion of the capital stock. Replacement is assumed to be distributed geometrically over time by

$$\mathrm{IR}_t = \delta I_{t-1} + \delta(1-\delta)I_{t-2} + \delta(1-\delta)^2 I_{t-3} + \ldots \tag{4.11}$$

where I is gross investment and IR is replacement investment.

Capital stock at the end of period t equals the sum of all previous net investment, i.e.,

$$K_t = \sum_{\tau=0}^{\infty} (I_{t-\tau} - \mathrm{IR}_{t-\tau})$$

$$= \sum_{\tau=0}^{\infty} (I_{t-\tau} - \delta I_{t-\tau-1} - \delta(1-\delta)I_{t-\tau-2} + \ldots) \tag{4.12}$$

$$\therefore\ (1-\delta)K_{t-1} = (1-\delta)\sum_{\tau=0}^{\infty} \{I_{t-\tau-1} - \delta I_{t-\tau-2} - \delta(1-\delta)I_{t-\tau-3} + \ldots\}$$

$$= \sum_{\tau=0}^{\infty} \{I_{t-\tau-1} - \delta I_{t-\tau-1} - \delta(1-\delta)I_{t-\tau-2} + \ldots\} \tag{4.13}$$

thus from (4.12) and (4.13)

$$K_t = I_t + (1-\delta)K_{t-1}$$

$$K_t - K_{t-1} = I_t - \delta K_{t-1}$$

$$\therefore\quad I_t = \mathrm{IE}_t + \delta K_{t-1} \tag{4.14}$$

and using (4.10)

$$I_t = \mu(\theta)\left[\frac{\alpha pX}{c}_t - \frac{\alpha pX}{c}_{t-1}\right] + \delta K_{t-1}\,. \tag{4.15}$$

In this model it would appear that financial considerations play little part in the firm's decision to invest. However, though the firm has no financial constraints, it does have to pay the going price to borrow, r, which is incorporated into the variable c. Given the assumption of certainty this is reasonable, but, as we have inferred before, there is likely to be other financial constraints in an uncertain situation. Let us now consider the effects of uncertainty.

4.3. Survey of the theory: uncertainty

A complete stochastic model in which a firm maximises its expected net worth to our knowledge has not been used for empirical research, presumably because of its intractability. One could appeal to the theory of certainty equivalence replacing expected values for the actual values in Jorgenson's equation, but it is unlikely that the conditions necessary for that are approximately fulfilled. Even so, it is then necessary to take a view on the generation of expectations. Early studies, in fact, used the actual values as proxies for the expected values, profits being a typical example. However, Grunfeld (1960) suggested that the stock market valuation should reflect expectations about a company's prospects.

4.3.1

The concept of the stock market valuation has also been used to capture some of the financial influences on investment. Most of the studies of investment which emphasise the financial aspects discuss the problem in terms of the rate of return on investment and the cost of capital. Duesenberry (1958) developed this approach and others, have extended it. Anderson (1967) indicates the connection with investment functions thus,

$$\text{mrr} = f_1(I, Z_1) \tag{4.16}$$

$$\text{mcf} = f_2(I, Z_2) \tag{4.17}$$

$$\text{mcf} = \text{mrr} \tag{4.18}$$

where

mrr = marginal rate of return;
mcf = marginal cost of capital;
I = level of investment;
Z_1 = vector of determinants of the marginal rate of return;
Z_2 = vector of determinants of cost of capital.
From (4.16)–(4.18) one derives

$$I = g(Z_1, Z_2) \tag{4.19}$$

which is the investment function. Analysing the investment decision in this manner is, a little artificial, but it does enable one to concentrate on the financial factors. The crucial concept here is the cost of capital, which appears in Jorgenson's model as r and affects investment via c the user cost of capital see (4.5). His measure is the long term bond rate on U.S. Government Securities, but many financial economists think that this does not adequately reflect the cost of capital in an uncertain world, believing it necessary to take into account the corporate structure of the firm.

4.3.2

Modigliani and Miller (1967) have developed a framework to do this. Their analysis rests on the central proposition that the value of a company facing a perfect capital market will be equal to its expected returns divided by a rate which incorporates interest and risk, i.e.,

$$V = S + D = \frac{\overline{X}}{\rho} \tag{4.20}$$

where
V = value of company;
S = value of equity;
D = value of debt;
$\overline{X}$ = expected income stream;
ρ = risk and interest factor.
They assume a constant certain income through time and that everyone concerned acts rationally. The proof of their proposition depends upon arbitrage in the capital market by investors. Consider two firms with same $\overline{X}$, let company 1 have only stock, whereas company 2 has some debt. Suppose the value of company 2 is V_2 and is larger than that of company 1, V_1. Consider an investor with s_2 dollars-worth of shares in company 2, representing α of S_2. The income from this portfolio, Y_2, is

$$Y_2 = \alpha(\overline{X} - rD_2) \tag{4.21}$$

where r is the rate of interest. Let the investor sell αS_2 and borrow αD_2 to buy s_1 dollars-worth of company 1 stock; i.e., $s_1 = \alpha(S_2 + D_2)$. His fraction of shares in company 1 is $s_1/S_1 = \alpha(S_2 + D_2)/S_1$. His income Y_1, will be

$$Y_1 = \frac{\alpha(S_2 + D_2)}{S_1}\overline{X} - r\alpha D_2$$

$$= \alpha\left(\frac{V_2}{V_1}\overline{X} - rD_2\right). \tag{4.22}$$

Thus comparing (4.21) and (4.22), provided $V_2 > V_1$, $Y_1 > Y_2$, i.e., it pays to move to company 1, which would bid down the value of company 2.

If $V_1 > V_2$ and an investor holds s_1 of company 1, representing the proportion α, then

$$Y_1 = \frac{s_1}{S_1}\overline{X} = \alpha\overline{X}. \tag{4.23}$$

Suppose he changes s_1 dollars-worth of shares for s_2 dollars-worth of shares in company 2, and d bonds, where $s_2 = (S_2/V_2)s_1$ and $d = (D_2/V_2)s_1$. The income from the new portfolio is

$$Y_2 = \frac{s_2}{S_2}(\overline{X} - rD_2) + rd = \frac{s_1}{V_2}(\overline{X} - rD_2) + r\frac{D_2}{V_2}s_1 = \frac{s_1}{V_2}\overline{X} = \alpha\frac{S_1}{V_2}\overline{X}$$

$$\therefore \quad Y_2 = \alpha\frac{V_1}{V_2}\overline{X}. \tag{4.24}$$

Therefore, comparing (4.23) and (4.24) if $V_2 < V_1$, $Y_2 > Y_1$, and arbitrage will take place. Modigliani and Miller's proposition implies that the debt–equity ratio does not affect the value of the firm. Their analysis also implies that dividend policy does not affect the value either, since investors counterbalance the loss of earned income by expected capital gain. If we assume that the firm will increase assets provided the present owners benefit, then it is possible to derive the lowest rate of return the company may earn and yet still expand. This rate of return is called 'the cost of capital'. Let

$$V = S^0 + D = \frac{\overline{X}}{\rho} \tag{4.25}$$

where S^0 is the value of present owners shares, and $\mathrm{d}A$ be the purchase cost of new assets. Then

$$\frac{\mathrm{d}V}{\mathrm{d}A} = \frac{\mathrm{d}S^0}{\mathrm{d}A} + \frac{\mathrm{d}S^n}{\mathrm{d}A} + \frac{\mathrm{d}D}{\mathrm{d}A} = \frac{\mathrm{d}\overline{X}}{\rho \cdot \mathrm{d}A} \tag{4.26}$$

wnere S^n is the value of new stock assuming that increasing A does not affect ρ.

$$\frac{\mathrm{d}S^0}{\mathrm{d}A} \geqslant 0 \quad \text{if} \quad \frac{\mathrm{d}\overline{X}}{\rho \cdot \mathrm{d}A} \geqslant 1 \qquad \text{since } \mathrm{d}A = \mathrm{d}S^n + \mathrm{d}D, \quad \text{i.e.,}$$

$$\frac{\mathrm{d}\overline{X}}{\mathrm{d}A} \geqslant \rho \tag{4.27}$$

$\therefore \rho =$ cost of capital.

Thus, the cost of capital is also independent of how the investment is financed. However, once taxation enters the model this rather simple situation disappears. This stems from the fact that debt payments are considered as costs and are usually deductable. Let τ be the tax rate on corporate income and P be the value of preferred stock which is non-deductable, then they (Modigliani and Miller, 1963) have shown that

$$V = S + D + P = \frac{\overline{X}(1-\tau)}{\rho} + \tau D\,. \tag{4.28}$$

Now

$$\frac{\mathrm{d}V}{\mathrm{d}A} = \frac{\mathrm{d}S^0}{\mathrm{d}A} + \frac{\mathrm{d}S^n}{\mathrm{d}A} + \frac{\mathrm{d}D}{\mathrm{d}A} + \frac{\mathrm{d}P}{\mathrm{d}A} = \frac{\mathrm{d}S^0}{\mathrm{d}A} + 1\,. \tag{4.29}$$

Thus, from (4.28) and (4.29)

$$\frac{\mathrm{d}V}{\mathrm{d}A} = \frac{\mathrm{d}\overline{X}}{\mathrm{d}A}(1-\tau)\frac{1}{\rho} + \frac{\tau \mathrm{d}D}{\mathrm{d}A} \quad \therefore \quad c = \rho\left(1 - \tau\frac{\mathrm{d}D}{\mathrm{d}A}\right). \tag{4.30}$$

Here the cost of capital is affected by the type of financing. If all finance is debt, the cost of capital is $\rho(1-\tau)$, but if it is all equity then it is ρ. Modigliani and Miller suggest that these financing decisions of a large corporation are of a long-run nature and as a result, the cost of capital can be represented in terms of a long-run desired debt/equity ratio, L, such that

$$c = \rho(1-\tau)L + (1-L)\rho$$

$$= \rho(1-\tau L)\,. \tag{4.31}$$

Thus provided L and τ are known, the cost of capital can be derived, provided ρ is known. The Modigliani and Miller approach is to derive estimates for ρ by estimating an equation similar to (4.28) but adjusted to take account of the growth potential and dividend policy effects on the value of the company. Modigliani and Miller claim that with perfect capital markets and rational behaviour, dividend policy will have no effect on the cost of capital unless there is tax discrimination or flotation costs. Since these are known to exist, dividends should be incorporated similar to the way in which the debt–equity ratio is included. Modigliani and Miller do not in fact estimate any investment functions but their work is a convenient starting point for a discussion of the financial aspects.

4.3.3

Since its original publication in 1958 the Modigliani–Miller model has been attacked by many financial economists, who believe that leverage and risk are connected. Lintner (1967) maintains that incorporating the assumption that risk rises with leverages, leads to a cost of capital function which rises with leverage, although he admits that some of this is offset by the taxation effect. This produces a U-shaped cost of capital schedule relative to leverage. Lintner also maintains that the marginal cost of retentions is a rising function of leverage. As a result the firm will use debt financing until it reaches a point where the marginal cost of debt equals that of retentions and hence where the marginal cost of funds is rising. This is the reverse of the Modigliani–Miller position. However, Lintner, and Modigliani and Miller all agree that the dividend-retention, the debt–equity, and the investment decisions are mutually determined in the long run. In the short run Lintner believes that dividends follow a distributed lag adjustment path to the desired long-run equilibrium position and that other decisions are then taken, given these dividends. Modigliani and Miller seem to suggest that the target debt–equity position is chosen and then the other decisions adjust. However, this does not affect the fact that the two models result in conflicting predictions for the signs of the effects on investment of using debt or retentions finance. These attempts to incorporate the interdependent nature of the dividend, external financing and investment decisions have led Dhrymes and Kurz (1967) to set up an interdependent system and estimate it by simultaneous methods. Earlier, Kuh (1963) attempted to compare a Lintner-type dividend equation with a Koyck-type investment function. We have already hinted that decisions have short-run and long-run aspects and this mention of Koyck-type investment function brings us to the problems of adjustment which are common to all the approaches we have considered so far.

4.4. Adjustment problems

Koyck (1954) organised his discussion of delay into subjective, technical and institutional factors. Subjective factors reflect psychological inertia due to habit or risk aversion, entrepreneurs, preferring to see more evidence of changed demand conditions than, say, one good month. Institutional factors causing lags in responses stem from such phenomena as decisions only being made at regular intervals. In modern industry one would not expect this factor to play much of a part in the actual investment decisions, but changes in wage and salary agreements may occur only after specific intervals, thus affecting investment decision. Technical lags are probably far more important, since the ordering, production and delivery of investment goods does take time. If one considers the possibility of a desired reduction in the capital stock, different factors enter the calculation. Reduction in the capital stock tends to depend on the rate of depreciation and obsolescence. Thus, the lags are probably asymetric with regard to an upward as opposed to a downward change in the desired capital stock.

Such asymmetry is rather awkward to handle mathematically and has been ignored by some investigators. With aggregate data and during periods of general expansion this may not be too damaging. However, Koyck did find evidence of such asymmetry in his work.

4.4.1

Given that these factors exist, they ought to be incorporated into the theoretical model of investment determination based on cost minimization. In order to do this the costs of adjustments need to be clearly specified and then taken account of. This has proved to be rather difficult. Eisner and Strotz (1963) presented a model which allowed for an extra cost being attributed to the speed of the increase in the capital stock. When solved, this reduced to the type of lag function used originally by Koyck. Lucas (1967) and others reported in Griliches (1967a) have extended analysis along the lines set out by Eisner and Strotz. Mundlak (1966) has indicated the interdependence of lagged responses involved when a number of factors are adjusting both in the short and long run. These suggest that the ad hoc adjustment scheme currently in use have very little theoretical basis. However, as yet few empirical investment studies embodying a rigorous adjustment theory have appeared and we content ourselves with a review of some ad hoc adjustment mechanisms.

4.4.2 †

The lagged effects of one variable on another can be represented thus

$$y_t = \beta(\mu_0 x_t + \mu_1 x_{t-1} + \mu_2 x_{t-2} + \dots) . \tag{4.32}$$

Usually the following restrictions are placed on the μ_i, namely,

$$\sum_{i=0}^{\infty} \mu_i = 1 \quad \text{and} \quad \mu_i \geqslant 0 .$$

Because of this, the μ_i can be regarded as probabilities and convenient use made of the probability generating function $\mu(z)$, i.e.,

$$\mu(z) = \mu_0 + \mu_1 z + \mu_2 z^2 + \mu_3 z^3 + \dots .$$

Koyck introduced the geometric lag distribution where $\mu_i = (1-\lambda)\lambda_i$ or

$$\mu(z) = (1-\lambda)[1 + \lambda z + \lambda z^2 + \dots]$$

$$= \frac{1-\lambda}{1-\lambda z} \qquad \text{taking } |z| \leqslant 1 .$$

Since z is an auxiliary variable we can use the variable θ instead, interpreting it either as a lag operator (see Section 4.2) or as an auxiliary variable. Hence

$$y_t = \beta\mu(\theta)x_t . \tag{4.33}$$

Thus, for the geometric lag

$$y_t = \beta\frac{1-\lambda}{1-\lambda\theta}x_t \tag{4.34}$$

or

$$(1-\lambda\theta)y_t = \beta(1-\lambda)x_t$$

$$y = \beta(1-\lambda)x_t + \lambda y_{t-1} . \tag{4.35}$$

† This section is based on Griliches (1967a).

The convenience of this transformation has accounted for the popularity of the geometric lag. Notice that it is a one-parameter lag function and hence involves estimating only one parameter. Yet it is very restrictive because it implies that the major impact comes immediately and the following impacts are less and less strong. If we think of a variable having to go through a two-stage process, both parts of which take time, then the lag distribution of the whole process will be a function of the two lag distributions of the individual stages. The whole process distribution will be the convolution of the stage processes. However, the probability generating function of the whole process will, in fact, be the product of those of the two stages. Thus, if the two stages involve the same lag, the process lag distribution will be

$$\begin{aligned}\mu(\theta) &= \mu(\theta)_1 \cdot \mu(\theta)_2 \\ &= (\mu(\theta)_2)^2 \\ &= \frac{(1-\lambda)^2}{(1-\lambda\theta)^2} \,. \end{aligned} \tag{4.36}$$

This is a Pascal distribution and no longer necessarily has the greatest impact in the first period. If there are r stages, then the distribution is

$$\mu(\theta) = \frac{(1-\lambda)^r}{(1-\lambda\theta)^r} \,. \tag{4.37}$$

Solow (1960a) suggested this form of lag distribution as being much less restrictive, yet involving only one more parameter, than the Koyck distribution.

With $r = 2$ the model reduces to

$$\begin{aligned}(1-\lambda\theta)^2 y_t &= \beta(1-\lambda)^2 x_t \\ (1-2\lambda\theta+\lambda^2\theta)y_t &= \beta(1-\lambda)^2 x_t \\ y_t &= \beta(1-\lambda)^2 x_t + 2\lambda y_{t-1} - \lambda^2 y_{t-2} \,. \end{aligned} \tag{4.38}$$

However, one problem in using this lag form is that it involves estimating an equation subject to nonlinear constraints. Jorgenson's approach is to generalise this form such that the roots of the lag polynominal need not be equal. Thus, with $r = 2$,

$$(1-\lambda_1\theta)(1-\lambda_2\theta)y_t = \beta(1-\lambda_1)(1-\lambda_2)x_t \tag{4.39}$$

which reduces to

$$y_t = \beta(1-\lambda_1)(1-\lambda_2)x_t + (\lambda_1+\lambda_2)y_{t-1} - \lambda_1\lambda_2 y_{t-2}\,. \tag{4.40}$$

Actually Jorgenson (1966) goes further allowing

$$\mu(\theta) = v(\theta)/w(\theta) \tag{4.41}$$

and shows that any arbitrary lag function can be approximated by a form such as this.

4.4.3

Although these sophisticated mathematical models of distributed lags bring about considerable simplification, their use does involve statistical problems. The estimation of the coefficient of lagged variables is but one of these and the extreme sensitivity of the time path to errors in these coefficients another. If one can specify the lag form a priori such estimation is not necessary, and it is possible to transform the data accordingly. De Leeuw (1962) uses the following weights

$$\mu_i = i+1 \qquad 0 \leqslant i \leqslant N/2$$

$$\mu_i = N-i \qquad i \geqslant N/2$$

$$\mu_i = 0 \qquad i \geqslant N$$

which produce an 'inverted V' form of lag distribution. Evans (1967b) suggests that a firm's decision process is essentially two-stage. He assumes that firms decide on investment but review plans six months later before final commitment. Then he assumes that the adjustment to each of these decisions is geometric. This produces a lag distribution with two peaks. He supports this type of function by reference to Almon (1965) who has suggested another type of distributed lag in which the finite length of the distribution and the number of coefficients to be estimated is under the control of the investigator. She suggests estimating a few points on the distribution and then using polynomial interpolation to find the rest. The actual combination of length and number of parameters is chosen empirically with regard to R^2 and the stability of the distribution. It was found that distributions with length

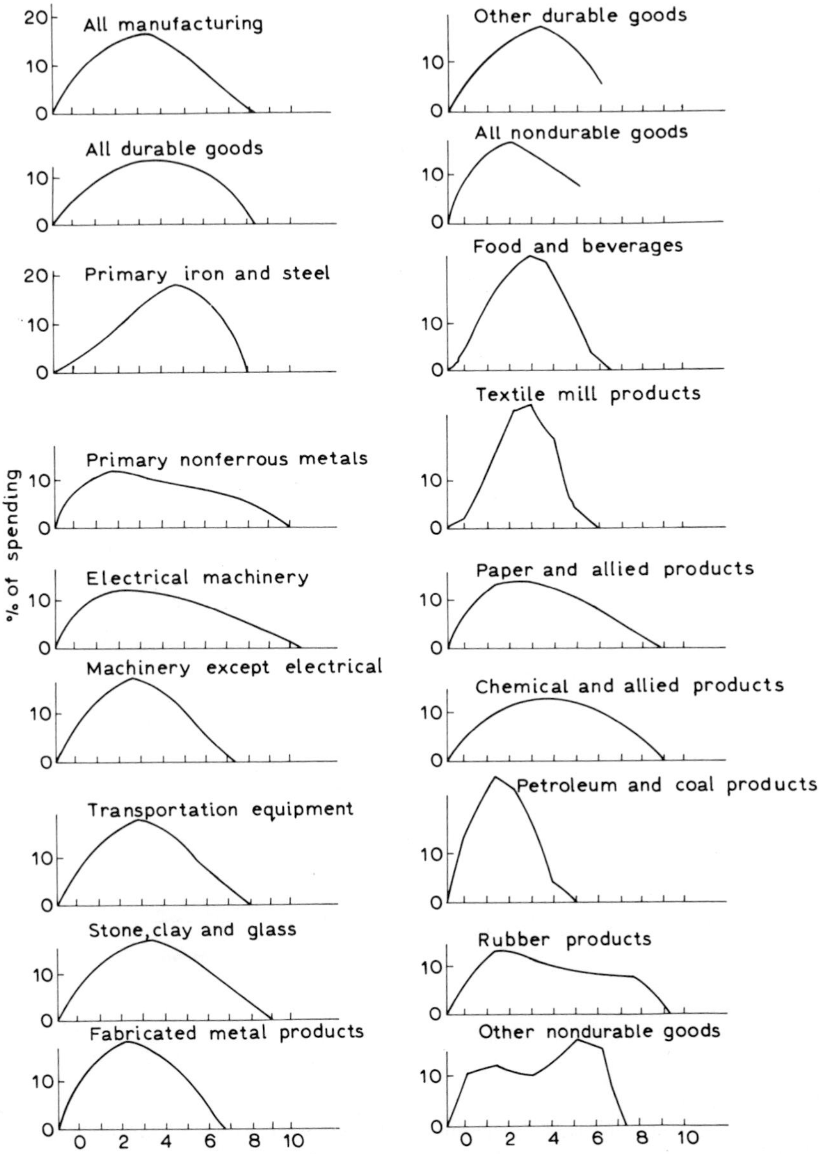

Fig. 4.1. The weights of Almon's best distributed lags. (Source: Almon, 1965.)

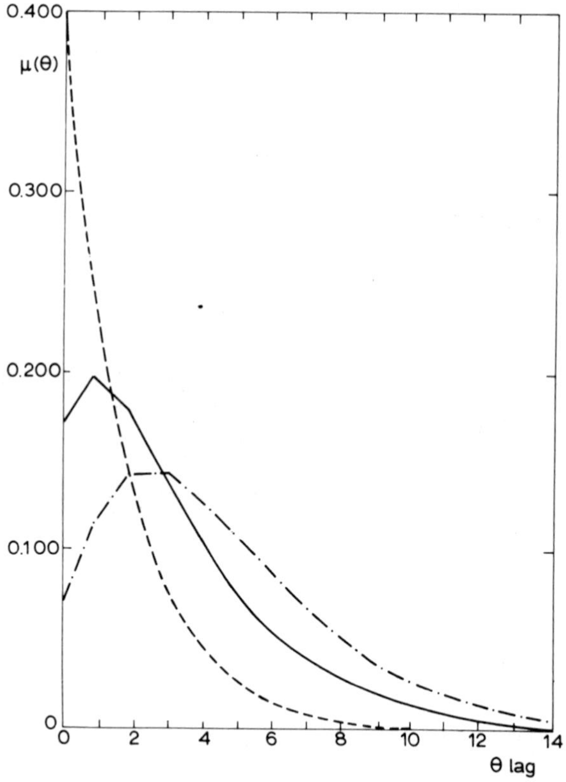

Fig. 4.2. Examples of Pascal distribution of different orders. – – – –, first order, $\mu(\theta) = 0.4/(1-0.6\,\theta)$; ———, second order, $\mu(\theta) = (0.4/(1-0.6\,\theta))^2 = 0.16/(1-1.20\,\theta + 0.36\,\theta^2)$; –·–·–·–, third order, $\mu(\theta) = (0.4/(1-0.6\,\theta))^3 = 0.064/(1-1.8\,\theta + 1.08\,\theta^2 - 0.216\,\theta^3)$. (Source: Griliches, 1967a.)

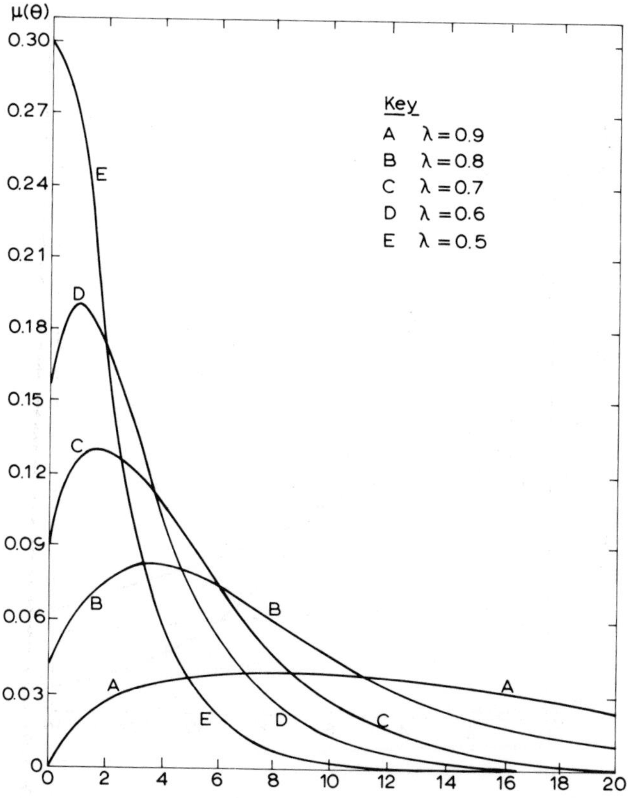

Fig. 4.3. Examples of second order Pascal distributions. $\mu(\theta) = a/(1 - \lambda\theta)^2$. (Source: Griliches, 1967a.)

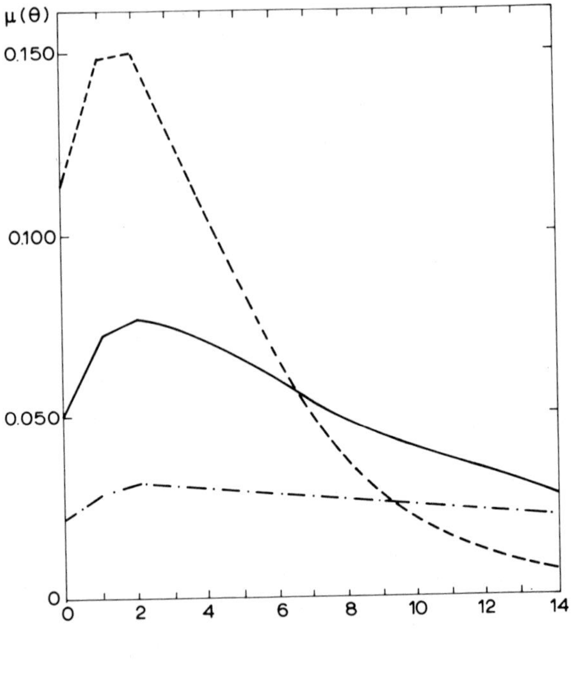

Fig. 4.4. Examples of second order lag distributions. – – –, $b = 1.34$, $c = -0.45$; ———, $b = 1.40$, $c = -0.45$; –·–·–, $b = 1.34$, $c = -0.36$. $\mu(\theta) = a/(1 - b\theta - c\theta^2)$. (Source: Griliches, 1967a.)

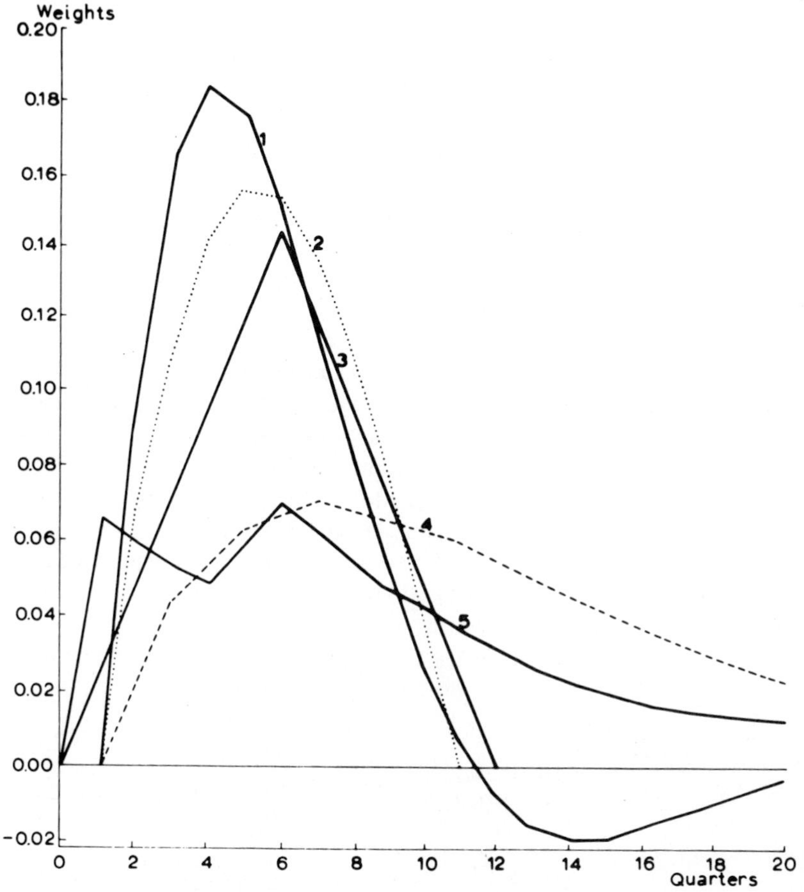

Fig. 4.5. Some empirical distributed lag functions. 1, Jorgenson (see Griliches and Wallace, 1965, footnote 21); 2, Almon (appropriations data); 3, De Leeuw 'V' peak at six six quarters; 4, Griliches–Wallace; 5, Evans (double distributed lag). (Source: Evans, 1967b.)

longer than that with the highest $\overline{R}^2$, tended to give some negative weights. The weights she estimated are given in fig. 4.1.

We end this section with a collection of diagrams illustrating different lag forms (figs. 4.2–4.5).

4.5. **Realisation functions**

Sophisticated as distributed lag models may become it is important to remember that they are rather mechanical tricks aimed at relating the investment decisions to the investment construction. This process may not be so simple that it can be represented by a probability distribution, but may involve explanatory factors as does the investment decision itself. The availability of data on stages prior to construction, e.g., capital appropriations, has encouraged research along this line as well as in the estimation of distributed lags. Investment anticipations are published in the U.S. *Survey of Current Business* and these have formed the basis of a number of 'realisation functions'. Such research has been mainly aimed at finding forecasting equations but it involves attempts to break the investment process down into parts which can be handled by recourse to other data. Modigliani and Cohen (1958) have set out the theoretical base for much studies, but we shall consider as an example of the realisation function approach, part of a study by Eisner (1965). He states that, given that desired K is a function of expected output, which itself is a function of expected sales, the discovery of a mistake in expected sales is likely to bring about a revision of investment plans. However, if business prospects are improving anyway, a firm may go ahead even if it felt it had made a mistake in the past.

Eisner's model estimated by least squares for all manufacturing industry from quarterly data 1948(iii)–1960(iv) is

$$\Delta\frac{I-\mathrm{IA}}{\mathrm{IA}} = -0.011 + \underset{(0.121)}{0.189}\,\frac{S_{t-2}-\mathrm{SE}_{t-2}}{\mathrm{SE}_{t-2}} + \underset{(0.048)}{0.182}\,\frac{Z_{t-1}-Z_{t-2}}{Z_{t-2}}$$

$$+ \underset{(0.048)}{0.078}\,\frac{Z_{t-2}-Z_{t-3}}{Z_{t-3}} - \underset{(0.125)}{0.507}\left[\frac{I-\mathrm{IA}}{\mathrm{IA}}\right]_{t-1} \qquad (4.41a)$$

$\overline{R}^2 = 0.392$
DW = 1.953

where

I = business gross investment
IA = current anticipated investment
S = sales
SE = expected sales
Z = profits

This involves a sales expectation error term, two lagged profit change terms, representing improving business prospects, and incorporates a Koyck distributed lag. However, the inclusion of the term $(I_{t-1} - \text{IA})/I_{t-1}$ improved the relationship to

$$\Delta \frac{I - \text{IA}}{\text{IA}} = -0.007 + \underset{(0.094)}{0.316} \frac{S_{t-2} - \text{SE}_{t-2}}{\text{SE}_{t-2}} + \underset{(0.036)}{0.190} \frac{Z_{t-1} - Z_{t-2}}{Z_{t-2}}$$

$$+ \underset{(0.037)}{0.108} \frac{Z_{t-2} - Z_{t-3}}{Z_{t-3}} + \underset{(0.073)}{0.435} \frac{I_{t-1} - \text{IA}}{I_{t-1}} \underset{(0.102)}{-0.751} \left[\frac{I - \text{IA}}{\text{IA}}\right]_{t-1} \tag{4.41b}$$

$\bar{R}^2 = 0.655$
DW = 1.943

As an attempt to test the usefulness of these equations Eisner calculates the within sample forecasts of business investment and compares them with the forecasts based solely on the anticipations data. The mean absolute errors and root mean square errors appear in table 4.1. These indicate the superiority of

Table 4.1
Comparison of within sample forecasts from anticipations data and the realisation functions.

	All manufacturing (million \$ 1954 prices)	
	Eq. (4.41a)	Eq. (4.41b)
Mean absolute error		
Anticipations data direct	519	519
Realisation function	395	255
Root mean squares error		
Anticipations data direct	670	670
Realisation function	500	355

Table 4.2
Forecast errors for four post sample periods of anticipation forecasts and realisation function forecasts.

	All manufacturing (million $ 1954 prices)	
	Anticipation data direct	Realisation function
1961(i)	−507	− 93
1961(ii)	−194	256
1961(iii)	−395	380
1961(iv)	−122	−187
Mean error	−304	−101
Mean absolute error	304	254

(4.41b), but within sample predictions are not very exacting tests so he also presents forecasts errors for post sample periods which appear in table 4.2. These results indicate that if we use anticipations data for forecasting investment the realisation function will provide better forecasts than the direct method. As yet very few macro models incorporate explicit realisation functions. Later we will show how Jorgenson incorporates anticipations data into the distributed lag approach.

4.6. **Empirical studies: time series data**

The number of empirical studies published on investment is very large and they cover different periods and levels of aggregation. Eisner and Strotz (1963) have reviewed many published at the time of their writing, but since that time many more have appeared. In the following sections studies are arranged according to type of data – aggregate in Sections 4.6.1–4.6.4; industry in Sections 4.6.5–4.6.8; and firm in Sections 4.6.10–4.6.11. Some aggregate results which are part of industry studies appear in Sections 4.6.5–4.6.8 and the Eisner–Nadiri–Bischoff discussion of Jorgenson's model is placed at the end of Section 4.6.9.

4.6.1. Hickman (1965) *annual data*, 1949–1960

Hickman wanted to explain why the U.S. economy since 1957 had operated below its potential and hence discover if it was likely to continue to do so for the rest of the sixties. He stresses the 'key role of business fixed investment demand' and concentrates his attention on explaining and predicting this component of aggregate demand.

He uses a capital stock adjustment model where the desired capital stock is determined by expected or 'normal' output, expected or 'normal' prices and the level of technology. 'Normal' output and prices are measured by weighted averages of the recent quantities where the weights are left to be determined by data. The level of technology is assumed to follow a smooth trend. Hickman adopts the non-linear form,

$$K^* = a_1 Y_t^{*a_2} P^{*a_3} e^{a_4 T} \tag{4.43}$$

where
K^* = desired capital stock;
Y^* = normal output;
P^* = normal relative price of capital;
T = trend;
transforms this into

$$\log K^* = \log a_1 + a_2 \log Y_t^* + a_3 \log P^* + a_4 T \tag{4.44}$$

and then defines

$$a_2 \log Y_t^* = a_{21} \log Y_t + a_{22} \log Y_{t-1} \tag{4.45}$$

$$a_3 \log P_t^* = a_{31} \log P_t + a_{32} \log P_{t-1} \tag{4.46}$$

which imply that normal variables are the geometric means of the current and previous year's actual quantities. The Koyck type of adjustment process is used in the form

$$\frac{K_t}{K_{t-1}} = \left(\frac{K_t^*}{K_{t-1}}\right)^b \tag{4.47}$$

and as a result the basic form of the equations used for the regression analyses is

$$\log K_t - \log K_{t-1} = b \log a_1 + ba_{21} \log Y_t + ba_{22} \log Y_{t-1} + ba_{31} \log P_t + ba_{22} \log P_{t-1} + ba_4 T - b \log K_{t-1} \tag{4.48}$$

where b is the adjustment coefficient and $a_{21} + a_{22}$ is the long-run elasticity of capital stock with respect to output.

The estimates of the capital stock were built up from figures of gross investment and useful lines using the perpetual inventory method. These useful lives embody not only physical depreciation but obsoloescence too. Hickman shows that his method of measuring capital stock plus the inclusion of the trend is essentially the same approach as that of Solow's vintage model (see Solow, 1960b). The data on output refer to real gross product originating in the sector concerned. If all industries are included the output figures would add up to gross national product in 1954 prices. However, in fact the coverage of the 'all industries' sector is 78% of gross national product in 1954. The relative price of capital is defined as the price of new capital goods multiplied by the depreciation rate plus the rate of interest all divided by the price of output, i.e., $P = P_k(\delta + r)/P_o$ (cf. Jorgenson's c/p).

Several variants of (4.4) are estimated using least squares and the results discussed on the basis of (a) their consistency with a priori knowledge on signs and implied elasticities and (b) statistical significance and goodness of fit. The best equations are:

All industries

$$\begin{aligned} \log K_t - \log K_{t-1} = \underset{(0.0970)}{0.0833} - \underset{(0.0434)}{0.2594} \log K_{t-1} - \underset{(0.0004)}{0.0016}\, T \\ + \underset{(0.0149)}{0.1235} \log Y_t + \underset{(0.0168)}{0.1157} \log Y_{t-1} \end{aligned} \qquad (4.49)$$

$$\bar{R}^2 = 0.966$$
$$\mathrm{DW} = 2.57$$

Manufacturing

$$\begin{aligned} \log K_t - \log K_{t-1} = \underset{(0.3454)}{-0.2999} - \underset{(0.1286)}{0.2731} \log K_{t-1} \\ - \underset{(0.0053)}{0.0035}\, T - \underset{(0.0002)}{0.0000}\, T^2 \\ + \underset{(0.0523)}{0.1896} \log Y_t + \underset{(0.0346)}{0.2311} \log Y_{t-1} \end{aligned} \qquad (4.50)$$

$$\bar{R}^2 = 0.951$$
$$\text{DW} = 2.71$$

The goodness of fit statistics are quite high but with the inclusion of a lagged endogenous variable very little significance can be given to the Durbin–Watson statistic. The estimates of the elasticities of capital with respect to output for the two equations is 0.9221 and 1.5405. If the inherent production function has constant returns to scale this elasticity should be 1. The figure 1.5405 reflects decreasing returns to scale. Hickman dismisses this as impossible in the long run as plants would be broken down into smaller units and so he decides to fix the elasticity at 1. This can be done by estimating the following equation.

$$\log K_t - \log K_{t-1} = \log c_1 + c_2 (\log Y_t - \log K_{t-1}) + c_3(\log Y_{t-1} - \log K_{t-1}) + c_4 T . \quad (4.51)$$

The results from this equation are

All industries

$$\log K - \log K_{t-1} = \underset{(0.0018)}{0.0337} + \underset{(0.0142)}{0.1236} (\log Y_t - \log K_{t-1}) + \underset{(0.0157)}{0.1141} (\log Y_{t-1} - \log K_{t-1}) - \underset{(0.0001)}{0.0018}\, T \quad (4.52)$$

$$\bar{R}^2 = 0.969$$
$$\text{DW} = 2.48$$

Manufacturing

$$\log K_t - \log K_{t-1} = \underset{(0.0043)}{-0.0265} + \underset{(0.0238)}{0.1529} (\log Y_t - \log K_{t-1}) + \underset{(0.0291)}{0.2173} (\log Y_{t-1} - \log K_{t-1}) + \underset{(0.0008)}{0.0007}\, T - \underset{(0.0001)}{0.0002}\, T^2 \quad (4.53)$$

$$\bar{R}^2 = 0.954$$
$$DW = 2.72$$

Hickman reports that in other regressions he tried, the price coefficients were either not significant or led to the 'wrong' sign or both. He points out that the trend coefficients in the results above may reflect other slow changing influences than technical progress including any scale effects, price effects and inter-industry shifts. Furthermore, since output is measured in value added terms and the capital stock is in total value terms, anything, e.g. vertical integration, which affects the ratio of total value to value added, could be reflected in the trend coefficients. These forms, i.e., (4.51) with and without T^2, are accepted because they also fit the individual industry data fairly well too. However, goodness of fit is not the only or even best test of a relationship. As a check on the usefulness of the results 1961 and 1962 capital stock figures are 'predicted', i.e., calculated from the regressions with unitary long run output elasticity, using the actual output figures on the righthand side of the equation. The following ratios are calculated, $100({}_AK_t - {}_AK_{t-1})/{}_AK_t$ and $100({}_PK_t - {}_AK_{t-1})/{}_AK_t$, where subscripts A and P reflect actual and predicted values, and the results for 1961 and 1962 are shown in table 4.3 along with those of a more naive predictor based on the assumption that net investment does not change.

Thus for the aggregate figures the regression forecasts do better than the naive, which is not the case for some of the individual industries. The equations do quite well when one considers their turning point accuracy too (see table 4.4).

In neither case is a turning point error made. These encouraging results

Table 4.3
Predicted and actual net investment as percentage of capital stock.

		All industries	Manufacturing
1961			
	Actual	1.0	0.2
	Regression predicted	1.2	0.7
	Naive predicted	1.5	1.2
1962			
	Actual	1.6	0.8
	Regression prediction	1.3	0.7
	Naive prediction	1.0	0.2

Table 4.4
Predicted and actual changes in net investment as percentage of capital stock.

	1960–1961		1961–1962	
	P	*A*	*P*	*A*
All industries	−0.3	−0.5	0.1	0.6
Manufacturing	−0.8	−1.0	0	0.6

lead us on to a discussion of the implications for the adjustment over time. Hickman shows the extent to which the influence of a change in output is spread over the first five years by a pair of diagrams (see fig. 4.6). These diagrams show the response each year as a proportion of the total long run response. They show that manufacturing industry tends to be faster in adjusting to changed circumstances than other sectors and this conforms to one's general expectations. Also, they show that it is in the second year that the greatest impact is felt though strong influence is still displayed in the fifth year. As well as using his equations to gain insight into why the U.S. economy has operated below its potential, Hickman presents some other interesting uses. In the model which he uses, there are lags in the effect of changes in output on the capital stock. These lags stem from two factors, adjustment lags due to businesses being slow to order machinery etc., and expectational lags inherent in the formation of 'normal' output. It is possible to separate the effects of these lags since

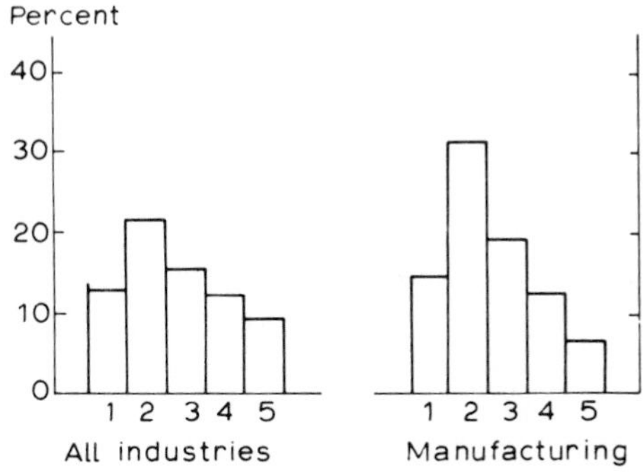

Fig. 4.6. Percentage response of investment to a change in output: aggregates.

$$\log K_t - \log K_{t-1} = b\,[\log a_1 + a_2 \log Y^* + a_2 \log P^* + a_4 T - \log K_{t-1}] \tag{4.54}$$

where $a_2 = a_{21} + a_{22}$.

Thus, setting $b = 1$ gives an estimate of investment if there are no adjustment delays, and $Y^* = Y$, a similar estimate if there are no expectation delays. The results show that the presence of these lags is very important for the stabilising of investment expenditures. Table 4.5 gives the estimated average amplitude of investment expenditures under alternative assumptions as to lags, and brings out strongly the stabilising influence of the lags.

Another use Hickman makes of his results is to develop a measure of capacity. Since (4.44) is derived from a minimisation procedure we can substitute the actual value of K in any one year to obtain an estimate of the output at which the existing plant would be optimally run, i.e., capacity output. Actually this estimate will involve some error for it is not legitimate to invert least squares estimated equations in this manner but since the fit of the original equation is high the error involved should be small. Using the 'normal' concept of output the rates of capacity utilisation are given in table 4.6. Hickman believes these are biased upwards since 'normal' output probably underestimates expected output. However, he indicates that this bias will not

Table 4.5
Estimated average amplitude of investment fluctuations.

	No lags	Expectational lag	Expectational and adjustment lags	Adjustment lag
All industries	3.8	2.0	0.5	0.6
Manufacturing	6.8	3.9	1.4	1.5

Table 4.6
Normal rates of capacity utilisation as percentage of capacity.

	1949	1950	1951	1952	1953	1954	1955
All industries	111	111	114	112	111	108	109
Manufacturing	105	105	113	112	112	109	105

	1956	1957	1958	1959	1960	1961	1962
All industries	111	108	103	103	106	105	102
Manufacturing	109	105	99	98	104	102	102

Table 4.7
Measures of the rate of capacity utilisation for total manufactures.

	Hickman	Federal reserve board	Wharton school	National industrial conference board	Fortune magazine	McGraw Hill
1948	100	97	99		94	
1949	90	88	88		86	
1950	101	98	96		97	
1951	104	102	98		100	
1952	101	101	97		99	
1953	104	103	100	103	102	
1954	92	92	91		92	91
1955	100	100	100	100	100	100
1956	98	99	101	94	98	93
1957	93	94	99	91	94	85
1958	83	84	89	90	85	87
1959	93	93	98	97	95	92
1960	93	92	98	96	94	84
1961	90	90	96	95	93	90
1962						

affect the changes in utilisation nor, therefore, the index of capacity. His measure is presented in table 4.7 along with other measures of spare capacity.

When he turns to his major task of explaining the less than full employment of the U.S. economy since 1957 he makes considerable use of his estimated equations. He shows that given that output grows at the rate of 3.5 percent per year, which is how the Economic Report of the President defined potential GNP, there will still be a shortage of aggregate demand unless the government uses fiscal or monetary policy to generate extra demand. He does this by calculating the ratio of investment to gross national product at potential GNP and noticing the gradual decline (see table 4.8). These figures, however, are a little academic since between 1957 and 1962 GNP did not follow the potential path. Hickman considers four alternative paths. Path A assumes immediate recovery to potential in 1963 and then follows the potential path. Path B assumes GNP rises steadily to the potential in 1966 and then continues at the potential till 1970. Path C assumes GNP grows steadily to the potential in 1970. Path D parallels potential till 1966 and then rises steadily to equal potential in 1970. The corresponding results are presented in table 4.9.

The policy implication that Hickman draws from his work stems from the fact that gross private savings seem to stay at a constant 15% of GNP. Thus

Table 4.8
Projection of potential gross business fixed investment as a percentage of potential GNP †.

1956	10.0	1963	9.2
1957	9.8	1964	9.2
1958	9.7	1965	9.1
1959	9.5	1966	9.1
1960	9.4	1967	9.1
1961	9.3	1968	9.1
1962	9.2	1969	9.1
		1970	9.0

† These figures, which take account of certain conceptual and statistical revisions in the GNP accounts, were kindly supplied by Professor Hickman. For an explanation of these revisions see Hickman (1966).

Table 4.9
The investment percentage of four alternative paths for GNP ‡.

	A	B	C	D
1963	9.2	9.0	9.0	8.9
1964	9.9	9.2	9.1	8.9
1965	9.7	9.5	9.2	9.0
1966	9.5	9.6	9.3	9.0
1967	9.4	9.6	9.3	9.0
1968	9.3	9.5	9.4	9.2
1969	9.3	9.4	9.4	9.4
1970	9.2	9.3	9.4	9.6

‡ These figures are taken from Hickman (1966).

there is considerable danger of a deficit of aggregate demand since other elements that make up aggregate demand are not likely to increase sufficiently to make up for the decline in the private investment proportion. Hickman is sceptical that monetary policy can be used to remedy the situation by increasing private investment because the rate of interest does not appear significant in his study. As to fiscal policy he states that he abstracted from this and so resort to other people's work is necessary for guidance in this matter. Hickman's own conclusion is that a government deficit will be needed in order to maintain full employment. Hickman's model is basically of the accelerator type involving no parameters through which the government can affect investment. Our previous discussion suggests that we may find that financial variables are important in determining investment and hence monetary policy may be effective. Anderson (1967) whose theoretical rationale we have already referred to has produced an annual model of the U.S. which includes financial variables.

4.6.2. Anderson (1967) *annual data*, 1941–1963 *excluding* 1957

Anderson's main aim is to show that financial variables are important in the determination of investment. His model is as follows:

$$\mathrm{mrr} = a_1 + a_2 \frac{I}{K} + a_3 \frac{Q}{K} \tag{4.55}$$

$$\mathrm{mcf} = b_1 + b_2 \frac{I}{K} + b_3 \frac{R}{K} + b_4 \frac{A}{K} + b_5 \frac{L}{K} + b_6 \frac{Q}{K} + b_7 s + b_8 r \tag{4.56}$$

where

mrr = marginal rate of return;
mcf = marginal cost of funds;
I = investment;
Q = output;
K = capital stock;
R = retained earnings;
A = non capital assets;
L = liabilities;
s = Moody's industrial dividend/price ratio;
r = Moody's industrial bond yield.

The variables in dollar values have been normalised for scale by dividing by the capital stock. Equating (4.55) and (4.56) and collecting terms gives

$$\frac{I}{K} = c_1 + c_2 \frac{Q}{K} + c_3 \frac{R}{K} + c_4 \frac{A}{K} + c_5 \frac{L}{K} + c_6 s + c_7 r\,. \tag{4.57}$$

The data for investment, capital and output are taken from the *Survey of Current Business*; retained earnings, non-capital assets and liabilities from the flow of funds accounts; and equity yield and bond yield are annual averages of Moody's industrial dividend price ratio and Moody's industrial bond yield. Anderson uses (4.57) to explain both net investment, I^{N}, and gross investment, I^{G}. He omits the depreciation rate from his regressions because its inclusion, though theoretically correct, raises substantially the standard errors of the coefficients without contributing much to compensate. His output variable is similar to Hickman's normal output but Anderson specifies weights of 0.5, i.e., $0.5\,Q_t + 0.5\,Q_{t-1}$. He also collapses his three financial variables into one by subtracting liabilities from assets and adding 'normal' retentions. This he does mainly because of data limitations but also because of the problem of collinearity, although he states that with regards to internal funds it is really only the net portion that is important for the cost of funds schedule. The two interest rates are lagged one year for he believes that decisions to finance by issuance of long term debt and shares are worked out quite far in advance of the spending. His estimating forms are written

$$\frac{I_t^{\mathrm{N}}}{K_{t-1}} = d_1 + d_2\, 0.5 \frac{Q_t + Q_{t-1}}{K_{t-1}} + d_3 \frac{A_{t-1} - L_{t-1} + 0.5\,[R_t + R_{t-1}]}{K_{t-1}}$$

$$+ d_4 s_{t-1} + d_5 r_{t-1} + d_6 t \tag{4.58}$$

$$\frac{I_t^{\mathrm{G}}}{K_{t-1}} = d_1' + d_2'\, 0.5 \frac{Q_t + Q_{t-1}}{K_{t-1}} + d_3' \frac{A_{t-1} - L_{t-1} + 0.5\,[R_t + R_{t-1}]}{K_{t-1}}$$

$$+ d_4' s_{t-1} + d_5' r_{t-1} + d_6' t\,. \tag{4.59}$$

The trend term is included to take account of changes in the productivity of capital and errors in the depreciation rate used in the measurement of the capital stock. When Anderson fitted these equations to the data he discovered about half the unexplained sum of squares was accounted for by a large error in 1957. Because he believed 'the continuation of the mid 1950's investment boom in 1957 was collective madness ex ante, not to mention ex post', he had 'little compunction about pulling the 1957 observation and refitting the equations without it'. Anderson estimates his equation using four different capital stock series based on four different depreciation methods. Though the results based on the different capital stock series do differ, none of them alter his conclusion, so only the results stemming from the use of the Department of Commerce capital stock series based on straight-line, Bulletin F lives, are reported in table 4.10.

Table 4.10 indicates that both accelerator and financial variables are significant in the determination of investment. The dividend/yield variable is also significant but this may reflect expectational influences incorporated in the market price. The rate of interest is also highly significant. The trend variable is not significant and Anderson suggests that Hickman's significant negative trend probably stems from mis-specifying the investment equation by ignoring the financial variables. However, as we have pointed out, annual aggregate functions are not rigorous tests of a theory, so that disaggregation with regards to time and coverage is desired. We shall first consider two quarterly studies of aggregate investment.

Table 4.10
Results of fitting (4.58) and (4.59) to U.S. all industries data.

	d_1	d_2	d_3	d_4	d_5	d_6	$\overline{R}^2$
Net investment	−0.1001	0.1392 (0.0332)	0.1395 (0.0298)	−0.0068 (0.0013)	−0.0168 (0.0024)		0.9716
	−0.1076	0.1493 (0.0394)	0.1257 (0.0420)	−0.0070 (0.0014)	−0.0155 (0.0037)	−0.0003 (0.0007)	0.9692
	d'_1	d'_2	d'_3	d'_4	d'_5	d'_6	
Gross investment	0.0103	0.1234 (0.0287)	0.1391 (0.0265)	−0.0077 (0.0013)	−0.0162 (0.0022)		0.9730
	0.0036	0.1323 (0.0350)	0.1268 (0.0374)	−0.0078 (0.0012)	−0.0151 (0.0033)	−0.0003 (0.0006)	0.9708

4.6.3. De Leeuw (1962) *quarterly data seasonally adjusted*, 1949–1959

The purpose of De Leeuw's paper is to confront the hypothesis that planned additions to stock are linearly related to the industrial bond yield, output, capacity and the flow of internal funds with quarterly data for all U.S. manufactures. This hypothesis is written in the following form,

$$D_{t+1} = a + b_c C_t + b_f F_t + b_r R_t + u_t \tag{4.60}$$

where

D_{t+1} = the backlog of investment projects decided upon less the amount already spent at the start of period t+1;

C_t = capital requirement in period t;

F_t = internal funds in period t;

R_t = industrial bond yield during period t.

If

N_t = new orders, net of cancellations, issued in period t;

I_t = investment expenditure in period t;

then

$$N_t = \Delta D_{t+1} + I_t$$

and

$$I_t = \sum_{i=1}^{n} k_i N_{t-i}$$

$$\therefore \quad I_t = \sum_{i=1}^{n} k_i \Delta D_{t+1-i} + \sum_{i=1}^{n} k_i I_{t-i}$$

i.e.

$$I_t - \sum_{i=1}^{n} k_i I_{t-i} = \sum_{i=1}^{n} k_i (b_c \Delta C_{t-i} + b_f \Delta F_{t-i} + b_r \Delta R_{t-i} + \Delta U_{t-i}).$$

The variable C, capital requirements, is used to take account of the influence of the difference between the desired and actual stock of capital. In a McGraw Hill survey of investment plans in 1957 the optimum capacity level equalled 111.1% of output. De Leeuw uses this to calculate capital requirements by multiplying the index of output by 111.1 and subtracting a capacity index. He also incorporates an allowance both for depreciation and for a prospective growth of output of 4% into his capacity requirements variable. In the final estimating equation is a set of weights k_i, which determines the adjustment

Table 4.11
De Leeuw's R^2 values for four lag distributions.

Length of total lag	Rectangular	'Inverted V'	Geometric
6	0.588	0.629	
8	0.751	0.726	
10	0.667	0.817	0.332
12	0.458	0.872	
14	0.348	0.865	

process (see Sections 4.4.2 and 4.4.3). De Leeuw fits his equation using geometric, rectangular and 'inverted V' weights. The value of R^2 for the different models is given in table 4.11. The total lag when using the inverted and rectangular weights has to be specified before. Since the total lag is unknown, results are quoted for five different lengths in quarters.

In addition to these rather unsatisfactory fits, the regressions using the rectangular and geometric weights produce 'wrong' signs for the coefficients of the bond yield and internal funds variables. Table 4.12 presents the result of three 'inverted V' regressions.

Since the dependent variable is the backlog of projects, the first equation implies that a rise of 1 billion dollars of capital requirements would increase the backlog of projects by $347 million. All the coefficients in table 4.12 are high relative to their standard errors but the presence of serial correlation does cast a shadow on these positive results. De Leeuw reports that two other explanatory variables were tried – net liquidity of manufacturing corporations – and the ratio of capital goods prices to wage rates. In both cases the

Table 4.12
De Leeuw's results for three 'inverted V' investment functions.

Total lag	b_c	b_f	b_r	DW
12 quarters	0.347 (0.035)	1.266 (0.594)	−4.892 (0.943)	0.42
10 quarters	0.326 (0.038)	0.615 (0.605)	−3.065 (0.944)	0.43
14 quarters	0.329 (0.042)	1.627 (0.699)	−7.586 (1.161)	0.33

sign of the coefficient was opposite to that expected. De Leeuw also presents a graph which shows the actual and calculated values of investment in the sample period and for 1960 and 1961, but no further analyses are carried out. On the basis of these results he concludes that data for all manufacturing for 1947–1959 are consistent with his hypothesis.

4.6.4. Lintner (1967) *U.S. manufacturing, quarterly data*, 1953–1963

Lintner, having presented a review of the theory of investment of corporate companies operating under uncertainty, comes to the conclusion (see Section 4.3.3) that financial and risk factors affect investment as well as capacity and accelerator factors. Specifically he states that leverage has a negative effect and retained funds a positive effect on investment. His statistical section is a regression analysis of this hypothesis, but since the theory is not explicit with regard to the form that the variables should take, he experiments with six capacity/accelerator variables and six leverage variables. Much of the data for the capacity variables he borrows from previous research, for instance, he uses a quarterly interpolation of Hickman's capital stock estimates, a slightly adjusted De Leeuw capacity variable and Jorgenson's output price to user cost of capital ratio. One of the interesting features of his work is that he uses the Almon weights to obtain a moving weighted average of all the explanatory variables. Because Almon's work relates to investment appropriations rather than decisions he introduces a further lag by using I_{t+1} as the dependent variable. In order to avoid the problem of collinearity between variables due to the occurrence of trends he deflates all variables not already in interest rate or ratio form by the capital stock. In his preliminary research serial correlation was evidently strong so he applies the transformation $1 - 0.9\theta$ (where θ is a lag operator) to all his variables.

Even though some of his variables are seasonally adjusted he includes seasonal dummy variables. He also includes 'time', but neither time nor the seasonal dummies contribute much more than 0.035 to R^2. The relation fitted is

$$\frac{I_{t+1}}{K_{t-1}} = \mathrm{SD} + b_1 + b_2 X_i + b_3 \frac{\mathrm{LTD} - \mathrm{RF}}{\mathrm{SP}} + b_4 r + b_5 tr(\Delta r)_{t-1} + b_6 T \tag{4.61}$$

where X_i represents the capacity/accelerator variable and SD represents seasonal dummies. The regression results for (4.61) appear in table 4.13 and for convenience we reproduce the following glossary of symbols.

Table 4.13
Regression coefficients, t-ratios, and partial correlation coefficients for interest rates and leverage, with alternative accelerator–capacity requirement variables.

Accelerator–capacity variable denoted by X_i	Constant	X_i	LTD-RF	r	$tr(\Delta r)_{t-1}$	Time	$\bar{R}^2_A$	$\bar{R}^2_B$	DW
O_t/K_{t-1}	0.011	0.1396	−0.3188	−1.7169	−10.9730	0.00001	0.827	0.955	1.71
		3.39	−5.24	−1.45	− 3.21	0.14			
		0.497	−0.663	−0.238	− 0.477	−0.024			
U_t	0.018	0.0636	−0.3853	−3.049	− 5.777	0.0002	0.720	0.955	1.64
		3.19	−5.66	−3.00	− 1.85	3.76			
		0.474	0.691	0.452	0.298	0.537			
$(CR)_t$	0.023	0.1614	−0.3019	−2.046	−10.698	0.0001	0.726	0.955	1.70
		3.34	−4.98	−1.80	− 3.14	2.01			
		0.491	−0.644	−0.291	0.469	0.322			
$J(O_t/K_{t-1})$	0.013	0.0093	−0.3196	−1.614	− 6.321	0.00013	0.656	0.935	1.41
		1.32	−4.47	−0.73	− 1.81	1.37			
		0.219	−0.603	−0.123	− 0.294	0.225			
$J(U)_t$	0.013	0.0099	−0.3079	−2.138	− 5.923	0.0002	0.651	0.935	1.38
		1.09	−4.37	−1.00	− 1.70	2.77			
		0.181	−0.595	−0.166	− 0.276	0.424			
$J(CR)_t$	0.023	0.0195	−0.2975	−2.269	−10.1674	0.0001	0.727	0.955	1.70
		3.35	−4.92	−2.06	− 3.05	2.18			
		0.492	−0.639	−0.329	− 0.458	0.346			

T = time;
I = deflated and seasonally adjusted plant and equipment outlay of manufacturing companies;
K = quarterly interpolation of Hickman's capital stock series;
O = unweighted average of the index of production over three months,
U = De Leeuw's index of utilisation of manufacturing capacity;
CR = capital requirements, $1.111\, U - 1 + d$, where d is the quarterly rate of depreciation inherent in Hickman's estimates;
J = Jorgenson's output price to user cost of capital ratio;
r = Moody's interest rate, average of monthly rates;
$tr(\Delta r)_{t-1} = 0.4(\Delta r)_{t-1} + 0.3(\Delta r)_{t-2} + 0.2(\Delta r)_{t-3} + 0.1(\Delta r)_{t-4}$;
LTD = long term debt;
RF = retained funds;
SP = market value of equity indexed by twice the Standard and Poor index of market prices of 425 industrial securities.

The regression results suggest that leverage is important in the determination of investment since, regardless of which capacity/accelerator variable is used, a significantly negative coefficient is found for the leverage variable. Two goodness of fit statistics are quoted. The first relates to the regressions actually fitted and since these are in first difference form, R_A^2 (corrected for degrees of freedom) understates the explanatory power of the regression. The other, R_B^2 (corrected for degrees of freedom), relates to the fit if these results are used to explain I_{t+1}/K_{t-1}. Although he experiments with different ways of measuring leverage these results are not significantly changed. He reports that he tried other variables reflecting relative real costs and profit margins but failed to find a significant relationship. One of his variants is to include a 'surprise' term involving expected minus actual output of the current period, which gives the equation a realization function flavour.

In this case too, the significance of the financial and risk coefficients reflect the Lintner hypothesis. Although encouraged by these results he admits that 'since the empirical work was confined to data for all manufacturing for the eleven years 1953–1963, with limited forecast periods beyond that period, the econometric results are not conclusive at this stage. Further work with individual industries, longer forecast periods, different time spans and other data will be required for that' (see Lintner, 1967, p. 250).

4.6.5. Hickman (1965) *annual U.S. industry data*, 1949–1960

We have already described Hickman's work involving aggregate data but an essential part of his study involves industry data. He uses industry investment functions to lend empirical support to his general approach and to check on the possibility that compositional changes will alter his conclusions. An example of his using the industry results to confirm his aggregate approach is his decision to restrict the output elasticity to unity. Judging by the results of the estimated investment functions for six major sectors with and without

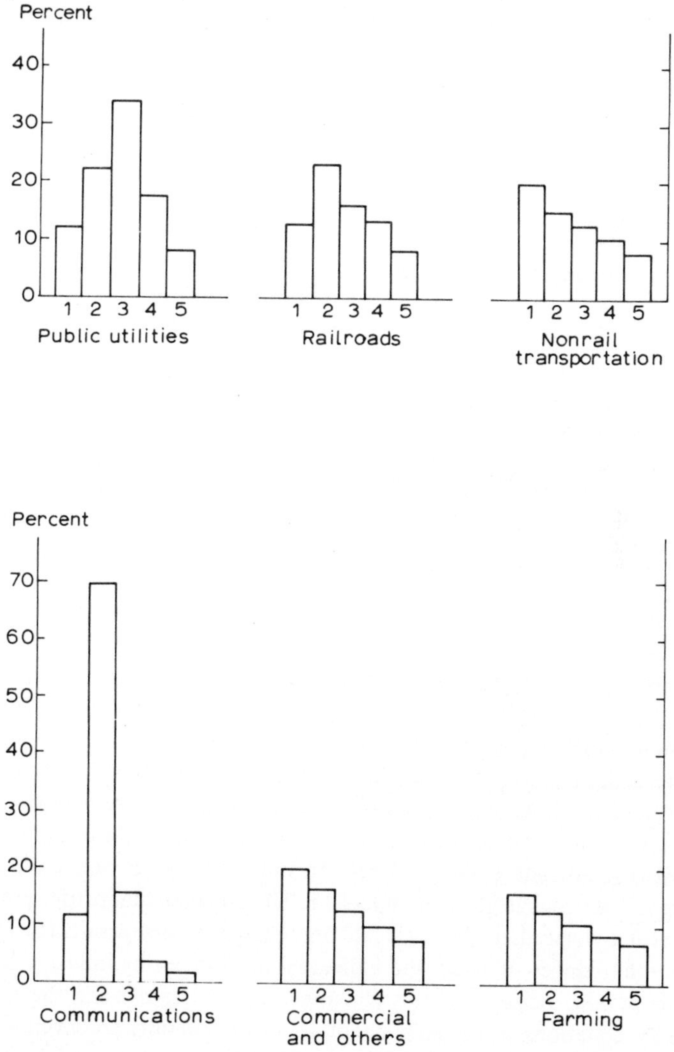

Fig. 4.7. Percentage response of investment to change in output: industries.

Table 4.14
Hickman's final set of investment regressions, all industries.

Industry or sector	Regression coefficients: Constant term	$\log K_{t-1}$	T	T^2	$\log Y_t$
All industries	0.0337	−0.2377	−0.0018		0.1236
Manufacturing	−0.0265	−0.3702	0.0007	−0.0002	0.1529
Primary metals	0.0036	−0.4790	0.0062		0.1297
Machinary	−0.0937	−0.2483	−0.0004		0.1508
Motor vehicles	−0.1029	−0.2991	0.0226	−0.0017	0.1132
Non-automotive transportation equipment	0.0293	−0.6316	−0.0214		0.2715
Stone, clay, and glass	−0.4207	−0.2512	0.0047		0.1837
Other durables	−0.1040	−0.3821	−0.0032		0.2597
Food and beverages	−0.0414	−0.3372	−0.0064		0.0029
Textiles	0.2538	−0.3687	−0.0016		0.1577
Paper	−0.0047	−0.4006	−0.0002		0.1685
Chemicals	0.1244	−0.6620	−0.0109	−0.0003	0.1317
Petroleum and coal	0.1598	−0.4142	−0.00002		0.1503
Rubber	−0.0574	−0.4427	−0.0033		0.2085
Other non-durables	0.0483	−0.3304	−0.0023		0.0816
Railroads	0.3337	−0.2473	−0.0011		0.0404
Non-rail transportation	0.1529	−0.1996	−0.0027		0.1996
Public utilities	0.5370	−0.5022	−0.0040		0.0763
Communications	0.2306	−0.7701	0.0023		0.1126
Commercial and other	0.0534	−0.2051	−0.0028	0.0001	0.2051
Farming	−0.0094	−0.1604	0.0002		0.1604

the restriction, only for 'public utility' and 'rail roads' is the restriction invalid. Restricting all industries but these two he estimates the 21 investment functions which appear in table 4.14.

The equations for the major sectors are quite good, but for the individual industries less so. As in Section 4.6.1, the price effect is very tentative, in fact, only seven equations include any price variables and, of these, only one coefficient is significant at the 5% level. An indication of the predictive accuracy of these equations is given in table 4.15. The individual industries predictions tend to be worse than the aggregate predictions. Similar results for 1962 also reflect the danger of using the individual manufacturing industry equations for prediction. Because of this Hickman refrains from using the individual industry equations in his later chapters. Further results are given in fig. 4.7 and table 4.16 (cf. Section 4.6.1).

Regression coefficients					Elasticity	R^2	DW
$\log Y_{t-1}$	$\log Y_{t-2}$	$\log P_t$	$\log P_{t-1}$	$\log P_{t-2}$			
0.1141					1	0.969	2.48
0.2173					1	0.954	2.72
0.2383	0.1110				1	0.534	0.86
0.0975					1	0.720	1.54
0.1859					1	0.868	2.28
0.0369	0.3232				1	0.876	2.74
0.0663	0.0012	−0.0703	−0.2339	−0.1367	1	0.871	2.63
0.1224					1	0.842	1.27
0.3343					1	0.924	1.62
0.1832	0.0278	0.0448	0.1222	0.0985	1	0.986	1.78
0.2321					1	0.398	1.11
0.3477	0.1826				1	0.933	2.74
0.2639					1	0.918	1.45
0.2342					1	0.738	2.13
0.2488		0.2030	0.0368		1	0.872	3.27
0.0388					0.32	0.855	1.75
		0.1547			1	0.800	2.13
0.1070	0.1631				0.69	0.843	1.22
0.6575			0.0615		1	0.941	2.72
		0.0941			1	0.812	2.89
		−0.0853			1	0.926	2.27

The variation between industries, with regard to response and fluctuation, highlights the importance of the composition of GNP. One of the main reasons for Hickman's study of individual sectors is to see what effect changing composition has had on aggregate investment. To see this he calculates what investment would have been if output in each industry had grown at the same speed. He compares this to the level of investment calculated on the basis of actual output changes. He concludes that the compositional changes that have taken place for 1949–1962 brought about $12.0 million (i.e., 13.7%) more real net investment than would have occurred if the changes had not occurred. Although we shall not report it here, Hickman also uses his sector equations to estimate indices of capacity for all industries. Other indices of capacity are available for some industries and where possible Hickman uses this outside information to support his estimates. In his later chapters Hickman is concerned

Table 4.15
Predicted and realized values of net investment, 1961 (in percent of capital stock).

Industry or sector	*P* (1)	*A* (2)	*N* (3)	*P–A* (4)	*N–A* (5)
1. All industries	1.2	1.0	1.5	0.2	0.5
2. Manufacturing	0.7	0.2	1.2	0.5	1.0
3. Primary metals	2.0	−0.4	2.8	2.4	3.2
4. Machinery	2.6	2.3	2.9	0.3	0.6
5. Motor vehicles	−4.3	−2.9	−1.3	−1.4	1.6
6. Non-automotive transportation equipment	−8.1	−2.9	−2.2	−5.2	0.7
7. Stone, clay, and glass	0.8	−0.6	2.5	1.4	3.1
8. Other durables	0.7	−0.1	1.1	0.8	1.2
9. Food and beverages	−1.7	0	−0.8	−1.7	−0.8
10. Textiles	−0.3	−0.7	0	0.4	0.7
11. Paper	4.0	1.8	3.5	2.2	1.7
12. Chemicals	1.1	1.3	1.3	−0.2	0
13. Petroleum and coal	1.7	0.6	0.7	1.1	0.1
14. Rubber	1.9	1.7	3.5	0.2	1.8
15. Other non-durables	2.1	1.7	2.0	0.4	0.3
16. Railroads	−1.2	−1.8	−1.0	0.6	0.8
17. Non-rail transportation	0	−1.3	−0.5	1.3	0.8
18. Public utilities	3.5	3.0	3.6	0.5	0.6
19. Communications	7.3	5.0	6.2	2.3	1.2
20. Commercial and other	2.2	1.9	1.9	0.3	0
21. Farming	0.7	0.5	0.3	0.2	−0.2
Root mean square					
Manufacturing				1.9	1.6
Nonmanufacturing				1.1	0.7
Total				1.7	1.4

P = predicted from regression; *N* = naive no change prediction; *A* = actual.

with projection into the future. He uses his sector results as a check on whether compositional changes are likely to disturb the conclusions reached by using his aggregate functions. The first step is to project sector output which is done by regressing each sector output on private GNP, government expenditure and time, using annual data 1947–1962 with all variables transformed into logarithms. On the assumption that both federal spending and private GNP increases at 3.8% in 1962–1963 and 5.1% in 1963–1966 he produces estimates of output and hence investment in each sector. The aggregate of these sector investment totals gives a figure for total investment which tends to be slightly higher than that derived from the aggregate equation.

Table 4.16
Estimated average amplitude of investment fluctuations under alternative assumptions as to lags (in percent).

Industry or sector	No lags	Expectational lag only	Expectational and adjustment lag	Actual investment	
				Net	Gross
	(1)	(2)	(3)	(4)	(5)
Component industries					
Manufacturing industries					
Primary metals	14.7	6.5	3.1	4.2	3.9
Machinery	11.8	8.1	1.9	2.4	2.2
Motor vehicles	18.9	12.1	3.9	4.5	4.1
Non-automotive transportation equipment	22.0	13.2	8.1	7.3	6.7
Stone, clay, glass	11.8	10.9	2.6	2.7	2.5
Other durables	6.7	4.3	1.6	1.9	1.7
Food and beverages	2.3	2.3	0.8	1.0	0.9
Textiles	4.9	3.6	1.5	1.5	1.3
Paper	6.4	4.2	1.7	2.0	1.9
Chemicals	7.4	3.5	2.3	2.4	2.2
Petroleum and coal	4.3	3.8	1.6	1.4	1.2
Rubber	8.9	5.2	2.3	2.6	2.3
Other non-durables	2.7	2.3	0.7	0.7	0.4
Railroads	2.1	1.7	0.5	0.6	0.6
Non-rail transportation	6.5	6.5	1.3	1.3	1.0
Public utilities	2.1	1.6	0.8	1.0	1.0
Communications	3.5	2.8	2.2	1.9	1.7
Commercial and other	2.8	2.8	0.6	0.6	0.6
Farming	4.1	4.1	0.6	0.6	0.6
Arithmetic mean of component industries	7.6	5.2	2.0	2.1	1.9
Standard deviation	5.7	3.4	1.7	1.6	1.5
Ratio of standard deviation to mean	0.75	0.65	0.84	0.76	0.78

However, since this excess is almost constant, Hickman's conclusion of Section 4.6.1 which depended on the trend of the investment to output ratio, is not materially affected.

4.6.6. Jorgenson (1965) *quarterly U.S. data, four main sectors*, 1952–1962 †

The major purposes of this study are to test the neoclassical theoretical

† 'Total regulated' and 'all other industries' are estimated from 1949–1962 data.

approach, to estimate time response paths, i.e., the effects over time of a change in the demand for capital, and to provide investment functions for the Brookings model. Jorgenson uses a sophisticated model based on the ideas of Sections 4.2 and 4.4 and specified in such a way that he is able to use anticipations data in its estimation. This is done by introducing a number of stages into the investment process.

It will be recalled that $\mathrm{IE}_t = \mu(\theta)\,\mathrm{IN}_t$, (see eq. (4.8)), where IE_t is the level of completions in period t. Between the initiation of projects and the actual investment expenditure he conceives intermediate stages consisting of, for example, the appropriation of funds, letting of contracts and issuing of orders. He assumes that each project must go through all stages and that transition times between stages are independent. Let IE_1 reflect projects having completed stage 1, IE_2 those completed stage 2 and IE, again, all three stages, then,

$$\mathrm{IE}_{1t} = v_1(\theta)\mathrm{IN}_t \tag{4.62}$$

$$\mathrm{IE}_{2t} = v_2(\theta)\mathrm{IE}_1 = v_2(\theta)v_1(\theta)\mathrm{IN}_t \tag{4.63}$$

$$\mathrm{IE}_t = v_3(\theta)\mathrm{IE}_2 = v_3(\theta)v_2(\theta)\mathrm{IE}_1 = v_3(\theta)v_2(\theta)v_1(\theta)\mathrm{IN}_t \tag{4.64}$$

where $v_1(\theta)$, $v_2(\theta)$, and $v_3(\theta)$ represent distributed lag functions. For instance,

$$v_1(\theta) = v_{10} + v_{11}(\theta) + v_{12}\theta^2 + \dots v_{1\tau}\theta^\tau \qquad \sum_{i=0}^{\tau} v_{1i} = 1$$

where

v_{1i} = the proportion of projects initiated in period t which completes stage 1 during period $t+i$.

Jorgenson combines this with an assumption to make replacement at any stage equal to δK_{t-1}. Thus gross investment completed at the various stages can be represented by the following six equations.

$$I_t = v_3(\theta)v_2(\theta)v_1(\theta)\left[\left(\frac{\alpha pX}{c}\right)_t - \left(\frac{\alpha pX}{c}\right)_{t-1}\right] + \delta K_{t-1} \tag{4.65}$$

$$I_{2t} = v_2(\theta)v_1(\theta)\left[\left(\frac{\alpha pX}{c}\right)_t - \left(\frac{\alpha pX}{c}\right)_{t-1}\right] + \delta K_{t-1} \tag{4.66}$$

$$I_{1t} = v_1(\theta)\left[\left(\frac{\alpha pX}{c}\right)_t - \left(\frac{\alpha pX}{c}\right)_{t-1}\right] + \delta K_{t-1} \tag{4.67}$$

$$I_t = v_3(\theta)v_2(\theta)[I_{1t} - \delta K_{t-1}] + \delta K_{t-1} \tag{4.68}$$

$$I_t = v_3(\theta)[I_{2t} - \delta K_{t-1}] + \delta K_{t-1} \tag{4.69}$$

$$I_{2t} = v_2(\theta)[I_{1t} - \delta K_{t-1}] + \delta K_{t-1}\,. \tag{4.70}$$

Before these equations can be fitted to data it is necessary to specify the form of the lags. Jorgenson uses different specifications for different sectors and industries. In Jorgenson (1965) no indication is given of how the form is chosen but elsewhere (Jorgenson and Stephenson, 1967) this is done by choosing that which has the lowest standard error for the regression. Each distributed lag is assumed to be a rational distributed lag and can be written as the ratio of two distributions. We illustrate the use of (4.65)–(4.70) for the total durables case as fitted in Jorgenson (1965). Consider (4.65), i.e.,

$$I_t = \frac{\gamma(\theta)}{w(\theta)}\left[\left(\frac{\alpha pX}{c}\right)_t - \left(\frac{\alpha pX}{c}\right)_{t-1}\right] + \delta K_{t-1}$$

where

$$\gamma(\theta) = \gamma_3\theta^3 + \gamma_4\theta^4 + \gamma_5\theta^5$$

$$w(\theta) = 1 + w_1\theta + w_2\theta^2\,.$$

Thus

$$\begin{aligned} I_t = {} & \alpha\gamma_3\left[\left(\frac{pX}{c}\right)_{t-3} - \left(\frac{pX}{c}\right)_{t-4}\right] + \alpha\gamma_4\left[\left(\frac{pX}{c}\right)_{t-4} - \left(\frac{pX}{c}\right)_{t-5}\right] \\ & + \alpha\gamma_5\left[\left(\frac{pX}{c}\right)_{t-5} - \left(\frac{pX}{c}\right)_{t-6}\right] - w_1[I_{t-1} - \delta K_{t-2}] \\ & - w_2[I_{t-2} - \delta K_{t-3}] + \delta K_{t-1}\,. \end{aligned} \tag{4.71}$$

For (4.66),

$$\gamma(\theta) = \gamma_2\theta^2 + \gamma_3\theta^3 + \gamma_4\theta^4$$

$$w(\theta) = 1 + w_1\theta + w_2\theta^2$$

and so

$$I_t = \alpha\gamma_2\left[\left(\frac{pX}{c}\right)_{t-2} - \left(\frac{pX}{c}\right)_{t-3}\right] + \alpha\gamma_3\left[\left(\frac{pX}{c}\right)_{t-3} - \left(\frac{pX}{c}\right)_{t-4}\right.$$

$$\left. + \alpha\gamma_4\left[\left(\frac{pX}{c}\right)_{t-4} - \left(\frac{pX}{c}\right)_{t-5}\right] - w_1[I_{t-1} - \delta K_{t-2}]\right.$$

$$- w_2[I_{t-2} - \delta K_{t-3}] + \delta K_{t-1}\,. \tag{4.72}$$

Notice that γ_2, γ_3 etc., are used as a convenient notation to indicate the coefficient of θ^2, θ^3, etc. and do not necessarily have the same value in (4.71) and (4.72). For (4.67),

$$\gamma(\theta) = \gamma_1\theta + \gamma_2\theta^2 + \gamma_3\theta^3$$

$$w(\theta) = 1 + w_1\theta + w_2\theta^2$$

Once these three cases are chosen the others must be consistent, thus for (4.68), $\gamma(\theta) = \gamma_2\theta^2$ and $w(\theta) = 1$; for (4.69) and (4.70) $\gamma(\theta) = \gamma_1\theta$ and $w(\theta) = 1$.

Using ordinary least squares (4.65)–(4.70) are estimated for four sectors, total durables, total non-durables, total regulated and all other industries. Since he uses the OBE-SEC Investment Survey these groups cover all business except agriculture, forestry, fishing, banking, insurance carriers, real estate, medical and legal services and non-profit organisations. The data are deflated by price indices to provide the figures of real investment used in the regressions. With the assumption of replacement investment being a fixed proportion of capital stock, one can relate terminal capital stock to that of beginning capital stock and intervening investment. Given the beginning and terminal values of capital stock and all the intervening values of investment it is possible to estimate all intervening levels of the capital stock and δ, i.e., the proportion which determines replacement investment. For the output series, data on sales and inventories were compiled from the *Survey of Current Business*, the U.S. *National Accounts and Statistics of Income* for 1947, 1953 and 1959. The most difficult measurement problem, however, arises with regard to c which Jorgenson takes to be equal to

$$q_t\left[\frac{1-u_tv_t}{1-u_t}\delta + \frac{1-u_tw_t}{1-u_t}r_t - \frac{1}{1-u_t}\frac{\Delta q}{q_t}\right]$$

where q_t is the investment deflator, r_t is the cost of capital taken to be equal to the U.S. Government long term bond rate, u is the ratio of direct taxes to profits before tax, v_t is that of capital consumption allowances to current replacement cost and w_t that of net monetary interest to the cost of total capital. Investment anticipations one quarter hence and two quarters hence are used to measure I_{2t} and I_{1t}. The result of the regressions for total durables are given in table 4.17.

The calculation of K produced an estimate of δ of 0.0279. Jorgenson claims that the regression estimate of δ reinforces this value and he performs statistical tests of the hypothesis $\delta = 0.0279$. Unfortunately Griliches (1968) has shown that this test has very low power in discriminating between alternative hypotheses about δ. Jorgenson, however, strong in his belief as to the value of δ, derives regression estimates of his equations with δ restricted by using $[I_t - \delta K_{t-1}]$ as the dependent variable. These results appear in table 4.18.

Jorgenson suggests that the models should be compared to certain 'naive' and 'forecasting' models from the point of view of the goodness of fit. The naive models corresponding to (4.65), (4.66) and (4.67) are

$$I_t = I_{t-1}, \quad I_{2t} = I_{2t-1}, \quad I_{1t} = I_{1t-1}$$

and those for (4.68), (4.69) and (4.70) which he calls forecasting models are

$$I_t = I_{1t-2}, \quad I_t = I_{2t-1} \quad \text{and} \quad I_{2t} = I_{1t} .$$

From table 4.18 the naive and forecasting models are clearly inferior with regard to goodness of fit. Another interesting conclusion from table 4.18 is that eq. (4.70) tends to be better than (4.66), and (4.69) better than (4.68) which in turn tends to be better than (4.65).

The main test of the theory of investment expansion is to compare the lag function estimated from the alternative data. The average lag can be derived for each distribution used. If we assume that the average lag between different stages is one quarter then it is possible to calculate from say the coefficients of (4.65), (4.66) and (4.67) three different estimates of the average lag between the demand for capital and investment expenditure. The average lag for a distribution can be derived as follows. Since

$$\mu(\theta) = \mu_0 + \mu_1\theta + \mu_2\theta^2 + \ldots \tag{4.73}$$

Table 4.17
Unrestricted estimates of regression coefficients.

Equation	$\alpha\gamma_1$	$\alpha\gamma_2$	$\alpha\gamma_3$	$\alpha\gamma_4$	$\alpha\gamma_5$	ω_1	ω_2	δ
				Total durables				
(4.65)			0.00088 (0.00035)	0.00077 (0.00036)	0.00038 (0.00039)	−1.26794 (0.14017)	0.44979 (0.13324)	0.02266 (0.00281)
(4.66)		0.00148 (0.00044)	0.00072 (0.00049)	0.00064 (0.00049)		−1.10844 (0.15188)	0.27190 (0.14608)	0.02685 (0.00363)
(4.67)	0.00099 (0.00040)	0.00079 (0.00043)	0.00054 (0.00040)			−1.24220 (0.14205)	0.39380 (0.13868)	0.02561 (0.00309)
(4.68)		0.80639 (0.04061)						0.01751 (0.00265)
(4.69)	0.84615 (0.03286)							0.01921 (0.00211)
(4.70)	0.95014 (0.03780)							0.02583 (0.00236)

$$\frac{\partial\mu(\theta)}{\partial\theta} = \theta\mu_1 + 2\mu_2\theta + 3\mu_3\theta^2 + \dots . \qquad (4.74)$$

Putting $\theta = 1$ in (4.74) gives the average lag. For total durables, the lag distribution of (4.65) is

$$\mu(\theta) = \frac{\gamma_3\theta^3 + \gamma_4\theta^4 + \gamma_5\theta^5}{1 + w_1\theta + w_2\theta^2}$$

since $\mu(1) = 1$

$$\gamma_3 + \gamma_4 + \gamma_5 = 1 + w_1 + w_2$$

$$= 1 - 1.29501 + 0.42764 = 0.13261$$

$$\alpha(\gamma_3 + \gamma_4 + \gamma_5) = 0.00210$$

$$\therefore \quad \alpha = 0.0158$$

$$\alpha\gamma_3 = 0.00096 \qquad \therefore \quad \gamma_3 = 0.0606$$

$$\alpha\gamma_4 = 0.00080 \qquad \therefore \quad \gamma_4 = 0.0505$$

$$\alpha\gamma_5 = 0.00034 \qquad \therefore \quad \gamma_5 = 0.0215$$

But

$$\frac{\partial\mu(\theta)}{\partial\theta} = \frac{3\gamma_3\theta^2 + 4\gamma_4\theta^3 + 5\gamma_5\theta^4}{1 + w_1\theta + w_2\theta^2} - \frac{(\gamma_2\theta^2 + \gamma_4\theta^4 + \gamma_5\theta^5)(w_1 + 2w_2\theta)}{(1 + w_1\theta + w_2\theta^2)^2}$$

$$\therefore \text{ av. lag} = \frac{3\gamma_3 + 4\gamma_4 + 5\gamma_6 - w_1 - 2w_2}{1 + w_1 + w_2}$$

$$= 7.02 .$$

For (4.66), total durables,

$$\gamma(\theta) = \gamma_2\theta^2 + \gamma_3\theta^3 + \gamma + \gamma_4\theta^4$$

$$w(\theta) = 1 + w_1\theta + w_2\theta^2$$

Table 4.18a
Results of restricted regression for total durables.

Equation	$\alpha\gamma_1$	$\alpha\gamma_2$	$\alpha\gamma_3$	$\alpha\gamma_4$	$\alpha\gamma_5$
(4.65)			0.00096	0.00080	0.00034
			(0.00036)	(0.00037)	(0.00040)
(4.66)		0.00151	0.00073	0.00065	
		(0.00042)	(0.00048)	(0.00048)	
(6.67)	0.00107	0.00060	0.00083		
	(0.00038)	(0.00038)	(0.00042)		
(4.68)		0.87721			
		(0.04209)			
(4.69)	0.90892				
	(0.03419)				
(4.70)	0.96437				
	(0.03391)				

Table 4.18b
Results of restricted regression for total non-durables.

	$\alpha\gamma_1$	$\alpha\gamma_2$	$\alpha\gamma_4$	$\alpha\gamma_5$	$\alpha\gamma_6$
(4.65)					0.00009
					(0.00033)
(4.66)				0.00046	
				(0.00031)	
(4.67)			0.00059		
			(0.00030)		
(4.68)		0.90064			
		(0.06159)			
(4.69)	0.93389				
	(0.04883)				
(4.70)	0.96100				
	(0.04441)				

w_1	w_2	Fitted model, restricted estimates $\bar{R}^2$	VN	Naive and forecasting models $\bar{R}^2$	VN
−1.29501 (0.14392)	0.42764 (0.13700)	0.94004 (0.91324)†	2.03829	0.78424	0.79207
−1.10756 (0.14993)	0.26338 (0.14128)	0.90740 (0.88374)	2.06095	0.75927	1.46256
−1.22784 (0.14001)	0.36394 (0.13200)	0.93133 (0.91546)	2.07754	0.79411	0.80835
		0.91183 (0.87243)	1.51790	0.23602	0.34349
		0.94391 (0.91183)	1.64228	0.37922	0.23286
		0.95062 (0.93799)	1.51000	0.78712	0.62739

w_1	w_2	$\bar{R}^2$	VN	$\bar{R}^2$	VN
−1.19735 (0.14940)	0.33170 (0.14799)	0.83970 (0.76686)	2.22230	0.71972	1.48236
−1.17952 (0.14695)	0.31465 (0.14586)	0.84818 (0.79167)	2.23447	0.73696	1.46801
−1.26339 (0.13848)	0.39227 (0.13656)	0.86424 (0.80597)	2.21971	0.73688	1.28823
		0.83584 (0.76125)	1.66458	0.38069	0.52702
		0.89698 (0.85017)	1.68629	0.16775	0.33628
		0.91768 (0.88704)	1.67710	0.73312	0.45940

† The dependent variable in the restricted regressions differs from that in the other regressions. In parentheses is an $\bar{R}^2$ value for this latter variable.

Table 4.18c
Results of restricted regression for total regulated.

Equation	$\alpha\gamma_1$	$\alpha\gamma_2$	$\alpha\gamma_3$	$\alpha\gamma_4$	$\alpha\gamma_5$	$\alpha\gamma_6$
(4.65)					0.00197 (0.00135)	0.00111 (0.00133)
(4.66)				0.00336 (0.00160)	0.00143 (0.00160)	0.00303 (0.00161)
(4.67)			0.00039 (0.00160)	0.00364 (0.00154)	0.00284 (0.00164)	
(4.68)		0.76935 (0.05969)				
(4.69)	0.83488 (0.06563)					
(4.70)	0.81282 (0.05946)					

Table 4.18d
Results of restricted regression for all other.

	$\alpha\gamma_1$	$\alpha\gamma_2$	$\alpha\gamma_3$	$\alpha\gamma_4$
(4.65)			0.00033 (0.00014)	0.00021 (0.00013)
(4.66)		0.00009 (0.00015)	0.00031 (0.00015)	
(4.67)	0.00033 (0.00016)	0.00023 (0.00016)		
(4.68)		0.68239 (0.06539)		
(4.69)	0.84426 (0.05254)			
(4.70)	0.77698 (0.06003)			

$\alpha\gamma_7$	w_1	w_2	Fitted model, restricted estimates $\bar{R}^2$	VN	Naive and forecasting models $\bar{R}^2$	VN
0.00118 (0.00134)	−1.00559 (0.13705)	0.27369 (0.13744)	0.69146 (0.83927)	2.02793	0.78530	1.58328
	−0.80923 (0.13406)	0.16287 (0.16287)	0.59149 (0.82308)	2.00217	0.75879	1.77829
	−0.86350 (0.13681)	0.14602 (0.13633)	0.66295 (0.82818)	1.9919	0.76424	1.81106
			0.75470 (0.87221)	1.72970	0.39813	0.72282
			0.74982 (0.86967)	1.74220	0.22932	0.35676
			0.77584 (0.90292)	1.73736	0.76973	0.87809

w_1	$\bar{R}^2$	VN	$\bar{R}^2$	VN
0.84109 (0.06137)	0.79045 (0.78094)	1.89495	0.72043	1.56218
0.85596 (0.06748)	0.75737 (0.74912)	1.89142	0.69910	1.92741
0.85413 (0.06717)	0.75923 (0.92082)	1.84890	0.66074	1.64256
	0.66855 (0.65350)	1.66517	0.59215	0.79450
	0.82703 (0.81918)	1.70611	0.84901	1.40133
	0.75626 (0.74797)	1.66049	0.83238	0.92488

$$\gamma_2 + \gamma_3 + \gamma_4 = 1 + w_1 + w_2$$

$$= 1 - 1.10756 + 0.26338 = 0.1558$$

$$\alpha(\gamma_2 + \gamma_3 + \gamma_4) = 0.00289$$

$$\alpha = 0.0186$$

$$\therefore \ \gamma_2 = 0.0814 \qquad \gamma_3 = 0.0394 \qquad \gamma_4 = 0.0351$$

$$\text{av. lag} = \frac{2\gamma_2 + 3\gamma_3 + 4\gamma_4 - w_1 - 2w_2}{1 + w_1 + w_2}$$

$$= 6.43 \, .$$

When a quarter is added to this it can be closely compared with that derived from (4.65). Another estimate can be derived from (4.67). Table 4.19 shows that the alternative estimates of the average lags are quite close to each other. A more precise comparison of the distributed lags can be achieved by actually calculating these from the alternative equations. For total durables the following alternative estimates can be obtained

$$\alpha v_3(\theta) v_2(\theta) v_1(\theta) = \frac{0.000960\theta^3 + 0.000800\theta^4 + 0.000340\theta^5}{1 - 1.295010\theta + 0.427640\theta^2}$$

$$v_3(\theta) \alpha v_2(\theta) v_1(\theta) = \frac{0.001370\theta^3 + 0.000600\theta^4 + 0.000590\theta^5}{1 - 1.107560\theta + 0.263380\theta^2}$$

$$v_3(\theta) v_2(\theta) \alpha v_1(\theta) = \frac{0.000940\theta^3 + 0.000530\theta^4 + 0.000730\theta^5}{1 - 1.227840\theta + 0.363940\theta^2} \, .$$

Table 4.19

Average lag between changes in demand for capital and actual investment expenditure.

	(4.65)	(4.66)	(4.67)
Total durables	7.02	7.43	6.58
Total non-durables	9.97	10.07	9.72
Total regulated	7.52	8.11	8.39
All others	8.68	9.72	9.27

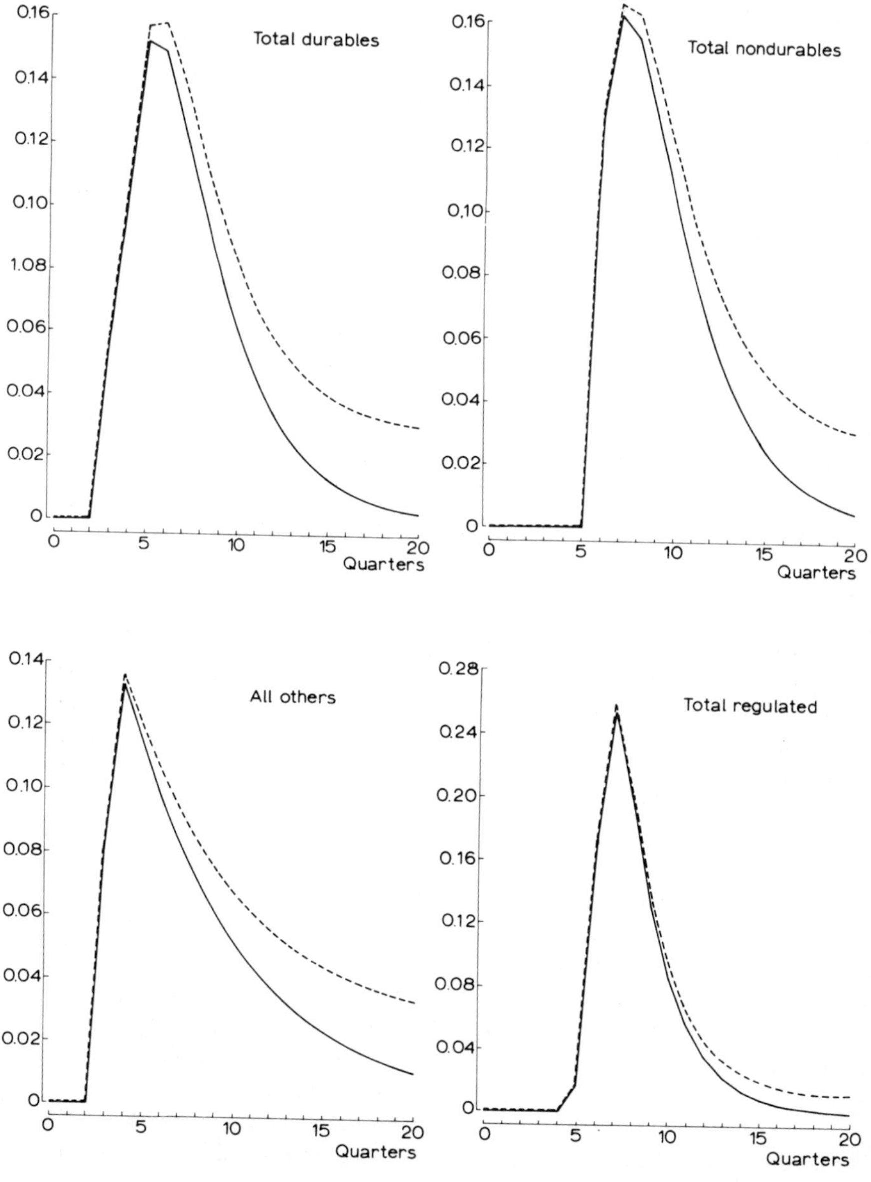

Fig. 4.8. Distributed lags and response paths for Jorgenson's four aggregates. Ordinate: investment as a proportion of the desired stock of capital, coefficients of $v_3(\theta)$ $v_2(\theta)$ $v_1(\theta)$. ———, distributed lag; – – –, time response path.

Jorgenson's theory is strongly supported by these results from which he goes on to calculate the response paths to a once and for all unit change in the desired capital stock. In fig. 4.8 we graph these paths for the four sectors and also the lag distributions. The lag distributions only take account of the investment for expansion and of course this tails off gradually, whereas the lagged response paths reflect the importance of replacement investment which eventually settles down to the value of δ. These time paths have been derived from regression estimates and, therefore, are themselves estimates. Griliches (1967a) has pointed out some difficulties concerned with such estimates. However, Jorgenson's estimates do bring out clearly the importance of taking account of the lags when discussing policies and the role of replacement. In the later section of his study he considers the reaction of investment to changes in certain policy instruments. These are all embedded in his variable c_t as is the rate of interest. Because of this it is not possible to isolate statistically the separate explanatory significance of each of these variables. Resek (1966) on the other hand, has followed an approach similar to Lintner's, i.e., fixing the distributed lags a priori (or rather accepting Almon's (1965) lags) and separating the effects of the rate of interest and liquidity position from that of output.

4.6.7. Resek (1966) *quarterly U.S. industries*, 1953–1962

This study aims to discover whether prices, the rate of interest, the cost of capital and the volume of unfilled orders have any effect on investment. Almon's (1965) lags are used in order to concentrate on the explanatory variables. Resek attempts to take account of the non-linearity of the cost of funds schedule by including in his investment function the inverse of $M-(D-F)/A$, where $D-F$ is debt at the beginning of the period minus retained earnings; A is the level of assets, which is taken as a measure of ability to bear debts; and M is a constant always larger than D/A. For the relative price variables he tries price of output, p, divided by $p_k^*(d+r)$ which is a simplified form of Jorgenson's c; and the wage rate, w, divided by $p_k^*(d+r)$. All of these variables are standard but one new element of this study is an attempt to take account of the fact that occasionally the capital goods industries will not be able to supply the goods ordered. These supply difficulties are likely to arise when the level of unfilled orders is high, which leads Resek to experiment with its inclusion in his investment function.

The data used for industry capital expenditures and capital stock are based on the same definition as Jorgenson's. The financial variables are taken from the FTC-SEC Quarterly Financial Report and are similar to those of Anderson. Output is the Federal Reserve Board's index of industrial production. The rate of interest is Moody's industrial and the earning–price ratio is Stan-

Table 4.20
Elasticities and t ratios of regression coefficients, for the following investment function for U.S. industries.

$$\frac{I}{K} = a_1 + a_2Q_2 + a_3Q_3 + a_4Q_4 + b_1\frac{O}{K} + b_2\frac{(\Delta O)}{K} + b_3r + b_4\left(\frac{1}{M-(D-F)/A}\right).$$

		b_1	b_2	b_3	b_4
Food	Elasticity	−0.34	3.24	0.13	0.18
	t	0.25	1.95	0.32	0.11
Textiles	Elasticity	4.30	−0.98	−1.86	−1.06
	t	5.55	1.89	3.41	2.93
Paper	Elasticity	−0.83	5.92	−0.64	−0.42
	t	0.89	7.83	3.35	2.22
Chemicals	Elasticity	1.50	1.68	−1.37	−2.82
	t	4.02	2.56	4.70	9.06
Petroleum	Elasticity	1.81	0.14	−1.31	−0.60
	t	3.64	0.22	−9.31	−1.91
Rubber	Elasticity	1.72	1.52	−1.30	−1.20
	t	1.74	2.05	2.58	2.57
Stone, clay and glass	Elasticity	−1.33	3.69	−1.97	0.71
	t	2.47	7.43	7.03	3.59
Iron and steel	Elasticity	0.56	0.94	0.06	−0.15
	t	0.52	1.39	0.12	0.54
Non-ferrous metals	Elasticity	8.14	−2.02	−1.07	13.73
	t	3.02	0.82	3.75	3.14
Non-electrical machinery	Elasticity	2.05	1.64	−0.50	−1.00
	t	4.27	6.46	2.46	3.05
Electrical machinery	Elasticity	−0.94	2.32	0.10	−0.38
	t	1.15	5.16	0.61	1.87
Motor vehicles	Elasticity	2.30	1.13	−3.02	0.41
	t	6.01	5.10	10.71	2.62
Other transportation	Elasticity	−1.05	−1.04	−1.99	0.04
	t	2.34	3.76	4.37	0.43
All manufacturing	Elasticity	0.81	1.73	−0.96	0.46
	t	1.10	3.14	−5.60	1.79

Table 4.21

Elasticities and t ratios of regression coefficients, for the following investment function for U.S. industries.

$$\frac{I}{K} = a_1 + a_2Q_2 + a_3Q_3 + a_4Q_4 + b_1\frac{O}{K} + b_3r + b_4\left(\frac{1}{M - (D-F)/A}\right) + b_5\mathrm{SP}\,.$$

		b_1	b_3	b_4	b_5
Food	Elasticity	0.34	−0.13	− 3.04	0.42
	t	0.33	−0.47	− 2.11	4.56
Textiles	Elasticity	1.03	−0.55	0.46	1.00
	t	2.55	−2.25	1.42	7.00
Paper	Elasticity	1.65	−2.27	− 0.39	0.81
	t	1.91	−5.70	− 1.80	6.53
Chemicals	Elasticity	1.47	−1.67	− 3.41	0.38
	t	4.54	−7.42	−12.32	3.41
Petroleum	Elasticity	1.84	−1.27	− 0.68	−0.05
	t	4.70	−7.49	− 1.95	−0.45
Rubber	Elasticity	1.57	−2.90	− 1.58	0.72
	t	0.95	−3.77	− 3.33	1.19
Stone, clay and glass	Elasticity	1.28	−3.20	0.68	1.26
	t	1.61	−6.65	2.82	5.22
Iron and steel	Elasticity	−0.06	−3.67	0.13	1.28
	t	−0.13	−5.37	0.81	6.61
Non-ferrous metals	Elasticity	3.51	−0.29	− 2.26	2.00
	t	2.99	−1.18	− 0.65	5.21
Non-electrical machinery	Elasticity	0.89	−2.67	− 0.12	1.11
	t	2.88	−9.02	0.52	10.41
Electrical machinery	Elasticity	1.95	−0.34	− 1.05	0.33
	t	2.90	−1.17	− 3.89	2.23
Motor vehicles	Elasticity	3.01	−3.05	0.36	0.02
	t	6.15	−6.17	1.80	0.10
Other transportation	Elasticity	−0.07	−2.90	0.32	0.81
	t	−0.22	−8.66	3.79	8.51
Manufacturing	Elasticity	2.32	−1.32	− 0.41	0.47
	t	7.44	−8.06	− 2.36	5.52

Table 4.22
Elasticities and t ratios of regression coefficients, for the following investment function for U.S. industries.

$$\frac{I}{K} = a_1 + a_2Q_2 + a_3Q_3 + a_4Q_4 + b_2\frac{\Delta O}{K} + b_3r + b_4\left(\frac{1}{M-(D-F)/A}\right) + b_5\text{SP}\,.$$

		b_2	b_3	b_4	b_5
Food	Elasticity	2.77	0.09	−3.50	0.41
	t	2.49	0.56	−3.73	4.92
Textiles	Elasticity	0.066	− 0.05	0.82	1.24
	t	0.26	− 0.27	2.62	9.35
Paper	Elasticity	3.84	− 1.80	−0.56	0.54
	t	9.06	− 9.33	−4.67	7.21
Chemicals	Elasticity	1.82	− 0.62	−3.00	0.41
	t	1.90	− 3.20	−6.78	2.21
Petroleum	Elasticity	1.67	− 0.76	−0.53	−0.18
	t	3.00	− 4.83	−1.34	−1.58
Rubber	Elasticity	1.71	− 2.14	−1.32	0.71
	t	2.63	− 3.12	−2.95	2.50
Stone, clay and glass	Elasticity	2.72	− 2.33	0.76	0.45
	t	4.03	− 5.17	3.80	2.02
Iron and steel	Elasticity	0.24	− 3.34	0.10	1.18
	t	0.83	− 6.21	0.59	6.44
Non-ferrous metals	Elasticity	2.82	− 3.97	−0.11	2.28
	t	2.80	− 3.98	−0.24	6.36
Non-electrical machinery	Elasticity	0.74	− 2.39	−0.10	0.89
	t	5.86	−11.22	−0.77	11.20
Electrical machinery	Elasticity	1.82	− 0.48	−0.73	0.37
	t	7.57	− 2.44	−3.78	3.80
Motor vehicles	Elasticity	1.72	− 1.29	−0.20	−0.41
	t	5.96	− 3.45	−1.42	−2.08
Other transportation	Elasticity	−0.38	− 2.92	0.32	0.74
	t	1.97	− 9.50	4.31	7.93
Manufacturing	Elasticity	1.82	− 1.38	0.23	0.38
	t	7.47	− 8.46	1.17	4.21

dard and Poor's end of quarter series. These data are available for thirteen industries from 1948 to 1962 but because of the Korean war Resek decides to exclude the first five years. With these data from thirteen industries Resek finds that neither prices nor unfilled orders consistently have the 'correct' sign and presents only the results of equations excluding these variables. The author uses three equation forms, which always include the rate of interest, and dent to assets ratio, but which, in any one equation, include only two of the following – output, change in output and the industry's stock price index. The latter variables are used to reflect the demand side of investment. He also deflates by K in a manner similar to Lintner. His results which appear in tables 4.20, 4.21, 4.22 and 4.23 support the view that careful attention should be paid to the finance variables. The significance of the stock price variable is a justification for our considering the study of Grunfeld (1960) which first suggested this variable. A further reason is that his study is based on firm data. However, before doing this we shall continue with industry studies since Jorgenson's model has been applied to industry data too.

4.6.8. Jorgenson and Stephenson (1967) *U.S. sixteen industries, quarterly, 1949(i)–1960(iv)*

This article subjects the Jorgenson approach outlined in Section 4.6.6 to the more rigorous test of satisfying industry data although the sophisticated use of anticipation data is not repeated. There are one or two changes from the previous article besides the data. Firstly the authors assume that capital gains are considered transitory and thus the implicit rental of capital, c, is defined, as

$$c = q\left[\frac{1-uw}{1-u}\,\delta + \frac{1-uw}{1-u}\,r\right].$$

Secondly the estimated coefficients of the lag distribution $\mu(\theta)$ satisfy certain constraints on the values of w_i and γ_i. These constraints have been specified fully in Jorgenson (1966) but in this context boil down to

$$-4w_2 \geqslant w_1^2 \tag{4.75}$$

and, the leading coefficient of

$$\gamma(\theta) > 0\,. \tag{4.76}$$

The distributed lag functions are chosen to fit (4.76) but not (4.75). When

Table 4.23
Goodness of fit statistics for the three functions in tables 4.20–4.22.

	Table 4.20		Table 4.21		Table 4.22	
	$\bar{R}^2$	DW	$\bar{R}^2$	DW	$\bar{R}^2$	DW
Food	0.240	0.60	0.484	1.01	0.567	1.25
Textiles	0.721	0.42	0.878	0.71	0.853	0.57
Paper	0.810	0.54	0.763	0.45	0.926	1.20
Chemicals	0.870	1.20	0.885	1.25	0.830	0.94
Petroleum	0.841	1.07	0.843	1.08	0.792	0.88
Rubber	0.619	0.96	0.588	0.83	0.651	1.00
Stone, clay and glass	0.756	1.23	0.641	0.76	0.742	1.11
Iron and steel	0.301	0.47	0.686	0.65	0.693	0.66
Non-ferrous metals	0.479	0.28	0.712	0.38	0.704	0.40
Non-electrical machinery	0.679	0.71	0.831	0.81	0.897	1.37
Electrical machinery	0.856	0.98	0.773	0.59	0.897	1.26
Motor vehicles	0.910	1.38	0.837	0.85	0.832	0.89
Other transportation	0.395	0.34	0.732	0.54	0.761	0.60
Manufacturing	0.818	0.55	0.889	0.67	0.889	0.76

the OLS estimates do not satisfy (4.75) the authors take the OLS value of w_1, calculate $w_2 = \frac{1}{4} - w_1^2$, and re-estimate with w_1 and w_2 fixed at these values. Where this process has been necessary is indicated by an asterisk in table 4.24. In Section 4.6.6 very little indication was given as to how the lags were chosen. In this article $w(\theta)$ is always of the form $1 + w_1\theta + w_2\theta^2$, then $\gamma(\theta)$ is chosen to minimise the standard error of estimate of the regression, given that (4.76) is satisfied. Another difference is that a constant term is allowed in the regressions which the authors interpret as the sample mean of the error in the equation. The results appear in table 4.24. In addition to providing these results the authors carry out tests for aggregation error. An aggregate equation implies that all industries investment functions have the same parameters, and their aggregation test is akin to Chow's test for the equality between set of coefficients (see Chow, 1968). They conclude that substantial aggregation errors occur when aggregates are used.

Unfortunately, their results indicate far too low a value for α, which it will be recalled is the exponent of K in the Cobb–Douglas production function. This leads the authors to doubt that production function coefficients can usefully be estimated in this way. It also indicates a weakness in their argument. Indeed Eisner and Nadiri (1968) have been led to question the whole basis of Jorgenson's thesis, i.e., the importance of relative prices.

Table 4.24
Quarterly investment functions U.S. industries.

$$I = \alpha\gamma(\theta)\left[\left(\frac{pX}{c}\right)_t - \left(\frac{pX}{c}\right)_{t-1}\right] + [1 - w(\theta)]\ [I_t - \delta K_{t-1}] + \delta K_{t-1} + \beta.$$

Industry	$\alpha\gamma_2$	$\alpha\gamma_3$	$\alpha\gamma_4$	$\alpha\gamma_5$	$\alpha\gamma_6$
Total manufacturing *			0.00305 (0.00077)	0.00153 (0.00076)	0.00190 (0.00070)
Total durables *			0.00095 (0.00073)	0.00070 (0.00073)	−0.00003 (0.00073)
Primary iron and steel				0.00372 (0.00119)	0.00221 (0.00179)
Primary non-ferrous metal *			0.00197 (0.00086)	0.00242 (0.00085)	0.00117 (0.00086)
Electrical machinery and equipment		0.00150 (0.00049)	0.00133 (0.00068)	0.00254 (0.00066)	0.00091 (0.00067)
Machinery, except electrical *		0.00138 (0.00062)	0.00011 (0.00068)	0.00160 (0.00070)	0.00033 (0.00073)
Motor vehicles and equipment		0.00160 (0.00113)	0.00316 (0.00136)	0.00279 (0.00139)	0.00189 (0.00115)
Transportation equipment excluding motor vehicles		0.00043 (0.00075)	0.00083 (0.00084)	−0.00032 (0.00087)	0.00087 (0.00087)
Stone, clay, and glass			0.00191 (0.00130)	0.00153 (0.00138)	0.00285 (0.00141)
Other durables *		0.00198 (0.00066)	0.00110 (0.00067)	−0.00011 (0.00070)	0.00136 (0.00070)
Total non-durables			0.00490 (0.00109)	0.00350 (0.00125)	0.00473 (0.00119)
Food and beverages			0.00028 (0.00073)	0.00129 (0.00076)	0.00000 (0.00082)
Textile mill products	0.00064 (0.00080)	0.00163 (0.00073)	0.00227 (0.00075)	0.00157 (0.00077)	
Paper and allied products		0.00165 (0.00081)	0.00312 (0.00134)	0.00255 (0.00167)	0.00211 (0.00155)
Chemical and allied products			0.00473 (0.00195)	0.00535 (0.00209)	0.00360 (0.00220)
Petroleum and coal products		0.02361 (0.00566)	0.02599 (0.00613)	0.01476 (0.00589)	0.01945 (0.00581)
Other non-durables *			0.00170 (0.00056)	0.00225 (0.00074)	0.00192 (0.00078)
			0.00084 (0.00052)	0.00073 (0.00052)	0.00053 (0.00056)

* Regression fitted with constraint.

$\alpha_{\gamma 7}$	ω_1	ω_2	δ	R^2	$S_{Y/X}$	DW
0.00270	−1.20525	0.36316	0.02084	0.96440	0.0915	1.9597
(0.00080)			(0.00178)			
0.00190	−1.42078	0.50465	0.02467	0.96430	0.0607	1.8748
(0.00193)			(0.00193)			
0.00265	−1.14061	0.30577	0.02170	0.85459	0.0327	2.2149
(0.00173)	(0.13929)	(0.13826)	(0.00634)			
	−1.34704	0.45362	0.00899	0.92632	0.0117	2.2760
			(0.00263)			
	−0.94305	0.17353	0.02591	0.91376	0.0076	1.9564
	(0.15902)	(0.14352)	(0.00310)			
	−1.17925	0.34765	0.03004	0.91967	0.0145	2.0502
			(0.00355)			
	−1.08317	0.19562	0.02622	0.90243	0.0296	2.0485
	(0.15442)	(0.15108)	(0.00429)			
	−1.17997	0.29782	0.03286	0.91863	0.0087	2.1081
	(0.15025)	(0.15974)	(0.00514)			
0.00292	−0.99115	0.24091	0.01583	0.85351	0.0118	2.2165
(0.00135)	(0.15386)	(0.14755)	(0.00313)			
	−0.90034	0.20265	0.02327	0.81336	0.0204	2.2219
			(0.00377)			
0.00337	−0.90959	0.08334	0.01192	0.90680	0.0550	2.1545
(0.00122)	(0.14323)	(0.13063)	(0.00331)			
0.00082	−0.73700	−0.02220	−0.00454	0.81078	0.0136	1.9917
(0.00073)	(0.15585)	(0.14573)	(0.01701)			
	−0.67278	−0.12027	0.03104	0.86022	0.0106	1.8911
	(0.16125)	(0.15566)	(0.00606)			
	−1.02962	0.16117	0.01857	0.94607	0.0080	2.1913
	(0.16444)	(0.16279)	(0.00343)			
0.00414	−1.00300	0.12911	0.01821	0.89297	0.0213	1.9677
(0.00211)	(0.14783)	(0.14827)	(0.00354)			
	−0.43799	−0.23425	0.01534	0.87697	0.0381	1.9521
	(0.13550)	(0.12397)	(0.00343)			
0.00085	−0.55106	−0.12307	0.00809	0.77128	0.0041	2.0019
(0.00061)	(0.16045)	(0.14833)	(0.00557)			
0.00002	−0.71888	0.12919	−0.06523	0.45361	0.0106	1.9810
(0.00055)			(0.06810)			

4.6.9. Eisner and Nadiri's *criticism of Jorgenson's thesis: a digression*

Jorgenson's assumption of a Cobb–Douglas production function necessarily implies that the optimal capital stock is directly related to relative prices and output in the following way

$$K^* = \frac{\alpha p X}{c}$$

i.e.,

$$\log K^* = \log \alpha + \log \frac{p}{c} + \log X \tag{4.77}$$

which means that the elasticity of capital with respect to both output and prices is unity. Thus the influence of relative prices enters by assumption. Eisner and Nadiri (1968) suggest the use of a CES production function (see Section 6.2.3), i.e.,

$$X = \gamma[\delta K^{-\rho} + (1-\delta)L^{-\rho}]^{-\mu/\rho}\,. \tag{4.78}$$

In this case the marginal productivity conditions lead to

$$K^* = b\left(\frac{p}{c}\right)^{1/(1+\rho)} X^{(\mu+\rho)/\mu(1+\rho)} \tag{4.79}$$

i.e.,

$$\log K^* = \log b + \frac{1}{1+\rho}\log \frac{p}{c} + \frac{\mu+\rho}{\tilde{\mu}(1+\rho)}\log X \tag{4.80}$$

and the elasticities of output and relative prices are different. If the production function has constant returns to scale, $\mu = 1$ and therefore the elasticity with respect to output is unity. The elasticity with respect to prices is equal to $1/(1+\rho)$ which is the elasticity of substitution (see Section 6.2.3). Jorgenson uses an arithmetic adjustment process, i.e.,

$$\Delta K = \mu(\theta)\Delta(K_t^* - K_{t-1}^*) \tag{4.81}$$

whereas Eisner and Nadiri use a geometric process† namely

$$\Delta \log K = \mu(\theta)\Delta \log K^*\,. \tag{4.82}$$

† See Section 4.6.1 especially (4.43)–(4.47) for a similar formulation.

This results in the following estimating form

$$\Delta \log K_t = \sum_{i=m}^{n} \left[\gamma_{pi} \Delta \log \left(\frac{p}{c}\right)_{t-i} + \gamma_{qi} \Delta \log X_{t-i} \right] + \sum_{j=1}^{s} w_j \Delta \log K_{t-i} + u_t \tag{4.8.2}$$

where

$\dfrac{\sum_{i=m}^{n} \gamma_{pi}}{1 - \sum_{j=1}^{s} w_j}$ is the elasticity with respect to prices;

$\dfrac{\sum_{i=m}^{n} \gamma_{qi}}{1 - \sum_{j=1}^{s} w_j}$ is the elasticity with respect to output;

m, n and s determine the length of the distributed lag.

Using Jorgenson and Stephenson's data for total U.S. manufacturing and experimenting with the length of the distributed lags, i.e. m, n and s, they produce the results reported in table 4.25.

Eisner and Nadiri conclude that not only is there little evidence to support the belief of unitary elasticity with regard to relative prices, but also that Jorgenson and Stephenson's time paths are not beyond question. Unitary elasticity with regard to output does seem to be consistent with the data though.

Jorgenson and Stephenson (1969) reply that the evidence for unitary elasticity of substitution from empirical production function studies is such that their assumption is reasonable. Bischoff (1969) takes issue with Eisner and Nadiri over their stochastic specification, and assuming serial correlation of the disturbance term reverses Eisner and Nadiri conclusions.

Instead of (4.82) Bischoff proposes

Table 4.25
Ordinary least squares estimates of the elasticity of investment with respect to relative price and output for different distributed lags.

n	m	s	Standard error of estimate	Price elasticity E_p	Output elasticity E_q
7	1	2	0.0012191	0.1470	0.6889
7	1	1	0.0012162	0.1576	0.8158
7	1†	2	0.0012073	0.1306	0.5873
7	2	2	0.0012791	0.1562	0.3444
7	3	2	0.0013415	0.1176	0.1539
7	4	1	0.0016711	0.1739	0.2433
7	4†	2	0.0014048	0.1714	0.1286
7	4	2	0.0013471	0.0844	0.0825
7	1	3	0.0012348	0.1492	0.7006
7	4	3	0.0013556	0.0701	0.0574

† Constant constrained to zero.

$$\log K_t = k + \sum_{i=m}^{n} [\gamma_{pi} \log \left(\frac{p}{c}\right)_{t-i} + \gamma_{qi} \log X_{t-i}]$$

$$+ \sum_{j=1}^{s} w_j \log K_{t-j} + w_t \,. \tag{4.83}$$

Even if the w_t are serially uncorrelated the same does not hold for the u_t in (4.82). Bischoff proposes

$$w_t = r w_{t-1} + \epsilon_t \tag{4.84}$$

where $0 \leqslant r \leqslant 1$, ϵ_t are serially independent. Thus if $r \neq 1$, least squares will not provide consistent estimates of (4.82). Bischoff sets $n = 8$, $m = 1$ and $s = 2$ in (4.83) and combines this with (4.84) to form,

$$\log K_t - r \log K_{t-1} = k(1-r) + \sum_{i=1}^{8} [\gamma_{pi\,i}\left(\log \left(\frac{p}{c}\right)_{t-i} - r \log \left(\frac{p}{c}\right)_{t-i-1}\right)$$

$$+ \gamma_{qi}(\log Q_{t-i} - r \log Q_{t-i-1})] + \sum_{j=1}^{2} w_j(\log K_{t-j} - r \log K_{t-j-i}) + \epsilon_t \,. \tag{4.85}$$

Table 4.26
Unitary elasticity tests under differing stochastic assumptions.

H	$r = 1$	$r = 0$	$0 \leqslant r \leqslant 1$
$E_p = 1$	reject	do not reject	do not reject
$E_q = 1$	do not reject	reject	do not reject
$E_p = E_q = 1$	reject	do not reject	do not reject

Searching over values of r, Bischoff estimates the maximum likelihood value of r to be 0.2, but claims that its variance is such that the evidence indicates that neither $r = 0$ nor $r = 1$ can be rejected. He goes on to test hypotheses about E_p, and E_q under alternative maintained hypotheses about r. His results appear in table 4.26. From table 4.26 he concludes that Eisner and Nadiri's conclusion is dependent on their stochastic specification.

He goes on to apply (4.85) to data of investment in equipment, U.S. private sector 1949(ii)–1966(iv). In this case $r = 1$ can be rejected but not $r = 0$. Proceeding on the basis that $r = 0$ he tests various models embodying assumptions about E_p and E_q against the alternative hypothesis of no restrictions on their values. All models implying $E_p = 0$ are rejected. The model embodying $E_p = E_q = 1$ is not rejected provided different distributed lags are assumed for the influence of relative prices and output. His own estimates suggest that the effect of prices is more delayed than that of output. Bischoff's general conclusion is to stress once more the importance of the stochastic specification of an econometric model. With so much disagreement at the industry level we pass on to firm data.

4.6.10. Grunfeld (1960) *annual data,* 1935–1954, *eight individual U.S. corporations*

Grunfeld is concerned with showing that profits should not be included in investment equations. We have already mentioned the theoretical aspects of his work which imply that the value of the company should be used to represent profit expectations, and liquidity should be represented by liquidity variables not profits. The data refer to eight companies namely: Atlantic Refining Company, U.S. Steel Corporation, Union Oil Company of California, Good-Year Tyre and Rubber Company, Diamond Match Company, American Steel Foundries, General Motors Corporation, General Electric Company. The definition of investment is gross additions to plant and equipment plus maintainance and repairs.

Grunfeld's first salvo is that although the zero order correlation between investment and profits might appear favourable, when one presents a model of the determination of investment and considers the partial correlations very little explanation can be attributed to profits. Grunfeld's first model relates investment to the excess of profits above normal profits, where normal profit is taken to be a constant proportion of the value of the capital stock. Thus

$$I_t = k(P_{t-1} - aM_{t-1}) \qquad k > 0 \tag{4.86}$$

where

I_t is gross investment in period t;

M_t is value of capital stock at the end of period t;

P_t is profit in period t.

This implies an estimating form

$$I_t = a + bP_{t-1} + cM_{t-1} \, . \tag{4.87}$$

From their low partial correlation with investment in table 2.7, it would appear that profits have a very small role to play in the determination of investment. This is not to say that expectations of future profits are not important; indeed Grunfeld suggests that these are measured by the market value of the company and he formulates a capital stock adjustment model where the desired stock of capital, ${}_{\mathrm{D}}M_t$, is a linear function of the value of the company V_t. Thus

$${}_{\mathrm{D}}M_t = a' + b'V_t$$

and

$$I_t = k({}_{\mathrm{D}}M_{t-1} - M_{t-1}) + gM_{t-1} \tag{4.88}$$

$$= ka' + kb'V_{t-1} + (g-k)M_{t-1} \tag{4.89}$$

where $k > 0$ and g represents the fraction of capital to be replaced.

The multiple and partial correlation coefficients which are given in table 4.27 provide much stronger support for this model. Since Modigliani and Miller have shown that the value of the company is equal to the expected future incomes divided by an interest and risk variable, Grunfeld attempts to separate off the effects of interest and expectation by multiplying V by Moody's index of bond rates, B, thus deriving an expectations variable, i.e. (BV). He then regresses I on $(BV)_{-1}$ B_{-1} and M_{-1}, the results of which (see table 4.28) suggest that both the rate of interest and the expectations variable have important and opposite effects on investment.

Table 4.27
Zero order, partial and multiple correlation coefficients of investment, lagged profits, value of company and capital stock for eight U.S. companies and their aggregate.

	GM	GE	USS	AR	UO	DM	GTR	ASF	Aggregate
$r^2_{IP_{-1}}$	0.235	0.376	0.414	0.460	0.270	0.196	0.524	0.049	0.420
$r^2_{IP_{-1} \cdot M_{-1}}$	(−)0.074	(−)0.009	0.211	0.086	(−)0.011	0.048	0.094	0.035	(−)0.010
$r^2_{IM_{-1} \cdot P_{-1}}$	0.790	0.459	0.067	0.340	0.637	0.573	0.160	0.001	0.834
R^2(4.87)	0.839	0.658	0.457	0.569	0.742	0.656	0.599	0.050	0.841
$r^2_{IV_{-1} \cdot M_{-1}}$	0.532	0.145	0.246	0.322	0.096	0.000	0.225	0.128	0.535
$r^2_{IM \cdot V_{-1}}$	0.851	0.671	0.306	0.000	0.756	0.640	0.337	0.067	0.882
R^2(4.89)	0.919	0.705	0.471	0.680	0.764	0.643	0.666	0.142	0.926

Table 4.28
Partial and multiple coefficients of determination in regression, including rate of interest as an independent variable.

	GM	GE	USS	AR	UO	DM	GTR	ASF	Aggregate
$r^2_{IB_{-1}}$	(−)0.025	(−)0.179	(−)0.107	(−)0.046	(−)0.113	(−)0.001	(−)0.235	(−)0.058	(−)0.072
$r^2_{IB_{-1} \cdot M_{-1}}$	(−)0.002	(−)0.056	(−)0.056	0.073	0.144	(−)0.017	(−)0.057	(−)0.043	0.005
$r^2_{IB_{-1} \cdot M_{-1}(BV)_{-1}}$	(−)0.182	(−)0.200	(−)0.152	(−)0.085	0.032	(−)0.020	(−)0.392	(−)0.037	(−)0.136
$r^2_{I(BV)_{-1} \cdot B_{-1}M_{-1}}$	0.502	0.267	0.203	0.292	0.021	0.004	0.399	0.092	0.496
$R^2_{I \cdot M_{-1}(BV)_{-1}B_{-1}}$	0.914	0.761	0.472	0.691	0.781	0.650	0.756	0.145	0.920

Having indicated the apparent usefulness of the model in explaining investment Grunfeld goes on to analyse the residuals arising from the least squares fit of (4.89). He compares his model with a 'naive' model which states that investment will be the same as last years. To compare the two models Grunfeld defines the coefficient of net gain as the difference between the sum of the absolute values of the predicted minus actual values, divided by the absolute values of the residuals from the regression equation. Thus the coefficient of net gain, G, is,

$$G = \frac{\sum_t |e_{Nt}| - \sum_t |e_{rt}|}{\sum_t |e_{rt}|}$$

where e_{Nt} = error in 'naive' prediction; e_{rt} = error in regression prediction.

Table 4.29 shows that in only one company is the naive model superior to the regression model on this criterion. Having considered the residuals of the whole sample period Grunfeld turns his attention to the turning points, since he feels that these and especially the peaks, are more important in testing whether his model has incorporated the expectation elements. It turns out that companies with a high net gain at the peaks are also those for which the regression fits are highest. One interesting result that emerges from the analysis of the residuals is that the aggregate equation (see AGG in table 4.29) does better in terms of fit and net gain than does a process of aggregating the predictions of the individual company equations (see ACC in table 4.29), but when one is concerned only with turning points this result is reversed.

So far, the discussion has been concerned with closeness of fit because Grunfeld's aim is to show the explanatory power of the value of the firm rather than produce a complete explanation. We reproduce his regression results in table 4.30. Two points arise out of these results that lead one to doubt that all the explanatory variables have been specified. Firstly, only in the case of the Atlantic Refining Corporation is it possible to reject the hypo-

Table 4.29
The coefficient of net gain for U.S. companies and their aggregate.

	GM	GE	US	AR	UO	DM	GTR	ASF	ACC	AGG
G	0.33	0.18	0.17	0.77	0.38	−0.08	0.18	0.17	0.26	0.72

Table 4.30
Partial regression coefficients of regression of investment on stock of plant and equipment and value of the firm. (Eight firms, 1935–1954.)

$$I = a + c_1 M_{-1} + c_2 V_{-1} \ .$$

	Corporation								
	GM	GE	USS	AR	UO	GTR	DM	ASF	Aggregate
c_1	0.400 (0.041)	0.152 (0.026)	0.390 (0.142)	0.003 (0.022)	0.124 (0.017)	0.082 (0.028)	0.437 (0.080)	0.084 (0.083)	0.281 (0.025)
c_2	0.116 (0.026)	0.027 (0.016)	0.175 (0.074)	0.162 (0.057)	0.087 (0.066)	0.075 (0.034)	0.005 (0.027)	0.065 (0.042)	0.097 (0.022)
r^2_{VM}	0.196	0.014	0.028	0.756	0.001	0.367	(–)0.022	(–)0.089	0.140
R^2	0.919	0.705	0.471	0.680	0.764	0.666	0.643	0.142	0.926
DW	0.88	1.07	1.12	2.37	0.76	1.08	1.25	0.99	1.26

thesis that positive serial correlation exists. Secondly, since $k > 0$ and $g > c_1$, the regression results imply that replacement investment as a proportion of capital stock is greater than 0.4, 0.39, and 0.43 for three companies. This is obviously too large.

Grunfeld is able to test his model with the post sample data of 1955 and 1956. Although the prediction errors (not reported here) are large for the majority of the corporations they are not such as would not be expected from the quality of the regressions. However, one rather disturbing fact comes to light from his analysis of the coefficient of net gain for these two years namely, 'those corporations for which we obtained the best fit in the regression yield the worst predictions'. One further section is devoted to fitting the model to the data for three more large corporations Chrysler, I.B.M., and Westinghouse – the results of which tend to confirm Grunfeld's view that although his model cannot be considered a complete explanation of investment, certainly, one that is, should include the value of the firm as a key variable. This early study of Grunfeld's has been 'revisited' by Griliches and Wallace (1965) who, using later data, compare the model unfavourably, on the whole, to that of Jorgenson. Jorgenson and Siebert (1968) have produced a fuller comparative study of investment models based on firm data.

4.6.11. Jorgenson and Siebert (1968) *fifteen U.S. corporations, annual time series*, 1949–1963

In this article the authors compare how well five investment models perform when faced with firm time series. The data are taken from company reports of fifteen large companies†. The calculation of the capital stock and the depreciation rate is the same as described in Jorgenson (1965). The investment good price index is based on the implicit deflators for structures and equipment taken from the U.S. Office of Business Economics *Business Statistics*. The five models are the neoclassical I, neoclassical II, accelerator, expected profit and liquidity models. The first two are the Jorgenson model with alternative measures of the implicit rental of capital services. For model I,

$$c_{\mathrm{I}} = \frac{q}{1-u}\,[1-uw)\delta + r - \frac{q_t - q_{t-1}}{q_t}]$$

For model II

† General Motors, Goodyear Tyre and Rubber, American Can, Pittsburgh Plate Glass, U.S. Steel, General Electric, Reynolds Tobacco, Dupont, Anaconda, Standard Oil N.J., International Paper, Westinghouse Air Brake, I.B.M., Swift and Company, Westinghouse Electric.

$$c_{\mathrm{II}} = \frac{q}{1-u}\,[1-uw)\delta + r]\ .$$

Model II assumes that firms consider capital gains as transitory phenomena and ignore them. The forms of the other models are as follows,

Accelerator	$K_t^* = \alpha X_t$
Expected profits	$K_t^* = \alpha V_t$
Liquidity	$K_t^* = \alpha L_t$

where
L = profits plus depreciation minus dividends paid, all deflated by q, the price of capital services;
V = market value of company (including debt) deflated by the GNP deflator;
X = value of output deflated by wholesale price index of firm's industry group.
Each of these forms is incorporated into

$$\Delta K_t = \frac{\gamma(\theta)}{w(\theta)}\,[K_t^* - K_{t-1}^*]$$

where $\gamma(\theta)$ and $w(\theta)$ are determined empirically (i.e. minimum residual variance) but each is restricted to a maximum of two lags.

The goodness of fit statistics appear in table 4.31 together with those of the following naive model,

$$I_t = \beta_0 + \beta_1 I_{t-1} + \beta_2 I_{t-2} + \beta_3 I_{t-3}\ .$$

In assessing these results the authors pay attention to the significance of α since without this the theories collapse to mere distributed lag functions. Table 4.32 gives the number of desired capital stock change coefficients appearing for each model.

Jorgenson and Siebert also consider the functioning of the model at turning points. The number of right, wrong and extra turning points attributed to each model are tabulated separately for peaks and troughs in table 4.33.

On the basis of these tables the authors conclude that the neoclassical model which allows for capital gains provides the best explanation of corporate investment.

Table 4.31
Goodness of fit statistics.

Firm and model	1949–1963		
	R^2	s ‡	DW
General Motors			
a. Neoclassical I	0.70	0.1765	2.03
b. Neoclassical II	0.89	0.1148	2.32
c. Accelerator	0.62	0.1920	2.21
d. Expected profits	0.64	0.1852	1.36
e. Liquidity model	0.61	0.2037	2.29
f. Naive model	0.47	0.2072	2.22
Good-Year			
a. Neoclassical I	0.73	0.0119	2.71
b. Neoclassical II	0.66	0.0127	2.14
c. Accelerator	0.61	0.0135	1.61
d. Expected profits	0.71	0.0118	2.16
e. Liquidity model	– *	–	–
f. Naive model	0.38	0.0157	2.02
American Can			
a. Neoclassical I	0.66	0.0087	2.21
b. Neoclassical II	0.44	0.0101	2.16
c. Accelerator	0.39	0.0105	1.73
d. Expected profits	0.27	0.0110	2.15
e. Liqudity model	– *	–	–
f. Naive model	0.04	0.0121	1.76
Pittsburgh Plate Glass			
a. Neoclassical I	0.72	0.0089	2.16
b. Neoclassical II	0.41	0.0129	1.86
c. Accelerator	0.51	0.01178	2.36
d. Expected profits	0.45	0.01180	1.91
e. Liquidity model	– *	–	–
f. Naive model	0.30	0.0127	1.83
U.S. Steel			
a. Neoclassical I	0.51	0.0801	1.46
b. Neoclassical II	0.50	0.0854	1.63
c. Accelerator	– *	–	–
d. Expected profits	0.69	0.0676	1.42
e. Liquidity model	0.46	0.0841	1.57
f. Naive model	0.39	0.0818	1.70

Table 4.31 (cont.)

Firm and model	1949–1963		
	R^2	$s^{\dagger}$	DW
General Electric			
a. Neoclassical I	0.72	0.0227	1.80
b. Neoclassical II	0.85	0.0173	1.37
c. Accelerator	0.58	0.0276	1.89
d. Expected profits	0.71	0.0244	2.27
e. Liquidity model	0.71	0.0240	2.58
f. Naive model	0.51	0.0272	1.71
Reynolds Tobacco			
a. Neoclassical I	0.85	0.0040	2.20
b. Neoclassical II	0.89	0.0034	2.28
c. Accelerator	0.92	0.0028	1.98
d. Expected profits	0.84	0.0039	1.87
e. Liquidity model	0.80	0.0043	2.03
f. Naive model	0.76	0.0044	1.73
Dupont			
a. Neoclassical I	0.60	0.0321	1.55
b. Neoclassical II	–*	–	–
c. Accelerator	0.63	0.0309	1.38
d. Expected profits	–*	–	–
e. Liquidity model	–*	–	–
f. Naive model	0.30	0.0407	1.42
Anaconda Company			
a. Neoclassical I	0.87	0.0078	1.06
b. Neoclassical II	0.78	0.0102	1.65
c. Accelerator	0.80	0.0098	2.48
d. Expected profits	0.87	0.0084	2.83
e. Liquidity model	0.85	0.0080	1.98
f. Naive model	0.54	0.0128	1.93
Standard Oil, N.J.			
a. Neoclassical I	0.86	0.0736	2.48
b. Neoclassical II	0.86	0.0755	2.25
c. Accelerator	0.69	0.1083	1.79
d. Expected profits	0.75	0.1022	2.24
e. Liquidity model	0.55	0.1249	1.62
f. Naive model	0.50	0.1258	1.67

Table 4.31 (cont.)

Firm and model	1943–1963		
	R^2	s †	DW
International Paper Company			
a. Neoclassical I	0.74	0.0105	2.01
b. Neoclassical II	0.77	0.0100	2.02
c. Accelerator	0.66	0.0121	1.72
d. Expected profits	0.72	0.0109	1.39
e. Liquidity model	0.79	0.0096	2.37
f. Naive model	0.14	0.0177	1.79
Westinghouse Air Brake Corp.			
a. Neoclassical I	0.61	0.00135	1.87
b. Neoclassical II	0.84	0.0009	1.76
c. Accelerator	0.55	0.0015	1.66
d. Expected profits	0.60	0.00137	2.08
e. Liquidity model	0.57	0.0016	1.71
f. Naive model	0.19	0.0018	2.01
International Business Machine			
a. Neoclassical I	0.93	0.0271	1.27
b. Neoclassical II	0.96	0.0208	2.57
c. Accelerator	0.95	0.0218	2.53
d. Expected profits	0.89	0.0313	1.91
e. Liquidity model	0.90	0.0306	2.38
f. Naive model	0.89	0.0324	1.90
Swift			
a. Neoclassical I	0.65	0.0049	1.37
b. Neoclassical II	0.53	0.00543	1.83
c. Accelerator	– *	–	–
d. Expected profits	0.59	0.0051	1.60
e. Liquidity model	0.49	0.00538	1.59
f. Naive model	0.42	0.0055	2.07
Westinghouse Electric			
a. Neoclassical I	0.64	0.0125	2.06
b. Neoclassical II	0.75	0.0110	1.56
c. Accelerator	0.58	0.01289	1.64
d. Expected profits	0.57	0.01293	1.70
e. Liquidity model	– *	–	–
f. Naive model	0.47	0.0131	1.78

* No K_t^* variable reduces the standard error of the regression.
† s = standard error of the regression.

Table 4.32
Desired capital stock change coefficients.

Model	1949–1963			
	ΔK_t^*	ΔK_{t-1}^*	ΔK_{t-2}^*	Total
Number of coefficients appearing (min. variance criteria)				
Neoclassical I	13	12	6	31
Neoclassical II	14	10	4	28
Accelerator	9	9	1	19
Expected profits	13	7	3	23
Liquidity	4	8	2	14
Number of coefficients not less than twice standard error				
Neoclassical I	10	8	2	20
Neoclassical II	10	7	1	18
Accelerator	5	6	0	11
Expected profits	9	6	1	16

4.7. Cross section data

When one considers the statistical problems involved in using time series data it is hardly surprising that econometricians are tempted to use cross section data if they are available. The statistical problems stemming from the existence of serial correlation and multicollinearity and the availability of only a small sample all seem to be lessened by use of an array across firms rather than over time. However, there are considerable dangers involved in trying to use cross-section data as a substitute for time series data and vice versa. Meyer and Kuh (1957), authors who have both jointly and separately published investment studies involving cross section data, have indicated some of these problems with regard to consumption studies (see Section 3.5).

One of the obvious dangers of cross section data is the low homogeneity of the sample. Eisner and Strotz (1963) have said that some investment studies are tantamont to assuming that the investment decisions of 'flower sellers' and industrial firms are similar, but Meyer and Glauber (1964, p. 37) maintain that by careful selection this can be overcome. Meyer and Kuh (1957) state that cross-section data tend to reflect long-run rather than short-run factors, whereas for time series data this is reversed. In the study of investment

Table 4.33
Prediction of direction of change of investment at turning points.

Model		Totals	
		P[a]	T[b]
Neoclassial I	R[c]	26	33
	W[d]	13	8
	E[e]	6	2
Neoclassical II	R	26	29
	W	13	12
	E	3	2
Accelerator	R	25	27
	W	14	14
	E	5	3
Expected profits	R	26	26
	W	13	15
	E	4	4
Liquidity model	R	16	18
	W	23	23
	E	7	3
Naive model	R	7	12
	W	32	29
	E	5	1

[a] Peak.
[b] Trough.
[c] Right direction
[d] Wrong direction.
[e] Extra turning points in regression prediction.

we have emphasised that adjustment through time is a very important influence and since the early cross-section studies failed to take this into account they must be suspect. However, Eisner (1964) has used cross-section data with a model carefully specified to allow for an adjustment mechanism. In this same article Eisner suggests an explanation for the earlier results of cross-section studies which underestimated the influence of the accelerator. His interpretation is that a firm with high sales relative to others in its industry, is not likely to take this as evidence of a permanent increase in demand and hence not grounds on which to increase investment whereas, if all firms' sales increase, this is a much firmer basis for such a supposition.

At the beginning of this section we indicated that cross-section samples are likely to be less troubled by certain problems than time series data but there are reasons to believe they are troubled by other problems. Heteroscedasticity is one of these and most studies try to lessen its effect by normalising variables by a convenient variable, often sales. One problem for which no easy answer is available is that the biases which affect the two types of data are not likely to be the same. For instance, let us consider a simple model where investment is determined by output and relative prices but where the relation is mis-specified by the omission of the relative price variable. In the time series study the disturbance term now including the effect of relative prices, will probably be correlated with the independent variable and hence lead to bias. In the cross-section case the correlation between output and price will depend on the extent of competition in the industry concerned, rather than on some inflationary mechanism relating total output and prices. One further problem with cross-section studies is that they refer to only one period of time and hence one cannot be very sure that the results obtained do not stem from an unrepresentative year. Because of these arguments Meyer and Glauber (1964) conclude: 'It would be extremely dangerous to construe in any very literal sense the regression estimates that follow as representing true structural parameters.' Kuh (1963) whose huge study of sixteen years of cross-section data on 60 firms allows him to compare the results of regression on both types of data, states that 'it must be concluded that estimates of micro or macro dynamic effects cannot typically rely on cross section estimates'. These gloomy quotations should not be taken as statements that nothing can be gained from cross section data. Meyer and Glauber, themselves, use such data as a preliminary analysis of the factors likely to affect investment. Provided one is aware of the problems involved it does seem reasonable to use whatever data is available. Furthermore, since Meyer and Glauber did have cross sections relating to four consecutive years, 1951–1954, some of these problems are lessened somewhat. Although Kuh felt that he could only rely on his time series results to draw economic implications he agrees that 'there is nothing in principle to prevent combination of the two types of information, but the warning is clear – differences in error generating mechanisms are often substantial so that it is careless to ignore them and difficult to make allowances explicitly'.

The warning, however, may not be relevant if one is trying to answer a question different from the type Kuh has in mind, namely, the determinants of investment from the aspect of macro dynamic models. Strotz and Eisner

(1963) suggest that cross-section studies perhaps indicate not the determinants of aggregate investment, but by which firms the investment is undertaken. This is a question to which econometricians have not in general applied themselves. Given the general sceptical nature of this discussion we will limit the review of cross-section studies to brief reports on a preliminary study by Eisner and an experimental one by Dhrymes and Kurz.

4.7.1. Eisner (1967)

In this article Eisner presents his permanent income hypothesis of investment. This states that firms have to be convinced that sales changes are here to stay before they expand capacity. One firm will be more impressed with increases in sales of the whole industry than with increases in its own sales. Thus a cross-section regression within industries should produce lower coefficients for sales change variables than a cross-section regression across industries. The permanent income hypothesis has a number of such implications for cross-section and time series data and Eisner checks these implications against such data.

The data he uses, arise from the McGraw-Hill capital expenditure surveys of 1955 to 1962. About 800 firms, divided into ten industries, are involved though not all provide observations for every year. The investment model that he uses involves seven change of sales variables, two profit variables and a depreciation variable. All the variables are normalised either by the capital stock or by average 1956–1958 sales. A selection of his results appear in table 4.34.

Eisner claims that the 'permanent hypothesis would require that the impact of sales changes should be lower in the firm 'within' regression than the 'across' '. Using the sum of the sales change coefficients as the index of this, the results of table 4.34 are consistent with this hypothesis. Similarly the fact that the corresponding coefficient in the industry cross section regression is higher than both, underlines Eisner's claim. When he compares the accelerator effect in the firm time series with that in the cross section of means regression, he again concludes this is consistent with his hypothesis.

4.7.2. Dhrymes and Kurz (1967) *ten years of cross sections of firms*, 1951–1960.

Dhrymes and Kurz's study concentrates on the interdependent decisions firms have to take when determining their investment. Previously we indicated the importance that others have attached to the dividend and financing decisions with regard to investment, even though none of them produced models where these variables are simultaneously determined. Dhrymes and Kurz present such a model involving five equations, which determine inven-

Table 4.34
Capital expenditure 1955–1962, firm and industry cross-section and time series regressions. Dependent variable I_t/K_{57}.

Variable	Firm within industry	Firm across industry	Industry cross section	Firm time series	Cross section firm means
$\frac{3(S_t - S_{t-1})}{S_{56}+S_{57}+S_{58}}$	0.088 (0.010)	0.086 (0.010)	−0.011 (0.089)	0.060 (0.010)	0.154 (0.056)
$\frac{3(S_{t-1} - S_{t-2})}{S_{56}+S_{57}+S_{58}}$	0.072 (0.009)	0.088 (0.009)	0.245 (0.070)	0.058 (0.010)	0.134 (0.059)
$\frac{3(S_{t-2} - S_{t-3})}{S_{56}+S_{57}+S_{58}}$	0.062 (0.009)	0.074 (0.009)	0.151 (0.061)	0.038 (0.010)	0.005 (0.063)
$\frac{3(S_{t-3} - S_{t-4})}{S_{56}+S_{57}+S_{58}}$	0.055 (0.009)	0.063 (0.009)	0.093 (0.059)	0.024 (0.010)	0.180 (0.056)
$\frac{3(S_{t-4} - S_{t-5})}{S_{56}+S_{57}+S_{58}}$	0.041 (0.010)	0.050 (0.010)	0.085 (0.062)	0.030 (0.010)	0.036 (0.058)
$\frac{3(S_{t-5} - S_{t-6})}{S_{56}+S_{57}+S_{58}}$	0.036 (0.010)	0.037 (0.010)	−0.011 (0.062)	0.021 (0.010)	0.042 (0.064)
$\frac{3(S_{t-6} - S_{t-7})}{S_{56}+S_{57}+S_{58}}$	0.007 (0.010)	0.012 (0.010)	0.018 (0.062)	0.011 (0.009)	0.079 (0.058)
$\frac{P}{K_{57}}$	−0.083 (0.027)	−0.085 (0.028)	0.309 (0.300)	−0.022 (0.031)	−0.100 (0.139)
$\frac{P_{t-1}}{K_{57}}$	0.166 (0.028)	0.136 (0.029)	−0.508 (0.312)	0.202 (0.028)	0.211 (0.146)
$\frac{D}{K_{57}}$	0.595 (0.048)	0.763 (0.041)	1.267 (0.176)	–	–
Sum of acceleration coefficients	0.361 (0.028)	0.410 (0.027)	0.533 (0.137)	0.244 (0.045)	0.629 (0.056)
Number of observations	3147	3147	80	3125	523
$\bar{R}^2$	0.162	0.244	0.629	0.055	0.264

S = sales; P = profits; D = depreciation.

tory investment, I_2, fixed investment, I_1, dividends, D, external financing, EF_2, and internal financing EF_1, plus a budget constraint equation. Unfortunately they do not explicitly present their model or derive their estimating model but the latter seems to be a reduced form version where I_2 and EF_2 have been eliminated leaving three interdependent equations in D, I_1 and EF_1. The influence of dividends and borrowing from outside stems from the existence of imperfect capital markets. Thus the easier the access to outside funds, the larger the investment programme a firm will undertake. Because of this the authors expect EF_1 to have a positive effect and D a negative effect in the investment equation. The external finance equation is expected to show a positive coefficient for investment and negative coefficients for the market interest rate, profits and depreciation. Little effect from dividends is expected.

The model describes a form in which the five decisions are taken simultaneously and although two equations have been eliminated the remaining three are still simultaneous. Because of this, although some preliminary estimation is done by ordinary least squares, the main results presented are in fact three stage least squares estimates. Three-stage least squares as opposed to two stage-least squares are used because the residuals from different equations are correlated. The data used in the estimation are taken from balance sheets and income statements of 181 firms, mostly medium and large sized. The sample includes firms of different industrial classification, and dummy variables are included in the regressions for the nine different industrial classes into which the firms are divided. Table 4.35 gives the class description, the number of firms in each class and the designated dummy variable.

The exogenous variables which appear in the investment equation are sales, S; book value at the beginning of period t, K_t; net profits before taxes, P; and the net current position of the firm, i.e. excess of inventories, cash, short term securities and accounts receivable over accounts payable and other short term liabilities, N. In order to reduce the heteroscedasticity stemming from using large and small companies in the same sample all endogenous variables are deflated by sales. The exogenous variables are also normalised and appear in the following form – an accelerator term denoted by S_{-2}, i.e. $(S_t - S_{t-3})/S_{t-3}$; P_{t-1}/K_{t-1}, the lagged rate of profit; and N/K which Dhrymes and Kurz maintain enters as a 'consequence of the use of the budget constraint to eliminate one of the equations'. The three-stage least squares results for the investment equation are given in table 4.36. The coefficients of the dummy variables C_9, C_8, C_7 and C_4 are consistently significant suggesting non-homogeneity with regard to investment behaviour between industries.

The coefficient of the accelerator variable tends to be significant in the

Table 4.35
Class descriptions of 181 firms in the sample.

Dummy variable	Class description	No. of firms
C_1	Transportation equipment	17
C_2	Retail trade stores	21
C_3	Alcohol, tobacco, food	21
C_4	Rubber, petrol, chemical products	30
C_5	Machine tools, agricultural equipment, and accessories	20
C_6	Electrical equipment and appliances	13
C_7	Building materials and equipment	18
C_8	Textile, glass, pulp and paper	25
C_9	Mining, steel, stell products, and non-ferrous metals	16
		181

years of boom and show some semblance of stability but that of the profits variable does not appear to have such properties. Dhrymes and Kurz argue, however, that the effect of profits on investment comes through the dividend variable, the coefficient of which is significant in the investment equation. Unfortunately no fit statistics are given for their three-stage least squares equations but those given for the ordinary least squares do not suggest that the fits would be high. However, Dhrymes and Kurz make no great claims for their results, stating that their study is a preliminary exploration into the topic of simultaneous determination of investment, dividend and external finance. Indeed their results do tend to suggest that significant interrelations are found in empirical data and that efficient estimation of such equations should use a full information method.

4.8. Conclusion

This chapter has surveyed many empirical studies of the determinants of investment. From these studies are there any propositions that would be generally accepted? Most researchers accept the dominant role of an accelerator variable in whatever disguise it appears, and all stress the need for a distri-

Table 4.36
Full information (3SLS) estimates, investment equation, 1951–1960.

Variable	1951	1952	1953	1954
C_0	0.0562	0.0360	0.0352	0.0779
	(2.9868)	(2.3605)	(1.7951)	(2.9383)
C_2	0.0009	0.0129	0.0076	0.0062
	(0.0507)	(0.9951)	(0.3759)	(0.2096)
C_3	−0.0024	0.0219	0.0133	0.0201
	(−0.1306)	(1.5934)	(0.5967)	(0.5855)
C_4	0.0822	0.0958	0.1135	0.1857
	(3.9719)	(5.1432)	(4.7983)	(4.6702)
C_5	0.0014	0.0314	0.0262	0.0604
	(0.0849)	(2.2174)	(1.3235)	(1.9267)
C_6	0.0002	0.0120	0.0098	0.0199
	(0.0149)	(0.8320)	(0.4483)	(0.5746)
C_7	0.1011	0.0781	0.0940	0.1639
	(4.4527)	(4.7017)	(3.9009)	(3.9948)
C_8	0.0462	0.0544	0.0606	0.1014
	(2.2504)	(3.9923)	(2.9593)	(2.9762)
C_9	0.1186	0.1314	0.1413	0.1918
	(3.9668)	(4.6803)	(5.0492)	(4.1124)
$(P/K)_{-1}$	0.0234	0.0042	0.1340	0.1842
	(0.4335)	(0.2297)	(1.9058)	(2.1315)
S_{-2}	0.0315	0.0071	0.0074	0.0143
	(1.9453)	(1.2251)	(0.9380)	(1.4220)
N/K	−0.0070	−0.0095	−0.0166	−0.0150
	(−1.5260)	(−2.5345)	(−2.3955)	(−1.7010)
D/S	−1.3758	−1.1043	−1.9639	−4.2004
	(−2.3716)	(−2.3017)	(−2.8860)	(−4.9679)
EF_1/S	−0.0943	0.3976	1.0322	1.0480
	(−0.4472)	(3.1588)	(3.0578)	(2.1296)

Note: Number in parentheses is t-ratio.

buted lag adjustment. In addition the influence of financing is generally accepted. Disagreements arise over the form of the distributed lag and whether it can usefully be estimated from the data. The disagreement over the form of the finance variable(s) is considerable. Jorgenson tends to play down the influence of finance variables by incorporating all effects into his implicit rental of capital variable whereas Lintner, Resek and others tend to put greater influence on firm liquidity and other financial variables.

Comparison of the performance of such competing models is by no means simple since the data and scope of the models are often very different. Unfor-

1955	1956	1957	1958	1959	1960
0.0313	0.0727	0.0463	0.0483	0.0657	0.0493
(2.1768)	(3.4825)	(2.0629)	(3.4706)	(2.9005)	(4.8220)
0.0172	−0.0080	0.0072	0.0023	0.0045	−0.0097
(0.8885)	(−0.3568)	(0.3238)	(0.1461)	(0.1980)	(−0.7771)
0.0261	0.0032	0.0233	0.0148	0.0220	0.0060
(1.2888)	(0.1358)	(1.0010)	(0.8151)	(0.9458)	(0.4448)
0.0918	0.1300	0.0942	0.0989	0.1344	0.0618
(4.6759)	(5.0582)	(3.2104)	(3.9044)	(2.8148)	(3.5059)
0.0481	0.0281	0.0146	0.0202	0.0328	0.0119
(2.5908)	(1.3977)	(0.6391)	(1.1669)	(1.0667)	(0.8567)
0.0198	0.0217	0.0212	0.0190	0.0261	0.0155
(0.9866)	(0.9607)	(0.8324)	(0.9917)	(0.9556)	(1.0980)
0.1147	0.1868	0.1689	0.1196	0.1275	0.0610
(5.6713)	(5.7198)	(4.1568)	(4.1999)	(2.5401)	(3.1452)
0.0623	0.1022	0.0709	0.0721	0.0721	0.0298
(2.9613)	(3.3186)	(2.7200)	(3.3576)	(2.1713)	(1.9612)
0.0844	0.1422	0.1428	0.1628	0.1528	0.0624
(3.6545)	(4.5389)	(3.4699)	(5.4355)	(3.3663)	(2.8230)
0.0806	0.1238	0.0090	0.1402	0.2418	−0.0108
(2.4284)	(2.4919)	(0.2099)	(2.1097)	(1.3015)	(−0.2809)
0.0627	0.0447	0.0357	0.0403	−0.0076	0.0241
(3.6952)	(2.6648)	(2.2093)	(2.0490)	(−0.1372)	(1.8978)
−0.0133	−0.0193	−0.0166	−0.0217	−0.0327	−0.0119
(−2.6445)	(−3.0976)	(−2.1921)	(−2.9701)	(−1.8591)	(−2.1800)
−1.3751	−2.3647	−0.8637	−1.6944	−2.6940	−0.4251
(−3.8710)	(−4.1750)	(−1.2435)	(−2.6593)	(−2.0022)	(−1.0417)
−0.1781	−0.8921	0.0912	−0.3760	0.4722	0.1064
(−0.4063)	(−1.1444)	(0.1626)	(−1.4426)	(0.4246)	(0.9507)

tunately there are very few studies comparing the performance of the alternative models available. Griliches and Wallace (1965) did compare the Grunfeld model with Jorgenson's and concluded that the latter was a better description of the investment process. Similarly the Jorgenson and Siebert article seems to support Jorgenson's model though the models of the 'opposition' are not exactly the same as those of Lintner, Resek, etc. Furthermore, Jorgenson's work involves the estimation of distributed lags which is known to cause bias. In addition Eisner's permanent income hypothesis casts doubt on whether firm time series are the appropriate data for such studies. However, a model can only be judged satisfactory on the basis of use. Jorgenson and Hall (1967) have used Jorgenson's model to analyse the impact of tax changes thus adding to the list of achievements of his model, but policy instruments can only make themselves felt in Jorgenson's model through c, which includes the cost of capital and the explanation of this is not particularly simple, as Modigliani and Miller (1967) have indicated. Indeed the explanation of the cost of capital may well include many of the financial variables which authors such as Lintner and Resek have incorporated into their investment functions. Thus although the latter school's results may appear less satisfactory, they are attempting to carry the determinants of investment beyond Jorgenson's results. From this it will be realised that there is still much disagreement in this field and much room for more research.

CHAPTER 5

INVENTORIES

5.1. Introduction

In recent times economists have stressed the role of inventory change as a destabilising element of aggregate demand. Certainly any short run model designed for aggregate forecasting and policy purposes will involve one or more inventory functions. To indicate the type of functions that have been provided will be the main aim of this chapter. Inventory accumulation is often called inventory investment which suggests that in this chapter we shall meet ideas similar to those in Chapter 4. This is true but inventory investment differs from fixed investment in some important ways. Some inventories are held because of uncertainty, not because they contribute inherently to the production process and when they are used they are actually used up rather than merely depreciated. Both of these features help to explain why inventories tend to fluctuate in the short run. A further difference from fixed investment is the phenomenon of passive investment. That is, it is possible because of decisions taken elsewhere in the economy, for inventories to rise and fall without this being a conscious decision. This aspect suggests that perhaps our attention should be concentrated on determining the production decision rather than thinking of an inventory decision. However, for the moment, let us continue to think of inventory changes as some form of investment, which is one of the theoretical approaches to inventory functions.

Inventories are difficult to handle in economic theory since one of their 'raisons d'être' stems from the presence of uncertainty. Firms are not sure when their goods will be required and hence hold stocks in order to satisfy demand as it occurs. Similarly firms may hold stock of raw materials because supplies are not certain. Although some stochastic theory is available uncertainty is more often allowed for by ad hoc devices because the former is difficult to handle. One important device which has been extensively used in inventory analysis is the concept of the 'desired level of stocks'. This is assumed to be proportionate to the level of sales or output. In this, however, we have an inventory–output ratio which plays the same role in inventory studies as the capital–output ratio does in investment studies. Since inventories are easily run down the traditional accelerator theory could be more useful than it is for fixed investment. This pseudo investment approach was used in early studies but later work seeks to introduce more variables, such as prices, the rate of interest and the level of unfilled orders.

An alternative approach is to view inventory holding much more as an element of production that involves certain costs and benefits to the firm. Seen from this angle it is the maximisation of profits (minimisation of costs) which determines the planned level of inventories. This approach corresponds to Jorgenson's theoretical approach to investment. In the same way that the capital–output ratio approach is a special case of Jorgenson's, so is the desired inventory–output ratio of this latter approach. However, for expository reasons we shall develop the simpler approach first but, before doing this, some other general features of inventory studies will be considered.

We have already emphasised the importance that uncertainty plays in inventory decisions. Thus the reader will not be surprised to find that in this chapter we shall consider further how expectations are handled by econometricians. Both anticipations data and various mechanical devices have been used to measure expectations in this context but at the moment there is little agreement as to the best method. More often than not the availability of data is a crucial factor.

The availability and form of the data also affects the degree of disaggregation that is possible. Although the aim is to determine the level of aggregate inventories we shall see that in order to use the a priori knowledge implicit in the theory, it will be necessary to disaggregate along less conventional lines than in the previous chapters.

Inventories consist of three types: finished goods, raw materials and goods in progress. We would expect each of these to be determined by different factors and hence this provides a possible form of disaggregation. One might think that it is an easy matter to determine which goods are raw material and which finished goods from published statistics. This is not so, for all intermediate goods can be thought to be either a finished goods or a raw materials depending upon who owns them. For example, a piece of sheet steel may be the finished good of the steel industry or a raw material of the motor industry. Obviously, such factors as these must be considered when the data are chosen. A further important distinction has been stressed by recent studies which have been concerned with the role of unfilled orders. This is the essential dissimilarity of inventory behaviour between firms which produce to order and those which produce to stock. In these studies, disaggregation to a level which will allow this distinction to become apparent is important. Before leaving the topic of aggregation it is important to emphasise that aggregation through time of an inventory function, i.e., whether we are dealing with monthly, quarterly or annual data, is rather different from that of a demand or investment function because of the possibility of negative inventory change. That is to say, inventory fluctuations are essentially short-run phenomena which may not be recorded in data pertaining to long periods. The earlier chapters of this book have already indicated that in the short run we can only expect partial adjustment to equilibrium and indeed this is an essential element of the study of inventories and our starting point for the discussion of the flexible accelerator approach.

5.2. The flexible accelerator approach

The flexible accelerator approach relates to finished goods inventories and hypotheses that there exists a desired (or optimal) level of inventories. This desired level of inventories will be different from the actual level of inventories and the firm will plan to increase or decrease its inventory according to the discrepancies. However, since changes in production are costly, the firm will not want to close the gap fully but only partially. Thus

$$H_t^{\mathrm{p}} - H_{t-1} = \delta(H_t^{\mathrm{d}} - H_{t-1}) + \epsilon_t \qquad 0 \leqslant \delta \leqslant 1 \tag{5.1}$$

where

H_t^{p} is the planned level of inventories at the end of period t;
H_{t-1} is the actual level of inventories at the end of period $t-1$;
H_t^{d} is desired level of inventories at the end of period t;
δ is the reaction coefficient;
ϵ_t is a random term.

This equation, it will be noted, can also be written in the alternative form

$$H_t^{\mathrm{p}} = \delta H_t^{\mathrm{d}} + (1-\delta)H_{t-1} + \epsilon_t \, . \tag{5.1a}$$

Eq. (5.1) is one formulation of the partial adjustment process but there are others that have been hypothesised. Johnston (1961) suggests the slightly more complicated formula

$$H_t^{\mathrm{p}} - H_t^{\mathrm{d}} = \gamma(H_{t-1} - H_{t-1}^{\mathrm{d}}) + \epsilon_t \, . \tag{5.2}$$

This implies that provided inventories are at the level desired at the beginning of the period, the firm will plan to produce sufficient to ensure that the optimal level of inventories exists at the end of the period. However, if the firm is not in this position at the beginning of the period, it will plan to make a partial adjustment within the period.

The desired level of inventories is assumed to depend upon the expected level of sales. One of the simplest forms that this relationship takes in empirical studies is

$$H_t^{\mathrm{d}} = \alpha + \beta \hat{S}_t \tag{5.3}$$

where $\hat{S}_t$ is the expected level of sales in period t.

This assumption is a little odd since one would think that a firm's desired level of stocks at the end of a period should relate to the expected sales in the following period. Johnston (1961) does use the following period but for the moment let us use (5.3). Although (5.3) allows us to substitute for the unobservable H^{d}, we are in fact left with two ex ante variables, i.e., $\hat{S}$ and H^{p}. The firm may plan to accumulate inventories but its plans may be upset. These upsets will be reflected by the extent to which their sales forecasts are in error. Thus if demand is greater than expected the firm will accumulate less inventories than it planned and the actual level of inventories at the end of the current period will be

$$H_t = \delta\alpha + \delta\beta\hat{S}_t + (1-\delta)H_{t-1} + \hat{S}_t - S_t + \epsilon_t \,. \tag{5.4}$$

This assumes that production decisions are taken at the beginning of the period and cannot be changed again until the end of the period. If, in fact, the firm's production process is more flexible, then, as the firm's forecasting error becomes apparent, some production changes will be possible and hence the error, being less serious, will have a smaller effect on the inventory position. This can also be incorporated into the model in the following way,

$$H_t = \delta\alpha + \delta\beta\hat{S} + (1-\delta)H_{t-1} + \lambda(\hat{S}_t - S_t) + \epsilon_t \qquad 0 \leqslant \lambda \leqslant 1 \,. \tag{5.5}$$

In this relation λ is the production flexibility coefficient, with $\lambda = 0$ representing the fact that the firm can adjust its production immediately.

Functions for raw material stocks can be developed along the same lines. Again there is assumed to be an optimal level of stocks which depends on output planned for the following period. Thus if stock decisions and purchases are made at the end of the period.

$$I_t^e = \alpha + \beta X_{t+1} \tag{5.6}$$

where
X_{t+1} is the level of output in period t+1;
I_t^e is the optimal level of raw materials at the end of period t.
Again using the partial adjustment argument

$$I_t - I_{t-1} = \delta(\alpha + \beta X_{t+1} - I_{t-1}) \tag{5.7}$$

i.e.

$$I_t = \alpha\delta + \beta\delta X_{t+1} + (1-\delta)I_{t-1}$$

where I_t is the actual level of raw material stocks at the end of period t. It will be appreciated that in this case we have assumed that the output level for t+1 is decided at the end of period t and not changed. Production adaption during a period is not so easily handled as in (5.5), since it is necessary to know the raw material content of each unit of production in order to translate change in output into changes in raw material stock. Eq. (5.6) stems from a very naive assumption about the factors influencing the optimal level of raw material stocks. In fact other variables can be introduced in an attempt to take account of other factors, such as price speculation, extra caution with regard to supplies in periods of quickly rising demand, and extra optimism stemming from the knowledge of the presence of unfilled orders.

Goods in progress have not had much separate attention. In fact Lovell (1961) combined goods in progress and raw material stocks together. Perhaps an assumption that goods in progress are a fixed proportion of output is a reasonable alternative procedure.

Although the flexible accelerator models are in some ways very convenient to estimate they do have the undesirable drawback that usually high collinearity exists between the explanatory variables. Although very few studies of the forecasting ability of flexible accelerator inventory models exist it does seem that they have not been very successful. From a theoretical point of view the introduction of unfilled orders to explain stocks of finished goods does seem to be inconsistent. Furthermore, the rather summary nature of the desired stock concept does not allow one to evaluate the effects of changes in costs or the degree of uncertainty. It is for these reasons that what we have referred to as the production decision approach was developed. Obviously, the flexible accelerator approach combined with the identity between production, sales and changes in inventory will also determine the level of production which shows that the essential difference between the two approaches lies in the detailed specification of the costs and the stochastic elements.

5.3. The production decision approach

Whereas the literature on the economic theory of the firm rather ignores the existence of inventories this cannot be said of the operations research literature. The production decision models of this section were inspired directly by this operations research literature, which is not surprising since economic theory involves deriving the actions of a rational firm and operations research involves urging rational behaviour on actual firms.

We have seen that inventory decisions involve uncertainty and dynamic elements which are not present in the traditional theory of the firm. In operations research these elements are usually dealt with by some form of stochastic dynamic programming, i.e., maximising the present value of a stream of discounted expected values of future profits when due allowance has been made for all the interrelations between variables in different time periods. General results are difficult to obtain but Mills (1962) has produced a model, inspired by dynamic programming, which provides a framework for analysing inventory and production decisions.

5.3.1

He postulates a form producing one commodity which faces a stochastic demand curve. The firm has two decisions to make, output and price, which are taken before sales are known. Since his model involves discrete time periods we can think of the firm deciding price and output at the beginning of the period. The random term in the demand function then determines the level of demand given the price. Sales and output then determine the change in inventories of finished goods. The firm is assumed to have a non-stochastic rising cost curve which depends on the level of output. Extra costs are incurred if the firm has to change its output from what it produced in the previous period. Furthermore, storage and deterioration imply that the holding of inventories causes the firm to incur costs. For the moment let us think of this firm being asked to plan its output and price for ten periods hence. If the demand is known exactly (i.e., no uncertainty) all ten periods price and output decisions could be taken immediately based on a complicated but exact analysis of all costs and revenues. When demand is uncertain an asymmetry between future and past events occurs. Future events are now uncertain where a past event is certain and known. Now the firm's best policy is not to decide all future output and prices in the first period but to take them sequentially at the start of each period because by doing this it will best use the information that is available to it.

For instance, if a firm decided to produce, say 100 units and there just happened to be an extraordinary high demand of 120 units that period, causing its inventories to fall drastically, the firm would know that its inventories ought to be higher. Thus the firm with an uncertain demand should take its price output decisions at the beginning of each period. The decision of any one period will still be influenced by those of other periods and we must consider how this influence is transmitted. If the firm always has sufficient goods available to satisfy the demand for its product, the influence of the past on the current decision can only come through the level of inventories at the beginning of the period. The influence of the future is more complicated, if marginal costs of producing in the future are higher than the current production plus storage costs it will pay the firm to produce now for future demand. This influence Mills accounts for by giving a value to inventories held at the end of the current period. However, future demand may be influenced by current decisions, for instance, if a firm is unable to satisfy all its customers in the current period they may not return in the future. This effect Mills approximates by putting a negative value (i.e., a cost) on shortages. Of course a high current price may have a similar effect but this is assumed not to be the case. With these approximations it is possible to consider a firm taking only one price-output decision at the beginning of the period, the implications for the future having been allowed for by the addition of inventory and shortage valuation functions. We shall now state Mills' model formally and derive his output functions.

Assume that the stochastic term enters the demand curve for the firm's product linearly, i.e.,

$$x = G(p) + u \tag{5.8}$$

where
x is the quarterly demand;
p is the price;
u is a stochastic term;
G is some function.
Let $f(u)$ be the distribution of u, given p, and $F(a) = \int_{-\infty}^{a} f(u)\,du$. Then

$$\int f(u)\,du = 1\,. \tag{5.9}$$

And, assuming u has zero mean,

$$\int u f(u)\,du = 0\,. \tag{5.10}$$

Let

$$Z = X + H_{t-1}$$

where
X is the amount produced;
H_{t-1} is the level of finished goods inventory at the beginning of the period. There will be unsatisfied demand if,

$$x < Z$$

i.e.,

$$u < Z - G(p)\,.$$

The mean amount of unsatisfied demand, $D(X, p)$ is given by,

$$D(X, p) = \int_{Z-G(p)}^{\infty} [G(p) + u - Z]\, f(u)\, du\,. \tag{5.11}$$

If $R(X, p)$ represents realized revenues,

$$R(X, p) = \begin{cases} px & x \leqslant Z \\ pZ & x > Z \end{cases}$$

then

$$E\{R(X, p)\} = p \int_{G(p)+u<Z} (G(p)+u) f(u)\, du + \int_{G(p)+u>Z} pZf(u)\, du$$

$$= p \int_{-\infty}^{\infty} [G(p)+u]\, f(u)\, du - p \int_{Z-G(p)}^{\infty} [G(p)+u-Z]\, f(u)\, du$$

$$= pG(p) - pD(X, p)\,, \tag{5.12}$$

using (5.11). Let $c(X)$ be the cost of producing X; $\phi(X - X_{t-1})$ be the cost of changing production; $\psi(X+H_{t-1}-x)$ be the inventory valuation and shortage cost function; and π be total profit. Then the expected value of profits, i.e.,

$$E(\pi) = pG(p) - pD(X, p) - c(X)$$

$$- \phi(X - X_{t-1}) + \int_{-\infty}^{\infty} \psi(X + H_{t-1} - x) f(u)\, du\,. \qquad (5.13)$$

Until specific forms are assumed for c, ψ and ϕ we cannot derive an explicit relation for output. To this end Mills suggests the following

$$c(X) = cX$$

where c is the marginal cost of production,

$$\psi(X{+}H_{t-1}{-}x) = \begin{cases} (c-r)(X{+}H_{t-1}{-}x) & X + H_{t-1} \geqslant x \\ k(X{+}H_{t-1}{-}x) & X + H_{t-1} < x \end{cases}$$

$$\phi(X{-}X_{t-1}) = \frac{g}{2}(X{-}X_{t-1})^2$$

where r is the marginal storage cost and g, c, r, k are all positive constants.

The first function is a simple linear cost function and the last is the simplest form that the ϕ function can take. The ψ function assumes that each lost sale involves the firm in a cost equal to k, but that a unit of inventory is worth the marginal cost of its production (in the future) minus the cost involved in its storage, i.e., r. In order to take account of the stochastic terms Mills assumes that u is distributed uniformly over the range $-\lambda$ to λ. Thus

$$F(X{+}H_{t-1} - G(p)) = \frac{X{+}H_{t-1} - G(p) + \lambda}{2\lambda}. \qquad (5.14)$$

Using these specifications (5.13) becomes

$$E(\pi) = pG(p) - pD(X, p) - cX - \frac{g}{2}(X{-}X_{t-1})^2$$

$$+ \int_{-\lambda}^{X+H_{t-1}-G(p)} (c-r)(X{+}H_{t-1} - G(p) - u) f(u)\, du$$

$$+ \int_{X+H_{t-1}-G(p)}^{\lambda} k(X{+}H_{t-1} - G(p) - u) f(u)\, du\,. \qquad (5.15)$$

Thus the first order conditions are

$$\frac{\partial E(\pi)}{\partial X} = p[1-F] - c + (c-r)F - g(X - X_{t-1}) = 0 \tag{5.16}$$

$$\frac{\partial E(\pi)}{\partial p} = G(p) - D(X,p) - kG'(p) + (p - c + r + k)G'(p)F = 0^{\dagger} \tag{5.17}$$

where $F = F(X + H_{t-1} - G(p))$.

Substituting (5.14) into (5.16) and simplifying gives

$$X = \frac{\lambda(p-c+k-r)}{p+k-c+r+2\lambda g} + \frac{p-c+k+r}{p-c+k+r+2\lambda g}G(p)$$

$$+ \frac{2\lambda g}{p-c+k+r+2\lambda g}X_{t-1} - \frac{p-c+k+r}{p-c+k+r+2\lambda g}H_{t-1} \tag{5.18}$$

i.e.

$$X = \beta_{10} + \beta_{11}G(p) + \beta_{12}X_{t-1} + \beta_{13}H_{t-1} \tag{5.19}$$

From (5.17)

$$(p - c + r + k)G'(p)F = -[G(p) - D(X,p) - kG'(p)]$$

$$\therefore \quad (p - c + r + k)G'(p)F < 0$$

since

$$G(p) - D(X,p) > 0$$

and

$$G'(p) < 0$$

$$\therefore \quad (p - c + r + k) > 0^{\ddagger}. \tag{5.20}$$

Also

$$p - c + r + k + 2\lambda g > 0. \tag{5.21}$$

† Since, if $z = \int_a^b f(xy)\,dy$, $dz/dx = \int_a^b (\partial f/\partial x)\,dy + f(x,b)\,db/dx - f(x,a)\,da/dx$.

‡ For the derivation of this condition from the first order condition I am indebted to Mr. M. Pearson of Manchester University. Mr. Ambalavanar also showed the author how to simplify the analysis.

From (5.18), (5.19), (5.20) and (5.21) we see

$$0 < \beta_{11}, \beta_{12}, -\beta_{13} < 1 \tag{5.22}$$

$$\beta_{11} + \beta_{12} = 1 \tag{5.23}$$

$$\beta_{13} = -\beta_{11} \tag{5.24}$$

The coefficients of (5.18) are functions of certain costs and prices. Mills suggests that the coefficients β_{ii} probably show a considerable degree of temporal stability, because they are ratios, and hence can be estimated as constants. It is not possible to derive estimates of c, r, k, p, λ, and g but the analysis does enable us to see what effects changes in costs, etc., might have on the coefficients.

5.3.2

Mills' model involves a number of approximations but it does place inventory functions in a more traditional decision framework. However, it relates only to finished goods inventories of a firm which produces to stock. It is of no help in analysing the role of unfilled orders which many believe to be important. Recent contributions by Belsley (1966), Childs (1967) and Courchene (1967) have concentrated on this aspect by distinguishing the behaviour of firms which produce to stock from those that produce to order. Belsley and Childs' models are in the same vein as Mills', i.e. based on a dynamic programming approach, but they do not allow the firm any control over revenue and hence their firms are cost minimisers rather than profit maximisers.

By distinguishing between production to stock and production to order the role of unfilled orders, or backlogs, can be seen to perform a similar role to the stock of inventories. Each is used as a buffer in order to prevent production from having to fluctuate as much as orders. Because of this, unfilled orders could be thought of as negative inventories but Belsley and Childs are opposed to such a view. Belsley in particular, emphasises that whereas inventories are likely to be more or less homogeneous, unfilled orders are likely to be heterogeneous because firms that produce to order usually produce to meet the particular requirements of each customer. Both Childs and Belsley emphasise that the costs of changes in inventories are quite different from those of changes in backlogs and these differences cause the firm to operate in different ways. One would assume that if the firm is producing to stock, unfilled orders cannot exist or if the firm is producing to order it will hold no finished goods. Belsley does in fact assume this but Childs maintains that even in production to order firms, stocks may exist because of cancellations or because the firm is waiting to accumulate a group of finished items that will make an optimal shipping load. Similar transportation consideration could cause a production to stock firm to have orders outstanding. We shall present Childs' model because by specifying that either unfilled orders or inventories are identically zero we can derive the forms that Belsley uses. Childs and Belsley also differ slightly in the way they specify the costs influence but this is not crucial.

Childs postulates a firm which produces one good and which has a linear cost curve. The costs incurred by changes in production are accounted for by a quadratic function. Thus if

X_t is the level of output in period t;
S_t is the level of shipments in period t;
O_t is the level of new orders received in period t;
H_{t-1} is the level of inventories at the end of period $t-1$;
U_{t-1} is the level of unfilled orders at the end of period $t-1$;
then the production costs for period t are

$$2c_{32}X_t + c_3(X_t - X_{t-1})^2 \,.$$

The holding of inventories helps the firm to avoid the costs involved with rapid changes in production or stock out costs but itself involves costs. Childs assumes that there is an optimal level of inventories, which is a linear function of new orders, and that deviations from this optimum involves quadratic increases in costs, i.e. $c_2(H_t - c_{21} - c_{22}O_t)^2$. The level of unfilled orders is dealt with in the same way. If backlogs are high, i.e., delivery dates are long, the firm may lose customers or have to resort to costly methods to satisfy the demand (e.g. subcontracting). Other backlog costs arise from the possibility that production costs may increase in the meantime, such that the firm makes less unit profit since its selling price was contracted earlier. Alternatively, if the firm is still involved with back orders and the market price of the good rises, the firm will also lose profits. However, backlogs enable the firm to use the optimal scheduling of jobs and thus save machine set up costs. These swings and roundabouts elements Childs again believes can be represented by the quadratic term

$$c_1(U_t - U_t^*)^2$$

where U_t^* is the optimal level of unfilled orders.

The optimal level of unfilled orders will depend on the firm's average lead time (delivery dates) vis à vis its competitors. However, as an approximation Childs assumes

$$U_t^* = c_{13} + c_{14}X_t \tag{5.25}$$

and hence the cost of backlogs is equal to

$$c_1(U_t - c_{13} - c_{14}X_t)^2 \, .$$

The firm's aim is assumed to be the minimisation of the expected value of present and discounted future costs, i.e.

$$\min C = \sum_{t=1}^{N} \lambda^t C_t$$

$$= \sum_{t=1}^{N} \lambda^t \{c_1(U_t - c_{13} - c_{14}X_t)^2 + c_2(H_t - c_{21} - c_{22}O_t)^2 + 2c_{32}X_t + c_3(X_t - X_{t-1})^2\} \tag{5.26}$$

where λ is the firm's discount rate, and C_t is total costs in period t, subject to

$$O_t - S_t = U_t - U_{t-1} \tag{5.27a}$$

and

$$X_t - S_t = H_t - H_{t-1} \qquad \text{for all } t \, , \tag{5.27b}$$

or

$$X_t = (H_t - H_{t-1}) - (U_t - U_{t-1}) + O_t \qquad \text{for all } t \, . \tag{5.27c}$$

It will be noticed that (5.26) involves future values of orders which cannot be known and are assumed to be stochastic variables. Simon (1956) has shown that with cost curves such as these the decision rules can be derived by replacing the stochastic variables by their expectations. Even so the solution of (5.26) and (5.27) is no simple matter. Childs dedicates a whole chapter to the derivation but we shall only reproduce his results. Assuming that $0 < \lambda < 1$, C_t is bounded and N is large, he derives the following decision rules.

$$U_t = \alpha_1 X_{t-1} + \alpha_2(H_{t-1} - U_{t-1}) + \sum_{i=0}^{N} \alpha_{3+i}\hat{O}_{t+i} + \alpha_0 \tag{5.28}$$

$$H_t = \beta_1 X_{t-1} + \beta_2(H_{t-1} - U_{t-1}) + \sum_{i=0}^{N} \beta_{3+i}\hat{O}_{t+i} + \beta_0 \tag{5.29}$$

where $\hat{O}_{t+i}$ represents expected new orders in period t+i. Using (5.27), (5.28) and (5.29)

$$X_t = \gamma_1 X_{t-1} + \gamma_2(H_{t-1} - U_{t-1}) + \sum_{i=0}^{N} \gamma_{3+i}\hat{O}_{t+i} + O_t + \gamma_0 \,. \tag{5.30}$$

Childs also derives the decision rules where the optimal level of inventories is assumed to be a linear function of S_t rather than O_t. The decision rules are similar to (5.28) and (5.29) except that the coefficients of H_{t-1} and U_{t-1} are not numerically equal.

The form of Belsley's models for firms producing only for stock and only for order, can be derived from (5.30) by specifying $U_{t-1} = 0$ for the former, and $H_{t-1} = 0$ for the latter. The coefficients also have different values since Belsley specifies that production costs for the two types of production are different, thus,

$$X_t^{\mathrm{s}} = \delta_0 + \delta_1 X_{t-1}^{\mathrm{s}} + \delta_2 H_{t-1} + \sum_{i=0}^{N} \delta_{i+3} O_{t+i}^{\mathrm{s}} \tag{5.31}$$

$$X_t^{\mathrm{o}} = \epsilon_0 + \epsilon_1 X_{t-1}^{\mathrm{o}} + \epsilon_2 U_{t-1} + \sum_{i=0}^{N} \epsilon_{i+3} O_{t+i}^{\mathrm{o}} \tag{5.32}$$

where the superscripts s and o signify production to stock and order respectively.

Both Belsley and Childs realise that the form of the data, i.e., industry totals, necessitates the consideration of industries producing both goods to order and goods to stock. Childs' approach is to consider this as an aggregation problem. Belsley proposes a model of a firm which produces both types of goods. His model consists of two equations which he hopes allows for the interdependence stemming from possible complementarity in production, or from capacity constraints. His equations are

$$X_t^{\mathrm{o}} = \zeta_0 + \zeta_1 X_{t-1}^{\mathrm{s}} + \zeta_2 X_{t-1}^{\mathrm{o}} + \zeta_3 H_{t-1} + \zeta_4 U_{t-1} + \sum_{i=0}^{N} \zeta_{5+i} \hat{O}_{t+i}^{\mathrm{s}} + \sum_{i=0}^{N} \zeta_{6+N+i} \hat{O}_{t+i}^{\mathrm{o}} + u_t \qquad (5.33)$$

and

$$X^{\mathrm{s}} = \eta_0 + \eta_1 X_{t-1}^{\mathrm{s}} + \eta_2 X_{t-1}^{\mathrm{o}} + \eta_3 H_{t-1} + \eta_4 U_{t-1} + \sum_{i=0}^{N} \eta_{5+i} \hat{O}_{t+i}^{\mathrm{s}} + \sum_{i=0}^{N} \eta_{6+N+i} \hat{O}_{t+i}^{\mathrm{o}} + w_t \qquad (5.34)$$

where u_t and w_t are disturbance terms. Childs does not attempt to take account of interdependence of the two types of production. Belsley's and Childs' work is similar in as much as both concentrate on finished goods inventory exclusively. Courchene's models, although they do not stem from an explicit decision process, are similar to Belsley's and Childs' in as much as they distinguish production to order and stock but have the additional feature of considering goods in progress and raw materials.

5.3.3

For his production to order model Courchene defines the change of goods in process to be equal to the input of materials, labour and capital minus the amount of completed production, i.e.,

$$\Delta I_{g_{\mathrm{p}}} = K_t + M_t - X_t \qquad (5.35)$$

where M_t is the input of raw material and K is input of capital and labour.

If each unit of production takes the same quantity of raw material and other inputs then

$$\Delta I_{g_{\mathrm{p}}} = \sum_{i=1}^{n} (k_i + m_i) X_{t+i} - X_t$$

where n is the number of periods necessary for production and k_i and m_i are the ith inputs of capital and materials for each unit of output.

Since future output determine the present inputs we can then write down that

$$I_{g_p} = \sum_{j=1}^{n} \sum_{i=j}^{n} (k_i + m_i) X_{t+j}$$

provided that k_i and m_i are fixed. This can be illustrated by considering a simple example of a good which involves three stages, each stage taking one time period to complete. Thus if we think of the firm starting with no production but wishing to produce X_3 in period 3, X_4 in period 4, etc, in period zero the firm will use up $(k_3 + m_3)X_3$ amount of inputs but final product will be zero. Hence $I_{g_p} = (k_3 + m_3)X_3$. In period 1 this inventory will be increased by $(k_3 + m_3)X_4 + (k_2 + m_2)X_3$. In period 2 a further increase of $(k_1 + m_1)X_3 + (k_2 + m_2)X_4 + (k_3 + m_3)X_5$. In period 3, X_3 is now subtracted, but $(k_3 + m_3)X_6 + (k_2 + m_2)X_5 + (k_1 + m_1)X_4$ is added to the level of inventories. We can list the change in the stock for each period as follows,

Change in I_{g_p} in period 0

$$(k_3 + m_3)X_3 \,.$$

Change in I_{g_p} in period 1

$$(k_3 + m_3)X_4 + (k_2 + m_2)X_3 \,.$$

Change in I_{g_p} in period 2

$$(k_3 + m_3)X_5 + (k_2 + m_2)X_4 + (k_1 + m_1)X_3 \,.$$

Change in I_{g_p} in period 3

$$(k_3 + m_3)X_6 + (k_2 + m_2)X_5 + (k_1 + m_1)X_4 - X_3 \,.$$

Change in I_{g_p} in period 4

$$(k_3 + m_3)X_7 + (k_2 + m_2)X_6 + (k_1 + m_1)X_5 - X_4 \,.$$

Since

$$X_3 = X_3 \sum_{1=i}^{3} (k_i + m_i)$$

$$X_4 = X_4 \sum_{1=i}^{3} (k_i + m_i)$$

$$I_{g_p} = (k_3 + m_3)X_{t+3} + [(k_3 + m_3) + (k_2 + m_2)]\, X_{t+2}$$
$$+ [k_3 + m_3 + k_2 + m_2 + k_1 + m_1]\, X_{t+1}\ .$$

Courchene does not use exactly this formulation but he proposes

$$I^{\mathrm{d}}_{g_p} = a + \sum_{i=1}^{n} d_i \hat{X}_{t+i} - d_0 X_t$$

where
$d_1 > d_2 > d_3 \ldots > d_n$;
$I^{\mathrm{d}}_{g_p}$ is desired level of goods in progress;
$\hat{X}_{t+i}$ is expected output in period $t{+}i$.
This involves $\hat{X}_{t+i}$ which are not known. However, assuming that there are three stages, i.e., $n = 3$, and that a firm begins production as soon as it receives an order then

$$X_{t+i} = O_{t+i-3}$$

$$\therefore\ I^{\mathrm{d}}_{g_p} = a + d_1 O_{t-2} + d_2 O_{t-1} + d_3 O_t - d_0 S_t \qquad d_1 > d_2 > d_3; d_0 > 0$$

since $X_t = S_t$.

If new orders are highly unstable production smoothing takes place, to approximate this Courchene suggests

$$I^{\mathrm{d}}_{g_p} = a + d_1 U_{t-2} + d_2 O_{t-1} + d_3 O_t - d_0 S_t \tag{5.36}$$

or

$$I^{\mathrm{d}}_{g_p} = b_1 + b_2 U_{t-2} + b_3 O_t - b_0 S_t \qquad b_2, b_3, b_0 > 0$$

or

$$I^{\mathrm{d}}_{g_p} = c_1 + c_2 U_{t-2} + c_3 (O_t - S_t) \qquad c_2, c_0 > 0\ .$$

These equations when combined with the flexible accelerator equation

$$\Delta I^{\mathrm{d}}_{\mathrm{gp}t} = \delta(I^{\mathrm{d}}_{\mathrm{gp}t} - I_{\mathrm{gp}t-1}) , \tag{5.37}$$

are the basis of Courchene's production to order model.

In production to stock industries, since the inventory turnover per quarter (i.e., S/H) is greater than unity only the next period's production is relevant. Thus Courchene's equation is the same as (5.6), i.e.,

$$I^{\mathrm{d}}_{\mathrm{gp}} = c_0 + c_1 \hat{X}_{t+1} .$$

He assumes that $\hat{X}_{t+1}$ depends on $\hat{S}_{t+1}$ and that this can be represented by S_t. Because of the continuous nature of the process, goods in progress follow a similar pattern to finished goods inventory, i.e. flexible accelerator and a passive inventory change due to mistaken expectations, hence,

$$\begin{aligned}\Delta I_{\mathrm{gp}t} &= \delta(I^{\mathrm{d}}_{\mathrm{gp}} - I_{\mathrm{gp}t-1}) + \lambda(S_t - \hat{S}_t)\\ &= \delta c_0 + \delta c_1 S_t - \delta I_{\mathrm{gp}t-1} + \lambda(S_t - S_{t-1}) .\end{aligned}$$

Raw material inventories are rather complex since we cannot assume that orders will be fulfilled immediately they are placed. Stocks increase with deliveries and fall with production as raw materials are used up. The following identity holds

$$I_{rt} \equiv I_{rt-1} + \mathrm{OPR}_t - M_t$$

where OPR is order of raw materials placed and received; M is materials used up in production.

If we assume that the delivery delay is s periods such that

$$\mathrm{OPR}_t = \mathrm{OP}_{t-s}$$

where OP is orders placed, then

$$I_{rt} = \mathrm{OP}_{t-s} - M_t + I_{rt-1}$$

and

$$I_{t+s} = I_{t-1} + (\mathrm{OPO}_{t-1} + \mathrm{OP}_t) - (M_t + \sum_{i=1}^{s} M_{t+i})$$

where OPO is outstanding orders of raw material. If

$$I^{\mathrm{d}}_{t+s} = c_3 + c_4\hat{M}_{t+s+1}$$

and

$$I^{\mathrm{d}}_{t+s} = I_{t+s}$$

then

$$I_{t-1} + \mathrm{OPO}_{t-1} + \mathrm{OP}_t = M_t + \sum_{t=1}^{s} M_{t+1} + c_3 + c_4\hat{M}_{t+n+1} \, .$$

Thus, in the determination of raw material inventory changes, the decision variable is orders placed (OP_t) but outstanding orders and the delivery delay also play a large part. Unfortunately data seldom exist on these variables and resort has to be made to what Courchene calls applied theory which is essentially the accelerator approach. This completes our review of the theory of inventories as used in econometric studies. Before looking at individual empirical studies however, we shall investigate two problems which all studies have to cope with – expectations and seasonal fluctuations.

5.4. Expectations

As will have become apparent inventory functions include ex ante variables such as expected sales, shipments and orders. Two approaches may be possible – the first is to actually use ex ante data and the second involves relating the ex ante variables to ex post data.

The use of ex ante data depends upon the availability of series which one feels reflect the attitude of the decision makers at the time they took the decisions. Most ex ante data that are available are open to question on this point. Some of the series do not relate to the same time, for instance, the U.S. Office of Business Economics short sales anticipations are produced halfway through the period to which they relate and hence may differ from the expectations on which the decisions are taken. Other anticipations series may be influenced by the fact that their original purpose was to indicate action to other companies, e.g. the shippers forecast of sales, analysed by Ferber (1953b) were meant to be a guide to the railway companies for the provision of transport capacity, and obviously their customers had an interest in being optimistic. Of course very few statistical series reflect exactly the concepts of theory but it does seem that anticipations are more subject to doubt on this account than most. If good series do not exist then necessarily we must follow the second approach. However, even if good anticipations data exist we may well wish to relate anticipations to ex post data. This would be so if we wished to simulate the model for a time period beyond the anticipations data horizon.

A number of models of expectation generation have been suggested and used. One of the most popular is Nerlove's adaptive expectations model. In this, firms change their expectations according to the mistake they made in their most recent forecast i.e.

$$\hat{X}_t - \hat{X}_{t-1} = B(X_{t-1} - \hat{X}_{t-1}) + \epsilon_t \tag{5.38}$$

hence

$$\hat{X}_t = \hat{X}_{t-1} + B(X_{t-1} - \hat{X}_{t-1}) + \epsilon_t$$

$$= B \sum_{i=1}^{\infty} (1-B)^{i-1} X_{t-i} + \sum_{j=0}^{\infty} (1-B)^j \epsilon_{t-j}$$

where ϵ_t is a stochastic variable with mean zero.

Thus the expected value can be expressed as a geometric distributed lag in actual quantities. Although this model has considerable appeal Mills (1962) points out that it is not rational for a firm to only take account of errors made in the most recent period. To put it another way why should the firm go on using a technique which has produced a whole series of errors in the past. Mills' own approach to the problem is to regard an expectation as a prediction which has statistical properties. He postulates that

$$\hat{X}_t = X_t + \epsilon\,. \tag{5.39}$$

That is, the expected value is equal to the actual value plus some error. This suggests that on average firms are correct in their expectations. Lovell (1961) suggests a form which implies that firms give more weight to the recent past Mills' form suggests, he uses

$$\hat{X}_t = \rho X_{t-1} + (1-\rho) X_t + \epsilon \qquad 0<\rho<1\,. \tag{5.40}$$

One criticism of both Mills' and Lovell's functions is that they do not allow temporal prediction of the expectation since the explanatory variable relates to the same period. The importance of this criticism will depend on what the investigator is attempting to do. In his study of railway shippers forecasts Ferber (1953b) implies that firms are influenced by the most recent data and by recent trends. Although Ferber's actual formula also takes in the complication of seasonal data, essentially his form is

$$\hat{X}_t = k + X_{t-1}\left[\lambda + \mu \frac{\Delta X_{t-1}}{X_{t-2}}\right] + \epsilon \,. \tag{5.41}$$

This, it will be appreciated, involves only past values on the right hand side of the equality sign and hence can be used for forecasting.

What evidence is available on these alternative schemes? The answer to this depends on what belief one has that anticipations data reflect expectations. If one is confident that they do then it is possible to test how well the alternatives do in explaining expectations. Hirsch and Lovell (1967) compare the use of (5.41), (5.38) and anticipations data and, although their results differ depending on the level of aggregation, conclude that the approaches are not mutually exclusive as all satisfy the data. If good anticipations data are not available then one is forced to judge the expectations hypotheses indirectly by seeing how well the inventory functions, which incorporate them, perform. Indeed, this is what one has to do even with anticipations data if one is not certain that they accurately reflect expectations. One such study is Modigliani and Sauerlender (1955) whose position is that although the sales anticipations data they use are very poor forecasts of sales, they are useful in explaining inventory movements.

So far we have only considered the problem of generating an expectation of the immediate period. Often the theory calls for expectations of a more distant period. Few studies have considered this problem. Most of the mechanical methods become rather cumbersome when applied in such a case. Occasionally anticipations data for two periods ahead are available and used.

5.5. **Seasonality**

This is a necessary evil with econometric inventory studies because they involve periods shorter than a year. Again there are a number of ways that this problem has been handled. Mills' approach is more or less to ignore it because he argues that seasonal fluctuation of demand is, after all, only fluctuation of demand. The only difference is that seasonal elements are a little easier to forecast. However, even series with strong seasonal elements include non-seasonal elements which are not easy to forecast. His model does depend upon the degree of uncertainty with which demand can be forecast but he feels that there is no evidence to suggest that series with strong seasonal patterns are any easier to forecast than those without. Thus Mills concludes that given this doubt one should see how well a simple model performs before embarking on a complicated one.

Modigliani and Sauerlender (1955) have taken explicit account of seasonal influences. Indeed their model 'assumes that the only function of inventories is to permit the firm to operate at a fairly uniform rate even though its shipments are subject to seasonal fluctuations'. They consider a year which is divided into seasons. The firm knows what inventory level it wishes to finish with at the end of the year and it knows its beginning stock. It has expectations of sales and production plans which can be flexible. The notation that the authors use is convenient and we shall adopt a slightly modified form here. The brackets following a symbol refer to the time dimension, stock variables have only one index whereas flow variables have two, denoting the end and the start of the period. Plans and expectations can be distinguished from actual quantities by the subscript which indicates the point of time when the plan or expectation is made. The beginning of the year is denoted by 0 and the end by t. This time interval is divided into seasons denoted by the subscript i. Thus

$X_0(i, i-1)$ is output for season i planned at the beginning of the year;

$S_i(t; i)$ is shipments from the end of the ith season to the end of the year, expected at the end of the ith season;

$H_i(t)$ is the desired level of inventories at the end of the year, viewed from the end of the ith season.

At the beginning of the year the firm plans its production for the ith season which will necessarily be a certain proportion of its planned production for the year.

$$X_0(i, i-1) = \gamma_i [S_0(t; 0) + H_0(t) - H(0)] \qquad (i = 1, 2, ..., t)$$

where $\sum_{j=1}^{t} \gamma_j = 1$, hence

$$X_0(t; i-1) = \sum_{j=i}^{t} \gamma_j [S_0(t; 0) + H_0(t) - H(0)]$$

and

$$\frac{X_0(i; i-1)}{X_0(t; i-1)} = \frac{\gamma_i}{\sum_{j=i}^{t} \gamma_j} .$$

We can also write the production for the rest of the year planned at the beginning of the ith period as

$$X_{i-1}(t;i-1) = S_{i-1}(t;i-1) + H_{i-1}(t) - H(i-1)\,.$$

However, to determine the planned production for individual seasons at this point of time, it is necessary to make one further assumption. Modigliani and Sauerlender assume that the firm would use the same proportion if it made the decision in the middle of the year as it did at the beginning, i.e.

$$X_{i-1}(i;i-1) = \frac{\gamma_i}{\sum_{j=i}^{t} \gamma_j} X_{i-1}(t;i-1) \tag{5.42}$$

$$= \frac{\gamma_i}{\sum_{j=i}^{t} \gamma_j} [S_{i-1}(t;i-1) + H_{i-1}(t) - H(i-1)]\,.$$

How is actual output related to planned output? This, as we have pointed out earlier in this chapter, depends on the extent to which expectations change throughout the period and the extent to which the firm can adjust its production within the period. In the case where expectations are continuously revised and production is completely flexible we can proceed as follows. Let expectations within the season be represented by the expected amount the firm will have to produce for the rest of the year. Thus at the beginning of the season this is

$$S_{i-1}(t;i-1) + H_{i-1}(t) - H(i-1)$$

whereas at the end of the season it is

$$S_i(t;i) + H_i(t) - H(i-1) + S(i;i-1)\,.$$

Within the season, expectations are assumed to follow a linear path, i.e.,

$$(1-m_i)[S_{i-1}(t;i-1) + H_{i-1}(t) - H(i-1)] + m_i[S_i(t;i) + H_i(t)$$
$$- H(i-1) + S(i;i-1)]$$

where $0 < m_i < 1$. It is this expectation that determines planned output (see (5.42)) and since planned and actual output are equal

$$X(i;i-1) = (1-m_i)\frac{\gamma_i}{\sum_{j=i}^{t}\gamma_j}[S_{i-1}(t;t-1) + H_{i-1}(t) - H_i(t) - H(i-1) + S(i;i-1)] \;. \tag{5.43}$$

If output is completely rigid then actual output will be equal to expected output at the beginning of the period, i.e.,

$$X(i;i-1) = \frac{\gamma_i}{\sum_{j=i}^{t}\gamma_j}[S_{i-1}(t;i-1) + H_{i-1}(t) - H(i-1)] \;. \tag{5.44}$$

If plans are neither completely fixed or completely flexible it seems reasonable to take a linear combination of (5.43) and (5.44) which when simplified becomes

$$X(i;i-1) = \frac{\gamma_i}{\sum_{j=i}^{t}\gamma_j}(1-a_i m_i)[S_{i-1}(t;i-1)+H_{i-1}(t)] + \frac{\gamma_i}{\sum_{j=i}^{t}\gamma_j}a_i m_i[S_i(t;i) + H_i(t)] + \frac{\gamma_i}{\sum_{j=i}^{t}\gamma_j}a_i m_i S(i;i-1) - \frac{\gamma_i}{\sum_{j=i}^{t}\gamma_j}H(i-1) \;. \tag{5.45}$$

This form includes anticipations variables referring to expectations for the rest of the year, the data for which are not in general available. To circumvent this problem Modigliani and Sauerlender assume that firms expect sales to follow a seasonal pattern, i.e.,

$$S_0(i;i-1) = s_i S_0(t;0) \qquad \sum_{i=1}^{t} s_i = 1$$

hence

$$S_0(t, i-1) = \sum_{j=i}^{t} s_j S_0(t, 0)$$

$$= \frac{\sum_{j=i}^{t} s_j}{s_i} S_0(i, i-1) \, .$$

This gives us the relationship between the expected sales in the *i*th period and expected sales for the rest of the year when viewed from the beginning of the year. If it is assumed that this same relationship holds, viewed from any point of time, we can write

$$S_{i-1}(t; i-1) = \frac{\sum_{j=i}^{t} s_j}{s_i} S_{i-1}(i, i-1) \, . \qquad (5.46)$$

One further variable in eq. (5.45) needs to be transformed. Planned end-of-year inventories are not usually known and so these are assumed to be proportional to the sales expected in the final season.

$$H_i(t) = \beta S_i(t, t-1)$$

i.e.,

$$H_i(t) = \beta s_t \frac{S_i(i+1, i)}{s_{i+1}} \dagger \, . \qquad (5.47)$$

† $S_0(t, t-1) = s_t S_0(t,0) = (s_t/s_i) S_0(i,i-1) = (s_t/s_{i+1}) S_0(i+1,i)$. But by the assumption embodied in (5.46) $S_i(t, t-1) = (s_t/s_{i+1}) S_i(i+1, i)$.

Using (5.46), (5.47) and (5.45) we obtain

$$X(i;i-1) = \frac{\gamma_i}{\sum_{j=i}^{t} \gamma_j}(1-a_i m_i)\left(\frac{\sum_{j=i}^{t} s_j}{s_i} + \frac{\beta s_t}{s_i}\right) S_{i-1}(i;i-1)$$

$$+ \frac{\gamma_i}{\sum_{j=i}^{t} \gamma_j} a_i m_i \left(\frac{\sum_{r=i+1}^{t} s_r}{s_{i+1}} + \beta \frac{s_t}{s_{i+1}}\right) S_i(i+1;i)$$

$$+ \frac{\gamma_i}{\sum_{j=i}^{t} \gamma_j} a_i m_i S(i;i-1) - \frac{\gamma_i}{\sum_{j=i}^{t} \gamma_j} H(i-1)\,. \tag{5.48}$$

This relates actual production in season i to shipments in season i, beginning inventories and expected shipments in seasons i and i+1. Notice that the coefficients change from season to season. This is one of the difficulties of models which take explicit account of seasonality, i.e., they involve more parameters even though more a priori information may also be present.

Very often the data are not plentiful enough to allow separate estimation for each season. In these cases resort is sometimes made to dummy variables or to seasonally adjusted data. That these techniques are necessarily approximate for this model can be seen from eq. (5.48) rewritten as,

$$\bar{X}(i;i-1) = \frac{(1-a_i m_i)}{\sum_{j=i}^{t} \gamma_j}\left(\sum_{r=i}^{t} s_r + \beta s_t\right) \bar{S}_{i-1}(i;i-1)$$

$$+ \frac{a_i m_i}{\sum_{j=i}^{t} \gamma_j}\left(\sum_{r=i+1}^{t} s_r + \beta s_t\right) \bar{S}_i(i+1;i) + \frac{a_i m_i}{\sum_{j=i}^{t} \gamma_j} S(i;i-1) - \frac{1}{\sum_{j=i}^{t} \gamma_j} H(i-1)\,.$$

Here the barred quantities represent seasonally adjusted variables according to the original definition of γ_i and s_i. The coefficients of this equation still vary with the season. Furthermore, it is obvious that the use of dummy variables is also invalid except as an approximation.

This completes our review of the theories of inventories that have been used in econometric studies of inventory movements. The empirical studies we shall report on will more or less follow the format that was used in this chapter so far. As far as possible we shall report on work produced since 1961 because Lovell (1964) has written good survey of work up to that date.

5.6. **Empirical studies based on the flexible accelerator approach**

5.6.1. Lovell (1961)

In this study Lovell uses quarterly U.S. data to investigate inventory functions based on a buffer stock motive. The data available allow the estimation of 'finished goods' and 'raw material and goods in progress' functions separately for total durable and non durable sectors of manufacturing. However, the individual industry data are only available for total inventories. Comparable sets of sales and unfilled orders are taken from the *Survey of Current Business* and deflated. Output is then defined as sales plus any increase in finished goods inventory.

Raw material and goods in progress at the beginning of the period are assumed to have an equilibrium level determined by current output, expected price changes, the change in output and unfilled orders. If output increases rapidly firms may be prepared to order raw materials in order to beat any shortages that may occur but delays in delivery may still occur. Unfilled orders may also cause a firm to be more prepared to order materials since unfilled orders represent almost firm evidence of future production. Expected price changes are a little difficult to measure and as a proxy Lovell uses the actual proportionate price change. Thus,

$$I^{\mathrm{e}}_{t-1} = \alpha + \beta_1 X_t + \beta_2 \Delta X_t + \beta_3 \frac{p_t - p_{t-1}}{p_t} + \beta_4 U_t$$

which, when combined with a partial adjustment mechanism, results in

$$I_{t-1} = \delta\alpha + \delta\beta_1 X_t + \delta\beta_2 \Delta X_t + \delta\beta_3 \frac{p_t - p_{t-1}}{p_t} + \delta\beta_4 U_t + (1-\delta) I_{t-2} + \epsilon_t$$

Table 5.1
Stocks of purchased materials and good in progress.

	Total manufacturing	Total durables	Total non-durables
Number of observations	29	29	29
$\delta\alpha$	4004	1412	−356.0
$\delta\beta_1$	0.062 (0.016)	0.053 (0.019)	0.023 (0.021)
$\delta\beta_2$	−0.100 (0.030)	−0.080 (0.030)	−0.037 (0.056)
$\delta\beta_3$	−0.320 (0.206)	0.039 (0.173)	0.148 (0.121)
$\delta\beta_4$	0.061 (0.005)	0.038 (0.004)	0.221 (0.051)
δ	0.458 (0.046)	0.363 (0.034)	0.097 (0.067)
R^2	0.993	0.994	0.970
DW	2.273	1.822	2.019
β_1	0.136	0.146	0.236
β_4	0.133	0.106	2.266

where ϵ_t is a random variable. The ordinary least squares results for this equation are presented in table 5.1. All coefficients are significant with the exception of that of the price expectation variable. The reaction coefficient, δ, for the non durable industries is unreasonably low. However, Lovell claims that these results are consistent with the theory he has outlined.

His finished goods equation is derived from (5.4) and (5.40) which can be combined to produce

$$H_t = \delta\alpha + \delta\beta S_t + (\delta\beta{+}1)\rho(S_{t-1} - S_t) + (1{-}\delta)H_{t-1} + u_t \,.$$

The ordinary least squares results appear in table 5.2. Notice that when (5.5) is used instead of (5.4) it is impossible to derive an estimate for ρ or λ, the production adaption coefficient. Lovell again indicates that the values of ρ and δ fit the a priori restriction of lying between zero and one.

Some industry data are available but only for total inventories i.e. $V =$

Table 5.2
Finished goods inventory.

	Total manufacturing	Total durables	Total non-durables
Number of observations	30	30	30
$\delta\alpha$	−258.2	−325.8	418.7
$\delta\beta$	0.042 (0.020)	0.055 (0.014)	0.006 (0.029)
$(\delta\beta+1)\rho$	0.132 (0.042)	0.097 (0.028)	0.170 (0.069)
$1-\delta$	0.848 (0.065)	0.817 (0.052)	0.935 (0.086)
δ	0.152	0.183	0.065
ρ	0.126	0.092	0.169
β	0.276	0.301	0.089
DW	1.39	1.33	1.57
R^2	0.958	0.966	0.947

$H_t + I_t$. The lack of finished goods data prevents us from ascertaining the production series. Lovell assumes that sales are a good proxy for production and proposes the following equation to explain total inventories.

$$V_t = \delta\alpha + \delta\beta_1 S_t + (1-\delta)V_{t-1} - (\delta\beta_1+1)\rho\Delta S_t$$

$$+ \delta\beta_2 U_{t+1} + \delta\beta_3 \frac{p_{t+1} - p_t}{p_{t+1}} + u_t\,.$$

Once again (see table 5.3), the coefficients have the signs one would expect. The reaction and expectations coefficients all lie between zero and one. The low expectations coefficients seem to support Mills' approach to expectations. The marginal desired inventory coefficients for 'primary metals' is the highest and that for 'machinery' the lowest. Again this is reasonable if 'machinery' tends to produce to order rather than stock. These results seem favourable but the presence of a lagged variable and most probably of multicollinearity among the explanatory variables, causes one to be a little reserved over Lovell's findings.

Table 5.3
Total inventories.

	Stone, clay, glass	Primary metal	Transportation equipment	Machinery	Other durables
Number of observations	33	30	31	31	29
$\delta\alpha$	27.38	−172.8	266.0	751.9	32.77
$\delta\beta_1$	0.109 (0.020)	0.063 (0.031)	0.083 (0.032)	0.035 (0.039)	0.122 (0.030)
$1-\delta$	0.733 (0.051)	0.945 (0.053)	0.684 (0.054)	0.701 (0.043)	0.806 (0.050)
$(\delta\beta_1+1)\rho$	0.234 (0.050)	0.0432 (0.032)	0.031 (0.046)	0.070 (0.065)	0.135 (0.048)
$\delta\beta_2$	*	0.018 (0.012)	0.032 (0.005)	0.059 (0.007)	*
$\delta\beta_3$	0.003 (0.020)	−0.036 (0.035)	0.006 (0.084)	0.029 (0.067)	*
δ	0.267	0.055	0.316	0.299	0.195
β_1	0.407	1.139	0.262	0.116	0.628
ρ	0.211	0.0406	0.028	0.067	0.120
R^2	0.978	0.939	0.990	0.991	0.960
DW	1.29	1.72	1.13	1.49	0.92

5.6.2. Ball and Drake (1963)

This paper is an attempt to explain the changes in 'physical stocks and work-in-progress' which appears in the U.K. National Accounts. The authors use a desired stock equation similar to (5.3) but involving quarterly dummies and expected sales, i.e.,

$$V_t^{\mathrm{d}} = a_1 + a_2 Q_{2t} + a_3 Q_{3t} + a_4 Q_4 + \beta \hat{S}_t$$

where $\sum_{i=1}^{4} a_i Q_i = 0$.

Although the U.K. data refer to goods in progress as well as finished articles they also use

$$V_t = V_t^{\mathrm{p}} + \hat{S}_t - S_t \; .$$

For their adjustment equation they suggest either (5.1) or (5.2). The model using (5.1) is called model A and that using (5.2) model B. Two alternatives are suggested for the expectations equations, namely Lovell's

$$\hat{S}_t = (1-\rho) S_t + \rho S_{t-1}$$

which is designated by an F and Nerlove's

$$S_t = \sum_{i=0}^{\infty} \tau^{i+1} S_{t-i}$$

which is designated by N. Thus it is possible to derive the following four models

$\mathrm{A^F}$ $\quad \Delta V_t = s_1 + \delta\beta S_t - \rho(1-\delta\beta)\Delta S_t - \delta V_{t-1}$

$\mathrm{A^N}$ $\quad \Delta V_t = s_1 + \{\tau(1+\delta\beta) - 1\} S_t + \tau S_{t-1} + (\tau-\delta) V_{t-1} - (1-\delta)\tau V_{t-2}$

$\mathrm{B^F}$ $\quad \Delta V_t = s_2 + \{(1-\rho)(1+\beta) - 1\} S_t + (1-\rho)(-\gamma)\beta$

$$+ \beta(1+\beta) S_{t-1} + \rho\beta(-\gamma) S_{t-2} - (1-\gamma) V_{t-1}$$

$\mathrm{B^N}$ $\quad \Delta V = s_2 + [(1+\beta)\tau - 1] S_t + \tau[\beta(-\gamma) + 1] S_{t-1}$

$$+ (\tau+\gamma-1) V_{t-1} - \tau(\gamma) V_{t-2}$$

where s_1 and s_2 represent seasonal effects.

These are fitted by least squares to data from the U.K. National Accounts (1956(i)–1961(iv), 'gross domestic product at 1954 prices' is used for S, 'physical increase in stocks and work in progress' for ΔV. The actual level of stocks is not available and in order to take account of this factor, Ball and Drake cumulated the ΔV series, thus the constant terms in the regressions include the levels of stocks at the beginning of the period. The results are

A^F

$$\Delta V_t = -\underset{(403.8)}{2050.2} + \underset{(35.5)}{282.5}\,Q_1 + \underset{(21.3)}{141.0}\,Q_2 + \underset{(22.2)}{164.5}\,Q_3 + \underset{(0.101)}{0.494}\,S_t - \underset{(0.090)}{0.009}\,\Delta S_t - \underset{(0.038)}{0.163}\,V_{t-1}$$

$$\bar{R}^2 = 0.81 \qquad \delta^2/s^2 = 1.61$$

B^F

$$\Delta V_t = -\underset{(459.2)}{2479.0} + \underset{(36.8)}{257.6}\,Q_1 + \underset{(24.7)}{117.0}\,Q_2 + \underset{(23.3)}{181.0}\,Q_3 + \underset{(0.082)}{0.415}\,S_t + \underset{(0.087)}{0.035}\,S_{t-1} + \underset{(0.091)}{0.157}\,S_{t-2} - \underset{(0.043)}{0.203}\,V_{t-1}$$

$$\bar{R}^2 = 0.83 \qquad \delta^2/s^2 = 1.76$$

A^N, B^N

$$\Delta V_t = -\underset{(459.7)}{1197.1} + \underset{(61.6)}{364.5}\,Q_1 + \underset{(30.1)}{103.2}\,Q_2 + \underset{(27.6)}{178.1}\,Q_3 + \underset{(0.082)}{0.421}\,S_t - \underset{(0.140)}{0.160}\,S_{t-1} + \underset{(0.227)}{0.433}\,V_{t-1} - \underset{(0.199)}{0.488}\,V_{t-2}$$

$$\bar{R}^2 = 0.88 \qquad \delta^2/s^2 = 2.26$$

where δ^2/s^2 is the Von Neuman ratio.

Ball and Drake consider these results from the point of view of the a priori restrictions, i.e.,

$$0<\delta<1, \qquad 0<\gamma<1, \qquad \beta>0, \qquad 0<\tau<1.$$

and construct table 5.4.

On this account one would only wish to rule out A^N. However, no account

Table 5.4
Consistency of coefficients with a priori restrictions for U.K. total inventories.

Model	S_t	S_{t-1}	S_{t-2}	ΔS	V_{t-1}	V_{t-2}
A^F	√	"	"	√	√	"
A^N	√	X	"	"	√	√
B^F	√	√	√	"	√	"
B^N	√	√	"	"	√	√

" not available; √ consistent with restrictions; X not consistent with restrictions.

has been taken of the internal consistency of the coefficients of an equation – a problem which becomes more apparent when one tries to derive estimates of the structural parameters i.e. of $\delta, \gamma, \beta, \rho$ and τ. If we use A^F it is possible to derive unique estimates from the least squares coefficients. The other forms lead to a problem of over-identification, for instance, for A^N we find

$$\hat{\tau} = -0.160$$
$$\hat{\tau} - \hat{\delta} = 0.433$$
$$(1-\hat{\delta})\hat{\tau} = -0.488$$

Thus we have three equations in two unknowns. Even if the first equation is ignored the remaining two equations involve a quadratic in $\hat{\tau}$ which has two solutions. There is nothing which forces these different estimates of $\hat{\tau}$ to be equal. Having discarded A^N on the grounds that the coefficient of S_{t-1} is 'wrong', they discard B^F because the underlying quadratic used to derive the structural estimates has imaginary roots. Thus only A^F and B^N are considered further.

The derivation of the structural coefficients for B^N hinges on solving the following equations

$$(1+\hat{\beta})\hat{\tau} - 1 = 0.421 \tag{5.49a}$$

$$\hat{\tau}[-\hat{\beta}\hat{\gamma}+1] = -0.160 \tag{5.49b}$$

$$\hat{\tau}+\hat{\gamma}-1 = 0.433 \tag{5.49c}$$

$$\hat{\tau}\hat{\gamma} = 0.488\ . \tag{5.49d}$$

The last two equations imply $\hat{\tau} = 0.88$ or 0.56. Ball and Drake choose the latter because

$$\hat{S} = \sum_{i=0}^{\infty} \tau^{i+1} S_{t-i}$$

and if sales are constant for a long time one would expect $\hat{S} = S$ but

$$\hat{S} = S \sum_{i=0}^{\infty} \tau^{i+1} ,$$

thus $\tau = 0.5$. In the light of this 0.88 for $\hat{\tau}$ seems too high. Furthermore, when $\hat{\tau} = 0.56$, and $\hat{\gamma} = 0.87$ are used with (5.49a) and (5.49b) to estimate $\hat{\beta}$, the two values are 1.54 and 1.48 which are remarkably close. The estimates for the structural parameters of A^F and B^N, i.e., the two models which appear to satisfy the a priori restrictions are as follows

A^F $\quad \hat{\beta} = 3.04 \quad \hat{\delta} = 0.16 \quad \hat{\rho} = 0.007$

B^N $\quad \hat{\beta} = \begin{matrix} 1.54 \\ 1.48 \end{matrix} \quad \hat{\gamma} = 0.87 \quad \hat{\tau} = 0.56 .$

In view of Lovell's results the numerical value of $\hat{\delta}$ and $\hat{\rho}$ in A^F do not seem unreasonable. With regard to B^N, $\hat{\gamma}$ could be a little high, as we shall see Johnston's figures are lower, but we really have very little reason to discard this result. The two models give very different values for $\hat{\beta}$. Since $\hat{\beta}/4$ is the ratio of the desired stock to normal output on an annual basis we see that B^N implies that in the long run stocks are approximately 38% of GDP. A rough check on this value is obtained by considering the change in inventories over the period 1948–1961 relative to the change in annual GDP over the same period. This results in an estimate of the long run stocks percentage of GDP as 43%, which would imply $\beta = 1.72$. On this basis Ball and Drake prefer B^N to A^N.

5.6.3. Johnston (1961)

In this article Johnston proposes a model similar to that of Modigliani and Sauerlender. He fits this to quarterly data of eight industries for the period 1946(i) to 1958(ii) and goes on to analyse the predictions for 1958(iii)–1959(i).

The model relates to inventories of finished goods. The desired level of inventories at the end of each quarter is assumed to be related to the desired inventory at the end of the year and the differences between sales and output. The seasonal pattern of sales and output differ because the firm wishes to smooth production. The seasonal variables are denoted as follows, $s_j S_t$ is the expected sales in quarter j, and $\sigma_j S_t$ is the corresponding level of planned production where $\hat{S}_t$ is the expected level of sales in the year. The desired end level of inventories for the first three quarters are as follows

$$H^{\mathrm{d}}_{t,1} = H^{\mathrm{d}}_{t,4} + (s_4 - \sigma_4)\hat{S}_t + (s_3 - \sigma_3)\hat{S}_t + (s_2 - \sigma_2)\hat{S}_t$$

$$H^{\mathrm{d}}_{t,2} = H^{\mathrm{d}}_{t,4} + (s_4 - \sigma_4)\hat{S}_t + (s_3 - \sigma_3)\hat{S}_t$$

$$H^{\mathrm{d}}_{t,3} = H^{\mathrm{d}}_{t,4} + (s_4 - \sigma_4)\hat{S}_t \,.$$

The ratios of desired inventories to next period sales are

$$\beta_2 = \frac{H^{\mathrm{d}}_{t,1}}{s_2\hat{S}_t} = \frac{H^{\mathrm{d}}_{t,4}}{s_2\hat{S}_t} + \frac{s_4 - \sigma_4 + s_3 - \sigma_3 + s_2 - \sigma_2}{s_2}$$

$$\beta_3 = \frac{H^{\mathrm{d}}_{t,2}}{s_3\hat{S}_t} = \frac{H^{\mathrm{d}}_{t,4}}{s_3\hat{S}_t} + \frac{s_4 - \sigma_4 + s_3 - \sigma_3}{s_3}$$

$$\beta_4 = \frac{H^{\mathrm{d}}_{t,3}}{s_4\hat{S}_t} = \frac{H^{\mathrm{d}}_{t,4}}{s_4\hat{S}_t} + \frac{s_4 - \sigma_4}{s_4}$$

$$\beta_1 = \frac{H^{\mathrm{d}}_{t,4}}{s_1\hat{S}_{t+1}} \,.$$

Johnston then assumes the β_j to be constants since the desired year and level of inventories is likely to vary with sales. Thus

$$H^{\mathrm{d}}_{tj} = \beta_{j+1}\hat{S}_{tj+1} \,.$$

Combining this with (5.2) and the identity between actual sales, output and change in inventories, produces

$$X^{\mathrm{p}}_{t,j} = \beta_{j+1}\hat{S}_{t,j+1} + (1-\gamma\beta_j)\hat{S}_{t,j} - (1-\gamma)H_{t,j-1} \,.$$

The expectations formulae that he uses for these two forecasts are akin to (5.41), in fact, because of the seasonal complication they are,

$$\hat{S}_{t,j} = S_{t-1,j}\left\{1 + \mu_1 \frac{S_{t,j-1} - S_{t-1,j-1}}{S_{t-1,j-1}}\right\} \qquad 0 < \mu_1 \leqslant 1$$

$$\hat{S}_{t,j+1} = S_{t-1,j+1}\left\{1 + \mu_2 \frac{S_{t,j-1} - S_{t-1,j-1}}{S_{t-1,j-i}}\right\} \qquad 0 < \mu_2 \leqslant 1 \,.$$

Planned output differs from actual output by random factors, hence

$$X_{t,j} = X^{\mathrm{p}}_{t,j} + u_{t,j} \,.$$

Substituting for these values produces

$$X_{t,j} = \beta_{j+1}(1-\mu_2)S_{t-1,j+1} + \beta_{j+1}\mu_2 \frac{S_{t-1,j+1}S_{t,j-1}}{S_{t-1,j-1}}$$

$$+ (1-\gamma\beta_j)(1-\mu_1)S_{t-1,j} + (1-\gamma\beta_j)\mu_1 \frac{S_{t-1,j}S_{t,j-1}}{S_{t-1,j-1}}$$

$$- (1-\gamma)H_{t,j-1} + u_{t,j} \,.$$

From the estimated coefficients of this equation we can derive estimates of the structural parameters. Indeed if each quarter is fitted separately it is possible to get two estimates for each $\beta_{t,j}$ and four for each μ_1, μ_2 and γ.

The data for petroleum and allied industries are taken from the U.S. Bureau of Mines Reports and those of the other three from Business Statistics Supplements to the *Survey of Current Business*. Six of the industries have exports and imports which can be either ignored or exports amalgamated with domestic sales and imports with production. Johnston does both but we shall only report the amalgamated version here. The fits are high which one might expect with only about a dozen observations and five independent variables. The DW statistics are not given for individual equations but Johnston reports that the majority indicate little serial correlation. The forecasts for 1958(iii)–1959(i) are not very satisfactory. The value of R^2 and percentage forecast error ((calculated – actual)/actual) are given for each industry in table 5.5. We noticed in the previous chapter when discussing Grunfeld's work that high R^2 is no guarantee of good ex sample forecasts. Johnston's results underline this fact.

Table 5.5
Goods of fit and forecast errors for the production equations of eight U.S. industries.

	R^2				% error		
	i	ii	iii	iv	1958(iii)	1958(iv)	1959(i)
Cement	0.954	0.961	0.986	0.952	−2.9	−15.0	−19.3
Gasoline	0.996	0.953	0.991	1.000	−4.6	8.7	− 3.2
Canadian newsprint	0.969	0.989	0.981	0.887	3.1	− 4.4	− 1.4
Fuel oil distillary	0.944	0.970	0.991	0.997	6.6	2.0	1.1
Fuel oil residual	0.905	0.790	0.746	0.862	2.8	− 1.8	..
Lubricants	0.958	0.811	0.930	0.794	9.7	− 4.5	0.9
Kerosene	0.528	0.507	0.954	0.842	6.8	1.1	6.7
Pneumatic tires	0.551	0.963	0.793	0.734	−2.8	−16.5	− 7.3

While the model may appear satisfactory from the point of view of fit, the estimates of the structural parameters derived from different quarters are not. In particular the values of μ_1 and μ_2 differ widely from quarter to quarter. Most of the other estimates lie in the bounds indicated by the a priori constraints but are subject to a great deal of inprecision. In an attempt to circumvent the problems of this model Johnston uses the sales-production-inventory change identity to transform (5.2) into

$$X^{\mathrm{p}}_{t,j} = \hat{S}_{t,j} + (H^{\mathrm{d}}_{t,j} - \gamma H^{\mathrm{d}}_{t,j-1}) - (1-\gamma)H_{t,j-1} \,.$$

If $(H^{\mathrm{d}}_{t,j} - \gamma H^{\mathrm{d}}_{t,j-1})$ is assumed constant then, using quarterly dummy variables, regression estimates of $(H^{\mathrm{d}}_{t,j} - \gamma H^{\mathrm{d}}_{t,j-1})$ can be made as well as of γ (from the coefficient of $H_{t,j-1}$) this time using all the data together. The way Johnston sets this up implies that the $H^{\mathrm{d}}_{t,j}$ (j=1, ..., 4) remain constant for all t. However, he relaxes the model somewhat by assuming that all the desired inventory levels increase by the same amount each year, and including a dummy variable, Q_5, which takes values 0,0,0,0, 1,1,1,1, 2,2,2,2 ... T,T,T,T, in his estimation equation,

$$X_{t,j} = (1-\mu_1)S_{t-1,j} + \mu_1 S_{t-1,j}\frac{S_{t,j-1}}{S_{t-1,j-1}} + c_1Q_1 + c_2Q_2 + c_3Q_3$$

$$+ c_4Q_4 + c_5Q_5 - (1-\gamma)H_{t,j-1} + u_{t,j} \,.$$

Table 5.6
Goodness of fit and percentage error in model II.

	R^2	DW	1958(iii)	1958(iv)	1959(i)
Cement	0.96	1.8	−16.1	−15.6	−12.8
Gasoline	0.98	1.5	4.3	3.7	4.9
Canadian newsprint	0.95	1.4	4.5	3.8	11.3
Fuel oil distillary	0.95	1.2	5.5	4.0	7.0
Fuel oil residual	0.88	1.5	− 4.1	− 7.2	..
Lubricants	0.79	1.9	0	− 0.5	5.3
Kerosene	0.74	1.2	9.9	1.2	5.5
Pneumatic tires	0.56	1.2	5.9	− 7.0	−14.4

We report the fit statistics and the percentage forecast error but not the parameter values for this equation, i.e. model II, in table 5.6. Comparing the results of models I and II reveals very little difference in their forecasting ability. If anything, model I is slightly better. Since nothing seems to be gained by altering the assumptions about the determination of desired inventories, Johnston tries an alternative form of generating sales expectations. This results in his model III but again the forecast errors suggest that there is little to choose between this and the earlier models. Although none of the three models is very successful all of them forecast better than two naive models. The naive models are

(a) $$X_{t,j} = X_{t-1,j}$$

(b) $$X_{t,j} = X_{t-1,j} \frac{X_{t,j-1}}{X_{t-1,j-1}} .$$

The average absolute percentage of errors and the frequency of best forecast for 1958(iii) to 1959(i) are presented in table 5.7 for the three regression and two naive models.

Table 5.7
Forecasting ability of alternative models.

Model	I	II	III	a	b
Average absolute % error	5.6	6.6	6.5	6.9	7.3
Frequency of best forecasts	10	2	3	5	3

Although this table provides a modicum of satisfaction for the econometrician it is only a modicum. Johnston concludes that progress in inventory/production functions probably depends on incorporating ex ante variables for sales expectations and more detailed analysis of individual firms behaviour. He also acknowledges that capacity and price considerations have been omitted from his models and that these might be important though a casual analysis of the residuals from his equation does not suggest that their influence is a simple matter. This interaction between price and output was at the heart of Mills' work as we have seen and this seems a convenient point to consider his empirical results.

5.7. Empirical studies based on the production decision approach

5.7.1. Mills (1962)

Mills' theoretical analysis (see Section 5.3.1) results in a linear production decision equation in expected sales, lagged output and inventories of finished goods at the beginning of the period, i.e.,

$$X_t = \beta_{10} + \beta_{11}\hat{S}_t + \beta_{12}X_{t-1} + \beta_{13}H_{t-1} \tag{5.19}$$

where

$$0 < \beta_{11}, \beta_{12}, -\beta_{13} < 1 \tag{5.22}$$

$$\beta_{11} + \beta_{12} = 1 \tag{5.23}$$

$$\beta_{13} = -\beta_{11}\,. \tag{5.24}$$

His empirical analysis is concerned with checking whether this is consistent with industry data. Because of the approximations that were applied in deriving his production equation he does not impose the constraints above exactly, but prefers to think of them as constraints that good estimates should approximately satisfy. The time period of his model is not specified but the shortest period for which data are available is a month. Thus three out of four of his studies are monthly studies. The other, cement, is based on quarterly data because he wishes to use the data that are available on expected sales. The four industries that he chooses, southern pine lumber, cement, pneumatic tires, and departmental store shoes are chosen mainly because of the availability of long series in these industries but also because their products tend to be clearly defined and subject to little quality change during the sample period.

Table 5.8
Production decision coefficients of four U.S. industries. Implicit expectations.

	β_{10}	β_{11}	β_{12}	β_{13}	R^2
Pine	93.287	0.443 (0.042)	0.511 (0.047)	−0.034 (0.023)	0.958
Cement	72.435	0.806 (0.030)	0.155 (0.031)	−0.266 (0.107)	0.964
Tires	52.489	0.389 (0.047)	0.559 (0.053)	−0.033 (0.023)	0.808
Shoe	4.855	0.850 (0.133)	0.420 (0.082)	−0.073 (0.027)	0.563
		Shippers forecasts			
Cement	166.703	0.748 (0.043)	0.127 (0.049)	−0.612 (0.173)	0.920

Mills further says that the movements of pine and cement are typical of many other industries, at least on the evidence of Abramowitz (1950).

The data, taken from Abramowitz for the pine, cement, and tire industries are physical volumes and hence avoid deflation problems. The sales and inventory data on shoes are taken from Mack (1956) and are deflated and seasonally adjusted. The 'production' data are also taken from Mack and they represent store receipts by department stores. Being independently estimated, they do not satisfy the $X–S = H_t – H_{t-1}$ identity. A number of the results quoted in Mills' book are in error †. In table 5.8 we present the corrected results.

These results seem to approximately satisfy the first two constraints but the third is not in general satisfied. However, as with all inventory equations multicollinearity is a problem. Some indication of this can be ascertained from the zero order correlations presented in table 5.9.

It might be claimed that with such correlations naive models, e.g. $X_t = X_{t-1}$ or $X_t = S_t$, will perform as well as Mills' models. Mills compares the within sample forecasts, i.e., the residuals, with the similar quantities derived from these two naive models. As a summary statistic he calculates the

† This was reported to the author by Mr. J. Bispham and later confirmed by Mills in correspondence.

Table 5.9
Zero order correlation coefficients.

	Pine				Cement			
	S	X_{t-1}	H_{t-1}		S	$\hat{S}$	X_{t-1}	H_{t-1}
X	0.95	0.95	−0.45	X	0.97	0.93	0.60	0.24
S		0.88	−0.39	S		0.96	0.47	0.37
X_{t-1}			−0.45	$\hat{S}$			0.47	0.45
				X_{t-1}				−0.15

	Tires				Shoes		
	S	X_{t-1}	H_{t-1}		S	X_{t-1}	H_{t-1}
X	0.81	0.85	0.46	X	0.66	0.63	0.32
S		0.70	0.52	S		0.57	0.60
X_{t-1}			0.51	X_{t-1}			0.49

Table 5.10
Average absolute percentage errors for three production models.

	Naive I $X_t = X_{t-1}$	Naive II $X_t = S_t$	Regression
Pine	6.78	8.14	4.64
Cement implicit	34.22	10.09	7.01
Cement expectation	34.22	14.00	10.62
Tires	11.52	12.78	9.47
Shoes	8.02	6.69	6.02

average absolute percentage forecasting error, i.e. $100\sum_{i=1}^{n} (X_i - X_{ci})/X_i n$ for each model (see table 5.10). These figures suggest that something is gained by the regression model but it must be remembered that these forecasts are within sample forecasts. The data appear to be consistent with Mills' theory, but his results for cement appear no more impressive than Johnston's who found that his equations forecast poorly outside the sample period. Furthermore, it is interesting to see that there is very little to indicate the best way to deal with expectations. Both the cement equations of Mills and those of Johnston appear equally 'successful'. Mills lack of concern over seasonality seems to be justified although lack of comparable results (except for cement) using an alternative approach, reduces the impact of this finding.

Mills' results, and Johnston's for that matter, refer to rather simple industries, i.e., where the product is homogeneous. In most industries this is not the case and the rather simple models of Mills and Johnston are likely to be of less value. Childs and Belsley have considered such industries and it is to their empirical work that we now turn.

5.7.2. Childs (1967)

The aim of this work is to develop explanations of inventories and unfilled orders. In Section 5.3.2 we saw how Childs distinguishes production to order from production to stock and then derives a rule for inventories, unfilled orders and production (see 5.28, 5.29 and 5.30). We also implied that slightly different rules result if the optimal level of inventories is assumed to depend on shipments rather than orders. Childs estimates both of these rules but we shall concentrate on the latter and we shall use Childs' notation throughout this section.

The data relate to four industries, 'primary metals', 'fabricated metals'. 'non-electrical machinery', and 'electrical machinery' and three aggregates 'all non-durables', 'all durables' and 'all manufacturing'. The series are monthly seasonally adjusted series from 1953 to 1964 and are taken from the U.S. Department of Commerce, Bureau of Census' *Manufacturers Shipments, Inventories and Orders. 1947–1963 Revised* and the Office of Business Economics *Business Statistics*.

These data, because they are seasonally adjusted, do not necessarily satisfy the identity relations between inventory, orders, production and shipments. Childs, however, derived his production and order series by using the identities so that necessarily his series do satisfy the constraints. The decision rules involve expected future orders. These are dealt with in two ways, one follows Mills, i.e. uses the actual values O_t, O_{t+1} and O_{t+2} – the other uses O_{t-1}, O_{t-2} and O_{t-3} which implies use of a generating function.

Because the industries and aggregates referred to above involve a number of firms producing different products, there are two aggregation problems. Given that Childs uses the function derived from his micro theory, aggregation bias will be very probable. The aggregation over products will probably involve aggregating over the two different types of production, i.e., to stock and to order. Because this distinction is at the root of Childs' work he spends a considerable effort to assess the impact of this aggregation on the signs of the coefficients of the decision rules. We shall try to highlight his discussion of this aspect before presenting some of his numerical results. His analysis is based on a result of Theil (1954) which shows that each macro least squares estimate depends on all of the micro parameters according to the relation between the micro variables and the macro variables. Let the micro relation be,

$$y_i = \alpha_i + \sum_{\lambda=1}^{L} \beta_{\lambda i} X_{\lambda i} + u_i$$

and the macro relation be

$$Y = \alpha + \sum_{\lambda=1}^{L} \beta_\lambda X_\lambda + u$$

where

$$Y = \sum_{i=1}^{I} y_i$$

$$X_\lambda = \sum_{i=1}^{I} X_{\lambda i} \ .$$

Then, upon estimation, β_λ are related to the micro parameters $\beta_{\lambda i}$ as follows

$$\beta_\lambda = \sum_{\lambda'=1}^{L} \sum_{i=1}^{I} B_{\lambda,\lambda' i} \beta_{\lambda' i} \tag{5.50}$$

where

$$X_{\lambda i} = A_{\lambda i} + B_{1,\lambda i} X_1 + \ldots + B_{L,\lambda i} X_L + V_{\lambda i}$$

$$(i=1, \ldots, I) \qquad (\lambda=1, \ldots, L)$$

i.e., the B's are the least squares coefficients of the regression of each micro variable on all macro variables. Furthermore, Theil shows that

$$\sum_{i=1}^{I} B_{\lambda,\lambda' i} \begin{matrix} = 1 & \text{if} & \lambda' = \lambda \\ = 0 & \text{if} & \lambda' \neq \lambda \ . \end{matrix} \tag{5.51}$$

It is (5.50) and (5.51) that Childs uses to assess the effect of aggregation over two products, one produced to order and the other to stock.

The micro relations for unfilled orders that he desires to aggregate are

$$U_t^s = a_{11}^s X_{t-1}^s + a_{12}^s H_{t-1}^s + a_{13}^s U_{t-1}^s + b_{10}^s \hat{O}_t^s + h_1^s + u_{1t}^s$$

$$U_t^o = a_{11}^o X_{t-1}^o + a_{12}^o H_{t-1}^o + a_{13}^o U_{t-1}^o + b_{10}^o \hat{O}_t^s + h_1^o + u_{1t}^o \,.$$

The macro relation is

$$U_t = a_{11} X_{t-1} + a_{12} H_{t-1} + a_{13} U_{t-1} + b_{10} \hat{O}_t + h_1 + u_{1t} \,.$$

For expositional simplicity only one expected orders variable is included. The auxiliary equations are

$$X_{t-1}^s = A_{11} + B_{1,11} X_{t-1} + B_{2,11} H_{t-1} + B_{3,11} U_{t-1} + B_{4,11} \hat{O}_t + V_{11t}$$

$$X_{t-1}^o = A_{12} + B_{1,12} X_{t-1} + B_{2,12} H_{t-1} + B_{3,12} U_{t-1} + B_{4,12} \hat{O}_t + V_{12t}$$

$$H_{t-1}^s = A_{21} + B_{1,21} X_{t-1} + B_{2,21} H_{t-1} + B_{3,21} U_{t-1} + B_{4,21} \hat{O}_t + V_{21t}$$

$$H_{t-1}^o = A_{22} + B_{1,22} X_{t-1} + B_{2,22} H_{t-1} + B_{3,22} U_{t-1} + B_{4,22} \hat{O}_t + V_{22t}$$

$$U_{t-1}^s = A_{31} + B_{1,31} X_{t-1} + B_{2,31} H_{t-1} + B_{3,31} U_{t-1} + B_{4,31} \hat{O}_t + V_{31t}$$

$$U_{t-1}^o = A_{32} + B_{1,32} X_{t-1} + B_{2,32} H_{t-1} + B_{3,32} U_{t-1} + B_{4,32} \hat{O}_t + V_{32t}$$

$$\hat{O}_t^s = A_{41} + B_{1,41} X_{t-1} + B_{2,41} H_{t-1} + B_{3,41} U_{t-1} + B_{4,41} \hat{O}_t + V_{41t}$$

$$\hat{O}_t^o = A_{42} + B_{1,42} X_{t-1} + B_{2,42} H_{t-1} + B_{3,42} U_{t-1} + B_{4,42} \hat{O}_t + V_{42t} \,.$$

Theil's result tells us,

$$a_{11} = B_{1,11} a_{11}^s + B_{1,12} a_{11}^o + B_{1,21} a_{12}^s B_{1,22} a_{12}^o + B_{1,31} a_{13}^s$$
$$+ B_{1,32} a_{13}^o + B_{1,41} b_{10}^s + B_{1,42} b_{10}^o$$

and

$$B_{1,11} + B_{1,12} = 1$$
$$B_{1,21} + B_{1,22} = 0$$
$$B_{1,31} + B_{1,32} = 0$$
$$B_{1,41} + B_{1,42} = 0 \,.$$

The B's are least squares coefficients but since these are not available Childs conjectures as to their signs, for instance, $B_{1,12} > 0$. Before doing this, however, he makes some assumptions which simplify the analysis but in one or two cases lead to further problems.

The assumptions are

(a) U^{s} and H^{o} are randomly and independently determined;

(b) $\hat{O}_t^{\text{s}}$ varies directly with $\hat{O}_t^{\text{o}}$; and

(c) X_t^{o} and U_t^{o} are independent of X_t^{s} and H_t^{s}, i.e., no complementarity exists nor are the two goods subject to a joint capacity constraint.

These assumptions, the Theil results, and a priori ideas of the signs of various coefficients, enables Childs to give some indication of the signs he expects in his regression results. We will illustrate the type of arguments he uses by considering a_{11}.

Since U^{s} is assumed to be random Childs assumes that $a_{11}^{\text{s}}, a_{12}^{\text{s}}, a_{13}^{\text{s}}, b_{10}^{\text{s}}$ and a_{12}^{o} are zero. Thus

$$a_{11} = B_{1,12}a_{11}^{\text{o}} + B_{1,32}a_{13}^{\text{o}} + B_{1,42}b_{10}^{\text{o}} \, .$$

Childs argues that since the decision rule is essentially a smoothing process, the decision variables X, U, and H will be serially correlated, thus $a_{13}^{\text{o}} > 0$. In addition, an increase in production in period $t-1$ will cause unfilled orders to be lower one period later, thus $a_{11}^{\text{o}} < 0$. Furthermore, $b_{10} > 0$ since an increase in orders will not be fully matched by shipments. Thus, he maintains that the expected sign of a_{11} is negative since

$$a_{11} = \underset{+}{B_{1,12}}\underset{-}{a_{11}^{\text{o}}} + \underset{(-)}{B_{1,32}}\underset{+}{a_{13}^{\text{o}}} + \underset{(+)}{B_{1,42}}\underset{+}{b_{10}^{\text{o}}} \, .$$

In a similar way he analyses each macro parameter of the following decision rules.

$$\begin{aligned}
U_t &= \underset{-}{a_{11}}X_{t-1} + \underset{*}{a_{12}}H_{t-1} + \underset{+}{a_{13}}U_{t-1} + \underset{+}{b_{10}}\hat{O}_t + h_1 + u_{1t} \\
H_t &= \underset{+}{a_{21}}X_{t-1} + \underset{+}{a_{22}}H_{t-1} + \underset{*}{a_{23}}U_{t-1} + \underset{(-)}{b_{20}}\hat{O}_t + h_2 + u_{2t} \\
U_t &= \underset{-}{\alpha_{11}}X_{t-1} + \underset{-}{\alpha_{12}}(H_{t-1} - U_{t-1}) + \underset{+}{\beta_{10}}\hat{O}_t + \gamma_1 + \mu_{1t} \\
H_t &= \underset{+}{\alpha_{21}}X_{t-1} + \underset{+}{\alpha_{22}}(H_{t-1} - U_{t-1}) + \underset{(-)}{\beta_{20}}\hat{O}_t + \gamma_2 + \mu_{2t} \, .
\end{aligned} \tag{5.52}$$

Table 5.11
All manufacturing.
Least squares regression estimates: decision rules for unfilled orders and inventories with implied rule for production. Desired level of inventories depends upon the rate of shipments.

Variable	Demand forecasts based on lagged orders			Perfect forecasts		
	U_t	H_t	X_t	U_t	H_t	X_t
Constant	1948.4 (653.6)	−428.1 (106.0)	−2376.5	−612.5 (501.5)	−498.4 (109.7)	114.1
X_{t-1}	−0.7995 (0.0869)	0.0123 (0.0141)	0.8118	−0.5170 (0.0475)	0.0178 (0.0104)	0.5348
H_{t-1}	−0.1325 (0.0668)	0.9713 (0.0108)	0.1038	−0.2171 (0.0474)	0.9712 (0.0104)	0.1883
U_{t-1}	0.9656 (0.0084)	0.0043 (0.0014)	0.0387	0.9893 (0.0064)	0.0051 (0.0014)	0.0158
O_{t-1}	0.6142 (0.0706)	0.0022 (0.0115)	−0.6120			
O_{t-2}	0.0754 (0.0783)	−0.0039 (0.0127)	−0.0793			
O_{t-3}	0.1851 (0.0713)	0.0149 (0.0116)	−0.1702			
O_t			1.0000	0.7513 (0.0543)	0.0069 (0.0119)	0.4356
O_{t+1}				0.0616 (0.0572)	−0.0205 (0.0125)	−0.0821
O_{t+2}				0.0455 (0.0481)	0.0221 (0.0105)	−0.0234
R^2	0.9943	0.9989		0.9973	0.9989	
s_e	550.7	89.3		404.9	88.6	
Mean of dependent variable	53,496	17,044		53,786	16,905	
Durbin-Watson	1.9538	1.5312		1.6928	1.5204	
d.f.	133	133		133	133	

Table 5.12
Primary metals.
Least squares regression estimates: decision rules for unfilled orders and inventories with implied rule for production. Desired level of inventories depends upon the rate of shipments.

Variable	Demand forecasts based on lagged orders			Perfect forecasts		
	U_t	H_t	X_t	U_t	H_t	X_t
Constant	507.4	− 47.4	−554.8	−113.4	− 37.3	76.1
	(170.0)	(18.4)		(135.4)	(21.6)	
X_{t-1}	−0.7290	0.0136	0.7426	−0.4849	−0.0024	0.4825
	(0.0877)	(0.0095)		(0.0535)	(0.0085)	
H_{t-1}	−0.2703	1.0248	0.2951	−0.2251	1.0120	0.2371
	(0.1092)	(0.0118)		(0.0770)	(0.0123)	
U_{t-1}	0.9282	0.0083	0.0801	0.9598	0.0056	0.0458
	(0.0190)	(0.0020)		(0.0132)	(0.0021)	
O_{t-1}	0.5785	0.0122	−0.5663			
	(0.0807)	(0.0087)				
O_{t-2}	0.2071	−0.0058	−0.2129			
	(0.1057)	(0.0114)				
O_{t-3}	0.0521	−0.0306	−0.0827			
	(0.0882)	(0.0095)				
O_t			1.0000	0.5668	−0.0077	0.4255
				(0.0652)	(0.0104)	
O_{t+1}				0.0663	0.0092	−0.0571
				(0.0742)	(0.0119)	
O_{t+2}				0.0904	−0.0005	−0.0909
				(0.0603)	(0.0096)	
R^2	0.9853	0.9940		0.9929	0.9934	
s_e	258.4	27.9		185.0	29.5	
Mean of dependent variable	6002.2	1350.5		6060.5	1333.0	
Durbin-Watson	1.8445	1.1282		1.7372	0.8934	
d.f.	132	132		132	132	

Table 5.13
Summary of signs and t ratios of regression coefficients in the rule for unfilled orders.

Independent variable and sign of coefficient		Number of coefficients with absolute value of t of				Total estimated coeffi-cients	Expected signs of		
		0–0.99	1–1.49	1.5–1.99	$\geqslant 2$		Corresponding micro-parameter	Bias from aggregation of products	Macro-parameter
X_{t-1}	positive	1	4	1	2	8	–	(u)	–
	negative	0	1	1	18	20			
$(H_{t-1} - U_{t-1})$	positive	0	0	0	0	0	–	u	–
	negative	0	0	0	14	14			
H_{t-1}	positive	0	0	0	0	0	none	u	u
	negative	0	1	2	11	14			
U_{t-1}	positive	0	0	0	14	14	+	+	+
	negative	0	0	0	0	0			
O_{t-1}	positive	0	2	2	10	14	+	n	+
	negative	0	0	0	0	0			
O_{t-2}	positive	5	0	2	6	13	+	n	+
	negative	1	0	0	0	1			
O_{t-3}	positive	3	2	3	5	13	+	n	+
	negative	1	0	0	0	1			
O_t	positive	0	0	0	14	14	+	u	+
	negative	0	0	0	0	0			
O_{t+1}	positive	5	1	0	0	6	u	u	u
	negative	4	2	0	2	8			
O_{t+2}	positive	7	1	1	0	9	u	n	u
	negative	4	1	0	0	5			

Table 5.14
Summary of signs and t-ratios of regression coefficients in the rule for inventories.

Independent variable and sign of coefficient		Number of coefficients with absolute value of t of				Total estimated coeffi-cients	Expected sign of		
		0–0.99	1–1.49	1.5–1.99	$\geqslant 2$		Corresponding micro-parameter	Bias from aggregation of products	Macro-parameter
X_{t-1}	positive	4	2	3	17	26	+	(u)	+
	negative	2	0	0	0	2			
$(H_{t-1} - U_{t-1})$									
	positive	1	0	1	12	14	+	u	+
	negative	0	0	0	0	0			
H_{t-1}	positive	0	0	0	14	14	+	u	+
	negative	0	0	0	0	0			
U_{t-1}	positive	3	1	2	8	14	none	u	u
	negative	0	0	0	0	0			
O_{t-1}	positive	4	1	0	0	5	–	n	(–)
	negative	4	0	1	4	9			
O_{t-2}	positive	7	1	0	0	8	–	n	(–)
	negative	6	0	0	0	6			
O_{t-3}	positive	4	4	4	0	12	–	n	(–)
	negative	1	0	0	1	2			
O_t	positive	4	1	0	0	5	–	+	(–)
	negative	6	3	0	0	9			
O_{t+1}	positive	6	0	0	0	6	u	n	u
	negative	6	1	1	0	8			
O_{t+2}	positive	7	0	1	1	9	u	n	u
	negative	3	1	1	0	5			

Brackets imply close to zero; u implies uncertain sign; n implies not discussed.

The signs he expects appear beneath the parameters. An unknown sign is signified by a * and a close to zero coefficient by a bracket. In the equations he estimates, three expectations variables occur rather than one. Childs believes that the lagged values O_{t-1}, O_{t-2}, O_{t-3} will have the same sign as O_t but that the signs of O_{t+1} and O_{t+2} are rather uncertain.

In the tables 5.11 and 5.12 are reproduced the results for (5.52) for 'all manufacturing' and 'primary metals'. The signs of the estimates are in line with those indicated in (5.52). It would take too much space to report all Childs results but tables 5.13 and 5.14 show that the signs of his empirical results tend to conform to the a priori information of (5.52).

Childs then, has produced inventory models which incorporate unfilled orders into the decision framework (as opposed to Lovell's ad hoc introduction into the final equations) and which seem to be consistent with the a priori restrictions and the data available. This seems more satisfactory than the earlier work, for instance, compare Childs' and Lovell's total manufacturing equations. Before leaving Childs' work we should mention that he looks at the stability of his system and finds that it is in accord with actual experience. Since his inventory, unfilled orders and production equations are interdependent difference equations they can be written as follows.

$$\begin{bmatrix} 1 & -1 & 1 \\ 0 & 1 & 0 \\ 0 & 0 & 1 \end{bmatrix} \begin{bmatrix} X_t \\ H_t \\ U_t \end{bmatrix} = \begin{bmatrix} 0 & -1 & 1 \\ a_{21} & a_{22} & a_{23} \\ a_{11} & a_{12} & a_{13} \end{bmatrix} \begin{bmatrix} X_{t-1} \\ H_{t-1} \\ U_{t-1} \end{bmatrix} + \begin{bmatrix} p(t) \\ g(t) \\ f(t) \end{bmatrix}$$

where $p(t)$, $g(t)$ and $f(t)$ are functions of t. Thus, given the values of the a_{ij} we can find the roots of this system. Childs does so and states that although no tests have been performed the results indicate that the general pattern is one of strongly damped fluctuations. This is what we would expect since the coefficients have been estimated from such data.

It would appear then that there is a complex interaction between unfilled orders and inventories, and that the production to order distinction is important. Childs has indicated this for a handful of industries. If we wish to see how the distinction fares in other industries we must turn to Belsley's work.

5.7.3. Belsley (1969)

In this study Belsley develops production decision rules for nineteen industries from monthly undeflated data obtained from the Bureau of the Census. Both seasonally adjusted and unadjusted data are used but here we only report the results based on the adjusted data. Six industries have no unfilled orders and these the author takes to be pure production to stock industries. All the other industries he assumes involve both production to stock and order. To proceed beyond the results of Section 5.3.2 he introduces the following assumptions.

Assumption 1

$S_t^s = O_t^s + \epsilon_t$ when ϵ_t is a stochastic term.

Assumption 2

$\hat{O}_t^s$ and $\hat{O}_t^o$ are so strongly auto correlated that

$$\sum_{i=0}^{N} \delta_{i+3} \hat{O}_{t+i}^s, \quad \sum_{i=0}^{N} \epsilon_{i+3} \hat{O}_{t+i}^o, \quad \sum_{i=0}^{N} \zeta_{5+i} \hat{O}_{t+i}^s,$$

$$\sum_{i=0}^{N} \zeta_{6+N+i} \hat{O}_{t+i}^s, \quad \sum_{i=0}^{N} \eta_{5+i} \hat{O}_{t+i}^s, \quad \text{and} \quad \sum_{i=0}^{N} \eta_{6+N+i} \hat{O}_{t+i}^o$$

can be replaced by $\delta_3 \hat{O}_t^s$, $\epsilon_3 \hat{O}_t^o$, $\zeta_5 \hat{O}_t^s$, $\zeta_6 \hat{O}_t^o$, $\eta_5 \hat{O}_t^s$ and $\eta_6 \hat{O}_t^o$. (Note that for convenience the subscripts of ζ_{6+N} and η_{6+N} are replaced by 6.)

Using assumptions 1 and 2, (5.31) becomes

$$X_t^s = \delta_0 + \delta_1 X_{t-1}^s + \delta_2 H_{t-1} + \delta_3 S_t + \epsilon_t \,.$$

Before estimating these coefficients he considers their likely values. The coefficient of X_{t-3}^s, i.e. δ_1, represents the influence of the cost of changing production, this he considers should lie between zero and unity, i.e. $0 < \delta_1 < 1$. Since H_{t-1} is a short-run buffer, a higher level of inventory, ceteris paribus, would imply less reason to hold the current production level, thus $\delta_2 < 0$. The less significant are the costs of holding inventories the closer δ_2 goes to zero. The more costly holding inventories becomes, the closer δ_2 goes to -1, since with very high cost of holding inventories production decisions will be reduced in order to wipe them out. We would expect that δ_3 also lies between zero and one since the firm will not fully adjust production according to new sales. The regression results are presented in table 5.15. These results suggest that production smoothing is not very important for this industry since δ_3 is

Table 5.15
Production decision for industries without unfilled orders. (162 observations.)

	δ_0	δ_1	δ_2	δ_3	$\bar{R}^2$
Food an kindred products	432.46 (138.68)	0.1037 (0.0604)	−0.5364 (0.1257)	0.9781 (0.0536)	0.9987
Tobacco manufactures	163.59 (76.00)	−0.1677 (0.1091)	−0.2418 (0.1024)	1.0492 (0.1285)	0.9251
Apparel	−32.83 (76.25)	0.0224 (0.0369)	−0.0673 (0.0628)	1.0053 (0.0361)	0.9808
Chemical and allied	−26.13 (16.07)	0.0881 (0.0236)	−0.1754 (0.0442)	0.9610 (0.0219)	0.9997
Petroleum and coal	134.97 (42.23)	0.1540 (0.0382)	−0.3620 (0.0848)	0.9004 (0.0346)	0.9969
Rubber and plastics	6.32 (13.13)	0.0630 (0.0397)	−0.1476 (0.0594)	0.9770 (0.0365)	0.9983

close to one and δ_1 is small. Although they are in the main significant, the coefficients of H_{t-1} are close to zero.

The other industries present us with data problems because if (5.33) and (5.34) are to be estimated even using assumption 2 we need series for X^{o}, X^{s}, $\hat{O}^{\mathrm{o}}$ and $\hat{O}^{\mathrm{s}}$. These are not available and, as a result, Belsley is forced to make some assumptions to circumvent the problem.

Using assumption 2, (5.33) and (5.34) become

$$X_t^{\mathrm{o}} = \zeta_0 + \zeta_1 X_{t-1}^{\mathrm{s}} + \zeta_2 X_{t-1}^{\mathrm{o}} + \zeta_3 H_{t-1} + \zeta_5 \hat{O}_t^{\mathrm{s}} + \zeta_6 \hat{O}_t^{\mathrm{o}} + w_t \tag{5.53}$$

$$X_t^{\mathrm{s}} = \eta_0 + \eta_1 X_{t-1}^{\mathrm{s}} + \eta_2 X_{t-1}^{\mathrm{o}} + \eta_3 H_{t-1} + \eta_4 U_{t-1} + \eta_5 \hat{O}_t^{\mathrm{s}} + \eta_6 \hat{O}_t^{\mathrm{o}} + u_t \,. \tag{5.54}$$

Since $S_t^{\mathrm{o}} = X_t^{\mathrm{o}}$, and $X_t^{\mathrm{o}} + S_t^{\mathrm{s}} = S_t$,

$$S_t = \zeta_0 + \zeta_1 X_{t-1}^{\mathrm{s}} + \zeta_2 X_{t-1}^{\mathrm{o}} + \zeta_3 H_{t-1} + \zeta_4 U_{t-1} + (1+\zeta_5)\hat{O}_t^{\mathrm{s}} + \zeta_0 \hat{O}_t^{\mathrm{o}} + (w_t + \epsilon_t) \,. \tag{5.55}$$

Also,

$$X_t = X_t^o + X_t^s = \theta_0 + \theta_1 X_{t-1}^s + \theta_2 X_{t-1}^o + \theta_3 H_{t-1}$$

$$+ \theta_4 U_{t-1} + \theta_5 \hat{O}_t^s + \theta_6 \hat{O}_t^o + (w_t + u_t) \qquad (5.56)$$

where $\theta_i = \zeta_i + \eta_i$. Thus from (5.55),

$$S_t = \zeta_0 + \zeta_2 X_{t-1} + (\zeta_1 - \zeta_2) X_{t-1}^s + \zeta_3 H_{t-1}$$

$$+ \zeta_4 U_{t-1} + (1 + \zeta_5 - \zeta_6) \hat{O}_t^s + \zeta_6 \hat{O}_t + (w_t + \epsilon_t) \qquad (5.57)$$

and from

$$X_t = \theta_0 + \theta_2 X_{t-1} + (\theta_1 - \theta_2) X_{t-1}^s + \theta_3 H_{t-1}$$

$$+ \theta_4 U_{t-1} + (\theta_3 - \theta_6) \hat{O}_t^s + \theta_6 \hat{O}_t + (w_t + u_t) \,. \qquad (5.58)$$

All series in (5.57) and (5.58) are observed except X_{t-1}^s, $\hat{O}_t^s$ and $\hat{O}_t$. At this point further assumptions are necessary. Of course a simple assumption would be that X_t^s is a fixed proportion of X_t but this would be too restrictive. A less restrictive approach is to assume that there is no effect on an aggregate variable, say X_t, if the two disaggregate variables change. Belsley in fact uses the following assumptions.

Assumption 3

$$\zeta_1 - \zeta_2 + \zeta_5 - \zeta_6 = -\sigma$$

and

$$\eta_1 - \eta_2 + \eta_5 - \eta_6 = \sigma$$

$$\therefore \quad \theta_1 - \theta_2 + \theta_5 - \theta_6 = 0$$

i.e.

$$(\theta_5 - \theta_6) = -(\theta_1 - \theta_2) \,. \qquad (5.59)$$

These restrictions imply that if X_{t-1}^s, X_{t-1}^o, $\hat{O}_t^s$ and O_t^o were changed by 1 unit the effect on X_t^o and X_t^s would be such that total production X_t would be unchanged.

Using (5.58) and (5.59),

$$X_t = \theta_0 + \theta_2 X_{t-1} + (\theta_1 - \theta_2)(X_{t-1}^s - \hat{O}_t^s) + \theta_3 H_{t-1}$$

$$+ \theta_4 U_{t-1} + \theta_6 \hat{O}_t + (w_t + u_t) .$$

This can be further simplified by

Assumption 4

$$\hat{O}_t^s \approx S_{t-1}^s \tag{5.60}$$

then,

$$X_t = \theta_0 + \theta_2 X_{t-1} + (\theta_1 - \theta_2)\Delta H_{t-1} + \theta_3 H_{t-1}$$

$$+ \theta_4 U_{t-1} + \theta_6 \hat{O}_t + (w_t + u_t) \tag{5.61}$$

since $X_{t-1}^s - S_{t-1}^s = \Delta H_{t-1}$.
This equation can be estimated from the data available, however, (5.55) needs a further assumption, the utility of which can be most easily seen if (5.55) is rewritten as,

$$S_t = \zeta_0 + \zeta_2 X_{t-1} + (\zeta_1 - \zeta_2) X_{t-1}^s + \zeta_3 H_{t-1} + \zeta_4 U_{t-1}$$

$$+ (1 + \zeta_5 - \zeta_6)\hat{O}_t^s + \zeta_6 \hat{O}_t + (w_t + \epsilon_t) . \tag{5.62}$$

Assumption 5

$$\sigma = 1$$

i.e.

$$\zeta_1 - \zeta_2 = -(1 + \zeta_5 - \zeta_6) . \tag{5.63}$$

Combining (5.62) and (5.63),

$$S_t = \zeta_0 + \zeta_2 X_{t-1} + (\zeta_1 - \zeta_2)[X_{t-1}^s - \hat{O}_t^s] + \zeta_3 H_{t-1}$$

$$+ \zeta_4 U_{t-1} + \zeta_6 \hat{O}_t + w_t + \epsilon_t .$$

This can be approximated as above by

$$S_t = \zeta_0 + \zeta_2 X_{t-1} + (\zeta_1 - \zeta_2)\Delta H_{t-1} + \zeta_3 H_{t-1}$$
$$+ \zeta_4 U_{t-1} + \zeta_6 \hat{O}_t + w_t + \epsilon_t \,. \qquad (5.64)$$

Belsley justifies assumption 5 on the following grounds. In the PTS case, the effect of lagged production and inventories is small. If the same is true for the PTS element of the mixed production firm it seems reasonable to assume that the cross effects in the X^s equation are small, i.e., η_2 and η_6 are small. Hence $\sigma \approx \eta_1 + \eta_5 \approx \delta_1 + \delta_3$. For five out of the six industries whose results are reported, $\delta_1 + \delta_3 \approx 1$, thus $\sigma = 1$ seems reasonable. Applying ordinary least squares to (5.64) where $\hat{O}$ is replaced by O produces estimates of ζ_i. Subtracting (5.64) from (5.61) gives

$$X_t - S_t = \Delta H_t = \eta_0 + \eta_2 X_{t-1} + (\eta_1 - \eta_2)\Delta H_{t-1}$$
$$+ \eta_3 H_{t-1} + \eta_4 U_{t-1} + \eta_6 \hat{O}_t + (u_t - \epsilon_t) \,. \qquad (5.65)$$

Thus applying least squares to (5.65) produces estimates of η_i. Before doing this, however, he discusses the prior restrictions that η_i and ζ_i should satisfy.

By analogy with the PTS case, $0 \leqslant \eta_1 \leqslant 1$, $-1 \leqslant \eta_3 \leqslant 0$ and $0 \leqslant \eta_s \leqslant 1$. It also seems reasonable that $0 \leqslant \zeta_2 \leqslant 1$, $0 \leqslant \zeta_6 \leqslant 1$ and $0 \leqslant \zeta_4 \leqslant 1$. The cross effects are far more complicated. The signs of the coefficients will depend on the type of interdependence that occurs. If capacity constraints exist then we would expect ζ_1 and η_2 to be negative (see (5.53) and (5.54)) and also ζ_5 and η_6. On the other hand ζ_3 would be positive since high inventories will cause production to stock to fall and hence production to order can rise. A similar argument makes η_4 negative. If, however, complementarity exists, i.e. the items of one type of production are used in the production of the other, then the expected signs differ. Let us assume that this period's production of PTO firms uses PTS products from inventory (i.e. case I). Thus an increase in PTO causes inventories to fall which stimulates PTS in the following period, i.e. $\eta_2 > 0$. Ceteris paribus, an increase in inventories will allow PTO to rise, hence, $\zeta_3 > 0$ and $\eta_4 > 0$, since an increase in unfilled orders is likely to stimulate production to stock, in anticipation of future demand. A similar argument gives $\eta_6 > 0$. If PTO items are used to produce stock products (i.e. case II) then ζ_1 and $\zeta_5 > 0$, but this case does not seem very likely. If a capacity constraint and complementarity of the first kind exists the only clear sign is that of ζ_3 which should be positive. For ease of reference, the expected signs and ranges of the coefficients of (5.53) and (5.54) are presented in table 5.16 and the corresponding regression estimates in tables 5.17 and 5.18.

Table 5.16
Sign and range of coefficients with capacity or complementarity constraints.

Own effect	ζ_2	ζ_4	ζ_6	η_1	η_3	η_5
		all numerically less than 1				
	+	+	+	+	–	+
Cross effects	ζ_1	ζ_3	ζ_5	η_2	η_4	η_6
Capacity	–	+	–	–	–	–
Complementarity						
case I	u	+	u	+	+	+
case II	+	–	+	u	u	u

Considering table 5.18 we see that η_3 like its counterpart δ_0, is significantly negative. The signs of η_1 and η_3 are not so certain but on the whole η_1 does seem to be close to zero and η_5 close to unity. These results are similar to the pure PTS results in table 5.15. Turning to the coefficients of the cross effects only η_2 is significant, with a tendency to be positive in the range 0 to 0.1. This is consistent with goods produced to stock being used in production to order (i.e. case I). Notice that unfilled orders have little direct effect on production to stock and that any indirect effect must come through their effect on production to order. Turning to table 5.17, we see that the coefficient of lagged production to order is significantly positive with values close to 0.5. This indicates that production smoothing is much more important for these types of goods, as we would expect. Almost as a corollary the effect of new orders is lower than with stock goods. Unfilled orders have a small but significant effect on production to order which is consistent with Lovell's earlier findings. Belsley believes that ζ_1 is biased upward, and ζ_5 biased downwards because of the assumptions that were made, and hence, thinks it is improbable that they would differ significantly from zero. However, ζ_3 is significantly positive which suggests that production to order goods are not used in the production of stock goods.

Belsley's empirical results provide evidence for the claim that production to stock and production to order do have essentially different determinants, unfilled orders being primarily associated with PTO. The stock of inventories is important for both PTO and PTS but in the case of PTO this effect stems from the fact that stock items are used in PTO production, rather than through a buffer motive.

Table 5.17

Estimated coefficients for industries with unfilled orders: production to order. Estimates for structural relation.

$$X_t^{\text{O}} = \zeta_0 + \zeta_1 X_{t-1}^{\text{S}} + \zeta_2 X_{t-1}^{\text{O}} + \zeta_3 H_{t-1} + \zeta_4 U_{t-1} + \zeta_5 \hat{O}_t^{\text{S}} + \zeta_6 \hat{O}_t^{\text{O}}$$

Industry	ζ_0	ζ_1	ζ_2	ζ_3	ζ_4	ζ_5	ζ_6
Textile mill products	–20.49	0.1655	0.6203	0.1149	0.0302	–0.2784	0.2669
	(20.77)	(0.1417)	(0.0456)	(0.0373)	(0.0123)	(0.1415)	(0.0306)
Lumber and wood products	–56.57	0.2037	0.4119	0.0227	0.1243	–0.2427	0.5490
	(26.92)	(0.0838)	(0.0463)	(0.0365)	(0.0343)	(0.0849)	(0.0422)
Furniture and fixtures	– 3.71	0.0992	0.3501	0.2124	0.0335	–0.2326	0.5164
	(7.69)	(0.1617)	(0.0483)	(0.0739)	(0.0129)	(0.1590)	(0.0365)
Paper and allied products	8.42	–0.3871	0.2585	0.0481	0.0721	0.3126	0.6670
	(7.49)	(0.1562)	(0.0350)	(0.0336)	(0.0226)	(0.1564)	(0.0307)
Printing and publishing	0.45	–0.1939	0.3859	0.2709	0.0585	0.0886	0.5087
	(19.56)	(0.1971)	(0.0521)	(0.0861)	(0.0236)	(0.1900)	(0.0439)
Leather and leather products	– 2.85	0.2735	0.6916	0.1782	0.0199	–0.3947	0.1873
	(9.18)	(0.1925)	(0.0472)	(0.0514)	(0.0127)	(0.1900)	(0.0322)
Stone, clay and glass	–53.74	0.0342	0.2330	0.1300	0.0910	–0.1903	0.6109
	(29.02)	(0.1654)	(0.0455)	(0.0272)	(0.0238)	(0.1615)	(0.0355)
Primary metals industries	–53.27	1.7577	0.4809	0.2671	0.0484	–1.9764	0.3003
	(102.26)	(0.4609)	(0.0508)	(0.0731)	(0.0124)	(0.4618)	(0.0309)
Fabricated metal products	104.54	–0.2940	0.4183	0.2527	0.0296	0.0124	0.3001
	(31.92)	(0.1740)	(0.0561)	(0.0541)	(0.0068)	(0.1755)	(0.0307)
Machinery, except electrical	15.47	0.2851	0.6558	0.1449	0.0080	–0.4354	0.1940
	(21.85)	(0.1865)	(0.0479)	(0.0360)	(0.0037)	(0.1899)	(0.0224)
Electrical machinery	–38.07	–0.0713	0.6882	0.1643	0.0080	–0.0354	0.2051
	(38.86)	(0.2426)	(0.0489)	(0.0577)	(0.0048)	(0.2442)	(0.0285)
Transportation equipment	345.62	4.3910	0.7088	0.4273	–0.0001	–4.5521	0.1301
	(114.23)	(1.0025)	(0.0528)	(0.1730)	(0.0038)	(1.0109)	(0.0311)
Instruments and related	– 1.15	–0.6699	0.6286	0.3184	0.0216	0.4316	0.1331
	(4.83)	(0.1957)	(0.0583)	(0.0674)	(0.0075)	(0.1968)	(0.0243)

Table 5.18

Estimated coefficients for industries with unfilled orders: production to stock. Estimates for structural relation.

$$X_t^s = \eta_0 + \eta_1 X_{t-1}^s + \eta_2 X_{t-1}^o + \eta_3 H_{t-1} + \eta_4 U_{t-1} + \eta_5 \hat{O}_t^s + \eta_6 \hat{O}_t^o$$

Industry	η_0	η_1	η_2	η_3	η_4	η_5	η_6
Textile mill products	−21.93	0.1254	0.0651	−0.0303	−0.0013	0.9215	−0.0182
	(12.29)	(0.0838)	(0.0271)	(0.0221)	(0.0074)	(0.0837)	(0.0182)
Lumber and wood products	41.83	0.2262	0.1325	−0.1237	−0.0122	0.8274	−0.0788
	(24.75)	(0.0768)	(0.0425)	(0.0335)	(0.0315)	(0.0781)	(0.0388)
Furniture and fixtures	− 0.81	−0.2260	0.0543	−0.1126	−0.0027	1.2892	0.0090
	(3.83)	(0.0806)	(0.0241)	(0.0368)	(0.0064)	(0.0792)	(0.0183)
Paper and allied products	−12.73	−0.0762	0.0514	−0.0351	0.0114	1.0982	−0.0294
	(3.83)	(0.0798)	(0.0179)	(0.0172)	(0.0115)	(0.0800)	(0.0157)
Printing and publishing	6.99	−0.1447	0.0091	−0.0258	−0.0081	1.1523	−0.0014
	(8.57)	(0.0864)	(0.0228)	(0.0378)	(0.0104)	(0.0833)	(0.0192)
Leather and leather products	− 3.57	−0.1378	0.0044	−0.0047	0.0012	1.1528	0.0106
	(4.09)	(0.0857)	(0.0210)	(0.0229)	(0.0056)	(0.0845)	(0.0143)
Stone, clay and glass	− 4.66	0.0645	0.0927	−0.0253	−0.0012	0.9663	−0.0619
	(14.34)	(0.0817)	(0.0225)	(0.0134)	(0.0117)	(0.0798)	(0.0175)
Primary metals industries	− 2.83	0.4245	−0.0052	0.0013	0.0027	0.5716	0.0013
	(16.67)	(0.0751)	(0.0083)	(0.0119)	(0.0020)	(0.0753)	(0.0051)
Fabricated metal products	−20.48	−0.0075	0.0531	−0.0635	0.0014	1.0563	−0.0043
	(14.97)	(0.0816)	(0.0263)	(0.0254)	(0.0032)	(0.0824)	(0.0144)
Machinery, except electrical	− 9.44	0.0508	−0.0050	−0.0261	0.0030	0.9685	0.0243
	(9.74)	(0.0831)	(0.0214)	(0.0160)	(0.0017)	(0.0846)	(0.0099)
Electrical machinery	10.38	0.1699	0.0487	−0.0717	0.0000	0.8708	−0.0080
	(11.26)	(0.0784)	(0.0158)	(0.0187)	(0.0016)	(0.0789)	(0.0092)
Transportation equipment	−26.35	0.0147	0.0086	−0.0429	0.0003	0.9987	0.0047
	(9.47)	(0.0831)	(0.0044)	(0.0143)	(0.0003)	(0.0838)	(0.0026)
Instruments and related	− 5.19	−0.2107	0.0192	−0.0456	0.0038	1.2455	0.0157
	(1.97)	(0.0800)	(0.0239)	(0.0276)	(0.0030)	(0.0812)	(0.0099)

5.7.4. Courchene (1967)

So far the studies which distinguish PTO and PTS have concerned U.S. data. This study involves Canadian data. Courchene analyses total manufacturing and the ten subsectors into which this is disaggregated. He realises that all of these sectors involve PTO and PTS but to differing degrees. Pure PTS involves no unfilled orders and pure PTO involves no inventories. Because of this he uses H/U averaged over the period 1955–1962 to rank the sectors as shown in table 5.19.

'Heavy transport', Courchene uses as an example of pure PTO whereas 'semi-durable consumer goods' is his pure PTS industry. 'Perishable consumer goods' is spurned on this account because perishable items are not governed by future demand. Throughout, the data used are seasonally adjusted on a monthly basis and summed to provide quarterly figures for the period 1955(i) to 1962(iv). The series are not deflated for price changes.

Finished goods inventories in pure PTO Courchene expects to be random, whereas in pure PTS he expects them to be explained by an equation similar to that used by Lovell, i.e.,

$$\Delta H = \delta\alpha + \delta\beta S_t + \lambda\Delta S - \delta H_{t-1} + u_t \, .$$

Data from high ranking industries should be consistent with this equation but not those from high ranking industries. The least squares results appear in table 5.20.

Two fit statistics are given, the first is the multiple correlation coefficient

Table 5.19
PTS and PTO rankings of Canadian subsectors.

	H/U	Ranking
Perishable consumer goods	20.20	10
Semi-durable consumer goods	1.63	9
Durable consumer goods	0.49	4
Heavy transport	0.014	1
Other capital goods	0.30	2
Construction goods	0.31	3
Largely export producing	1.03	8
Motor vehicles and related	0.95	7
Intermediate goods and supplies	0.92	6
Unclassified	0.88	5
Total manufacture	0.58	

Table 5.20
Finished goods inventories. (Figures in parentheses are t ratios.)

Industry ranking	$\alpha\delta$	$\beta\delta$	λ	δ	$\bar{R}$	$\bar{R}_2$
1	0.319 (1.82)	−0.012 (1.70)	−0.007 (1.01)	0.099 (0.80)	0.18	0.83
2	2.550 (3.24)	0.126 (4.70)	+0.133 (2.72)	0.610 (5.32)	0.71	0.92
3	−0.085 (0.06)	0.055 (1.26)	+0.100 (1.98)	0.193 (2.52)	0.38	0.95
4	−0.548 (0.79)	0.095 (2.41)	+0.256 (3.93)	0.185 (3.58)	0.63	0.97
5	−3.334 (0.93)	0.151 (2.12)	−0.064 (0.63)	0.467 (2.60)	0.44	0.90
6	−1.909 (1.36)	0.093 (2.86)	+0.165 (2.76)	0.237 (2.81)	0.47	0.98
7	−0.460 (0.49)	0.046 (2.26)	+0.058 (2.48)	0.188 (2.83)	0.53	0.92
8	−2.200 (0.88)	0.040 (1.33)	+0.094 (2.19)	0.076 (1.15)	0.22	0.96
9	−0.587 (0.79)	0.118 (3.23)	+0.181 (4.00)	0.307 (3.91)	0.63	0.97
10	2.198 (1.67)	0.076 (2.46)	−0.044 (0.64)	0.561 (2.89)	0.42	0.92
Total manufacture	−22.89 (3.46)	0.114 (5.39)	+0.1399 (3.57)	0.311 (5.95)	0.73	0.99

when ΔH is the dependent variable, the second is the corresponding coefficient for H. The buffer stock motive does not seem to be operative for industry 1, whereas for most of the others there does seem to be some influence from this aspect. Courchene introduces some more explanatory variables into some of these equations, but in essence they remain of the buffer stock variety.

In Section 5.3.3 we developed Courchene's theory for goods in progress, and it will be recalled that an important aspect is the time that the production process takes to complete. Once again Courchene ranks his industries, this time according to X_t/U_t, to get some idea of those with the long production processes. The one with the longest by this criterion is 'heavy transport' and in the interests of brevity we shall only report the results for this industry. In fact, Courchene presents an equation for each of his 10 subsectors and total manufacturing, although these differ from each other as he introduces a number of different explanatory variables. However, to illustrate his emphasis on the PTS–PTO distinction one result will suffice. From Section 5.3.3,

$$\Delta I_{g\mathrm{p}} = \delta(I^{\mathrm{d}}_{g\mathrm{p}t} - I_{g\mathrm{p}t-1}) \qquad (5.37)$$

$$I^{\mathrm{d}}_{g\mathrm{p}} = a + d_1 U_{t-2} + d_2 O_{t-1} + d_1 O_t - d_0 S_t \qquad (5.36)$$

$$d_1 > d_2 > d_3; \quad d_0 > 0 .$$

To this last equation Courchene adds a trend and an interest rate variable (the corporate bond rate lagged one period) and produces the following least squares regression equation.

$$\Delta I_{g\mathrm{p}} = \underset{(2.15)}{5.36} + \underset{(8.19)}{0.295}\, U_{t-1} + \underset{(7.83)}{0.241}\, O_{t-1} + \underset{(5.41)}{0.142}\, O_t$$

$$- \underset{(3.75)}{0.307}\, S_t - \underset{(4.50)}{2.43}\, r^{\mathrm{c}}_{t-1} + \underset{(5.26)}{0.278}\, T - \underset{(6.55)}{0.549}\, I_{pgt-1} \; ^{\dagger}$$

$$\bar{R} = 0.91 \qquad \mathrm{DW} = 2.39 .$$

All these coefficients are significant and satisfy the constraints above.

Courchene does go on to estimate functions for raw material inventories but he himself warns that they are only statistical relations which do not capture the underlying behaviour. He also shows that if one is only interested in goodness of fit, there is little to be gained by disaggregating total inventories into finished goods, goods in progress and raw materials, but that the aggregate relations can give a distorted view of the size of the structural parameters.

The work of Belsley, Courchene, and Childs is very persuasive of the need to distinguish production to stock and order. Much of the earlier work, e.g. that of Mills and Johnston, is still useful since the industries they were dealing with were mainly pure PTS industries. One aspect that was discussed in the

† Figures in parentheses are t ratios.

theoretical section above, but which we have not dealt with except in passing is the use of anticipations data. There have been a few studies which have used such data and it is to these that we now turn. In those studies we shall be considering whether meaningful results can be achieved by using anticipations data. Mills believed that the shippers' forecast for cement were of such poor quality that they could not be used but his corrected results show that he may have been wrong on this account. Modigliani and Sauerlender also used this series and it is to their work that we now turn.

5.8. **Empirical studies based on anticipations data**

5.8.1. Modigliani and Sauerlender (1955)

The cement industry, as we have already seen in discussing Mills' work, provides long series of seasonally unadjusted data as well as the shippers forecasts. As we might expect the forecasts are not exactly the most desirable series and one problem is that of timing. The forecasts relate to a quarter which is between four and six weeks into the future, thus they are not exactly what the authors require for the theory. In order to use these shippers forecasts Modigliani and Sauerlender re-define a season to be a three month period starting two months before the calendar quarter covered by the forecast data. Production is defined to be shipments plus increase in stock and includes cement and clinker production.

The equation (see (5.48)) for the ith season is of the form

$$X_j = a_0\hat{S}_i + a_1\hat{S}_{i+1} + a_2S_i - a_3H_{i-1}$$

where $\hat{S}_{i+1}$ represents the expected sales at the end of the current season for the following season. Least squares fitting of this equation for the first season produces

$$X_1 = \underset{(0.13)}{0.52}\,\hat{S}_i + \underset{(0.04)}{0.32}\,\hat{S}_{i+1} + \underset{(0.11)}{0.43}\,S_i - \underset{(0.09)}{0.50}\,H_{i-1}$$

$$R = 0.996\,.$$

This appears to be satisfactory although the authors do not discuss the magnitude of the individual coefficients, neither do they present results for the other seasons. They do, however, calculate the zero order correlation matrix (table 5.21) and conclude from it that the role of anticipations is stronger

Table 5.21
Zero order correlation matrix. Cement industry season I.

	H_{i-1}	$\hat{S}_i$	S_i	$\hat{S}_{i+1}$
X	−0.71	0.97	0.94	0.86
H_{i-1}		−0.67	−0.72	−0.33
$\hat{S}_i$			0.93	0.80
S_i				0.70

than that of actual shipments. Modigliani and Sauerlender also look at aggregate inventories but on these we report Pashigian's results instead.

5.8.2. Pashigian (1965)

In this study Pashigian does something which is rather unusual – he varies the period of his analysis. He compares the inventory change over the first three, six, and nine months. The data that he uses refer to 'all manufacturing', 'total durables', and 'total non-durables' for the U.S. 1948–1960. Here, we shall concentrate on his 'all manufacturing' analysis. The anticipated sales that are used in this study are taken from the *Survey of Current Business* and relate to manufacturers anticipated annual sales. These are expressed as a monthly average and Pashigian informs us that they appear to be better forecasts for the early months than for the later months of the year.

The model is the familiar flexible accelerator but without any undesired or passive inventory changes. Namely,

$$\Delta H_t^{\mathrm{p}} = \delta(H_t^{\mathrm{d}} - H_{t-1})$$

$$H_t^{\mathrm{d}} = \beta \hat{S}_t$$

$$\therefore \quad \Delta H^{\mathrm{p}} = \delta\beta\hat{S} - \delta H_{t-1} \,. \tag{5.66}$$

Into this model Pashigian introduces the concept of an expost optimal level of inventories which is related to actual sales as follows

$$H_t^{\mathrm{o}} = \beta S_t \,.$$

The adjustment mechanism is assumed to be to that above

$$\therefore \quad \Delta H_t^{\mathrm{o}} = \delta\beta S_t - \delta H_{t-1}\,. \tag{5.67}$$

It is then proposed that firms will lie between these two extremes i.e. (5.66) and (5.67), which implies that some production adaption occurs. Thus,

$$\Delta H_t = a\Delta H^{\mathrm{p}} + (1-a)\Delta H^{\mathrm{o}} \qquad \text{where } 0 \leqslant a < 1$$

$$\therefore \quad H_t = \beta a\delta\,\hat{S}_t + \beta\delta(1-a)S_t + (1-\delta)H_{t-1}\,.$$

The higher the value of a, the more important are anticipations in the determination of stock changes.

Thinking of the 3, 6, and 9 month inventory changes as separate equations we get the following three estimating equations

$$\begin{aligned} H(3) &= \beta a\delta\,\hat{S}_t + \beta\delta(1-a)S(3) + (1-\delta)H(1) \\ H(6) &= \beta a'\delta'\hat{S}_t + \beta\delta'(1-a')S(6) + (1-\delta')H(1) \\ H(9) &= \beta a''\delta''\hat{S}_t + \beta\delta''(1-a'')S(9) + (1-\delta'')H(1)\,. \end{aligned} \tag{5.68}$$

Since the anticipations surveys were carried out mainly in February Pashigian uses the level of inventories at the end of January to measure H_{t-1}. The latest actual monthly sales are used for S_t and the anticipations variable is the expected average monthly sales for the year.

The desired stock ratio β should not alter as we look at these three different models, but it is to be expected that $\delta < \delta' < \delta''$ since in a longer period a larger proportion of the discrepancy between desired stock and January stocks should have been made up. Furthermore, we would expect that anticipations would be more important earlier in the year which implies $a > a' > a''$.

Normalising the three equations by dividing by $H(1)$ gives an alternative form and we reproduce the corresponding regression results in table 5.22. When the equations are fitted directly the R^2's are of the order of 0.99. The coefficients follow the pattern that the a priori considerations suggest. The fact that a is close to one, suggests anticipations are important in determining inventories early in the year. In fact if $a = 1$ is imposed the standard error of estimate falls for case 3 and 6 to 0.0080 and 0.0251, but rises for case 9 to 0.0424, while the β and δ coefficients retain their pattern. Similar results are obtained for the 'total durables' category but the 'non-durables' results are rather unsatisfactory.

Whether the use of anticipations data is better than some form of proxy,

Table 5.22
Inventory–sales anticipations equations. For 3, 6, and 9 month periods. All manufacturing.

Period in months	3	6	9
Intercept	0.713 (0.057)	0.193 (0.167)	−0.191 (0.245)
coefficient of $\frac{\hat{S}}{H(1)}$	0.492 (0.168)	1.296 (0.413)	1.779 (0.524)
coefficient of $\frac{S(i)}{H(1)}$	0.032 (0.097)	0.167 (0.198)	0.369 (0.245)
R^2	0.78	0.77	0.75
Standard error of estimate	0.0084	0.254	0.0402
β	1.83	1.81	1.80
$\delta, \delta' \delta''$	0.29	0.81	1.19
a, a', a''	0.94	0.89	0.83

is investigated by his using three proxies for $\hat{S}$. The three proxies are (1) extrapolation of January's sales, (2) a weighted average of recent sales and (3) a weighted average of past annual sales. Of these, (1) turns out to be the most successful and we shall concentrate on this. Substituting

$$S = (1 + r)S(1)$$

into the estimating equations and then re-estimating he obtains table 5.23.

It will be noticed that the standard error of estimate is lower for the 6 and 9 month models than for the anticipations model. The January extrapolation model not only has a high standard error of estimate but also implies less reasonable values for the structural parameters. Because it is impossible to unscramble the structural coefficients without some further restriction, Pashigian imposes the constraint that β equals the average actual stock-sales ratio, i.e. 1.80, which results in the estimates reproduced in table 5.24.

It is strange that $1 + \hat{r}$ falls through the year, since one would expect businessmen to expect sales to grow. Pashigian also considers the extent to which anticipations have succeeded in forecasting actual sales vis à vis the success of forecasts based on $(1 + \hat{r})S(1)$. The latter, overall, are more accu-

Table 5.23
Inventory equations with January. Extrapolation proxy. All manufacturing.

Month	3	6	9
Intercept	0.804 (0.038)	0.389 (0.085)	0.054 (0.126)
Coefficients of $\frac{S(1)}{H(1)}$	0.417 (0.169)	1.042 (0.233)	1.408 (0.263)
Coefficient of $\frac{S(i)}{H(1)}$	−0.050 (0.142)	0.084 (0.162)	0.323 (0.179)
R^2	0.76	0.85	0.86
Standard error of estimate	0.0089	0.0206	0.0300

Table 5.24
Structural coefficients when $\beta = 1.80$.

Model	3	6	9
$1 + \hat{r}$	1.036	1.026	1.019
$\delta, \delta', \delta''$	0.20	0.61	0.95
a, a', a''	1.14	0.92	0.81

rate, but tend to persistently over-estimate, especially the March sales. In view of all the above considerations Pashigian believes that the use of the anticipations data is justified though he underlines the rather tentative character of this finding. Perhaps this was wise since Orr (1967) using Pashigian's own empirical results concludes that Pashigian is wrong.

5.8.3. Orr (1967)

Orr maintains that if one incorporates the concept of unplanned inventories into Pashigian's model, his results can be interpreted differently.

If we let $\Delta H'$ stand for actual change in inventories in Pashigian's first polar case, i.e. no revision of plans then,

$$\Delta H' = \Delta H^{\mathrm{p}} + \hat{S} - S \, .$$

Data on $\hat{S}_t$ for each month are not available and this is serious because of the role of $(\hat{S}_t - S_t)$. Orr approximates $(\hat{S}_t - S_t)$ by $n(\hat{S} - S(i))$, where $n = 2$, 5 and 8. The estimating equation now becomes

$$H = a(\delta\beta + n)\hat{S} + (1-\delta)H_{t-1} + [(1-a)\beta\delta - an]\,S(i)\,.$$

Since this is the same form as (5.68) Orr re-interprets Pashigian's results. The values of β and δ are the same but the value of a differs from Pashigian's. The difference is considerable since Orr finds $a = 0.20$, $a' = 0.20$ and $a'' = 0.18$. These values suggest that the anticipations data are nowhere near as useful as Pashigian's work suggests.

Orr also compares Pashigian's approach (which itself stems from Modigliani and Sauerlender's) to production adaption, with that of Lovell, see (5.5). Their equations, if we set $\alpha = 0$, are as follows:

Pashigian $\quad H_t = \beta a\delta\,\hat{S}_t + \beta\delta(1-a)S_t + (1-\delta)H_{t-1}$

Lovell $\quad H_t = (\delta\beta + \lambda)\hat{S}_t - \lambda S_t + (1-\delta)H_{t-1}\,.$

Since $0 \leqslant \beta, \delta, a, \lambda \leqslant 1$ there is a conflict since the coefficients of S_t are expected to have different signs. Obviously Pashigian's model allows firms to overadjust for wrong expectations, i.e., in Lovell's terms $\lambda < 0$. There seems to be no reason why firms should not do this, thus $0 \leqslant \lambda \leqslant 1$ is too rigid a constraint. Indeed Lovell himself in a more recent study, to which we now turn, has followed this approach.

5.8.4. Lovell (1967)

In this study Lovell makes use of quarterly data of manufacturers anticipations of sales and inventories to review his previous findings. These new data refer to fourteen U.S. industries and originate from surveys carried out by the Office of Business Economics. Although twenty-one surveys were carried out during the period of Lovell's sample only 18 observations can be used since the first three surveys omitted certain questions. The surveys asked firms, for the actual level of inventories at the beginning of the current and previous quarter, the expected level of inventories at the end of the current and following quarter, and the expected level of sales during the current and following quarter. Although the surveys covered different industries only the aggregate figures are broken down according to the stage of fabrication. Previously we said that anticipations data should reflect the variables which decision makers actually take account of. Interviews conducted by the Office of Business

Economics confirmed that these sales expectations lie at the heart of most companies future plans.

Early anticipations data analysed by Ferber, Mills and Modigliani and Sauerlender proved to be poor forecasts of actual sales. Lovell's first finding is that these new data are in fact very good forecasts of actual sales. Compared to a naive forecasting model the average absolute error of the short (i.e. current periods) and long (i.e. next periods) anticipations were worse than the naive in only three out of thirty-six cases. If the anticipations are good forecasts, and further analysis by Lovell tends to support this, then the anticipations data may not be particularly useful vis à vis proxies (cf. Mills) in inventory models. This is the opposite view from that of Modigliani and Sauerlender who found that the shippers' forecasts were poor forecasts but useful in explaining inventories.

As we suggested when discussing Orr's study, Lovell's model, in this later study, follows the Modigliani and Sauerlender approach to production flexibility. However, in other respects, it is similar to his own earlier model. Desired inventories are assumed to be a linear function of current and future sales, i.e.,

$$H_t^{\mathrm{d}} = \beta_1 + \beta_2 S_t + \beta_3 S_{t+1} + \epsilon_1 \,.$$

Thus, anticipated desired inventories are a function of short and long sales anticipations.

$$\hat{H}_t^{\mathrm{d}} = \beta_1 + \beta_2 \hat{S}_t + \beta_3 \hat{\hat{S}}_{t+1} + \epsilon_2 \tag{5.69}$$

where $\hat{\hat{S}}_{t+1}$ represents long anticipations. Combining this with the reaction equation (5.1) we get

$$H_t^{\mathrm{p}} = \delta\beta_1 + \delta\beta_2 \hat{S}_t + \delta\beta_3 \hat{\hat{S}}_{t+1} + (1-\delta)H_{t-1} + \epsilon_3 \,. \tag{5.70}$$

If no production flexibility is possible

$$H_t = H_t^{\mathrm{p}} - (S_t - \hat{S}_t) \tag{5.71}$$

but if complete flexibility is possible

$$H_t = \delta\beta_1 + \delta\beta_2 S_t + \delta\beta \hat{S}_{t+1} + (1-\delta)H_{t-1} + \epsilon_4 \,. \tag{5.72}$$

Then the linear combination of (5.71) and (5.72) gives

$$H_t = a(H^p + \hat{S}_t - S_t) + (1-a)\delta\beta_1 + (1-a)\delta\beta_2 S_t + (1-a)\delta\beta_3 \hat{S}_{t+1}$$

$$+ (1-a)(1-\delta)H_{t-1} + (1-a)\epsilon_4 . \qquad (5.73)$$

Using (5.70), (5.73) can be transformed to

$$H_t = H^p + [(1-a)\delta\beta_2 - a](S - \hat{S}) + (1-a)\delta\beta_3(\hat{S}_{t+1} - \hat{\hat{S}}_{t+1}) + \epsilon_6 . \qquad (5.74)$$

This equation is a realisation function and Lovell estimates it using anticipated inventories for H^p. Substituting for H^p gives,

$$H_t = \delta\beta_1 + a(1 + \delta\beta_2)\hat{S}_t + a\delta\beta_3 \hat{\hat{S}}_{t+1} + (1-a)\delta\beta_3 \hat{S}_{t+1}$$

$$+ [\delta\beta_2 - a(\delta\beta_2 + 1)] S + (1-\delta)H_{t-1} + \epsilon_7 . \qquad (5.75)$$

Firstly he considers the case where $\beta_3 = 0$ to allow comparison with his previous results. Using finished goods inventories for total durables and total non-durables he estimates,

durables

$$\Delta H_t = \underset{(1089.7)}{53.0} + \underset{(0.035)}{0.080}\, S_t - \underset{(0.139)}{0.047}\, (S_t - \hat{S}_t) - \underset{(0.166)}{0.330}\, H_{t-1}$$

$$\bar{R}^2 = 0.290 \quad DW = 1.52 \quad S_u = 280.9$$

$$\hat{\delta} = 0.330, \quad \hat{\beta}_1 = 160.5, \quad \hat{\beta}_2 = 0.242, \quad \hat{a} = 0.044.$$

non-durables

$$\Delta H_t = \underset{(540.0)}{449.0} + \underset{(0.021)}{0.089}\, S_t - \underset{(0.048)}{0.103}\, (S_t - \hat{S}_t) - \underset{(0.097)}{0.457}\, H_{t-1}$$

$$\bar{R}^2 = 0.551 \quad DW = 1.47 \quad S_u = 104.3$$

$$\hat{\delta} = 0.457, \quad \hat{\beta}_1 = 981.6, \quad \hat{\beta}_2 = 0.194, \quad \hat{a} = 0.095.$$

In both cases the low value of $\hat{a}$ suggests high flexibility. In the durable case the surprise coefficient, i.e. that of $(S - \hat{S})$ is half its standard error. Hence the buffer stock principle seems to be far less important than Lovell's earlier work suggested. When β_2 is not fixed at zero, the structural parameters are 'overidentified', so Lovell chooses the values which minimise the standard error of estimate. In this case the estimates of $\hat{a}$ are 0.06 and 0.13 for durables and non-durables. Thus the inclusion of the long sales anticipations does not do much to alter the conclusion that production is very flexible in both durable and non-durable industries.

Using either of the following proxies

$$\hat{S}_t = S_{t-1}$$

$$\hat{S}_t = \rho S_t + (1-\rho)S_{t-1}$$

in (5.75) when $\beta_3 = 0$ results in an equation the empirical results of which are:

durables

$$\Delta H = \underset{(1133.6)}{180.7} + \underset{(0.039)}{0.062}\, S_t + \underset{(0.031)}{0.011}\,(S_t - S_{t-1}) - \underset{(0.161)}{0.268}\, H_{t-1}$$

$$\bar{R}^2 = 0.290 \qquad \mathrm{DW} = 1.58 \qquad S_u = 280.9$$

non-durables

$$\Delta H = \underset{(567.9)}{306.9} + \underset{(0.030)}{0.047}\, S_t + \underset{(0.041)}{0.064}\,(S_t - S_{t-1}) - \underset{(0.132)}{0.248}\, H_{t-1}$$

$$\bar{R}^2 = 0.488 \qquad \mathrm{DW} = 1.60 \qquad S_u = 111.3\,.$$

Two points are noted from these equations. Firstly for durables the use of anticipations data as opposed to these proxies does not bring any decrease in the standard error of estimate, but in the case of non-durables there is a decrease. Secondly, the coefficients of $(S_t - S_{t-1})$ have the opposite sign to those which Lovell achieved using 1948–1955 data (see table 5.2). Thus the 1958–1963 data is consistent with the Modigliani and Sauerlender production adaption approach, but not with the early Lovell formulation, presumably because of the over-adjustment of production to sales forecast error.

The data on anticipations are available for seven durable and seven non-durable industries. Using anticipated inventories for planned inventories he estimates eqs. (5.70) and (5.74) with $\beta_3 = 0$. The results of these regressions are mixed and we shall not reproduce them there. However, Lovell is interested in the value of a and neither (5.70) nor (5.74) enable him to estimate this. Of course values of a can be derived using the same process as that used for the aggregates, but he prefers one which enables him to use more information. Notice that (5.73) can be rewritten

$$H_t - a(H^{\mathrm{p}} + \hat{S}_t - S_t) = \delta\beta_1(1-a) + \delta\beta_2(1-a)S + \delta\beta_3(1-a)\hat{S}_{t+1} + (1-\delta)(1-a)H_{t-1} + \epsilon_5 \qquad (5.76)$$

thus for a given value of a, the parameters of (5.76) are exactly the same as eq. (5.70). Thus, for a given value of a, all the data can be combined to give estimates of δ, β_1, β_2, and β_3. Subject to the constraints that $\beta_2, \beta_3 \geqslant 0$, Lovell searches over values of a between zero and one, to obtain maximum

Table 5.25
Maximum likelihood estimates of total inventory parameters of 7 durable, 7 non-durable, total durable and total non-durable industries, 1948–1963.

	a	$\delta\beta_1$	$\delta\beta_2$	$\delta\beta_3$	δ	S_u
Primary iron and steel	0.10	371.9	0	0.043	0.205	116.2
Primary non-ferreous	0.08	2.5	0.086 *	0	0.106	24.5
Electrical machinery	0.68	171.1	0.158 *	0.143 *	0.507	102.4
Machinery excluding electrical	0	1709 *	0.054	0.151 *	0.554	131.1
Motor vehicle and equipment	0	600.9 *	0.020	0.089 *	0.412	140.0
Transportation equipment	0.08	66.2	0.009	0.058	0.095	99.8
Other durables	0	309.6	0	0.052	0.175	97.4
Total durables	0	2374 *	0.098 *	0.072 *	0.341	363.9
Food and beer	0.10	409.8	0.200 *	0	0.664	204.0
Textile	0	803.8	0	0	0.298	110.3
Paper	0.05	187.9 *	0	0.161 *	0.451	30.9
Chemical	0.15	1926 *	0	0.243 *	0.900	91.3
Petroleum	0.14	1472 *	0	0.125	0.800	80.2
Rubber	0.22	229.8 *	0	0.224 *	0.515	37.2
	0.11	724.5 *	0	0.270 *	0.881	151.0
Total non-durables	0	1597	0.067	0	0.226	258.7

* Coefficient greater than twice its standard error.

likelihood estimates of a, δ, β_1, β_2 and β_3. The results appear in table 5.25. The values of a are very low, underlining Lovell's general theme. Zero values of $\delta\beta_2$ seem quite reasonable, especially when combined with significant values for $\delta\beta_3$. On this account the non-durable results seem to provide evidence supporting Lovell's desire to dismantle his earlier theory. The durable results in view of Belsley, Childs, and Courchene's work, one would not expect to be very successful.

5.9. Conclusion

The theoretical and empirical sections of this chapter have described many problems involved in explaining inventory movements. What general conclusions can we draw? We started with a rather simple explanation of inventories and this has had to be altered and occasionally scrapped altogether. The simple buffer stock–production smoothing model seems to be useful for pure production to stock industries when monthly data are available. If proxies are used to represent expectations this conclusion seems to be valid for quarterly data too. Lovell and Orr, who made use of anticipations data, concluded that firms do not make as many errors, or are as slow to adjust production as was previously thought. Their conclusions are based on quarterly data. When attention is turned to firms which have more complex products the simple buffer stock model is no longer appropriate. Belsley, Childs and Courchene have produced alternative inventory functions for the more complex industries which are consistent with the data.

So far, very little use has been made of the more sophisticated inventory functions of this chapter but the simple buffer stock functions, have been used in large and small scale macro models, for instance, Duesenberry et al. (1965) incorporates a set of such equations to which various other variables, e.g. unfilled orders, have been added. Most of these inventory equations have been included because of their effect on aggregate output, however, Liu (1963) attempts, not very successfully, to relate price changes to inventory movements. In addition there has been some research of their effect on imports (see Godley and Shepherd, 1965).

In the studies included in this chapter it would appear that only slight success in forecasting inventory changes has been achieved. Most studies, however, do present predictions. Stekler (1969) has re-estimated and tested the predictions of eleven aggregate inventory models of the buffer stock variety. His conclusion is that although the econometric inventory forecasts are not good they are better than naive extrapolations and no worse than some judgemental forecasts. Thus judgement sums up the present state of econometric inventory functions.

CHAPTER 6

PRODUCTION FUNCTIONS

6.1. Introduction

In previous chapters we have been considering practical questions of demand, i.e., given a level of incomes and prices, what will be the quantity of goods demanded. In this chapter we turn to questions of the generation and distribution of income. An important question for an economy is what is the maximum level of real income per head attainable with the present resources. How this income is to be distributed is also important. One might also wish to know what other alternative growth paths for real income per head and the corresponding income distributions are available to an economy. Real income is generated by the transformation of the services of humans (labour), goods (capital), and land into other goods and services. To obtain the services of these factors their owners have to be compensated and thus an important determinant of the distribution of income to respective factors is the form of the transformation process. This is also important in determining the various growth paths available since one set of inputs, i.e., goods (capital) is an output of previous periods' transformations. If the transformation process involves few goods, then the growth paths would be less easy to change since economists usually confine their attention to affecting the production of goods rather than humans. Furthermore, increasing the number of humans will itself tend to cause real income per head to fall. Thus the form of the transformation process, especially with regard to the role of the services of goods vis à vis humans, is of crucial importance. This transformation process can be considered as being composed of a number of determinants which are technical, behavioural, organizational, and legal in character.

The physical aspect of transformation relates to what is technically feasible, i.e., technically infeasible transformations are ruled out. Other transformations may be ruled out by legal or moral considerations, for instance, some combinations of capital and labour may be too dangerous to humans to be considered. Of all the legally and technically feasible means of transformation some will be obviously wasteful, i.e., involve more of some factors and no less of others. If all these are discarded what is left constitutes what the economist calls a production function. The transformation process also involves behavioural and organizational aspects. If two economies have the same production function and different organizational structures, e.g. a monopolistic as opposed to a competitive structure of industry, their transformation processes may differ. A further element of the transformation process is the behaviour current in the economy. This is normally linked with the organizational element. In a decentralised economy where production takes place in firms, the behaviour of each firm, e.g. profit maximisation, will effect the overall transformation process. However, the behaviour of each firm is constrained by its own technical constraints. Thus, although the questions with which we started this chapter call for consideration of the aggregate transformation process, in a decentralised economy we are forced to consider the micro elements of the process, for it is in these that our a priori knowledge of behaviour is embedded.

This situation runs parallel with the demand analysis of Chapter 3 for there also the a priori knowledge stemmed from the assumed behaviour of the individual, operating subject to his utility function. The direct estimation of the utility function was ruled out by the lack of any measurable variable for utility. In the case of the production function, however, measurable quantities of production are available and the direct estimation of production functions is not automatically ruled out. Although we have suggested that it is the behavioural aspect of the transformation process which has forced us to consider the micro unit, it is also true that much of our a priori knowledge of the technical possibilities relate to the firm or even a lower level of aggregation. For instance, the textbook justifications for diminishing marginal productivity usually refer to the simple case of adding labour to one machine. Furthermore, considering the firm level production function may enable us to make use of other non-statistical information in the form of engineering data.

So far, we have referred to the production function without being very specific, however, in the rest of this chapter we shall mean by this term a continuous twice differentiable function between inputs and outputs. This implies that we are excluding from this chapter the activity analysis and input output approaches. Even so the literature on the production function is so vast that we cannot hope to produce a comprehensive survey. Fortunately, a number of surveys already exist to which the reader can refer (see Walters, 1963; Hildebrand and Liu, 1965; and Nerlove, 1967). This field is all the more difficult because there is very little agreement on anything but the magnitude of the problem of estimating production functions. Certainly there is little agreement on the actual estimates of particular features of the empirical production functions. Indeed Brown (1967, p. 3) summing up a recent National Bureau of Economic Research Conference states:

"... there was real dissatisfaction as a result, and it was intensely expressed – in fact, the day and a half conference seemed like a winter of discontent with production economics. I would say, that its sources were the following; the inability to derive in the recent past acceptable production function estimates from engineering data and, hence, in some people's opinion, to obtain structural or stable estimates; the wide and irreconciled disparities of estimates of the elasticity of substitution taken from intercountry, interregional, interindustry, cross-section and time series data, and between small differences in time periods, thus casting doubt on the specification and results of production studies; the uncertainty that the elasticity of substitution is even pertinent to growth analysis in the short and medium run; the role of two new 'impossibility' theorems which place certain restrictions on the estimation of production functions and on their interpretation; the inability to evaluate from empirical studies of production functions whether an increase in technological change since World War II has actually occurred; and the essential lack of usefulness of the empirical results for policy purposes."

With such clear warnings the reader will appreciate why this chapter will appear to be a catalogue of the problems of econometric production functions with very little suggestion of corresponding solutions. This chapter is organised to explain these problems one at a time. We have already explained why a micro approach is useful and we start by considering the form of the production function for a firm and then introduce the complications arising from technical progress. Following this the behaviour of the firm is postulated and embedded in a number of models. There follows a discussion of the problems of identification, the measurement of variables and estimation, if firm data are available. This is followed by some discussion of aggregation problems before we report on some empirical studies.

6.2. **The form of the production function**

The general form of the production function is,

$$G(X_1, X_2, ..., X_n, \quad Y_1, Y_2, ..., Y_m, \quad L_1, L_2, ..., L_r, \quad K_1, K_2, ..., K_s) = 0 \tag{6.1}$$

where

X_i is output of good i;
Y_j is input of good j;
L_k is input of labour services of type k;
K_l is input of capital services of type l.

Land is excluded as a factor as this is usually considered constant. Eq. (6.1) is still too general and involves too many variables for any possibility of estimation to exist. The standard simplification involves the aggregation of the arguments of the function. A natural way to combine X_i and Y_j is to use their prices to give a value added variable,

$$V = F(L_1, L_2, ..., L_r, \quad K_1, K_2, ..., K_s) \tag{6.2}$$

where

$V = \sum_{i=1}^{n} p_{i0}X_i - \sum_{j=1}^{m} p_{j0}Y_j$, and

p_{i0}, p_{j0} are fixed base period prices.

Notice that the V is not the usual concept of value added since prices are not allowed to vary. In fact V represents real income originating in the firm. The production function still contains too many factors for us to handle so further grouping is necessary. In Section 6.1 we emphasised the inherent differences of capital and labour for growth theory so this distinction is usually kept. The type of production function estimated by econometricians is,

$$V = f(K, L) \tag{6.3}$$

where

$$K = K(K_1 K_2 ..., K_s) \tag{6.4}$$

and

$$L = L(L_1 L_2 ..., L_r) \tag{6.5}$$

It can be shown (see Green, 1964, p. 12) that this aggregation is possible, i.e., f is a single valued function, if and only if the marginal rate of substitution between any two types of labour (capital) is independent of any type of capital (labour). Furthermore (Green, 1964, p. 25), if the aggregation functions $K(K_1 K_2 ..., K_s)$ and $L(L_1 L_2 ..., L_r)$ are homogeneous of degree one, the aggregates K and L can be dealt with as though they are actual individual inputs.

6.2.1

Econometric theory provides some restrictions on the general shape of f in the very simple case where only one good is produced by the services of one piece of capital and one type of labour. The marginal products of each factor one would expect to be positive and decreasing, i.e.,

$$\frac{\partial V}{\partial L}, \frac{\partial V}{\partial K} > 0 \tag{6.6}$$

and

$$\frac{\partial^2 V}{\partial L^2}, \frac{\partial^2 V}{\partial K^2} < 0 . \tag{6.7}$$

Furthermore, as one factor is increased, output should approach a finite limit, i.e.,

$$V \to M_1 \quad \text{as} \quad L \to \infty \quad \text{and} \quad V \to M_2 \quad \text{as} \quad K \to \infty \tag{6.8}$$

where M_1 and M_2 are finite positive constants. Eq. (6.3) involves composite output, capital and labour but aggregation theory indicates that (6.6) and (6.7) are satisfied provided (6.2) satisfies the Hicksian stability conditions and (6.4) and (6.5) are homogeneous of degree one (see Green, 1964, p. 29). In fact many empirical studies use prices to aggregate types of capital by including the value of capital in their function. Not only does this not satisfy the homogenity condition but it also destroys the technical purity of the production function. In spite of such problems the users of production functions have believed that (6.3) should satisfy (6.6)–(6.8). Economic theory also indicates certain other concepts in production analysis which are useful. These are economies of scale, the degree of substitutability of the factors, the extent to which the production process is capital or labour intensive, and the efficiency of the process. If we can find a mathematical form whose parameters reflect these concepts especially if the parameters are pure numbers, i.e., do not depend upon the units in which the variables are measured, this form should be very convenient. A number of alternative forms are available and we shall now consider the more popular of these.

6.2.2

The Cobb–Douglas function is the most popular form for it has been and continues to be useful and convenient for empirical work. Its form is

$$V = AL^{\alpha}K^{\beta} \tag{6.9}$$

and the marginal products are

$$\frac{\partial V}{\partial L} = \alpha \frac{V}{L} \qquad \frac{\partial V}{\partial K} = \beta \frac{V}{K} . \tag{6.10}$$

Notice that

$$\frac{\partial^2 V}{\partial L^2} = \frac{\alpha(\alpha-1)}{L} \cdot \frac{V}{L} \quad \text{and} \quad \frac{\partial^2 V}{\partial K^2} = \frac{\beta(\beta-1)}{K} \cdot \frac{V}{K}. \tag{6.11}$$

Thus, (6.6) and (6.7) are satisfied but (6.8) is not. From (6.10) it can be seen that α and β are elasticities of output with regard to labour and capital. Furthermore $\alpha + \beta$ is a measure of the economies of scale where $\alpha + \beta = 1$ reflects constant returns to scale. The degree of factor substitutability involved in a production function is measured by the elasticity of substitution which is defined as

$$\sigma = \frac{\mathrm{d}(K/L)}{K/L} \bigg/ \frac{\mathrm{d}(-\partial K/\partial L)}{-\partial K/\partial L} \tag{6.12}$$

$$= \frac{\mathrm{d}\log(K/K)}{\mathrm{d}\log(-\partial K/\partial L)}.$$

However,

$$\frac{\partial K}{\partial L} = -\frac{\partial V}{\partial L} \bigg/ \frac{\partial V}{\partial K}.$$

Thus, for the Cobb–Douglas function,

$$-\frac{\partial K}{\partial L} = \frac{\alpha K}{\beta L}$$

$$\therefore \quad \log\left(-\frac{\partial K}{\partial L}\right) = \log\frac{\alpha}{\beta} + \log\frac{K}{L}$$

$$\mathrm{d}\log\left(-\frac{\partial K}{\partial L}\right) = \mathrm{d}\log\frac{K}{L}$$

$$\sigma = 1\,.$$

That is, the Cobb–Douglas function restricts the substitution between factors such that the elasticity of substitution is always unity. The coefficient of efficiency is A, since two functions which have identical elasticities may still have different outputs if they have different values of A. The degree of factor intensity can be assessed by the ratio of α to β. A production function with a higher α/β ratio represents a more labour intensive technique than a function with a low α/β ratio. Thus the Cobb–Douglas function offers parametric representation for three out of the four economic concepts. Only in the realm of substitutability does this function fail us. It does, of course, have the characteristic of being linear in the logarithms which is convenient for estimation purposes.

6.2.3

The constant elasticity of substitution or the CES function, provides a function, which though more complex than the Cobb–Douglas, does allow the elasticity of substitution to differ from unity. The CES function is

$$V = \gamma[\delta K^{-\rho} + (1-\delta)L^{-\rho}]^{-\upsilon/\rho} \tag{6.13}$$

which has marginal productivities

$$\frac{\partial V}{\partial L} = \upsilon(1-\delta)\gamma^{-\rho/\upsilon}\,\frac{V^{1+\rho/\upsilon}}{L^{1+\rho}}. \tag{6.14}$$

$$\frac{\partial V}{\partial K} = \upsilon\delta\gamma^{-\rho/\upsilon}\,\frac{V^{1+\rho/\upsilon}}{K^{1+\rho}}. \tag{6.15}$$

Obviously the CES function satisfies (6.6). It can also be shown to satisfy (6.7) if $\upsilon = 1$. It is just possible that if υ is large, (6.7) is not satisfied but such large values of υ are not likely. If $\rho > 0$ the CES function even satisfies (6.8) (see Brown, 1966, p. 50). However, it is in the interpretation of its parameters that this function really shines. Obviously υ represents the economies of scale, γ the efficiency and δ the capital intensity of the production process. The elasticity of substitution of the function can be derived as follows from (6.14) and (6.15)

$$-\frac{\partial K}{\partial L} = \frac{1-\delta}{\delta}\left(\frac{K}{L}\right)^{1+\rho} \tag{6.16}$$

$$\therefore \quad \log\left(-\frac{\partial K}{\partial L}\right) = \log\frac{1-\delta}{\delta} + (1+\rho)\log\frac{K}{L}$$

$$\mathrm{d}\log\left(-\frac{\partial K}{\partial L}\right) = (1+\rho)\,\mathrm{d}\log\frac{K}{L}$$

$$\therefore \quad \sigma = \frac{1}{1+\rho}. \tag{6.17}$$

Thus the parameter ρ reflects the extent of substitution and can take any value. This is where the CES function gains over the Cobb–Douglas. In fact it is possible to show that when $\sigma = 1$, i.e., $\rho = 0$, the CES reduces to a CD function. It is worthwhile to develop the relation between the two functions and at the same time derive an approximation which will be used later. Let

$$Z(\rho) = \delta K^{-\rho} + (1-\delta)L^{-\rho} \tag{6.18}$$

and

$$\phi(\rho) = \log Z(\rho) \tag{6.19}$$

$$\therefore \quad \phi'(\rho) = \frac{Z'(\rho)}{Z(\rho)} \tag{6.20}$$

and †

$$Z'(\rho) = -[\delta K^{-\rho} \log K + (1-\delta)L^{-\rho} \log L] \tag{6.21}$$

$$\phi''(\rho) = \frac{Z''(\rho)}{Z(\rho)} - \frac{Z'(\rho)^2}{Z(\rho)^2} \tag{6.22}$$

$$Z''(\rho) = \delta K^{-\rho} \log^2 K + (1-\delta)L^{-\rho} \log^2 L\,. \tag{6.23}$$

But

$$\begin{aligned}
\phi(\rho) &= \phi(0) + \rho\phi'(0) + \frac{\rho^2}{2}\phi''(0) + \dots \\
&= \log Z(0) + \rho\frac{Z'(0)}{Z(0)} + \frac{\rho^2}{2}\left[\frac{Z''(0)}{Z(0)} - \frac{Z'(0)^2}{Z(0)^2}\right] + \dots \\
&= -\rho[\delta \log K + (1-\delta)\log L] \\
&\quad + \frac{\rho^2}{2}[\delta \log^2 K + (1-\delta)\log^2 L - \{\delta \log K + (1-\delta)\log L\}^2] + \dots \\
&= -\rho[\delta \log K + (1-\delta)\log L] + \frac{\rho^2\delta(1-\delta)}{2}[\log K - \log L]^2 + \dots\,.
\end{aligned} \tag{6.24}$$

† $dK^{-\rho}/d\rho = -K^{-\rho} \log K$ since if $y = K^x$, $\log y = x \log K$ and $1/y\,(dy/dx) = \log K$ $\therefore dy/dx = K^x \log K$.

∴ Taking logs of (6.13)

$$\log V = \log \gamma - \frac{v}{\rho} \log Z(\rho) ,$$

i.e.,

$$\log V = \log \gamma + v\delta \log K + v(1-\delta) \log L$$

$$- \frac{v\rho\delta(1-\delta)}{2} [\log K - \log L]^2 + \dots \tag{6.25}$$

Setting $\rho = 0$ in (6.25)

$$\log V = \log \gamma + v\delta \log K + v(1-\delta) \log L . \tag{6.26}$$

Thus when $\sigma = 1$ the CES function is a CD function.

Unfortunately, the CES function does have a number of drawbacks. Quite apart from the obvious difficulties involved in its estimation it also has theoretical limitations. The value of the parameter δ depends on the units of measurement of the variables, which is unfortunate. More restricting though, is the constancy of the parameters over the whole range of output. It might be desirable to have a production function which exhibits increasing returns at low levels of output and decreasing returns at high levels. The CES is not such a function. Similarly one might wish to allow the elasticity of substitution to vary with the factor proportions. These criticisms also relate to the CD function.

6.2.4

There have been a number of extensions of the CD and CES functions though few empirical studies have yet appeared. One such extension to the CD is the transcendental production function which has the form

$$V = cL^{\alpha_1} e^{\alpha_2 L} K^{\beta_1} e^{\beta_2 K} . \tag{6.27}$$

This has the characteristic of allowing marginal products to rise before eventually falling (see Halter et al., 1957). A function which allows the elasticity of substitution to vary with output was introduced by Lu and Fletcher (1968). Their VES constant returns to scale has the form

$$V = \gamma[\delta K^{-\rho} + (1-\delta) \left(\frac{K}{L}\right)^{-c(1+\rho)} L^{-\rho}]^{-1/\rho} . \tag{6.28}$$

Sato and Hoffman (1968) have also produced a VES function where σ varies with the ratio of capital to labour. Functions which allow the returns to scale to vary with output have also been developed. One such has been proposed by Soskice (1968). His approach can be appreciated by deriving the returns to scale from the CES function in the following way. Using (6.13) and (6.18)

$$V = \gamma Z^{-\upsilon/\rho}$$

$$\therefore \quad \frac{\mathrm{d}V}{\mathrm{d}Z}\left[\frac{\partial Z}{\partial K}\frac{K}{V} + \frac{\partial Z}{\partial L}\frac{L}{V}\right] = -\rho\frac{\mathrm{d}V}{\mathrm{d}Z}\left[\frac{\delta K^{-\rho}}{V} + (1-\delta)\frac{L^{-\rho}}{V}\right]$$

$$= -\rho\frac{\mathrm{d}V}{\mathrm{d}Z}\cdot\frac{Z}{V}$$

$$= \upsilon\,.$$

If, however, the returns to scale are specified as a quadratic function of output then,

$$-\rho\frac{\mathrm{d}V}{\mathrm{d}Z}\cdot\frac{Z}{V} = \upsilon_0 + \upsilon_1 V + \upsilon_2 V^2$$

and the following production function can be derived

$$V|V-k_1|^{b_0}|V-k_2|^{b_1} = \gamma[\delta K^{-\rho} + (1-\delta)L^{-\rho}]^{-\upsilon_0/\rho} \tag{6.29}$$

where k_1 and k_2 are the roots of $\upsilon_0 + \upsilon_1 V + \upsilon_2 V^2$.

A more general class of production functions has been suggested by Clemhout (1968). Her general form is

$$V = F(f[K, L]) = F(X) \tag{6.30}$$

where F is monotomic in $f(K, L)$, f is homogeneous of degree one in K and L, and the elasticity of substitution is constant on a ray from the origin through the isoquants but the elasticities for different rays are not necessary equal. Clemhout shows how to estimate X from the relative share of labour and capital, output, and the ratio of capital to labour, assuming the firm is maximising profits. Thus F can be chosen to allow for varying returns to scale. There have been other extensions of the CD and CES functions, which incorporate more inputs than one capital and one labour. These functions involve difficulties in terms of the definition of the elasticities of substitution, unless all pairs of factors have the same elasticity. As we indicated previously little empirical use has been made of any of these more complicated functions. This is not the case, however, with regard to extensions of the CD and CES functions which allow for technical change.

6.3. Technical progress

It is very unlikely that the technical relations which we are studying will not change. This phenomenon can be approached from three viewpoints. We can think of our production function changing, or we can discard our (6.3) in favour of

$$V = \phi(K, L, T) \tag{6.31}$$

where T represents the level of technology, or we can consider the technical change operating to augment the variables L and K, i.e.,

$$V = f(a(t)K, b(t)L)\,. \tag{6.32}$$

The theory of marginal productivity contains certain concepts which are used to analyse the effects of technical change on factor incomes. For this reason technical change has been classified according to its neutrality with regard to these concepts. For instance 'Hicks neutral' implies that the technical change does not affect the marginal rate of substitution of capital for labour. There are many such definitions, Sato and Beckmann (1968) list fourteen, but we shall not discuss them further here. Diamond (1965) has suggested measuring technical progress in terms of two indices, one showing the effect on output and the other the effect on the marginal rate of substitution, the latter he calls the 'bias'.

If we conceive of technical progress altering the production function, i.e., from the first viewpoint, then the parameters of that function must change, e.g., in the CES case ρ, δ, γ and v. Any one of the parameters can be thought of as a smooth function of time, or of other variables, e.g. research or certain proxy variables, or even changing with discreet jumps. The latter case is used by Brown (1966) who refers to technical epochs. The second viewpoint, i.e. using (6.31) can be illustrated by the CD function

$$V = AL^{\alpha}K^{\beta}\,\mathrm{e}^{\gamma T} \tag{6.33}$$

where T is a trend variable. This was one of the first econometric formulations of technical change. A very simple example of the third approach is

$$V = A(QL)^{\alpha} K^{\beta} \tag{6.34}$$

where Q is an index of the quality of labour.

A specification such as this forces us to distinguish between an input measured in some physical term, e.g. man hours, and the services stemming from that physical input. So far we have not really faced the issue as to how the inputs are measured. We will return to this later but for the moment let us continue to ignore this problem and turn to another, i.e., how to introduce behaviour.

6.4. Models of firm behaviour

The neo-classical theory assumes that an entrepreneur faced with market prices which he cannot affect, arranges the inputs of capital and labour to maximise his profits. The entrepreneur is someone who provides services which cannot be bought. Walters refers to entrepreneurship as an admission of ignorance since without such a concept the existence of firms cannot be justified. Entrepreneurial services or expertise can be thought of as having technical and economic aspects. His technical expertise will enable him to get more output out of a given set of inputs than can another entrepreneur (in another firm) with less technical ability. This ability will show up in the production function, i.e., the production function of his firm may have a higher $A(\gamma)$ if the production is CD (CES). His economic expertise involves his ability to choose the right quantities of inputs when prices are brought into the reckoning.

6.4.1

If perfect knowledge and perfect economic ability is assumed the entrepreneur will operate as the neoclassical theory of the firm dictates. Under perfect competitive conditions this can be derived as follows, since

$$\pi = pV - wL - rK \, , \tag{6.35}$$

where π is profits, w is the price of labour services, r is the price of capital services, to maximise profits subject to the production function we form

$$\pi^* = pV - wL - rK - \lambda(V - f) \tag{6.36}$$

where $f = f(K, L)$. The first order condition for (6.36) to be at a maximum is

$$\begin{aligned} d\pi^* &= (p - \lambda)dV + (\lambda f_L - w)dL + (\lambda f_K - r)dK + (V - f)d\lambda \\ &= 0, \qquad \text{for all } dV, dL, dK, \text{ and } d\lambda \end{aligned} \tag{6.37}$$

which implies,

$$\begin{aligned} p &= \lambda \\ w &= \lambda f_L \\ r &= \lambda f_L \\ V &= f . \end{aligned} \tag{6.38}$$

The second order condition is

$$d^2\pi^* < 0 \tag{6.39}$$

where (6.38) is also satisfied. Thus substituting into (6.36)

$$\pi^* = p(-f_L L - f_K K + f) \tag{6.40}$$

if f is homogeneous of degree k

$$\therefore \quad \pi^* = p(1 - k)f \tag{6.41}$$

and

$$d^2\pi^* = p(1 - k)d^2 f . \tag{6.42}$$

Since f is homogeneous of degree k

$$[L \;\; K] \begin{bmatrix} f_{LL} & f_{KL} \\ f_{KL} & f_{KK} \end{bmatrix} \begin{bmatrix} L \\ K \end{bmatrix} = k(k - 1)V . \tag{6.43}$$

Thus $\begin{bmatrix} f_{LL} & f_{KL} \\ f_{KL} & f_{KK} \end{bmatrix}$ is negative definite if $(1 - k) > 0$, and positive definite if $(1 - k) < 0$.

Thus d^2f and $(1-k)$ will be of opposite sign, however, d^2f cannot be positive definite since $f_{LL}, f_{KK} > 0$ therefore k is less than 1. This shows that if the production is homogeneous of a positive degree at the maximum profit point then it must be of degree less than one. This implies that the data generated by this model will always give the appearance of a production function with decreasing returns to scale.

6.4.2

From (6.38) we can derive the demand for labour, the demand for capital and the supply of output equations. To illustrate this we use the CD functions. Substituting (6.10) into (6.38) we find

$$V = AL^{\alpha}K^{\beta}$$
$$\frac{w}{p} = \frac{\alpha V}{L}$$
$$\frac{r}{p} = \frac{\beta V}{K}\,. \tag{6.44}$$

These can be written

$$\begin{aligned} x_0 - \alpha x_1 - \beta x_2 &= \log A \\ x_0 - x_1 \qquad &= \log \frac{w}{p\alpha} \\ x_0 \qquad - x_2 &= \log \frac{r}{p\beta} \end{aligned} \tag{6.45}$$

thus,

$$\begin{bmatrix} x_0 \\ x_1 \\ x_2 \end{bmatrix} = \begin{bmatrix} 1 & -\alpha & -\beta \\ 1 & -1 & 0 \\ 1 & 0 & -1 \end{bmatrix}^{-1} \begin{bmatrix} \log A \\ \log \dfrac{w}{p\alpha} \\ \log \dfrac{r}{p\beta} \end{bmatrix} \tag{6.46}$$

where
$x_0 = \log V$;
$x_1 = \log L$;
$x_2 = \log K$.

For one firm, one set of prices w, r and p will generate one point on the production function from which it is impossible to discern the production function. However, if prices vary over time, this firm's time series data will lie exactly on the production function and there will be no estimation problem. If we consider a number of firms each with the same production function and again perfect competition and knowledge is assumed, then, at any point of time when prices are fixed, each firm will produce exactly the same amount. If we were trying to estimate the production function from this cross section the task would be impossible again. This model is obviously too restrictive, for different firms do have different outputs and inputs even when confronted with the same set of prices.

6.4.3

Let us conceive of our firm as being a typical firm of an industry. We will maintain the perfect competition assumption, i.e., firms face fixed prices of factors and outputs. Firms, although basically the same, differ from each other in the sense that some entrepreneurs are better than the typical and others are worse. The econometrician does not know to what extent, but he assumes that the technical abilities of the entrepreneurs are distributed randomly around the typical firm's ability. Thus the ith firm's production function is

$$V_i = f(K_i, L_i, u_i)$$

when u_i is a random variable. Although the econometrician does not know the value of u_i it is assumed the entrepreneur himself does. Entrepreneurs' economic expertise, i.e., their reaction to prices, may also vary. Thus we should introduce a disturbance term into each of the marginal productivity equations. To illustrate this with the CD function consider the following:

$$V_i = A_i L_i^{\alpha} K_i^{\beta} \tag{6.47}$$

where

$$A_i = A\, e^{u_{0i}}, \tag{6.48}$$

i.e.,

$$V_i = A L_i^{\alpha} K_i^{\beta}\, e^{u_{0i}}. \tag{6.49}$$

The stochastic equivalents of (6.44) are,

$$w = \frac{p\alpha V_i \mathrm{e}^{-u_{1i}}}{L_i} \tag{6.50}$$

$$r = \frac{p\beta V_i \mathrm{e}^{-u_{2i}}}{K_i} \tag{6.51}$$

where u_{1i} and u_{2i} are stochastic variables and the negative sign is introduced for later convenience, or using the log form,

$$x_{0i} - \alpha x_{1i} - \beta x_{2i} = \log A + u_{0i} \tag{6.52}$$

$$x_{0i} - x_{1i} = \log \frac{w}{p\alpha} + u_{1i} \tag{6.53}$$

$$x_{0i} - x_{2i} = \log \frac{w}{p\beta} + u_{2i} \,. \tag{6.54}$$

One further simple extension to this model is to allow for the fact that all firms may not be able to satisfy the marginal productivity constraints exactly. This can be achieved by introducing two constraints R_1 and R_2 such that

$$R_1 w = \lambda f_L \tag{6.55}$$

$$R_2 r = \lambda f_K \,. \tag{6.56}$$

Incorporating this into the CD case we get

$$x_{0i} - \alpha x_{1i} - \beta x_{2i} = \lambda_0 + u_{0i} \tag{6.57}$$

$$x_{0i} - x_{1i} = \lambda_1 + u_{1i} \tag{6.58}$$

$$x_{0i} - x_{2i} = \lambda_2 + u_{2i} \tag{6.59}$$

where

$\lambda_0 = \log A$;

$\lambda_1 = \log \dfrac{R_1 w}{p\alpha}$;

$\lambda_2 = \log \dfrac{R_2 r}{p\beta}$.

If our data are cross section observations over firms, then the λ_i will be constants and we have a simultaneous system without any exogenous variables to help identification. We will return to this problem later. It will also be appreciated that the disturbance terms are likely to be correlated since if an entrepreneur has a production function which differs from the average, his behaviour is likely to, also. This correlation affects the estimation as we will see later.

6.4.4

What problems arise if (6.57), (6.58) and (6.59) are thought of as a model of one firm through time? In this case λ_1 and λ_2 will be exogenous variables, and $u_{0i} = u_{1i} = u_{2i} = 0$ unless random factors through time affect the production function and the firm's behaviour. Zellner et al. (1966) have suggested a model along these lines. That is, they have introduced factors which are assumed to be unknown to the entrepreneur as distinct from the econometrician. Consider u_{0i}, this can be interpreted as the effects of factors, such as weather, which the entrepreneur does not know when he takes his decisions. The firm is no longer operating in certainty and it is necessary to assume a new motive. Zellner et al. assume that the firm maximises expected profits. If u_{0i} is assumed to be normally distributed, the expected value of V is

$$E(V) = AL^{\alpha}K^{\beta}\,\mathrm{e}^{\frac{1}{2}\sigma_{00}} \tag{6.60}$$

where σ_{00} is the variance of u_{0i}. Maintaining the assumption that prices are known exactly, maximising expected profits produces

$$R_1 w = \frac{\alpha p\,\mathrm{e}^{\frac{1}{2}\sigma_{00}}V}{\mathrm{e}^{u_{0i}}L} \tag{6.61}$$

and

$$R_2 r = \frac{\beta p\,\mathrm{e}^{\frac{1}{2}\sigma_{00}}V}{\mathrm{e}^{u_{0i}}K}. \tag{6.62}$$

However, if there are random factors which affect the entrepreneur's economic activity we have to introduce random terms into (6.61) and (6.62). These occur, for instance, if the firm does not know prices exactly but bases its decision on anticipated prices which are randomly distributed around the actual prices. Thus (6.61), (6.62) and (6.49) are the structural equations for a firm operating under uncertainty and maximising expected profits. Transferring to the logarithmic form we get

$$x_{0i} - \alpha x_{1i} - \beta x_{2i} = \log A + u_{0i} \tag{6.63}$$

$$x_{0i} - x_{1i} = k_1' + u_{0i} + u_{1i} \tag{6.64}$$

$$x_{0i} - x_{2i} = k_2' + u_{0i} + u_{2i} \tag{6.65}$$

where

$$k_1' = \log\left(\frac{wR_1}{\alpha p}\right) - \tfrac{1}{2}\sigma_{00};$$

$$k_2' = \log\left(\frac{rR_2}{\beta p}\right) - \tfrac{1}{2}\sigma_{00}.$$

The reduced form equations are

$$x_{0i} = \frac{[\log A - \alpha k_1' - \beta k_2' + (1-\alpha-\beta)u_{0i} - \alpha u_{1i} - \beta u_{2i}]}{1 - \alpha - \beta} \tag{6.66}$$

$$x_{1i} = \frac{[\log A + (\beta-1)k_1' - \beta k_2' + (\beta-1)u_{1i} - \beta u_{2i}]}{1 - \alpha - \beta} \tag{6.67}$$

$$x_{2i} = \frac{[\log A - \alpha k_1' + (\alpha-1)k_2' - \alpha u_{1i} + (\alpha-1)u_{2i}]}{1 - \alpha - \beta}. \tag{6.68}$$

Notice that x_{1i} and x_{2i} are not functions of u_{0i} †, therefore, provided u_{0i} and u_{1i} and u_{2i} are not correlated, least squares applied to (6.63) will not produce inconsistent estimates. That these disturbances are not correlated could be a reasonable assumption though one can imagine situations when they are correlated. With cross-section data this model can be used and least squares will give consistent estimates of the production function provided we assume that the production function only varies from firm to firm because of unexpected factors.

6.4.5

We have illustrated the simultaneous model with the CD function but the

† This can be seen very easily by noticing that u_{0i} always appears with x_0 and thus will be eliminated in the solution.

same ideas have been used with other functions. From (6.13), (6.14) and (6.15) we see that the equivalent CES model is

$$V = \gamma e^{u_0} [\delta K^{-\rho} + (1-\delta)L^{-\rho}]^{-v/\rho} \tag{6.69}$$

$$\frac{R_1 w}{p} = v(1-\delta)\gamma^{-\rho/v} \frac{V^{1+\rho/v}}{L^{1+\rho}} e^{-u_1} \tag{6.70}$$

$$\frac{R_2 r}{p} = v\delta\gamma^{-\rho/v} \frac{V^{1+\rho/v}}{K^{1+\rho}} e^{-u_2}\,. \tag{6.71}$$

This can be simplified somewhat if we use (6.25) to approximate the production function. Thus,

$$x_0 - v(1-\delta)x_1 - v\delta x_2 + \tfrac{1}{2}\rho v\delta(1-\delta)(x_1 - x_2)^2 = k_0 + u_0 \tag{6.72}$$

$$\left(1 + \frac{\rho}{v}\right) x_0 - (1+\rho)x_1 = k_1 + u_1 \tag{6.73}$$

$$\left(1 + \frac{\rho}{v}\right) x_0 - (1+\rho)x_2 = k_2 + u_2 \tag{6.74}$$

where

$k_0 = \log \gamma$

$k_1 = \log \dfrac{R_1 w}{p} - \log\, [v(1-\delta)^{-\rho/v}]\,;$

$k_2 = \log \dfrac{R_2 r}{p} - \log\, [v\delta\gamma^{-\rho/v}]\,.$

So far all the models we have considered have involved instantaneous reactions. In Chapter 4 we stressed the fact that with regard to investment a firm takes time to adjust. Thus we used distributed lag models to relate the actual capital stock to the desired. Similar techniques can be applied to the marginal productivity equations. This produces an ad hoc adjustment process into the model of the firm. It would be more satisfying if a dynamic programming model of the firm had been developed for this purpose but as yet econometric studies have not used such a model.

All the models we have considered so far have taken the prices facing the firm as fixed. If the firm's action affects the price as in imperfect competition, it is necessary to allow for this. Marschak and Andrews (1944) showed how this could be done by introducing functions to represent the demand for output and the supply of factors. Most models assume that the supply of factors is infinitely elastic to the firm or industry but some studies have taken account of imperfection in the output market. The effect of this imperfection is incorporated by including

$$p = \xi V^{-1/\eta} \tag{6.75}$$

where η represents the elasticity of demand for output. Thus, the marginal productivity conditions for the certainty case become

$$w = pf_L \left(1 - \frac{1}{\eta}\right) \tag{6.76}$$

$$r = pf_K \left(1 - \frac{1}{\eta}\right) . \tag{6.77}$$

The two uncertainty models can also be extended to include (6.75).

6.5. Identification problems

So far we have not discussed the identification of the models suggested. Obviously this can be a very complex matter but here we shall concentrate on the model defined by (6.52), (6.53) and (6.54) to illustrate the issues. If relative prices vary exogenously over the sample then the necessary condition for the identification of (6.63) is satisfied. However, if relative prices do not vary there are no exogenous variables in the system and (6.63) will not be identified unless special restrictions are placed on the variance-covariance matrix of the stochastic terms.

Let $\boldsymbol{\Sigma} = [\sigma_{ij}]$ be the variance-covariance matrix of the stochastic terms $(i, j = 0, 1, 2)$ and $\boldsymbol{\psi} = [\psi_{ij}]$ be the corresponding reduced form matrix. Thus

$$\boldsymbol{\Sigma} = \mathbf{B}\boldsymbol{\psi}\mathbf{B}'$$

where

$$\mathbf{B} = \begin{bmatrix} 1 & -\alpha & -\beta \\ 1 & -1 & 0 \\ 1 & 0 & -1 \end{bmatrix}.$$

That is,

$$\sigma_{10} = -\alpha(\psi_{00} - \alpha\psi_{01} - \beta\psi_{02}) - \psi_{10} + \alpha\psi_{11} + \beta\psi_{12} \tag{6.78}$$

$$\sigma_{20} = -\beta(\psi_{00} - \alpha\psi_{01} - \beta\psi_{02}) - \psi_{20} + \alpha\psi_{21} + \beta\psi_{22} \tag{6.79}$$

$$\sigma_{12} = -\beta(\psi_{00} - \psi_{01}) - (\psi_{20} - \psi_{21}) \tag{6.80}$$

$$\sigma_{21} = -\alpha(\psi_{00} - \psi_{02}) - (\psi_{20} - \psi_{12}). \tag{6.81}$$

Since $\sigma_{12} = \sigma_{21}$, and $\psi_{12} = \psi_{21}$

$$\frac{\alpha}{\beta} = \frac{\psi_{00} - \psi_{01}}{\psi_{00} - \psi_{02}}. \tag{6.82}$$

If $\sigma_{10} = 0$ and $\sigma_{20} = 0$ then,

$$\alpha(\psi_{00} - \alpha\psi_{01} - \beta\psi_{02}) = -\psi_{10} + \alpha\psi_{11} + \beta\psi_{12} \tag{6.83}$$

$$\beta(\psi_{00} - \alpha\psi_{01} - \beta\psi_{02}) = -\psi_{20} + \alpha\psi_{21} + \beta\psi_{22}. \tag{6.84}$$

Therefore (6.83)÷(6.84) gives

$$\frac{\alpha}{\beta} = \frac{-\psi_{10} + \alpha\psi_{11} + \beta\psi_{12}}{-\psi_{20} + \alpha\psi_{21} + \beta\psi_{22}}. \tag{6.85}$$

Substituting (6.82) into (6.85)

$$\frac{\psi_{00} - \psi_{01}}{\psi_{00} - \psi_{02}} = \frac{-\psi_{10} + \alpha\psi_{11} + \beta\psi_{12}}{-\psi_{20} + \alpha\psi_{21} + \beta\psi_{22}}. \tag{6.86}$$

Using (6.82) and (6.86) we can solve for α and β. Thus $\sigma_{10} = \sigma_{20} = 0$ is sufficient to identify α and β since $\mathbf{\Sigma}$ is symmetric. This means that we can identify the production function (6.52) if economic efficiency is not correlated with technical efficiency.

As we have stated before, identification can be a very complex matter, especially when technical progress is present. In fact it can be shown that it is impossible to identify a constant returns to scale production function with arbitrary technical progress. Nerlove (1967) reports Arrow's proof of the Diamond McFadden impossibility theorem for CES functions but shows that the production function is identified if the technical change is either (i) not factor augmenting; or (ii) wholly factor augmenting and exponential. Brown's (1966) assumption of technological epochs also circumvents the impossibility theorem. Even when the hurdle of identification has been crossed we have to consider how the actual variables are to be measured.

6.6. Measurement of the variables

In the discussion so far, K and L have stood for capital and labour services used. In relating these to statistical concepts various difficulties arise. Let us first consider labour. The obvious choice is number of man hours. This assumes that men are homogeneous and that there is no disguised unemployment. That is, men are fired when redundant and not kept on the books. However, through time or between different firms men may not be homogeneous. Increased education may cause the quality of labour to rise, or certain firms may attract better workers. One way of handling this is to include a variable which reflects these quality differences but such variables are difficult to find. Usually the problem is ignored. Similarly if men are employed but not used, the number of manhours will not reflect the provision of labour services. Even within firms there are different types of labour and the question arises of how to aggregate. Walters (1968, p. 324) suggests that weighting by a base year's marginal products (represented by wages) is the most appropriate method but most empirical studies use an unweighted sum.

When we turn to the capital variable the problems of measurement are even greater. If no firm owned its capital then each machine etc. would have to be rented. Presumably we would have statistics on machine hours and rentals and thus the problem of constructing an index for capital would be the same as it is for labour. Since firms tend to own their own capital it is necessary to impute these values. This is complex because the number of machine hours depends on the rate of utilisation, and rentals will be effected by original costs, the capital loss, the rate of depreciation and the rate of interest (see Griliches and Jorgenson, 1966). Few studies have followed this approach but it highlights the problems involved in using a stock of capital measure. For one thing the problem of utilisation is more important than in the case of labour, as firms are much more reluctant to discard or sell unused machines or plant. Furthermore, the problem of quality is also likely to be more acute. Old and new machines are not likely to provide the same services since machines deteriorate and obsolesce. However, models have been designed in order to take some account of different utilisation rates and of capital with different vintages, see Section 6.10.3. Turning to the output or value added variable, we have already seen that value added in constant prices approximates the concept of output when raw material inputs are excluded from the production function. It is convenient too, in terms of the ultimate aggregate aim of production function analysis since value added reflects national output.

Discussing how to measure the variables of the production function may appear academic since in very few cases will the data allow much choice. This point is still important because we may be able to get some idea of the direction and magnitude of the bias which is introduced by using faulty or approximate measures of the variable. Occasionally these biases can be assessed by using Theil's specification error analysis (for an example see Griliches, 1957).

6.7. **Estimation methods**

In this section we discuss the methods of estimation for the CD and CES functions, maintaining the fiction that we are estimating an individual firm's production function.

6.7.1

Let us consider the CD function. Its log linear form allows direct application of ordinary least squares. However, if the underlying model of behaviour is (6.57)–(6.59), then the OLS estimates will be biased and inconsistent. This model is one that has been used often and as a result econometricians have tried to find estimates which are at least consistent. We have already seen that assumptions on the shape of the variance-covariance matrix of disturbances are necessary for α and β to be identified from cross section data. These restrictions can simplify maximum likelihood estimation. Kmenta (1964) shows that two estimation methods for α and β are in fact equivalent to the maximum likelihood method. The simpler of these is the indirect least squares. This method involves using the regression,

$$x_0 = b_0 + b_1(x_1 - x_0) + b_2(x_0 - x_0) + \mathrm{e}$$

to estimate b_0, b_1, b_2 and then putting

$$\hat{\alpha} = \frac{b_1}{1 + b_1 + b_2} \quad \text{and} \quad \hat{\beta} = \frac{b_2}{1 + b_1 + b_2}.$$

With the model suggested by Zellner et al. i.e. (6.63)–(6.65), the application of least squares does not result in inconsistent estimates. In fact they showed that the least squares estimator is the maximum likelihood estimator and is both consistent and unbiased.

Models which allow for lagged reaction, imperfect competition and technical change, in as much as they involve more exogenous variables, are more easily identified and estimated. When time series are available the inclusion of price variables also helps.

6.7.2

Turning to the CES function, the estimation procedures are more complicated because the CES function is nonlinear in the parameters. Direct estimation of the production function may be achieved as follows. Since

$$V = \gamma[\delta K^{-\rho} + (1-\delta)L^{-\rho}]^{-\upsilon/\rho}$$

$$V = f(\gamma, \upsilon, \delta, \rho)\,.$$

Thus

$$V \approx f^0 + f^0_\gamma(\gamma - \gamma_0) + f^0_\delta(\delta - \delta_0) + f^0_\upsilon(\upsilon - \upsilon_0) + f^0_\rho(\rho - \rho_0)$$

where superscripts indicate the functions are evaluated at the point $(\gamma_0, \delta_0, \upsilon_0, \rho_0)$ and the subscripts on f indicate partial derivatives.

Making a guess at $\gamma_0, \delta_0, \upsilon_0$ and ρ_0 we can obtain OLS estimates for γ, δ, υ and ρ. These can then be used to repeat the process. If the subsequent estimates of γ, δ, υ and ρ converge these are the estimated coefficients of the CES function. Another approach suggested by Kmenta (1967) is to estimate not the exact CES function but the following approximate form (see (6.25))

$$\log V = \log\gamma + \upsilon\delta \log K + \upsilon(1-\delta)\log L - \frac{\upsilon\rho\delta(1-\delta)}{2}[\log K - \log L]^2\,. \quad (6.87)$$

Applying ordinary least squares provides estimates from which consistent estimates of γ, υ, δ and ρ can be derived. These direct methods of estimation ignore the behavioural models of Section 6.4 and may give rise to inconsistent estimates.

6.7.3

The estimation methods for the CES function involving a whole system, can be divided according to whether they are applicable to cross section or time series data. Kmenta has produced a modified indirect least squares approach which produces maximum likelihood estimates of (6.72)–(6.74) provided (a) the disturbance of the production function is interpreted as embodying differences in efficiencies which are known to the entrepreneur but unknown to the econometrician, and (b) the variance–covariance matrix of the disturbances is diagonal. Kmenta's method involves forming

$$z_{1i} = Fx_{0i} - x_{1i}$$

$$z_{2i} = Fx_{0i} - x_{2i}$$

$$z_{3i} = (x_{1i} - x_{2i})^2$$

where $F = \dfrac{\rho/\upsilon + 1}{\rho + 1}$

then using the regression coefficients of

$$x_{0i} = a_0 + a_1 z_{1i} + a_2 z_{2i} + a_3 z_{3i} + \mathrm{e} \tag{6.88}$$

to produce those of the production function from the following,

$$\log \gamma = \frac{a_0}{1 - Fa_1 - Fa_2}$$

$$\upsilon(1-\delta) = \frac{-a_2}{1 - Fa_1 - Fa_2}$$

$$\upsilon\delta = \frac{-a_2}{1 - Fa_1 - Fa_2}$$

$$-\tfrac{1}{2}\rho\upsilon\delta(1-\delta) = \frac{a_3}{1 - Fa_1 - Fa_2}$$

and

$$a_3 = -\tfrac{1}{2}(F-1)a_1 a_2 \,. \tag{6.89}$$

Eqs. (6.73) and (6.74) imply that z_1 and z_2 are functions of u_1 and u_2 and hence are not correlated with u_0. This means that the application of least squares to (6.88) subject to (6.89) will provide consistent estimates of the coefficients of (6.88) which in turn lead to consistent estimates of the production function. However, we need to know F. From (6.73) and (6.74)

$$Fx_0 - x_1 = \frac{k_1}{1+\rho} + \frac{u_1}{1+\rho}$$

and

$$Fx_0 - x_2 = \frac{k_2}{1+\rho} + \frac{u_2}{1+\rho}.$$

Imposing the constraint that the sample disturbances should be uncorrelated gives

$$0 = \hat{F}^2 M_{00} - \hat{F}(M_{10} + M_{20}) + M_{12}$$

where the M's are the sample moment of the x's and $\hat{F}$ is an estimate of F.

This equation will give two estimates of F, but whichever produces the lowest sum of squared residuals in the regression of (6.88), is used.

6.7.4

When there is variation in the relative prices, (6.72)–(6.74) become

$$x_0 - v(1-\delta)x_1 - v\delta x_2 + \tfrac{1}{2}\rho v\delta(1-\delta)(x_1 - x_2)^2 = k_0 + u_0 \qquad (6.90)$$

$$\left(1 + \frac{\rho}{v}\right)x_0 - (1+\rho)x_1 = \log\frac{R_1 w}{p} + k_1'' + u_1 \qquad (6.91)$$

$$\left(1 + \frac{\rho}{v}\right)x_0 - (1+\rho)x_2 = \log\frac{R_2 r}{p} + k_2'' + u_2 \qquad (6.92)$$

where
$k_1'' = -\log[\gamma^{-\rho/v}v(1-\delta)]$;
$k_2'' = -\log[\gamma^{-\rho/v}v\delta]$.

If $v = 1$, from (6.91),

$$x_0 - x_1 = \frac{1}{1+\rho}\log\frac{R_1 w}{p} + \frac{k_1''}{1+\rho} + \frac{u_1}{1+\rho}. \qquad (6.93)$$

Hence least squares will give a consistent estimate of ρ. This estimate which does not depend on any approximation is the approach used by Arrow et al. (1961). It has the advantage that no capital data are required. If v is not specified as unity,

$$x_0 - x_1 = \frac{1}{1+\rho} \log \frac{R_1 w}{p} + \frac{\rho}{1+\rho}\left(1 - \frac{1}{v}\right) x_0 + \frac{k_1''}{1+\rho} + \frac{u_1}{1+\rho} \tag{6.94}$$

but x_0 and u_1 are correlated and OLS will produce inconsistent estimates. However, subtracting (6.92) from (6.91) gives

$$x_2 - x_1 = \frac{1}{1+\rho} \log \frac{\delta}{1-\delta} \frac{R_1}{R_2} + \frac{1}{1+\rho} \log \frac{w}{r} + \frac{1}{1+\rho}(u_1 - u_2) \tag{6.95}$$

which can be used to get a consistent estimate of ρ. The disadvantage here is that we now need capital data. If $R_1 \equiv R_2$, we can also estimate δ from this equation. To estimate the other coefficients of the production function Kmenta suggests a two stage least squares method. The production function is rewritten in the following form

$$x_0 = \log \gamma + v\delta(x_2 - x_1) + vx_1 - \tfrac{1}{2}\rho v\delta(1-\delta)(x_2 - x_1)^2 + u_0 \tag{6.96}$$

and the corresponding reduced form equations are (6.95) and

$$x_2 = b_0 + b_1 \log \frac{r}{p} + (b_2) \log\left(\frac{r}{w}\right) + b_3 \left[\log \frac{r}{w}\right]^2 + b_4 v_1^2 + v_2 \tag{6.97}$$

where

$$v_1 = \frac{u_1 - u_2}{1+\rho}, \text{ and}$$

v_2 is a linear combination of all disturbances.

The method involves applying least squares to (6.95) and (6.97) to get calculated values for $(x_2 - x_1)$, $(x_2 - x_1)^2$ and x_2 which are then used as regressors to estimate the coefficients of (6.96).

6.7.5

Quite obviously the estimation of CES functions is much more difficult than that of CD functions. Is the extra effort worth it? If one were to use a

CD function in a CES world would the error be serious? Obviously the elasticity of substitution may well be in error but Nelson (1965) has suggested that from the point of view of growth the influence of the elasticity of substitution is negligible. Nerlove (1967), says that Nelson's argument rests on aggregate conventionally measured concepts and that differences in the elasticity of substitution among industries may have an important effect on the rate of growth. However, even if we are not too interested in the value of σ, will not a misspecification of this parameter cause others, e.g. the returns to scale parameter, to be biased? This is an issue which Maddala and Kadane (1967) consider. They assume that the true function is a CES function but fit a CD function. If the approximation for the CES function is close, one can use Theil's specification analysis in the following way. If $\hat{\alpha}$ and $\hat{\beta}$ are the least squares estimates of the CD function parameter then,

$$E(\hat{\alpha}) = \upsilon(1-\delta) - \tfrac{1}{2}\rho\upsilon\delta(1-\delta)\theta_1$$

$$E(\hat{\beta}) = \upsilon\delta - \tfrac{1}{2}\rho\upsilon\delta(1-\delta)\theta_2$$

where θ_1 and θ_2 are the least squares coefficients of $(\log K - \log L)^2$ on $\log L$ and $\log K$. If θ_1 and θ_2 are zero, then $E(\hat{\alpha}+\hat{\beta}) = \upsilon$, and there is no bias in the estimate of the returns to scale. Maddala and Kadane show that if L and K follow independent but similar log normal distributions, $\theta_1 \equiv \theta_2 \equiv 0$, and the CD estimates will give a true indication of the factor intensities but if these distributions are uniform, the bias can be made arbitrarily large. Similar conclusions are arrived at from a Monte Carlo experiment where the exact as opposed to the approximate CES function is used with differing values of σ. Thus, provided the distributions of L and K are independent, log normal and similar, using a CD function to estimate the returns to scale will not result in much bias. Further experiments by Maddala and Kadane suggest that even if the distributions of K and L are uniform, the method suggested by Kmenta produces good estimates of υ even though those of σ may be poor. As we shall see in many empirical studies the estimated value of σ is close to unity which suggests that the CD function is reasonable.

6.8. Aggregation

So far we have been concerned with the production function of a single firm. In this section we turn our attention to the possibility of a production function for a whole industry or country. Given the existence of firm production functions, the question is whether a unique function which relates some aggregate output to some aggregates of capital and labour exists. This should not be confused with the aggregation question discussed in 6.2 which relates to the aggregation of inputs within an individual firm. If an aggregate production function exists the next step is to consider the meaning of the aggregate parameters in terms of the micro parameters. Klein (1946) showed that given a set of CD micro production functions

$$V_1 = A_1 L_1^{\alpha_1} K_1^{\beta_1}$$

$$V_2 = A_2 L_2^{\alpha_2} K_2^{\beta_2}$$

$$\vdots$$

$$V_n = A_n L_n^{\alpha_n} K_n^{\beta_n}$$

then

$$\log V = \log A + \alpha \log L + \beta \log K$$

if

$$\log V = \frac{1}{n} \sum \log V_i$$

$$\log A = \frac{1}{n} \sum \log A_i$$

$$\alpha = \frac{\sum \alpha_i \log L_i}{\sum \log L_i}$$

$$\beta = \frac{\sum \beta_i \log K_i}{\sum \log K_i}.$$

Thus, if the micro functions are CD and the aggregates are geometric means, then there exists an aggregate CD function, the parameters of which are weighted averages of those of the micro functions. Since data are seldom published in such form, let us see what is implied if the aggregation procedure for output is specified to be a summation.

Consider a set of n production functions

$$V_1 = f_1(K_1 L_1)$$

$$V_2 = f_2(K_2, L_2)$$

$$\vdots$$

$$V_n = f_n(K_n, L_n)\,.$$

If

$$V = \sum V_i$$

then

$$V = f_1(K_1, L_1) + f_2(K_2, L_2) + \ldots + f_n(K_n, L_n)$$

$$= G(K_1, K_2, \ldots, K_n, \quad L_1, L_2, \ldots, L_n)\,.$$

The necessary and sufficient conditions for this to be written

$$V = F(K, L)$$

where
$K = \psi(K_1, K_2, \ldots, K_n)$;
$L = \phi(L_1, L_2, \ldots, L_n)$
are (see Green, 1964, p. 12)

$$\left(\frac{\partial G/\partial K_i}{\partial G/\partial K_j}\right) = h_{ij}(K_1, K_2, \ldots, K_n)$$

and

$$\left(\frac{\partial G/\partial L_i}{\partial G/\partial L_j}\right) = g_{ij}(L_1, L_2, \ldots, L_n) \qquad \text{for all } i, j$$

$$\therefore \quad \frac{\partial G}{\partial K_i} = h_{ij}(K_1, K_2, \ldots, K_n)\frac{\partial G}{\partial K_j} \qquad \text{for all } i, j\,.$$

But

$$\frac{\partial G}{\partial K_j} = m_j(K_j, L_j)$$

$$\therefore \quad \frac{\partial f_i}{\partial K_i} = \frac{\partial G}{\partial K_i} = h_{ij}(K_1, K_2, \ldots, K_n)m_j(K_j, L_j)$$

$$\therefore \qquad \frac{\partial}{\partial L_i} \frac{\partial f_i}{\partial K_i} = 0 \qquad \text{for all } i\,.$$

Similarly

$$\frac{\partial}{\partial K_i}\left(\frac{\partial f_i}{\partial L_i}\right) = 0 \qquad \text{for all } i$$

thus f_i must be expressible as

$$f_i = g_1(K_i) + g_2(L_i)$$

where g_1 and g_2 are functions.

This condition is called additive separability and is very restrictive. Notice that neither CD nor CES is additive separable. If we further require that $L = \sum L_i$ then $g_2(L_i) = cL_i$, where c is a constant and is the same for all firms, similarly for K.

An aggregate production function can be thought of as something slightly different from the summation of individual production functions. A micro production function is the relationship between inputs and the maximum output achievable from those inputs. A macro production function should then be the relationship between a set of inputs and the maximum output achievable from those inputs. That is, it bears the implicit assumption that each micro unit is producing efficiently, i.e., that the factors are allocated such that each firm is producing efficiently. This necessarily brings in economic as well as technical efficiency. Thus the concept of the production function loses some of its purity. In practice of course it is very difficult to distinguish between institutional and technical barriers to production.

This changed definition of aggregation allows slightly more freedom to the form that the production functions can take and still be capable of aggregation. It can be shown that if both capital and labour can move between firms then each individual production function must be expressible in terms of a common function, f, which is homogeneous of degree one, i.e.,

$$\begin{aligned} V_i &= f_i(K_i, L_i) \\ &= g_i\,[f(K_i, L_i)] \end{aligned}$$

where f is homogeneous of degree one.

A very simple example is an industry of two CD firms

$$V_1 = A_1 K_1^{\beta} L_1^{\alpha}$$

$$V_2 = A_2 K_2^{\beta} L_2^{\alpha}$$

where $\alpha + \beta = 1$.

More recently Fisher (1969) has deduced the conditions for the existence of an aggregate production function where capital is not freely movable, i.e., is specific to each individual firm. Fisher shows that in the case of all firms having constant returns to scale the necessary and sufficient conditions for the existence of an aggregate production function are that the individual functions can be written thus

$$f_i(K_i, L_i) = f(b_i K_i, L_i)\,.$$

That is, that the difference between firms can be thought of in terms of augmenting capital. The actual form of the aggregate function is not simple however. Fisher (1969) gives the function for two firms as

$$V = f(\lambda J, \lambda L) + f((1-\lambda)J, (1-\lambda)L)$$

where
$J = b_1 K_1 + b_2 K_2$;
$L = L_1 + L_2$;
$\lambda = L_1/L$.
Another of Fisher's conclusions is that although firms may have different capital mixes they are not allowed to have different labour mixes.

The depressing conclusions to be drawn from this section is that even assuming constant returns and optimal allocation, firms have to be very similar for even complicated aggregate production functions to exist †. Furthermore we have not considered the problem of how production functions for intermediate goods are aggregated to produce functions for final goods (see Black, 1969).

† Houthakker (1955–1956) shows that it is possible to derive an aggregate CD function for a set of fixed proportions productive units (firms) but that the coefficients of the production function reflect the coefficients of the distribution of the units.

6.9. Empirical studies

The number of published studies is enormous and because of this we shall try to keep to the more recent work and make use of survey articles. The basic plan will be to consider aggregate functions first, looking first at time series studies and then cross section. Later we shall move on to industry studies. In each section we shall deal with the CD functions first and then the CES.

6.10. Aggregate time series

6.10.1. Douglas (1948)

Much of the work on the aggregate production function has been stimulated by the early estimates of the CD function produced by Professor Douglas and his associates. His article in 1948 reviews the numerous studies associated with that function. All of these early studies produced single equation least squares estimates based on rather dubious data. Indeed, in this article, Douglas presents four estimates for the U.S., each using different data. The time period is 1899–1922 and the function fitted is the original CD function with no allowances for technical progress. Douglas also reports functions based on Australian and New Zealand data (see table 6.1).

The U.S.I data are, for L, average number of employed wage earners, i.e., salaried staff and working proprietors were excluded; for K, value of plant, buildings, tools and machinery taken from censuses and adjusted for investment deflated by a specially constructed price index based on the price of metals, building materials and labour; and for V, the original Day index of production. In the U.S.II model, L includes clerical and salaried staff and V is the Day–Thomas index of production. In U.S.III, the changes in the length of the standard working week are allowed for to give a better indication of manhours worked. In U.S.IV, all three time series used in U.S.II are purged of trend. Douglas suggests that the production series, which is based on materials used, probably underestimates production because of the trend towards more manufactured goods and because new goods are slow to appear in the index. The Australian series used are, for L, average numbers of persons employed including wage earners, salaried employees, supervisory officials and working employees; for K, fixed capital deflated but excluding land and working capital, and for V, index of physical production using 1911 value weights. The New Zealand I series are the total man hours worked, the value of fixed capital with annual increments of investment deflated by a cost of investment

Table 6.1
Time series estimates of aggregate CD production functions.

	α	β	A	$\alpha+\beta$	W/P †	N ‡
U.S. I 1899–1922	0.81 (0.15)	0.23 (0.06)	0.84	1.04	0.605	24
U.S. II 1899–1922	0.78 (0.14)	0.15 (0.08)	1.38	0.93	0.605	24
U.S. III 1899–1922	0.73 (0.12)	0.25 (0.05)	1.12	0.98	0.605	24
U.S. IV 1899–1922	0.63 (0.15)	0.30 (0.05)	1.35	0.93	0.605	24
Victoria 1907–1929	0.84 (0.34)	0.23 (0.17)	0.71	1.07		22
New South Wales 1901–1927	0.78 (0.12)	0.20 (0.08)	1.14	0.98		26
New Zealand I 1915–1916 1918–1935	0.42 (0.11)	0.49 (0.03)	2.03	0.91	0.52	18
New Zealand II 1923–1940	0.54 (0.02)				0.54	18

† Average share of wages.
‡ Number of observations.

series, and the deflated value of production. The New Zealand II series are, the number of persons employed; the value of land, machinery, building and plant minus depreciation plus money values of investment; and value added by manufacturing deflated by the price of locally produced goods.

Douglas' conclusions from these (and the cross-section results he presents) are that there are indeed general laws of production which suggest constant returns to scale and that factors are paid as we would expect under perfect competition. Of course, these studies are subject to all the problems we have enumerated above and this makes the similarities between countries and the agreement of the cross-section studies even more startling. However, Douglas' apparent success could stem from the form of the data. It may be that the data are defined such that

$$p_i V_i \equiv w_i L_i + r_i K_i \, .$$

If p_i, w_i and r_i are constant then,

$$V_i \equiv \frac{w}{p} L_i + \frac{r}{p} K_i \tag{6.98}$$

and any linear production function fitted will produce estimates of the relative prices and have exceptionally high R^2. Douglas et al. did not use a linear but a log linear form, but Cramer (1969) shows that if the variation in V, K and L is not too great then Douglas' results could stem from a similar source. If the true production function is CD then,

$$\log \frac{V_i}{\bar{V}} = \alpha \log \frac{L_i}{\bar{L}} + \beta \log \frac{K_i}{\bar{K}}$$

where $\bar{V}, \bar{L}$, and $\bar{K}$ are geometric means. Since

$$\log \frac{V_i}{\bar{V}} \approx \frac{V_i}{\bar{V}} - 1 \; ^{\dagger}$$

we find

$$\frac{V_i}{\bar{V}} - 1 \approx \alpha \frac{L_i}{\bar{L}} - \alpha + \beta \frac{K_i}{\bar{K}} - \beta ,$$

i.e.,

$$V_i \approx \alpha \frac{L_i \bar{V}}{\bar{L}} + \beta \frac{K_i \bar{V}}{\bar{K}} + (1 - \alpha - \beta) \bar{V} .$$

Thus a least squares fit of a CD function to data satisfying (6.98) would give $\alpha \bar{V}/\bar{L} = w/p$, $\beta \bar{V}/\bar{K} = r/p$, $\alpha + \beta \approx 1$ as well as a good fit, i.e., all of Douglas' results. In fact in the period that Douglas considered there was considerable fixity of relative prices, i.e., w/p. In Section 6.5 using a simple simultaneous model we showed that a difficult identification problem is present if prices are fixed. Thus with little variation in relative prices one feels dubious at putting much store by Douglas' conclusions.

6.10.2. Brown (1966)

Brown's aim is to measure technical progress in the U.S. by epochs, that is

† By Taylor series, $\log (1 + x) = x - \frac{1}{2}x^2 + \ldots \approx x \therefore \log V_i/\bar{V} \approx V_2/\bar{V} - 1$ by setting $1 + x = V_i/\bar{V}$.

he wants to fit production functions using the data in blocks. He also tries to overcome the utilisation problem by adjusting the net capital stock by a utilisation index. The data he uses are taken from Kendrick (1961). The series are gross production in 1929 prices, net capital stock in 1929 prices, man hours employed in millions, and they relate to the U.S. private domestic non-farm sector 1890–1960. Brown, in fact, extends Kendrick's series using the relevant Department of Commerce series. The function that he fits is

$$\Delta \log V = k_0 + \alpha \Delta \log L + \beta \Delta (\log s + \log K) . \qquad (6.99)$$

Capacity utilisation, s, is measured according to the Wharton School method, which is, roughly speaking, that output peaks are connected linearly and the ensuing path denoted as full capacity, from which the percentage of underutilisation is calculated. Brown realises that this is not perfect and resorts to checking the correlation of $\log s$ with the residuals obtained from fitting (6.99). Finding the correlation significant, Brown concludes that the utilisation index was not fully satisfactory. The slope coefficient in the regression of the residuals on $\log s$ is 0.3557 and this value is used to adjust the utilisation index. The final form of the estimated production function is

$$\Delta \log V = \underset{*(4.4913)}{0.0061} + \underset{*(3.6860)}{0.3253}\, \Delta \log L + \underset{*(11.4081)}{0.5521}\, \Delta(1.3556 \log s + \log K)$$

$$R^2 = 0.8873 \qquad \text{DW} = 1.49 .$$

This function is successful by statistical criteria but Brown's main aim is to derive a utilisation index which he can use to search for epochs. However, it is interesting to note that over this longer period, with some allowances made for utilisation and technical progress via a trend term, Douglas' results are not upheld.

Brown goes on to check for structural breaks in the period. This is done by using the Chow test and finally he produces the epochal estimates which appear in table 6.2.

Brown's results for 1890–1906 and 1947–1960 are similar to those of Douglas, but for the periods in between the similarity disappears. It could be argued that the years between were unusual years but if the production function is supposed to reflect technical relations then it should hold up under diverse conditions.

* t ratios.

Table 6.2
Epochal estimates of CD production functions for the U.S.

	α	β	k_0	$\bar{R}^2$	DW	$\alpha+\beta$
1890–1906 *	0.6904	0.4156	0.0018	0.867	1.98	1.1060
	(3.0016)	(4.5047)	(0.5287)			
1907–1920	0.1272	0.7347	0.0018	0.998	2.40	0.8619
	(2.5843)	(3.0538)	(5.1583)			
1921–1939 *	0.3829	0.5046	0.0077	0.928	1.81	0.8875
	(2.3622)	(5.0394)	(3.0268)			
1940–1960 *	0.4531	0.4891	0.0069	0.775	1.27	0.9422
	(2.5825)	(3.7431)	(2.6790)			
1947–1960 *	0.6590	0.3791	0.0062	0.891	1.90	1.0381
	(3.3895)	(3.3861)	(3.0099)			
1940–1960 †	0.5282	0.4243	0.0059	0.998	1.94	0.9525
	(2.3381)	(2.4297)	(3.8121)			

* Fitted in first difference form.
† Theil and Nagar (1961) method of allowing for serial correlation.
Numbers in parenthesis are t ratios.

6.10.3. Solow (1957, 1960b, 1962)

Solow's approach to technical progress and utilisation is different from Brown's. In Solow (1957) he produces a measure of disembodied technical progress for the U.S. using the CD form of (6.31) i.e.

$$V = A(t)K^{\beta}L^{1-\beta}$$

which can be written as

$$\frac{\Delta V/L}{V/L} = \frac{\Delta A_t}{A_t} + \beta\,\frac{\Delta K/L}{K/L}.$$

Taking β equal to the share of property income in non-farm material income enables him to generate a series for $\Delta A_t/A_t$ and hence a measure of technical progress. In Solow (1960b) he presents a model where all technical progress is capital augmenting and in Solow (1962) he extends this model, using it to investigate how much investment is necessary to sustain alternative rates of growth of potential output in the U.S.

He assumes that capital goods produced in any one year are 100 λ per cent more productive than those produced the year before. Thus it is necessary to differentiate pieces of capital according to their vintage. If $I(v)$ is the gross investment in year v and $B(t-v)$ is the proportion surviving in year t, then the equivalent stock of capital in year t is,

$$J(t) = \sum_{v=-\infty}^{t} (1+\lambda)^v B(t-v) I(v) .$$

Provided one knows the survival curves for pieces of capital one can calculate different series for $J(t)$ for different values of λ. Assuming that labour is allocated between machines of different vintage so as to maximise output, it can be shown that potential output, V_{pot}, can be written as

$$V_{\text{pot}} = F(J, L)$$

or assuming a CD form

$$V_{\text{pot}} = A\, J^{\beta} L^{1-\beta} . \tag{6.100}$$

In order to estimate this function, however, we need to relate potential output to actual output. Solow assumes that the unemployment rate can be used in the following way

$$V = 10^{b+cu+du^2}\, V_{\text{pot}} \tag{6.101}$$

where u is the unemployment rate. This assumption he justifies on the basis of it being better than a linear relation and yet workable. Combining (6.100) and (6.101) produces

$$V = A\, 10^{b+cu+du^2}\, J^{\beta} L^{1-\beta}$$

i.e.

$$\frac{V}{L} = A\, 10^{b+cu+du^2} \left(\frac{J}{L}\right)^{\beta}$$

or

$$\log\left(\frac{V}{L}\right) = \log A + b + cu + du^2 + \beta \log \frac{J}{L} . \tag{6.102}$$

From (6.101) it can be seen that at full employment, i.e.

$$V = V_{\text{pot}}\,, \qquad b + cu + du^2 = 0\,.$$

Solow defines 'full employment' to be that where $u = 0.04$, thus $b = -(0.04c + 0.0016d)$. This enables him to identify b from the least squares estimates of the coefficients of (6.102).

The data that he uses are all expressed in 1954 prices. Each of the J series is computed with different values of λ for plant and for equipment, each with its own mortality curve. Solow's aim is to reflect the privately owned production process and so religious, educational, hospital and institutional construction is excluded, as are dwellings. Similarly in the output figures that he uses, national production originating in government, government enterprises, households, institutions and the rest of the world is ignored, as are the services of houses. The unemployment rate he uses is the difference between full employment supply of man hours and the number of man hours actually worked, expressed as a ratio of the full employment supply (all figures relating to the private sector). Actually Solow adds 0.130 to this value when fitting the function presumably to ensure that the calculations are performed on positive data. The results appear in table 6.3.

Solow points out that low values for the improvement factor λ result in values for β that are too high. Furthermore, the value of β tends to depend more on the improvement factor for equipment than that for plant. Table 6.3 also indicates that the estimated curve relating actual and potential output is not very sensitive to the value of λ assumed.

Solow uses these results to estimate the investment percentage necessary to sustain certain rates of growth of output, given certain growth rates in the supply of man hours to the private sector. These results, which appear in table 6.4, are based on full employment, i.e., $u = 0.04$. From table 6.4 it appears that if the rate of growth is to rise from 3½% to 4½%, the percentage of business gross national production devoted to investment has to rise from about 10% to about 12%. Solow also estimates a disembodied technical progress production function but finds that it implies that a 4% rate of growth would need 20% of output devoted to investment which he claims is wholly unrealistic.

Solow realises, of course, that the economy may not be free to move back and forth along his estimated production function. He cites the possibility of premature scrapping of machines, the slowness of adjustment and the possibility of compositional changes as three factors which could prevent the naive application of his work. However, his study does illustrate both the type of

Table 6.3
Solow's embodied technical progress production function.
$\log (V/L) = \log A + b + cu + d(u + 0.130)^2 + \beta \log (J/L)$.

λ plant	λ equipment	$\log A$	b	c	d	β	R^2
0	0	−0.4179	0.0460	−0.1244 (0.2016)	−1.344 (0.413)	1.2377 (0.0993)	0.9622
0.02	0.02	−0.3934	0.0395	−0.2814 (0.1524)	−0.979 (0.315)	0.6323 (0.0364)	0.9789
0.02	0.03	−0.3328	0.0382	−0.3187 (0.1465)	−0.879 (0.304)	0.4990 (0.0274)	0.9806
0.02	0.04	−0.2956	0.0370	−0.3386 (0.1398)	−0.813 (0.291)	0.4026 (0.0221)	0.9825
0.03	0.03	−0.3888	0.0387	−0.3097 (0.1427)	−0.909 (0.295)	0.5054 (0.0270)	0.9816
0.03	0.04	−0.0375	0.0375	−0.3319 (0.1381)	−0.838 (0.287)	0.4160 (0.0214)	0.9828

Table 6.4
Investment percentage required for alternative rates of growth of labour and output.

Rate of growth of man hours (%)	Plant λ	Equipment λ	Rate of growth of output 3%	3½%	4%	4½%
0.65	0.02	0.04	9.9	11.2	12.4	13.8
1	0.02	0.04	9.2	10.4	11.7	13.1
0.65	0.03	0.03	9.0	10.2	11.4	12.5
1	0.03	0.03	8.5	9.8	10.9	12.0
0.65	0.03	0.04	10.1	11.3	12.6	13.9
1	0.03	0.04	9.4	10.8	12.0	13.3

question we would like to be able to answer and two gadgets which attempt to circumvent the problem of technical progress and utilisation. More recently attention has concentrated on the CES function and it is to this that we now turn.

6.10.4. Arrow et al. (1961)

In one section of this paper the authors estimate an aggregate production function for the U.S. non-farm sector. The data are taken from Solow (1957) and relate to 1909–1949. Technical progress is assumed to enter only through the efficiency parameter γ, such that

$$\gamma(t) = \gamma_0 10^{\lambda t}.$$

From (6.93), setting $R_1 = 1$, we can derive,

$$\log \frac{wL}{pV} = (1-\sigma) \log \frac{w}{p} + (\sigma-1) \log \gamma + \sigma \log (1-\delta) - \frac{u_1}{1+\rho} \tag{6.103}$$

$$= (1-\sigma) \log \frac{w}{p} + (\sigma-1) \log \gamma_0 + \sigma \log (1-\delta) - (1-\sigma)\lambda t - \frac{u_1}{1+\rho}.$$

Performing the regression,

$$\log \frac{wL}{pV} = \alpha_0 + \alpha_1 \log \frac{w}{p} + \alpha_2 t \tag{6.104}$$

where
$\alpha_0 = \sigma \log (1-\delta) + (\sigma-1) \log \gamma_0$
$\alpha_1 = 1-\sigma$
$\alpha_2 = -\lambda(1-\sigma)$
produces estimates of 0.595 and 0.008 for σ and λ, respectively. This value for λ corresponds to an annual rate of growth of productivity of 1.83 per cent. The CD function implies that (wL/pV) is constant thus the significance of the regression ($R = 0.74$) leads the authors to reject this possibility.

To estimate δ the authors manipulate the production function into the following form,

$$\frac{\delta}{1-\delta} = \frac{\gamma_0^\rho}{1-\delta} 10^{\lambda t \rho} \left(\frac{K}{V}\right)^\rho - \left(\frac{K}{L}\right)^\rho \tag{6.105}$$

then since from (6.104),

$$\frac{\gamma_0^\rho}{1-\delta} = \frac{1}{\text{anti} \log (\alpha_0/\sigma)}$$

the right-hand side of (6.105) is known. Using (6.105) it is possible to check on the constancy of δ and, using mean sample values, to derive the estimate, $\delta = 0.519$. From (6.105) an estimate of γ_0 can be derived. The resulting production function is

$$V = 0.584\,(1.0183)^t\,(0.519\,K^{-0.756} + 0.481\,L^{-0.756})^{-1.322}\,.$$

Notice that although capital stock figures are not used to estimate ρ and λ they are used to estimate δ and γ_0. The authors do not calculate the fit statistics for this function but state that out of forty-one years the residual error is not more than 4% in twenty-two years and not more than 8% in thirty-one years. The maximum errors are −13.3% in 1933 and +10.7% in 1909.

Since capital stock figures are available the authors also attempt to use these directly in the estimation of ρ and δ. From (6.95), setting $R_1 = R_2 = 1$,

$$\log \frac{wL}{rK} = \log \frac{1-\delta}{\delta} + \rho \log \frac{K}{L} + u_2 - u_1\,. \qquad (6.106)$$

Applying least squares Arrow et al. find a value for ρ (−0.095) which contradicts their earlier finding. The authors believe that the reason for this discrepancy lies in the different assumptions about the error terms which are implied in the different estimation methods.

6.10.5. Kmenta (1967)

Kmenta, using U.S. non-farm data for 1947 to 1960, presents single equation estimates of (6.87). Direct application of least squares to (6.87) will provide estimates of the production function but because of multicollinearity he prefers to accept the Arrow et al. estimate of δ (i.e., 0.519) and then apply least squares. The resulting estimates are:

$$\gamma = 0.1112 \qquad \underset{(0.1487)}{v = 1.1785} \qquad \underset{(0.4398)}{\rho = 0.4884}\,.$$

The implied value of σ, 0.6719, is not significantly different from unity. This contradicts Arrow et al.'s first finding. On the surface it would appear that Kmenta has not allowed for technical progress but, in fact, he adjusted the capital and labour data to allow for quality improvements at an annual rate of 1.5% and 1%, respectively. He does not fix the returns to scale a priori, but his results do not suggest any significant difference from constant returns to scale.

6.10.6. Brown and De Cani (1963a,b)

In an earlier section we described how Brown calculated CD production functions for different epochs for the U.S. In these two articles Brown and De Cani are trying to trace the effects of technological change on employment and the distribution of income. Their approach is to derive and estimate a demand for labour function and an income distribution function for three epochs. The changes in coefficients of these functions reflect the technological change and hence the authors can analyse its effect. Our immediate interest in their work stems from the fact that their functions are derived from a CES production function. The authors introduce a geometric distributed lag to take account of the inertia of entrepreneurs and hence are able to derive short-run and long-run estimates of the elasticity of substitution. From (6.95),

$$\log\left(\frac{L}{K}\right) = \sigma \log \gamma_2 + \sigma \log\left(\frac{r}{w}\right) + \sigma(u_2 - u_1) \tag{6.107}$$

where $\gamma_2 = (1-\delta)/\delta$.

Brown and De Cani assume that the labour/capital ratio responds not only to immediate relative prices but also to all past relative prices. That is, they assume that,

$$\log\left(\frac{L}{K}\right) = \sigma \log \gamma_2 + \sigma \log\left(\frac{r}{w}\right)^* \tag{6.108}$$

where

$$\log(r/w)^* = (1-\lambda)\log(r/w) + (1-\lambda)\lambda \log(r/w)_{-1} + (1-\lambda)\lambda^2 \log(r/w)_{-2} + \ldots \text{ and } 0<\lambda<1\,. \tag{6.109}$$

Thus

$$\log\left(\frac{L}{K}\right) = \sigma(1-\lambda)\log\gamma_2 + \sigma(1-\lambda)\log\left(\frac{r}{w}\right) + \lambda\log\left(\frac{L}{K}\right)_{-1}\,. \tag{6.110}$$

In this equation σ is obviously the long-run elasticity of substitution, the equivalent short-run concept is $\sigma(1-\lambda)$. The distribution function that they use is obtained by subtracting $\log(r/w)$ from both sides of (6.110). Using data pertaining to U.S. private domestic non-farm sector the authors present the results reproduced in table 6.5.

Table 6.5 indicates considerable changes in the production function from epoch to epoch. Furthermore, the estimates of the elasticity of substitution

Table 6.5
OLS estimates of the labour–capital expansion path for the U.S.

	$\log \gamma_2$	σ	$\sigma/(1-\lambda)$	λ	R^2
1890–1918	−0.8865	0.3453	0.55	0.3764	0.847
	(0.437)	(0.123)		(0.169)	
1919–1937	−7.1660	0.0779	0.31	0.7462	0.730
	(5.360)	(0.098)		(0.221)	
1938–1958	−2.9275	0.1112	0.47	0.7623	0.861
	(1.450)	(0.038)		(0.159)	

are the lowest we have yet seen. Certainly they differ considerably from Kmenta's estimate.

With these estimates of δ and σ it would be possible to go on to estimate the production function. Brown and De Cani (1963b), however, proceed to derive and estimate a demand for labour equation. Dividing (6.71) by (6.70) setting $R_1 = R_2 = 1$ and ignoring the stochastic terms

$$\frac{r}{w} = \frac{1}{\gamma_2}\left(\frac{L}{K}\right)^{1/\sigma} \tag{6.111}$$

thus

$$\frac{L}{K} = \gamma_2^{\sigma}\left(\frac{r}{w}\right)^{\sigma}$$

and

$$K = L\gamma_2^{-\sigma}\left(\frac{r}{w}\right)^{-\sigma}. \tag{6.112}$$

Substituting (6.112) into the CES function and solving for L gives

$$L = \left(\frac{V}{\gamma}\right)^{1/v}\left[\delta\left(\gamma_2\frac{r}{w}\right)^{\rho\sigma} + (1-\delta)\right]^{\rho}$$

i.e.

$$\log L - \rho\log\left[\delta\left(\gamma_2\frac{r}{w}\right)^{\rho\sigma} + (1-\delta)\right] = -\frac{1}{v}\log\gamma + \frac{1}{v}\log V. \tag{6.113}$$

The authors introduce technical progress directly into (6.113) by letting

$$\gamma = \gamma_1 t^{\beta v} .$$

Substituting the available estimates for parameters (6.113) becomes

$$\log L - \hat{\rho} \left[\hat{\delta} \left(\hat{\gamma}_2 \frac{r}{w} \right)^{\hat{\rho}\hat{\sigma}} + (1-\hat{\delta}) \right] = -\frac{1}{v} \log \gamma_1 + \frac{1}{v} \log V - \beta \log t . \quad (6.114)$$

Applying least squares to (6.114) produces estimates of the returns to scale and efficiency parameters which appear in table 6.6. Table 6.6 suggests that before 1938 the U.S. was operating under increasing returns to scale and thus casts doubt on the wisdom of Arrow et al. in assuming constant returns to scale.

The CES studies we have considered so far have produced conflicting results. Nerlove (1967), concentrating mainly on the elasticity of substitution estimates, surveys a number of CES aggregate production function studies all relating to the U.S. and comes to the same conclusion. He presents a collection of estimates of σ which varies from 0.068 to 1.16. This variety of results leads one to be very suspicious of attributing much meaning to aggregate production functions based on time series data.

6.11. Aggregate cross-section studies

Cross-section data have also been used to estimate aggregate production functions. Censuses of production data for different industries have been used to estimate production functions. Douglas (and his associates) (1948) pro-

Table 6.6
CES estimates of the returns to scale and efficiency parameters. U.S. non-farm sector.

	$-\frac{1}{v} \log \gamma_1$	$\frac{1}{v}$	v	$-\beta$ *	$\bar{R}^2$
1890–1918	0.9912 (0.0481)	0.5867 (0.0420)	1.7044	0.1091 (0.1186)	0.9893
1919–1937	1.9863 (0.0931)	0.6393 (0.0531)	1.5641	−0.0406 (0.0099)	0.9053
1939–1958	0.8196 (0.0991)	1.2456 (0.1673)	0.8028	−0.1873 (0.0539)	0.9506

* t equals 1 in the first year of each sample.

duced numerous studies of this kind. We shall not report their results, however, because it is very difficult to interpret them since they make no allowance for different qualities of inputs or for different technologies between industries. The type of data that would be acceptable for cross section studies is that which refers to units that have similar technology. Thus perhaps data from states within the U.S. or from different countries may be acceptable. On the whole this type of data has been used to estimate industry functions. One study which does use interstate and interindustry data for aggregate production functions is Griliches (1967).

6.11.1. Griliches (1967)

This article is part of a major programme of research on the sources of productivity changes in the U.S. In agriculture Griliches believes that most of the technical progress has come from the improvement in the quality of labour, the existence of economies of scale and public research. In this article he is preparing the way for similar research into manufacturing industries by producing an aggregate production function which involves a measure of the influence of the quality of labour and economies of scale. He admits to considerable 'fishing in the data' taken from the 1958 Census of Manufactures and 1960 Census of Population to produce his results, stating that these results will have to be tested on new data, i.e., 1963 Census of Manufactures.

The production function that he estimates is of CD form which includes measures of capital and labour quality, Z_{hij}, and dummy variables d_j and d_i to take account of interstate and interindustry differences. The actual form is

$$\log \left(\frac{pV}{L}\right)_{ij} = a_0 + \beta \log \left(\frac{K}{L}\right)_{ij} + h \log L_{ij} + \sum_r \mu_1 Z_{rij}$$

$$+ d_i + d_j + u_{ij} \,. \tag{6.115}$$

The meaning of this equation can be appreciated by considering the CD function

$$V = A\,(KZ_1)^{\beta}\,(LZ_2)^{\alpha}\,\mathrm{e}^{u}$$

where

Z_1 is a quality variable for capital; and

Z_2 is a quality variable for labour.

This can be written,

$$\log\left(\frac{V}{L}\right) = \log A + \beta \log\left(\frac{K}{L}\right) + (\alpha+\beta-1)\log L$$

$$+\beta \log Z_1 + \alpha \log Z_2 + u\ .$$

Thus Griliches' function assumes that the CD function coefficients are the same for all industries and all states except for the constant term. The coefficient of $\log L_{ij}, h$, represents the extent to which the economies of scale differ from constant returns (i.e. $\alpha + \beta = 1$). The assumption that each industry has the same α and β he justifies on two grounds. He is attempting to produce an aggregate function and this assumption is inherent. If the parameters do in fact vary, his estimates should represent some sort of average, which is what he is after. However, he reports that he fitted equations which did allow α and β to vary for different industries and that the variation was not great. The introduction of varying intercepts does help to soften this assumption a little.

The estimation technique he uses is ordinary least squares. He has two justifications for not using a simultaneous method. A possible model embodying the production function is (6.52)–(6.54) which can be estimated by indirect least squares (the reduced form is obtained from (6.66)–(6.68)). Unfortunately, this approach produces implausible estimates with very high standard errors. Another possible model is one which allows for an adjustment lag which introduces lagged values as exogenous variables. This model can be estimated by two stage least squares but he believes that these estimates will not differ much from the OLS estimates (see Section 6.13.3).

The data are taken from the 1958 U.S. Census of Manufactures and the 1960 Census of Population. Using seventeen industries from forty-nine states (although some small states were combined) led to a sample of 417 observations on the average establishment. The variables are defined as follows,

pV – value added;

K – the flow of capital services, i.e., the sum of insurance premiums, rental payments, property taxes paid, depreciation and depletion charged in 1957 and 6% gross book value on December 31st, 1957;

L – total payroll divided by average wage rate per hour of production workers;

w – total wages divided by total man hours of production workers.

No allowance is made for the fact that different vintages of capital may not be equally productive. This was weakly tested by including the ratio of net to gross capital stock in the regressions. No significant influence was found.

The quality of labour variables, taken from the Census of Population, relate to age, sex, colour and occupation. Occupation mix is used because education is not available. These variables are defined as,

Age = median age of employed males;

P White = white as a fraction of total males;

P Female = female as a fraction of total employees;

O_{ij} = $\sum_k Y_k O_{kij}$, where O_{kij} is the fraction of males in occupation k in industry i, state j, Y_k is mean income of all males, twenty-five and over, in this occupation.

All quality variables are transformed to logarithms except P White, P Female and the dummy variables. Much of the variation in the quality variables and in the wage rate is regional and for this reason Griliches wishes to use the state dummy variables sparingly. The results appear in table 6.7. Once again Griliches admits to a great deal of pretesting and points out that the word 'significant' should be taken with 'more than usually large chunks of salt'.

The capital coefficient, β, is between 0.39 and 0.23 which fits with the a priori notions of this coefficient. The returns to scale parameter, h, is always significant and always positive suggesting increasing returns to scale. This finding is consistent with that of Hildebrand and Liu (see Section 6.13.3). The quality of labour variables have the expected signs and are significant, although this significance tends to be eroded by the introduction of the dummy variables. Griliches' conclusions from these results are that differences in the quality of labour are an important factor in explaining differences in productivity and that there are mildly increasing returns to scale in U.S. industry. One might be surprised to find that Griliches has used a CD function rather than a CES. In fact, he justifies this choice by considering the findings of other studies, by producing estimates of the elasticity of substitution and by estimating the approximate aggregate CES function.

Using his data, i.e., 417 observations, the approximate aggregate CES function is estimated to be

$$\log\left(\frac{pV}{L}\right) = \underset{(0.03)}{0.64} + \underset{(0.037)}{0.422}\log\frac{K}{L} + \underset{(0.014)}{0.050}\log L + \underset{(0.018)}{0.030}\left[\log\frac{K}{L}\right]^2$$

$$R^2 = 0.55\,.$$

The coefficient of $\log^2 K/L$ is insignificant and remains so even if industry dummy variables are included. He points out that this is not a very good test, however, because the coefficient of $\log^2 K/L$ is likely to be small anyway. Consider the coefficient of $\log^2 K/L$ when $v = 1$, $\delta = 4$, $\rho = 1$ (i.e., $\sigma = 0.5$) (see (6.87)). In this case the coefficient is -0.12 and given the usual standard

Table 6.7

Griliches production function estimates, U.S. manufacturing, 1958.

	440 observations		417 observations								
Coefficients of:	1	2	3	4	5	6	7	8	9	10	11
K/L	0.358 (0.023)	0.297 (0.023)	0.392 (0.018)	0.388 (0.018)	0.382 (0.075)	0.351 (0.019)	0.252 (0.022)	0.258 (0.021)	0.261 (0.020)	0.235 (0.021)	0.229 (0.021)
L	0.058 (n.c.)			0.056 (0.013)	0.070 (0.012)	0.078 (0.012)	0.032 (0.015)	0.047 (0.015)	0.055 (0.016)	0.058 (0.016)	0.054 (0.015)
R(Age K)	0.053 (0.058)	0.013 (0.043)									
Occupation					0.952 (0.079)	0.992 (0.098)	0.352 (0.092)		0.391 (0.177)	0.419 (0.174)	0.289 (0.180)
Age						−0.672 (0.128)					0.067 (0.139)
P White						0.092 (0.056)	0.196 (0.046)				0.134 (0.047)
P Female						−0.120 (0.030)	−0.261 (0.069)			−0.238 (0.066)	−0.245 (0.059)
Industry dummies		yes					yes	yes	yes	yes	yes
State dummies								yes	yes	yes	yes
R^2	n.c.	0.781	0.528	0.547	0.665	0.697	0.823	0.852	0.854	0.860	0.862
O_{ij}	0.1090	0.0772	0.1073	0.1052	0.0907	0.0865	0.0672	0.0629	0.0626	0.0616	0.0611

n.c. – not computed. These estimates are from log V dependent regressions. While the coefficients are the same or related, the R^2's are not comparable with the log (V/L) forms.

errors this is not likely to be 'significant'. The situation is worse as σ gets close to unity. His method of estimating σ is similar to that of Section 6.7.4. From (6.93)

$$\log \frac{V}{L} = \rho \log \gamma - \log (1-\delta) + \sigma \log \frac{w}{p} + \frac{u_1}{1+\rho}. \tag{6.116}$$

If there is a geometric adjustment lag one should estimate

$$\log \frac{V}{L} = (1-\lambda)\,[\rho \log \gamma - \log (1-\delta)] + (1-\lambda)\,\sigma \log \frac{w}{p}$$

$$+ \lambda \log \left(\frac{V}{L}\right)_{t-1} + \frac{u_{1t} - \lambda u_{1t-1}}{1+\rho}. \tag{6.117}$$

If, however, there is no adjustment lag but u_1 is serially correlated because of excluded variables (e.g. quality of labour), then

$$\log \frac{V}{L} = (1-r)\,[\rho \log \gamma - \log (1-\delta)] + \sigma \log \frac{w}{p}$$

$$- r\sigma \log \left(\frac{w}{p}\right)_{t-1} + r \log \left(\frac{V}{L}\right)_{t-1} + \epsilon_t \tag{6.118}$$

if $u_t = ru_{t-1} + \epsilon_t$.

Using the 417 observations† to estimate (6.116)–(6.118) Griliches gets

$$\log \frac{pV}{L} = A_1 + 1.198 \log w \qquad R^2 = 0.606$$

$$\log \frac{pV}{L} = A_2 + 0.273 \log w + 0.827 \log \left(\frac{pV}{L}\right)_{t-1} \qquad R^2 = 0.890$$

$$\log \frac{pV}{L} = A_3 + 1.056 \log w + 0.855 \log \left(\frac{pV}{L}\right)_{t-1} - 0.900 \log w_{t-1}.$$

$$R^2 = 0.918$$

† Griliches' data is in fact in money terms, i.e. pV and w replace V and w/p (see Section 6.12.2).

The adjustment model produces a very low rate of adjustment (17% per annum) and a value for the long run elasticity of substitution of 1.35. The serial correlation model produces an estimate of σ which is not significantly different from unity. Griliches accepts the serial correlation model since all the signs and magnitudes of the coefficients are consistent with the theory.

Griliches repeats this exercise for the industry (two-digit level) data. Also he incorporates the quality of labour variables and dummy variables in (6.116), (6.117) and (6.118). On the basis of these results and after considering the substitution elasticity estimates of other studies, he concludes that there is no strong evidence against the CD function for manufacturing industry.

6.12. **Industry time series**

6.12.1. Walters (1963)

In this survey of econometric production functions Walters refers to very few time series studies of CD functions. Presumably this shortage stems from the unavailability of annual capital data for industries. However, we reproduce the results he collected in table 6.8.

It will be immediately realised that these show wildly different estimates between industries in the same country and between the same industries in different countries. Walters points out that Tintner's results for U.S. agriculture and Lomax's results for U.K. agriculture are simply not acceptable. These results rightly cause Walters to be sceptical that any meaningful results are achieved from such studies. Of course, these studies were based on dubious capital series and relate to periods of generally depressed economic conditions. These problems are probably less acute for the CES industry studies which have appeared since 1961. Nerlove (1967) has surveyed the studies which relate to two digit manufacturing industries in the U.S.

6.12.2. Nerlove (1967)

This article concentrates on the estimates of the elasticity of substitution. Table 6.9 reproduces Nerlove's summary table of time series estimates from six studies together with the standard errors presented by Ferguson (1965).

Kendrick's figures are based on only two years 1953–1957 and subject to uncertainty and we will not discuss them further. Lucas (1963), McKinnon (1962) and McKinnon (1963a) are all estimated in basically the same way. From (6.93) setting $R_1 = 1$ we get

Table 6.8
Production functions for industries: time series estimates.

Country and period	α	β	γ_3 (raw material)	$\alpha + \beta$ $(+ \gamma_3)$		Reference
U.S. agriculture 1920–1941	1.70	0.81		2.51 with exponential trend	1.6% p.a.	Tintner (1952, p. 303)
U.K. agriculture 1924–1947	0.18	0.37		0.55	1.03% p.a.	Lomax (1949)
U.K. cotton industry 1948–1952	0.33	0.70 (loom hours)	0.26	1.29	0.45% p.a.	Lomax (1953)
U.K. coal	0.79	0.21		(restricted)		Lomax (1950)
Canada automobiles 1918–1930	0.96	0.41		1.37	exp trend $-0.034t$ $+0.00134t^2$	Smith (1945)

$$\log \frac{V}{L} = \rho \log \gamma - \log (1-\delta) + \sigma \log \frac{w}{p} + \frac{u_1}{1+\rho}. \tag{6.119}$$

Technical progress and a distributed lag can be incorporated into (6.119). Although only McKinnon (1962) uses a distributed lag, all of them make some allowance for technical progress. Although the actual sources of data differ, one feels that the differences in the estimates are too large to be attributed to this. The major difference in the three studies relates to the extent to which their data are affected by recession conditions. Lucas's data, 1931–1958, is obviously heavily affected whereas McKinnon (1963a) uses mainly years of high economic activity, i.e., 1899, 1909, 1919, 1927, 1937, 1948, 1953, and 1957. McKinnon (1962) relates to 1947–1958.

Ferguson, while using a similar sample period to McKinnon (1962), in fact, 1949–1961, uses undeflated data. The likely effect of this can be seen from (6.119) by adding $\log p$ to both sides of the equation, i.e.,

$$\log \frac{pV}{L} = \rho \log \gamma - \log (1-\delta) + \sigma \log w + (1-\sigma) \log p + \frac{u_1}{1+\rho}. \tag{6.120}$$

Thus Ferguson's model involves a specification error. If $\log w$ and $\log p$ are positively correlated then Ferguson's method will produce an estimate of σ biased toward unity. Comparing Ferguson's results to those of McKinnon (1962), in fifteen out of eighteen industries the estimates of the former are closer to unity. Thus the differences here can be reconciled, Maddala who also deals with post-war deflated data, 1947–1958, uses another estimation method. He regresses $\log (K/L)$ on $\log (w/r)$ and vice versa (see 6.107) thus providing a range in which σ should lie. Maddala's estimates differ quite considerably from McKinnon (1962).

In conclusion it would appear that for similar data and sometimes similar methods one can get widely differing estimates of a crucial parameter of the CES function. Could these differences stem from the fact that some of the studies are more subject to the influences of recession than others? Nerlove tries to reconcile the differences on this account but is unable to. It would appear that the CES studies based on U.S. industry data encourage scepticism on the possibility of estimating economic production functions. If the different estimates are due to the rate of utilisation or due to the different specification of technical progress perhaps cross-section data will provide meaningful estimates, since, presumably, these will be less subject to such factors. Unfortunately, as was pointed out in Section 6.5, the problem of identification is greater when cross-section data are used.

Table 6.9
Summary of time series estimates of the elasticity of substitution between capital and labour for two-digit manufacturing industries.

Industry	McKinnon (1962)	McKinnon (1963a)	Kendrick (1964)	Ferguson (1965)	Maddala (1965)	Lucas (1963)	Ferguson (1965) Standard errors
Food and kindred products	0.37	n.o.	0.25	0.24	0.03– 0.14	0.40	0.20
Tobacco manufactures	0.92	n.o.	0.88	1.18	0.09– 0.46	0.15	0.46
Textile mill products	0.16	0.44	0.58	1.10	0.06– 0.10	0.13	0.44
Apparel, etc.	0.69	1.44	0.09	1.08	−0.05– −0.13		0.16
Lumber and timber	0.80	0.56	0.40	0.91	0.17– 0.26	0.48	0.07
Furniture and fixtures	1.02	0.91	1.86	1.12	0.11– 0.21		0.05
Paper, etc.	0.09	0.94	0.55	1.02	0.17– 0.23	0.51	0.06
Printing and publishing	0.84	0.94	0.18	1.15	−0.04– −0.10	0.49	0.31
Chemical, etc.	−1.11	1.12	0.65	1.25	0.10– 0.22	0.68	0.07
Petroleum and coal	n.o.	n.o.	0.51	1.30	0.27– 0.37	0.38	0.15
Rubber and plastics	0.35	n.o.	0.35	0.76	0.19– 0.34	0.32	0.56
Leather, etc.	0.25	0.52	0.47	0.87	−0.01– −1.32	0.41	0.14
Stone, clay, glass	−1.12	1.08	0.89	0.67	0.27– 0.40	−0.21	0.47
Primary metals	0.03	n.o.	0.81	1.20	0.22– 0.27	0.64	0.11
Fabricated metal products	0.33	n.o.	0.78	0.93	0.04– 0.41		0.26
Non-electric machinery	0.75	n.o.	0.50	1.04	0.15– 0.25	0.48	0.04
Electrical machinery	0.43	0.64	0.80	0.64	0.11– 0.22		0.36
Transportation equipment	0.18	n.o.	0.65	0.24	0.05– 0.46	0.73[b]	0.56
Instruments	0.38	n.o.	−0.14	0.76	0.42– 0.58	n.o.	0.29

n.o. = not obtained.

[a] Based on a comparison of the United States and Japan only.

[b] Automobiles only.

6.13. Industry cross-section studies

The data available for studies of this kind are either international or interstate data. Relative prices vary between countries and between states which lessens the problem of identification. Arrow et al. use international data but many studies have been based on U.S. interstate data.

6.13.1. Arrow et al. (1961)

In this article the authors find an empirical relationship between the output–labour ratio and the average money wage for data from different countries relating to twenty-four industries. To explain these findings they derive the CES function and perform a number of tests on their results. Given the existence of the CES function they are able to indicate what biases may be present in their estimates of the elasticity of substitution. They assume that competitive markets and profit maximising equilibria exist.

We shall not explain the derivation of the CES function but the tests they use need a little explanation. Their starting point is the relation,

$$\log \frac{V}{L} = a + b \log \frac{w}{p} . \tag{6.121}$$

Remember at this point they do not assume that a CES function exists. Now consider,

$$c = \left(\frac{V}{K}\right) \left[1 - a^{-1/b} \left(\frac{V}{L}\right)^{(1-b)/b}\right]^{b/(1-b)} \tag{6.122}$$

i.e.

$$V = [c^{(b-1)/b} K^{(b-1)/b} + a^{-1/b} L^{(b-1)/b}]^{b/(b-1)} .$$

It can be shown that b is the elasticity of substitution, σ, and thus

$$V = [c^{-\rho} K^{-\rho} + a^{-1/b} L^{-\rho}]^{-1/\rho} . \tag{6.123}$$

Given that a and b are constants then, if c is a constant, (6.123) is a production function with constant returns to scale. Introducing the notation $\phi = a^{-1/b}$, $\psi = c^{-\rho}$, (6.123) becomes

$$V = [\phi K^{-\rho} + \psi L^{-\rho}]^{-1/\rho} . \tag{6.124}$$

Finally putting $\phi + \psi = \gamma^{-\rho}$ and $\phi\gamma^{\rho} = \delta$ brings (6.124) into the standard CES form

$$V = \gamma\,[\delta K^{-\rho} + (1-\delta)L^{-\rho}]^{-1/\rho}\,. \tag{6.125}$$

This analysis shows us that if c, which can be calculated if we know a and b, is constant then the function has constant returns to scale, and that ψ and hence γ and δ are constant. This is the first test that Arrow et al. perform. With negative results for this test they use the assumptions of constant returns to scale and $b = \sigma$ to test whether ϕ, ψ or δ is constant. Values of δ_i and γ_i can be calculated from,

$$\frac{\delta}{1-\delta} = \left(\frac{r}{w}\right)\left(\frac{K}{L}\right)^{1+\rho} \tag{6.126}$$

and (6.125), and from these, values of a_i and b_i can be constructed. However, let us turn our attention to their empirical analysis.

The data are derived from industrial censuses for nineteen countries. These countries and the average wage are listed in table 6.10. Values are translated into U.S. dollars via the official exchange rates. The average wage, w, is measured by total wages bill divided by the number of employees, output, pV, is represented by the value added in U.S. dollars and the labour input, L, is measured in man years. Using this data the least squares regressions of $\log (pV/L)$ on $\log w$ gives the results which appear in table 6.11.

The fits are quite high and there is an indication that most of the elasticities of substitution differ significantly from unity. To perform the tests outlined above it is necessary to have data on the capital stock. The authors were able to assemble comparable information on the rate of return, r, and hence the capital stock, $K = (V - wL/r)$ for four industries for certain countries. To get an indication of the constancy of c, the value for each observation is divided by the geometric mean, in the case of δ, a and b, the coefficient of variation is also calculated. The values are reproduced in table 6.12.

On the basis of table 6.12, Arrow et al. reject the hypothesis that c is constant and this, as can be seen from (6.123), implies that efficiency varies from country to country. However, they accept the hypothesis that δ is constant since the variation of δ is less than that of ϕ and ψ. The constancy of δ implies that only γ varies from country to country, i.e., that the variation in efficiency is neutral. Comparing (6.121) with (6.119) brings to light the fact that if γ is positively correlated with the real wage then the least squares coefficient of $\log (w/p)$ will give an estimate of σ which is biased towards unity.

Table 6.10
Countries in the sample used by Arrow et al.

Country	Year of census	Average wage [a] (current dollars)	Number of industries used
1. United States	1954	3841	24
2. Canada	1954	3226	23
3. New Zealand	1955/56	1980	22
4. Australia	1955/56	1926	24
5. Denmark	1954	1455	24
6. Norway	1954	1393	22
7. Puerto Rico	1952	1182	17
8. United Kingdom	1951	1059	24
9. Colombia	1953	924	24
10. Ireland	1953	900	15
11. Mexico	1951	524	21
12. Argentina	1950	519	24
13. Japan	1953	476	23
14. El Salvador	1951	445	16
15. Brazil	1949	436	10
16. S. Rhodesia	1952	384	6
17. Ceylon	1952	261	11
18. India	1953	241	17
19. Iraq	1954	213	2

[a] Unweighted average of wages in industries in sample.

This bias is likely to be increased due to the fact that Arrow et al. use money values (see Section 6.12.2).

This very impressive article leaves one with the feeling that the CES function is very useful for industry production functions and that the elasticity of substitution is typically less than one. This article stimulated more studies based on rather less dubious data. Unfortunately, the results of the later studies are not all consistent. This has been brought home strongly by Nerlove (1967).

6.13.2. Nerlove (1967)

The author finds that the estimates of the elasticities of substitution based on international data are more or less consistent with each other (cf. Murata and Arrow, and Arrow et al. in table 6.13). However, those based on U.S. state data differ considerably from each other and from those based on international data. Table 6.13 reproduces Nerlove's summary of the cross-section estimates for two digit manufacturing industries.

Table 6.11
Results of regression analysis.
$\log (pV/L) = \log a + b \log w$.

Industry	Regression equations log a	Regression equations b	Standard error S_b	Coeff. of deter. R^2	Test of significance on b: Degree of freedom	Test of significance on b: Confidence level for b different from 1
Dairy products	0.419	0.721	0.073	0.921	14	99%
Fruit and vegetable canning	0.355	0.855	0.075	0.910	12	90
Grain and mill products	0.429	0.909	0.096	0.855	14	*
Bakery products	0.304	0.900	0.065	0.927	14	80
Sugar	0.431	0.781	0.115	0.790	11	90
Tobacco	0.564	0.753	0.151	0.629	13	80
Textile – spinning and weaving	0.296	0.809	0.068	0.892	16	98
Knitting mills	0.270	0.785	0.064	0.915	13	99
Lumber and wood	0.279	0.860	0.066	0.910	16	95
Furniture	0.226	0.894	0.042	0.952	14	95
Pulp and paper	0.478	0.965	0.101	0.858	14	*
Printing and publishing	0.284	0.868	0.056	0.940	14	95
Leather finishing	0.292	0.857	0.062	0.921	12	95
Basic chemicals	0.460	0.831	0.070	0.898	14	95
Fats and oils	0.515	0.839	0.090	0.869	12	90
Miscellaneous chemicals	0.483	0.895	0.059	0.938	14	90
Clay products	0.273	0.919	0.096	0.878	11	*
Glass	0.285	0.999	0.084	0.921	11	*
Ceramics	0.210	0.901	0.044	0.974	10	95
Cement	0.560	0.920	0.149	0.770	10	*
Iron and steel	0.363	0.811	0.051	0.936	11	99
Non-ferrous metals	0.370	1.011	0.120	0.886	8	*
Metal products	0.301	0.902	0.088	0.897	11	*
Electric machinery	0.344	0.870	0.118	0.804	12	*

* Not significant at 80% or higher levels of confidence.

Table 6.12
Tests of the CES production function.

	Spinning and weaving					Basic chemicals				
	$c_i/\bar{c}$	δ_i	γ_i	ϕ_i	ψ_i	$c_i/\bar{c}$	δ_i	γ_i	ϕ_i	ψ_i
U.S.	1.72	0.54	1.02	0.46	0.53	2.31	0.77	1.02	0.23	0.77
Canada	1.16	0.58	0.77	0.45	0.61	2.01	0.77	0.84	0.24	0.80
U.K.	1.44	0.60	0.88	0.41	0.62	–	–	–	–	–
Japan	0.55	0.65	0.43	0.43	0.79	0.70	0.73	0.57	0.30	0.83
India	0.63	–	–	–	–	0.51	0.75	0.44	0.30	0.88
mean		0.59		0.44	0.64		0.75		0.27	0.82
Coefficient of variation †		5.85%		4.17%	11.85%		1.72%		11.19%	8.04%
	Iron and steel					**Metal products**				
	$c_i/\bar{c}$	δ_i	γ_i	ϕ_i	ψ_i	$c_i/\bar{c}$	δ_i	γ_i	ϕ_i	ψ_i
U.S.	2.96	0.61	1.73	0.34	0.54	2.35	0.51	1.74	0.46	0.48
Canada	2.13	0.64	1.38	0.34	0.59	1.37	0.54	1.29	0.45	0.53
U.K.	0.62	0.56	0.86	0.46	0.58	–	–	–	–	–
Japan	0.49	0.58	0.69	0.44	0.65	0.31	0.49	0.62	0.54	0.52
India	0.53	0.60	0.67	0.44	0.66	–	–	–	–	–
mean		0.60		0.41	0.60		0.51		0.48	0.51
Coefficient of variation †		3.55%		12.84%	6.77%		3.50%		7.41%	3.79%

† Defined as $\sum_{i=1}^{n} |X_i - \bar{x}|/N.\bar{x}$ where X_i is the value of country i, $\bar{x}$ is the industry mean and N is the number of observations.

Some of Minasian and Solow's results are very different, (e.g. 'tobacco' and 'electrical machinery'). They use different data – Minasian uses individual states, 1957, and Solow uses aggregates of states, 1956 – but Nerlove is unable to explain the differences on these accounts. Dhrymes' results are based on essentially the same data as Minasian but again his results differ considerably. Although his second set of results are based on the capital marginal product equation his first set of results are based on the same method of estimation as Minasian's, i.e., via the labour marginal product equation. Arrow and Murata's estimates, which are based on international data, are in general less than those based on interstate data (e.g. Solow and Minasian). Nerlove

Table 6.13
Summary of cross-section estimates of the elasticity of substitution between capital and labour for two-digit manufacturing industries.

Industry	Arrow et al. (1961)	Minasian (1961)	Solow (1964)	Liu–Hildebrand (1965)		Murata–Arrow (1965) Intercountry data 1953/1956	Murata–Arrow (1965) Intercountry data 1957/1959	Dhrymes (1965)
Food and kindred products	0.93	0.58	0.69	2.15	1.29	0.72	0.73	0.56–0.97
Tobacco manufactures	n.o.	3.46	1.96	n.o.	n.o.			n.o.
Textile mill products	0.80	1.58	1.27	1.65	2.08	0.79	0.83	0.68–1.03
Apparel, etc.	n.o.	n.o.	1.01	1.43	2.38	0.66	0.80	0.54–1.03
Lumber and timber	0.84	0.94	0.99	0.99	0.91	0.82	0.92	0.78–1.1
Furniture and fixtures	n.o.	1.09	1.12	0.92	0.96			0.70–1.39
Paper etc.	1.14	1.60	1.77	1.06	0.71	0.90	0.79	0.20–0.64
Printing and publishing	1.21	n.o.	1.02	n.o.	n.o.	0.84	0.93	0.68–1.11
Chemicals, etc.	0.90	n.o.	0.14	1.25	0.88	0.84	0.83	0.31–1.03
Petroleum and coal	n.o.	−0.54	1.45	n.o.	n.o.			0.11–1.31
Rubber and plastics	0.98	0.82	1.48	1.45	1.39	0.83	0.77	0.40–1.04
Leather, etc.	0.72	0.96	0.89	0.79	0.93	0.71	0.70	0.51–1.13
Stone, clay, glass	1.08	0.59	0.32	1.28	1.44	0.85	0.86	0.49–0.89
Primary metals	n.o.	0.92	1.87	0.99	1.00	0.86	0.87	0.10–0.97
Fabricated metal products	n.o.	n.o.	0.80	0.70	0.45	0.92	0.92	0.40–0.95
Non-electric machinery	0.97	0.31	0.64	0.60	0.41	n.o.	n.o.	0.12–0.25
Electrical machinery		1.26	0.37	0.78	1.10	n.o.	n.o.	0.19–0.62
Transportation equipment	1.04	2.04	0.06	2.01	1.91	n.o.	n.o.	n.o.
Instruments	n.o.	n.o.	1.59	1.24	1.65	n.o.	n.o.	n.o.

reports McKinnon's (1963b) justification for this; namely, that rates of return vary markedly between countries but not between states. Since wages vary this implies that product prices must vary more between states than between countries. Thus there will be more bias on this amount in the interstate estimates, i.e., the estimates will be higher (see Section 6.12.2). In spite of this case of reconciliation, one of Nerlove's conclusions is:

'What remains striking is the diversity of results and their sensitivity to small changes in the specification of the equation fitted or of the data used.'

6.13.3. Hildebrand and Liu (1965)

This monograph formulates and estimates production functions for two-digit U.S. industries based on data taken from three U.S. Bureau of Census publications. Its aims are to estimate industry production functions without recourse to assumptions of perfect competition in both factor and product markets, profit maximising equilibrium, constant returns to scale, and neutral technical progress.

Before they present their own model of production, Hildebrand and Liu review the earlier research and especially Arrow et al. (1961). They make a number of criticisms as may be expected from their own aims. A fundamental criticism is that the empirical base on which Arrow et al. built their CES function is very uncertain. Hildebrand and Liu claim that if one is attempting to explain movements in value added per man then capital per man should be included as an explanatory variable in addition to the average wage. Using their data they compute this regression and the results appear in table 6.14 along with the coefficient of determination, R^2, for the Arrow et al. regression. Nerlove (1967) reports that Bruno (1962) has derived the production function for this expanded empirical base. Nerlove himself derives the corresponding elasticity of substitution and it is this which is recorded in table 6.13. Actually Hildebrand and Liu repeat the exercise excluding non-production workers from the labour and wage variables, hence the two estimates. Having listed their objections to the Arrow et al. model the authors specify their own model.

The special features of their production function are the presence of two labour variables, production and non-production workers and the allowances for improved quality of labour and technical progress in capital via the exponents of the input variables. Thus

$$V = aL_p^{b \log q} L_n^c K^{e \log R} u \tag{6.127}$$

where L_p and L_n represent the input of production and non-production

Table 6.14

Tests of the empirical basis of the 'new class of production function', developed by Arrow et al. using U.S. Census of Manufactures, 1957.

pV/L = value added per man-hour of all employees; w = average salary and wage rate; K/L = capital per man-hour.

	No. of observations (states)	Coefficients of determination between pV/L and w	Regressions of pV/L on w and K/L: Regression coefficients of w	Regression coefficients of K/L	Coefficient of determination
Food and kindred products	35	0.401	0.407 (0.177)	0.446 (0.139)	0.548
Textile mill products	18	0.651	0.975 (0.175)	0.160 (0.109)	0.695
Apparel and related products	18	0.641	1.071 (0.263)	0.097 (0.086)	0.660
Lumber and wood products	14	0.943	0.990 (0.135)	0.002 (0.070)	0.943
Furniture and fixtures	19	0.819	1.258 (0.128)	−0.154 (0.072)	0.859
Pulp, paper and products	28	0.253	0.386 (0.322)	0.331 (0.050)	0.730
Chemicals and products	31	0.309	0.866 (0.231)	0.201 (0.085)	0.424
Petroleum and coal products	18	0.062	0.180 (0.716)	0.282 (0.224)	0.152
Rubber products	16	0.522	1.278 (0.553)	0.018 (0.217)	0.523
Leather and leather goods	15	0.357	0.890 (0.457)	−0.050 (0.113)	0.368
Stone, clay and glass products	25	0.251	0.539 (0.177)	0.295 (0.065)	0.611
Primary metal products	28	0.075	0.298 (0.704)	0.321 (0.141)	0.234
Fabricated metal products	32	0.180	0.401 (0.207)	0.178 (0.068)	0.336
Machinery except electrical	25	0.146	0.222 (0.263)	0.258 (0.100)	0.343
Electrical machinery	22	0.068	0.300 (0.210)	0.278 (0.071)	0.483
Transportation equipment	26	0.234	1.008 (0.448)	0.214 (0.060)	0.504
Instruments and related products	12	0.556	0.601 (0.294)	0.217 (0.116)	0.681

labour; and q and R are indices of the improvement in labour and capital. Imperfect competition is allowed for by incorporating a demand function which allows the price of the commodity to vary with the quantity

$$V = dp^{-h} \tag{6.128}$$

where h is the industry's elasticity of demand.

This equation stems from the assumption that industries are made up of either many firms of the same size or of few firms and their prices moved proportionally in 1957. The profit maximising position in such conditions, is where marginal revenue product of labour equals the money wage, i.e.,

$$\frac{\partial pV}{\partial L_p} = \frac{\partial (d^{1/h} V^{1-1/h})}{\partial L_p} = \frac{pVb \log q(1-1/h)}{L_p} = w_p \tag{6.129}$$

and

$$\frac{\partial pV}{\partial L_n} = \frac{pVc(1-1/h)}{L_n} = w_n \, . \tag{6.130}$$

Into these exact conditions are introduced stochastic disturbance terms as well as distributed lags. Within an industry, firms will diverge from the optimal condition according to their knowledge and skill. Hildebrand and Liu assume that this will be related to the size of the firm and to the wage rate. Large firms are likely to have better information and research activities and, therefore, be better informed – although this could be counter-balanced by their less flexible organisation. Firms paying high wages may obtain superior labour or may have greater incentive to achieve the optimum position. However, the more efficient firms may have located in low wage areas. High quality of labour is probably also correlated with efficiency. The extensions to (6.129) and (6.130) incorporating these disturbance terms are,

$$\frac{V(1-1/h)\, b \log q}{L_p^*} = w_p f_1 w_p^{-g_1} k_1 V^{m_1} l_1 (\log q)^s z_p \tag{6.131}$$

$$\frac{V(1-1/h)c}{L_n^*} = w_n f_2 w_n^{-g_2} k_2 V^{m_2} z_n \tag{6.132}$$

where L_p^* and L_n^* are the optimal inputs of labour; $f_1, g_1, k_1, m_1, l_1, s, f_2, g_2, k_2$, and m_2 are all constants; and z_p, z_n are stochastic terms.

Finally, the model has two adjustment equations,

$$\frac{L_p}{L_{p,t-1}} = \left[\frac{L_p^*}{L_{p,t-1}}\right]^{\lambda_p} \qquad (6.133)$$

$$\frac{L_n}{L_{n,t-1}} = \left[\frac{L_n^*}{L_{n,t-1}}\right]^{\lambda_n} . \qquad (6.134)$$

Eqs. (6.127), (6.131), (6.132), (6.133) and (6.134) represent the basic model but four estimating versions of this are considered.

Version I

$$\log pV = \log A + b \log q \log L_p + c \log L_n + e \log R \log K + \log u \qquad (6.135)$$

$$\log L_p = \lambda_p \log B + (1-\lambda_p) \log L_{p,t-1} + (1-m_1)\lambda_p \log pV$$
$$- (1-g_1)\lambda_p \log w_p + (1-s)\lambda_p \log \log q - \lambda_p \log z_p \qquad (6.136)$$

$$\log L_n = \lambda_n \log C + (1-\lambda_n) \log L_{n,t-1} + (1-m_2)\lambda_n \log pV$$
$$- (1-g_2)\lambda_n \log w_n - \lambda_n \log z_n \qquad (6.137)$$

where
$A = ap$ †;

$$B = \frac{b}{f_1 k_1 l_1}\left(1 - \frac{1}{h}\right);$$

$$C = \frac{c}{f_2 k_2}\left(1 - \frac{1}{h}\right).$$

Version II

This is the same as version I except that $\log q = 1$ and $B = b(1-1/h)/f_1 k_1$.

† p is taken to be constant since observations on p are not available. This will bias the estimates somewhat but hopefully not too much.

Version III

Production and non-production workers are not distinguished, hence

$$\log pV = \log A + b \log L + e \log R \log K + \log u \tag{6.138}$$

$$\log L = \lambda \log B + (1-\lambda) \log L_{t-1} + (1-m)\lambda \log pV$$

$$- (1-g)\lambda \log w - \lambda \log z \tag{6.139}$$

where $B = \frac{b}{fk}\left(1 - \frac{1}{h}\right)$.

Version IV

This is the same as version III but with $\log R = 1$, i.e., no technical progress.

All four versions are simultaneous models but all are identified and the authors estimate the coefficients by OLS and TSLS. Basically the production function is a CD function with various modifications for technical progress, which is measured by a number of proxies.

Hildebrand and Liu use two proxies for technical change, i.e., R. These are (1) the ratio (X 100) of the value of equipment to the value of plant and (2) the ratio of the net value of assets (gross value minus accumulated depreciation) to the gross value of assets. The former is based on the belief that progressive firms tend to use the same or similar buildings with more elaborate i.e. expensive, machines inside. The second measure reflects the 'average age' of capital. The full list of variables used is as follows:

pV : value added per establishment in the state in thousands of dollars in 1957;

L_p : employment of production workers in the state in thousands of man hours in 1957;

L_n : employment of non-production workers in the state in thousands of man hours in 1957;

L : $L_p + L_n$;

K : gross book value of plant and equipment per establishment in the state in thousands of dollars at the beginning of 1957;

K' : K plus the corresponding data on rental payments for plant and equipment after dividing the latter by 0.05 (i.e., an assumed discount of 5%);

R : the ratio of net to gross book value in the state at the beginning of 1957 multiplied by 100;

W : average wage rate in the state in 1957 in dollars per hour;

q : median school years completed by persons twenty-five years old and over in the state in 1960 in index numbers (average of all states = 10).

The authors produce sixteen estimated production functions for each industry. For each version there are single equation and two stage least squares estimates with two alternative measures of capital. The choice between these functions is taken on the basis of plausibility. The authors discussion of the results always starts with the TSLS estimates of version I using K', or, in their notation, (I,B,2) †.

To judge the plausibility they first find the relationship between the marginal revenue product of production workers per dollar of wage cost, ϕ_p, and the elasticity of demand, h. If the firm is at the profit maximising point, $\phi_p = 1$ (see (6.129)) and a corresponding estimate of h is derived. Overemployment exists if ϕ_p, is greater than unity and vice versa. If it is believed that there are plausible values of ϕ_p and h which satisfy the estimated relation, the authors go on to consider what change in ϕ_p, and hence L_p would be necessary to bring ϕ_p to unity in the conditions existing in 1957. Thus, as it were, the desired change in L_p is derived and, using the speed of adjustment, λ_p, estimated via the demand for labour equation, the authors calculate the 1957 change in L_p which their results suggest. Comparing this with the change which actually occurred in 1957 gives then a further indication of the plausibility of their results. This approach is repeated for the non-production workers. The authors also consider the plausibility of the capital coefficient but it will help if we explain the plausibility analysis more fully.

Using the definitions above, and (6.129)

$$\phi_p = \frac{\partial pV}{\partial L_p} \cdot \frac{1}{w_p} \tag{6.140}$$

$$= \left(1 - \frac{1}{h}\right) \frac{b\,(\log q)\, pV}{L_p\, w_p}\,. \tag{6.141}$$

Thus we have the relationship between ϕ_p and h. To find the relationship between the proportionate change in ϕ_p and that in L_p we can use (6.141).

$$\log \phi_p = \log b \left(1 - \frac{1}{h}\right) \log q + \log pV - \log L_p - \log w_p\,. \tag{6.142}$$

† B refers to K', if K is used the symbol is A. 2 refers to TSLS, if OLS is used the symbol is 1.

Substituting for pV and assuming changes in L_p only,

$$\mathrm{d}\log\phi_p = [b\log q\left(1-\frac{1}{h}\right) - 1]\ \mathrm{d}\log L_p$$

i.e.

$$\frac{\mathrm{d}L_p}{L_p} = \frac{1}{b\log q(1-1/h) - 1}\,\frac{\mathrm{d}\phi_p}{\phi_p}. \tag{6.143}$$

If we have a plausible value for h (6.143) can be used to estimate the proportionate change needed in production workers to bring ϕ_p to unity. The equivalent equations for ϕ_n and $\mathrm{d}L_n/L_n$ are

$$\phi_n = \frac{c(1-1/h)pV}{L_n w_n} \tag{6.144}$$

and

$$\frac{\mathrm{d}L_n}{L_n} = \frac{1}{c(1-1/h) - 1}\,\frac{\mathrm{d}\phi_n}{\phi_n}. \tag{6.145}$$

To judge the plausibility of the capital coefficients the capital–output and technology–output (see below) elasticities are computed as is the marginal revenue product per dollar of capital cost, i.e., ϕ_k. The marginal productivity of capital is derived as follows, holding L_n, L_p, and u constant, from (6.127),

$$\mathrm{d}\log V = \mathrm{d}\,(e\log R\log K_g)$$

i.e.

$$\frac{\mathrm{d}V}{V} = e\log R\,\frac{\mathrm{d}K_g}{K_g} + e\log K_g\,\frac{\mathrm{d}R}{R} \tag{6.146}$$

but

$$R = \frac{K_n}{K_g}\cdot 100$$

$$\therefore\quad \mathrm{d}R = \frac{K_g\,\mathrm{d}K_n - K_n\,\mathrm{d}K_g}{K_g^2}\cdot 100\,.$$

At a given point of time

$$\mathrm{d}K_n = \mathrm{d}K_g$$

$$\therefore \quad \frac{\mathrm{d}R}{R} = \frac{100 - R}{R} \frac{\mathrm{d}K_g}{K_g} . \tag{6.147}$$

Substituting (6.147) into (6.146)

$$\frac{\mathrm{d}V}{V} = e \log R \frac{\mathrm{d}K_g}{K_g} + \mathrm{d} \log K_g \frac{100 - R}{R} \frac{\mathrm{d}K_g}{K_g}$$

$$\therefore \quad \frac{\partial V}{\partial K_g} = e \frac{V}{K_g} \log R + \frac{eV}{K_g} \frac{100 - R}{R} \log K_g . \tag{6.148}$$

From (6.146) it is easy to see that, with constant technology ($\mathrm{d}R = 0$), $(eV)/(K_g \log R)$ is the marginal product of capital or the quantity effect. The other term in (6.148) is the technology effect. Thus the corresponding elasticities are $e \log R$ and $(1/R)\, e(100-R) \log K$. These, Hildebrand and Liu call the capital output elasticity and the technology output elasticity. The marginal revenue product of capital per dollar of capital cost is ϕ_k.

$$\phi_k = \frac{\partial pV}{\partial K_g} \tag{6.149}$$

$$= p \left(1 - \frac{1}{h}\right) \frac{\partial V}{\partial K_g}$$

$$= \frac{pV}{K_g} \left(1 - \frac{1}{h}\right) \left[e \log R + \frac{e(100-R)}{R} \log K_g \right] . \tag{6.150}$$

To allow for property tax, T, and depreciation, D, the authors use $(pV - T - D)$ instead of pV in (6.150), i.e.,

$$\phi_k = \frac{pV - T - D}{K_g} \left(1 - \frac{1}{h}\right) \left[e \log R + \frac{(100-R)}{R} \log K_g \right] . \tag{6.151}$$

It will be impossible to trace through all their results but it is worthwhile considering their food results which are reproduced in table 6.15.

Starting with equation (I,B,2) we find, using (6.141),

$$\phi_p = \left(1 - \frac{1}{h}\right) 1.11 . \tag{6.152}$$

Table 6.15
Hildebrand and Liu results for food production functions.

Version I				
(I,A,1)	$\log V =$ 0.307 $\log q \log L_p$	+ 0.433 $\log L_n$	+ 0.302 $\log R \log K_g$	
	(0.086)	(0.070)	(0.048)	$R^2 =$ 0.89
(I,A,2)	0.299	+ 0.421	+ 0.307	
	(0.096)	(0.077)	(0.053)	0.86
(I,B,1)	0.323	+ 0.408	+ 0.304 $\log R \log K'_g$	
	(0.092)	(0.074)	(0.055)	0.87
(I,B,2)	0.315	+ 0.397	+ 0.309	
	(0.100)	(0.081)	(0.059)	0.85
Version II				
(II,A,1)	$\log V =$ 0.685 $\log L_p$	+ 0.274 $\log L_n$	+ 0.208 $\log R \log K_g$	
	(0.139)	(0.077)	(0.052)	$R^2 =$ 0.91
(II,A,2)	0.692	+ 0.256	+ 0.209	
	(0.161)	(0.089)	(0.060)	0.89
(II,B,1)	0.733	+ 0.244	+ 0.195 $\log R \log K'_g$	
	(0.147)	(0.080)	(0.059)	0.90
(II,B,2)	0.743	+ 0.228	+ 0.195	
	(0.165)	(0.088)	(0.065)	0.88
Version III				
(III,A,1)	$\log V =$ 0.916 $\log L$	+ 0.234 $\log R \log K_g$		
	(0.087)	(0.042)		$R^2 =$ 0.91
(III,A,2)	0.894	+ 0.241		
	(0.100)	(0.048)		0.88
(III,B,1)	0.908	+ 0.237 $\log R \log K'_g$		
	(0.095)	(0.048)		0.89
(III,B,2)	0.891	+ 0.242		
	(0.106)	(0.053)		0.87
Version IV				
(IV,A,1)	$\log V =$ 0.536 $\log L$	+ 0.618 $\log K_g$		
	(0.139)	(0.112)		$R^2 =$ 0.90
(IV,A,2)	0.467	+ 0.665		
	(0.154)	(0.123)		0.89
(IV,B,1)	0.401	+ 0.724 $\log K'_g$		
	(0.176)	(0.146)		0.89
(IV,B,2)	0.336	+ 0.773		
	(0.190)	(0.156)		0.89

Table 6.15 (cont.)

Demand functions for labour

$$(\mathrm{V}_p)\ \log L_p = \underset{(0.123)}{0.837}\ \log L_{p,-1} + \underset{(0.112)}{0.153}\ \log V - \underset{(0.085)}{0.210}\ \log W_p + \underset{(0.239)}{0.390}\ \log(\log q) \qquad R^2 = 0.98$$

$$(\mathrm{V}_n)\ \log L_n = \underset{(0.047)}{0.963}\ \log L_{n,-1} + \underset{(0.057)}{0.103}\ \log V - \underset{(0.107)}{0.197}\ \log W_n \qquad R^2 = 0.97$$

If $\phi_p = 1$ the elasticity of demand for food (h) is 9.9 which appears too high. The authors believe that $\phi_p = 0.85$ and $h = 4.2$ are plausible values for the food industry. This high elasticity they believe is reasonable for modern food products which are no longer mainly subsistence products. Taking $\phi_p = 0.85$ the percentage change needed to reach unity, i.e., the profit maximising point, is 0.176. Thus (6.143) implies that the employment of production workers should fall by 23% for the conditions prevailing in 1957. The speed of adjustment indicated by the demand for production workers equation is 0.16 (i.e. 1 – 0.84). This implies that one should expect a fall in the employment of production workers of 3.7% (i.e. 23% × 0.16). In actual fact it fell by 3.1% from 1956 to 1957. Turning to non-production workers, if $h = 4.2$ then $\phi_n = 1.547$ from (6.144). Using (6.145) full adjustment to profit maximizing would imply an increase of 15%. However, since $\phi_n = 0.04$ the annual increase should be about 2%. In fact, from 1956 to 1957 non-production workers increased by 2.6%. The capital–output and technology–output elasticities were 0.53 and 0.76 in 1957. The adjusted marginal revenue product was 1.02 per dollar invested before business income tax.

Version II produces a value of $\phi_n = 0.44$ when $\phi_p = 0.8$. The authors dismiss this as implausible since it suggests very great over-employment of non-production workers. Version III results are similar to version I and are ignored since they do not give as much information, similarly for version IV. In fact, version IV seems to be estimated only to show to what extent the omission of the technical progress factor produces biased estimates of the capital–output elasticities.

The approach described here for food is carried out for fifteen two-digit manufacturing industries. The production functions they finally accept appear in table 6.16.

From these they calculate the output elasticities with respect to the input. These appear in table 6.17 together with their sum, i.e., the estimate of the returns to scale. One noticeable feature is the size of the returns to scale. Even

Table 6.16
Production functions for 15 two-digit manufacturing industries 1957.

Industry	$\log L$	$\log q \log L_p$	$\log L_p$	$\log L_n$	$\log R_{-1} \log K_{-1}$	R^2
Food products		0.315		0.397	0.309	
		(0.100)		(0.081)	(0.059)	0.85
Apparel		0.591		0.258	0.114	
		(0.125)		(0.117)	(0.068)	0.94
Lumber products	0.792				0.183	
	(0.336)				(0.073)	0.83
Paper products			0.547	0.270	0.159	
			(0.115)	(0.107)	(0.028)	0.98
Chemicals		0.348		0.570	0.156	
		(0.213)		(0.202)	(0.045)	0.89
Petroleum and		0.274		0.500	0.136	
coal products		(0.230)		(0.268)	(0.164)	0.91
Rubber products	0.851				0.140	
	(0.102)				(0.054)	0.98
Leather products	0.849				0.041	
	(0.124)				(0.041)	0.86
Stone, clay, and		0.671		0.299	0.077	
glass products		(0.175)		(0.180)	(0.037)	0.92
Primary metals	0.958				0.099	
	(0.114)				(0.045)	0.91
Fabricated metal			0.529	0.337	0.086	
products			(0.143)	(0.123)	(0.039)	0.92
Machinery		0.467		0.272	0.190	
		(0.125)		(0.143)	(0.035)	0.96
Electrical			0.410	0.244	0.171	
machinery			(0.133)	(0.078)	(0.043)	0.96
Transportation		0.415		0.284	0.187	
equipment		(0.243)		(0.174)	(0.043)	0.90
Instruments	0.668				0.254	
	(0.019)				(0.072)	0.97

Table 6.17

Output elasticities with respect to labour, capital and technology and the returns to scale.

Industry	Output elasticities of					Returns to scale
	L_p		L_n	K	R	
Food products	0.31		0.40	0.53	0.76	2.0
Instruments		0.67		0.44	0.56	1.67
Transportation equipment	0.41		0.28	0.32	0.52	1.53
Petroleum and coal products	0.27		0.50	0.23	0.51	1.51
Rubber products		0.85		0.23	0.49	1.57
Chemicals	0.34		0.57	0.27	0.48	1.66
Machines	0.47		0.27	0.33	0.45	1.52
Primary metals		0.96		0.16	0.42	1.54
Electrical machinery	0.41		0.24	0.30	0.39	1.34
Paper products	0.55		0.27	0.28	0.37	1.47
Lumber products		0.79		0.31	0.32	1.42
Apparel	0.58		0.26	0.20	0.24	1.28
Lubricated metal products	0.53		0.34	0.15	0.19	1.21
Stone, clay and glass products	0.66		0.30	0.13	0.19	1.28
Leather products		0.85		0.07	0.13	1.05

if the technology component is excluded, all but two of the industries are operating under increasing returns to scale. Another important feature is the size of the influence of technology. Perhaps their most important result is that regarding the extent to which firms are over-employing production workers. As we have seen, 1957 conditions should have led to a reduction of 23% for the food industry. The corresponding figure for other industries varies from 64% for 'transportation equipment' to 9.7% for 'rubber products'. Because of the slow speed of adjustment the authors estimate that all industries were overemploying non-production workers in the late fifties. They also analyse the extent to which U.S. industries were not operating at a Pareto optimum point, based on their estimates of the marginal physical products. On this basis they conclude that there was considerable underemployment in U.S. industries in 1957.

Criticism of Hildebrand and Liu can be made on a number of grounds some of which they accept. They admit that their estimates contain aggregation bias, but point out that in production function studies disaggregation to a much greater level, e.g. four-digit industry level, would be meaningless because production is mainly multiproduct and it is impossible to allocate capital and labour to individual products. Their use of book values for the quantity of capital in use obviously introduces error, but they point out that if the rate of utilisation is constant from state to state, or if it is not correlated with capital and labour, then the labour and capital output elasticities will not be biased on that account. Their failure to deflate, they explain, is due to the lack of good price data for capital. With regard to their adjustment for the quality of labour, in seven out of fifteen industries it produced plausible results, but this they do not find satisfactory since they are unable to explain why the quality of labour is important for some and not for other industries. Griliches (1966) questions the usefulness of the technical progress variable R and the plausibility of the low adjustment coefficients. Another criticism that has been levelled against Hildebrand and Liu's results is that, on statistical grounds alone, there is very little to choose between their different versions, and that the CD functions estimated by OLS look as good as those functions that are actually used in their monograph. These CD functions give much lower estimates of the returns to scale. Thus their important results must be judged mainly on the plausibility of their model. One further criticism is that their model is based on the behaviour of the firm yet, basically, they use industry data. This criticism can be levelled at all the studies of this section so far. Presumably with a model of firm behaviour one should use firm data. Walters (1963) provides a summary of such studies and we shall end this chapter with it.

6.14. **Firm cross-section studies**

6.14.1. Walters (1963)

All of the functions in table 6.18 are CD and are estimated by ordinary least squares mainly from firm cross-section data. The values produced indicate near constant returns to scale. The estimates for the same Indian industries are very different for 1950 and 1951. This leads one to be very suspicious that Murty and Sastry have really isolated technical relationships. Indeed, these results do nothing to dispel the scepticism arising from previous sections.

Table 6.18
Inter-firm studies of industries values of Cobb–Douglas coefficients.

	Labour α	Capital β	Raw materials γ_3	Total $\alpha+\beta+\gamma_3$	Reference
			Utilities, railways		
France					
1945 Gas	0.83	0.10		0.93	Verhulst (1948)
	0.80	0.14		0.94	
U.S.A					
1936 Railroads	0.89	0.12	0.28	1.29	Klein (1953, pp. 226–236)
			Other extractive and manufacturing industries		
U.K.					
Coal	0.79	0.29		1.08	Lomax (1950)
Coal	0.51	0.49		1.00	Combined cross-section time-series. Leser (1955)
U.S.A.					
1909 Clothing	0.98	−0.07		0.91	Bronfenbrenner
Foods	0.72	0.35		1.07	and
Metals and machinery	0.71	0.26		0.97	Douglas (1939)
			Share of wages	Total	
India					
1951 Cotton	0.92	0.12	0.63	1.04	
1952 Cotton	0.66	0.34	0.75		
1951 Jute	0.84	0.14	0.60	0.98	
1952 Jute	0.91	0.34	0.71		
1951 Sugar	0.59	0.33	0.30	0.92	
1952 Sugar	0.24	0.94	0.32		
1951 Coal	0.71	0.44	0.57	1.15	Murti and Sastry (1957)
1952 Coal	0.58	0.58	0.55		
1951 Paper	0.64	0.45	0.41	1.09	
1952 Paper	0.59	0.49	0.39		
1951 Basic	0.80	0.37	0.37	1.17	
1952 Chemicals	0.82	0.40	0.48		
1951 Electricity	0.20	0.67	0.30	0.87	
1952 Electricity	0.02	1.00	0.30		

6.15. Conclusion

Early in this chapter we explained why production functions are so tempting to econometricians. If a simple form can be estimated which reflects the technology under which a whole economy operates so many questions can be answered. Unfortunately the problems of such a task are as numerous as the possibility is tempting, technical progress and under utilisation creating special difficulties in addition to the problems of aggregation, identification and estimation which occur in all econometric fields. These problems have been handled with considerable ingenuity, but it seems that little trust can be placed in the empirical results obtained. In none of the other fields we have reviewed has so little agreement occurred. In this chapter the degree of aggregation over variables and over firms has been high in spite of considerable warnings about the restrictive conditions that are necessary. If aggregation over variables is not possible the whole concept of the production function appears very shaky and indeed a considerable battle rages in economic theory on this very question.

We can introduce this criticism of the production function concept by considering a problem we have not referred to earlier. Most of the production functions we have reviewed have assumed some degree of substitution between capital and labour. Ex ante this seems reasonable, but once the capital is built and installed, one would imagine the degree of substitution is limited. Thus perhaps we need to distinguish ex ante and ex post production functions – the latter involving fixed proportions of factors. If this is the type of technology entrepreneurs face the investment decision can be thought of as the choice of technique. In this kind of world the linear programming type of model would seem more appropriate than the neoclassical production function.

Other attacks against the production function concept have been mounted using this approach which has the definite advantage that a number of inputs can be handled conveniently. Furthermore, the general equilibrium framework of linear economics circumvents some of the aggregation over firms. Using this linear-process–general-equilibrium approach it can be shown that the production function involving composite capital does not necessarily have the same properties as one involving only one capital input. First of all consider the simplest neoclassical production function involving one output, one type of capital and labour. This smooth production function can be thought of as representing an infinite number of linear techniques. At low level of w a labour intensive technique will be chosen, and at high levels of w, a capital intensive technique will be chosen. Higher and higher levels of w will be associated with more and more capital intensive techniques. There will never be a technique which is associated with both a high and a low level of w, unless it occurs at all levels of w between these two levels. Using the linear–general-equilibrium approach it is possible to show that the choice of technique does not in general follow such a simple pattern if more than one type of capital is used. A simple example has been devised by Morishima. There are two products M_1, M_2 and the production process for M_2 is

$$0.2 M_1 + 1 L \rightarrow 1 M_2$$

but production of M_1 can be done in two ways

$$(1) \qquad 0.5 M_1 + 0.1 M_2 + 0.5 L \rightarrow 1 M_1$$

$$(2) \qquad 1 M_2 + 0.2 L \rightarrow 1 M_1 \, .$$

At low levels of w, method (2) is preferred. At middle values of w, method (1) is preferred, but at very high levels of w, method (2) comes back into its own. This phenomenon is that of 'double switching' and it is glossed over in the production-function approach because the outputs and inputs are aggregated. Throughout this chapter implicitly outputs and capital inputs have been aggregated via prices, either current or fixed base period prices. The 'double switching' problem in a production function setting can be viewed from the point of view of what happens to prices and hence the aggregates. When w changes, since capital inputs are themselves produced by the use of labour, equilibrium capital input prices will change. Now consider a production function with two capital inputs which we would presumably aggregate into one capital variable. If prices of capital are used for this aggregation and if these prices are sensitive to changes in the wage rate, then the measure of capital will vary, even though there may have been no physical change in the capital inputs. The marginal product of composite capital will be different depending on whether the change stems from physical changes or price changes. Certainly we are not free to restrict the production function according to (6.6)–(6.8), and the form of a single valued production function becomes either very complex or even non-existent.

A tempting solution is to use base period constant prices in the aggregation process. In growth- and distribution-theory this only pushes the problem forward one step, inasmuch as how much current output (and its mix) goes to capital expansion is determined by current prices. We have concentrated on the aggregation of capital, but a similar problem exists with regard to the aggregation of output. In fact, Green (1964, p. 83) has shown that if the outputs aggregation function is homogeneous of degree one, then with a homogeneous production function and competitive conditions, a necessary condition for the existence of an aggregate production function is that relative prices must be constant.

Obviously the 'double switching' attack on the production function depends on the extent to which capital input prices change. Any attempt to use production functions for long-run purposes seems bound to fail. Thus, the answers to the grandiose questions of economic growth and income distribution with which we began this chapter do not seem to lie in econometric production functions. In short-run situations, where it can be assumed that labour prices are independent, the production function concept may still be of use as a theoretical short cut to the decisions of entrepreneurs. There will still be aggregation problems but these will be less important in certain cases; for instance, if all the prices of outputs of the firm move together as do the prices of capital inputs. Unfortunately, the empirical results for industry production functions do not suggest that we have isolated anything even approximating the technical relations that the conceptual production function envisages.

CHAPTER 7

SUMMARY AND CONCLUSIONS

The aim of this book has been to survey the literature of applied econometrics. Obviously, this task was too great and we have had to be content with certain areas where econometric studies abound. The basic philosophy of the book has been to use economic theory as a frame work into which to file the individual studies and to show their relationship to the theory. Whilst performing this survey function an attempt has been made to illustrate some of the "tricks of the trade". In this final chapter we summarise the points made in earlier chapters and make some rather general observations stemming from the surveys.

Before briefly summarising the findings from the earlier chapters, let us consider those areas of applied econometrics which have been omitted. Econometric methods can be applied to most if not all fields of applied economics and so it does not really make sense to talk of omitted areas; however, some areas do lend themselves to econometric methods more than others and there are certain fields where econometric studies abound. The first chapter illustrates the use of econometric models for macro policy-making and forecasting. This is a very important and large area of applied econometrics. Although we have dealt with a few of the major components of such models, except for that illustrative chapter we have not considered any actual macro econometric models. The reason is that anything like a comprehensive survey of such models would double or treble the length of the book. Other areas that some would have liked to see included are inflation (wage-price models) and money. The controversies in the area of money and inflation are such that it would be difficult to deal effectively with these topics without necessarily becoming involved with macro econometric models. Thus, macro models, inflation and money, while important areas of applied econometrics, are best left to another book. Turning to the areas we did cover, a number of points can be made.

The consumption function has been an important concept of Keynesian economics and it is not surprising that a great deal of effort has been expended in this area. The early studies illustrate the dangers of accepting models on the basis of good statistical properties. The consumption function chapter also shows how a priori information is essentially micro in nature and hence how important aggregation problems can be. Observationally, the three modern hypotheses, i.e., the permanent income, the life cycle and the wealth hypotheses, are very similar which leads to difficulties in choosing between them given the quality of data that are available. One positive conclusion from this chapter is that some permanent concept is necessary to explain both the time-series and cross-section data that are available.

Chapter 3 concentrates on the allocation decision of consumers which is important from a number of policy angles. In this chapter there is a clear division between models which are based on static consumer theory and those which allow explicit dynamic elements. Some of the former are the most sophisticated of all applied econometric studies showing how economic theory can be incorporated to improve estimation. However, the main point arising from this chapter is that prices are significant only when one uses the constraints of static theory. In dynamic formulations the influence of prices tends to be very small. A desirable development in this field would be the formulation of constraints similar to those stemming from classical static theory for dynamic functions. Chapter 3 also illustrates some uses of cross-section data and the care that is necessary in comparing results derived from such data with those derived from time series data. Other intriguing topics are suggested in this chapter, including the incorporation of uncertainty via stochastic utility functions from which is derived the form of the variance–covariance matrix of the disturbance term of the demand functions.

Chapter 4 (investment) illustrates alternative ways of handling uncertainty although the most apparently successful model of investment behaviour is derived on the basis of certainty. Uncertainty in investment studies has been handled by introducing certain institutional variables, such as the stock market. Indeed, much of the disagreement in that field centres on the role of the finance variables. On the technical side, chapter 4 illustrates the use of distributed lags in applied econometric studies. Jorgenson's study not only presents a sophisticated class of distributed lags but also ingeniously incorporates anticipations data into the estimation method. From these distributed lag models it is possible to derive time response paths which are important from the point of view of policy. Unfortunately, these estimates are subject to wide confidence intervals.

Inventory investment is quite different from fixed investment and chapter 5 brings out the differences quite clearly. In this field uncertainty is very important and chapter 5 illustrates other ways by which econometricians try to cope with expectations. Here the relative merits of explicit expectation generating functions, as opposed to implied expectations, are considered. Inventories present a number of other problems which are not present in other fields and which arise from the essentially short run nature of their movements and the existence of 'passive' changes. This short run feature forced us to consider the influence of seasonality and how it is handled in econometric studies. No one way of handling seasonality can be adjudged to be best; each model should be dealt with on its own scope and purpose. Another technical topic illustrated at length in this chapter was that of aggregation, or more specifically, Theil's approach to linear aggregation. The survey of inventory studies also indicated the heterogeneous nature of the concept and how important it is to distinguish production to order and to stock.

Chapter 6 (production functions) turned out to be the most disappointing from the point of view of empirical results because so little agreement exists among studies based on similar data. However, important problems were illustrated including a number of aggregation, identification and estimation problems. In this chapter we met simultaneous models which illustrate a number of problems that econometric theory has high-lighted. Perhaps the most important lesson that arose from chapter 6 was the dangers involved in complete commitment to a seductive theory.

In all the surveys we have been confronted with many models, often of the same phenomenon. This raises the question of how different researchers choose their models. There are two views on how to choose a model. In fact, few people would accept either in its extreme form, but it will help the exposition if we state the two approaches starkly. Method 1 starts with a maintained hypothesis which embodies all the prior knowledge that we have. This hypothesis will be maintained regardless of the data. A typical form is that y and X are related in the following way

$$y_t = \mathbf{X}_t\boldsymbol{\beta} + u_t$$

where u_t is normally distributed with zero mean and $\mathbf{X}_t$ is a vector of explanatory variables. The data are then used to estimate (or test hypotheses about) $\boldsymbol{\beta}$ and the parameters of the distribution of u_t. All these inferences and tests are based on the assumption that the maintained hypothesis is true. This approach has been criticised on grounds that our state of knowledge in economics is such that it is not possible to put forward such unassailable maintained hypotheses. The alternative approach is called the experimental method. This implies a trial and error approach in which if the maintained hypothesis results in a poor fit, insignificant parameters or implausible values, it is discarded and another hypothesis tried. If this is found to be unsatisfactory it, too, is discarded. Thus, eventually, hopefully, a satisfactory hypothesis will be found.

In order to assess these two methods it will be useful to review the aims of applied econometrics. In practical terms, in any one particular study, we are faced with finding a structure, i.e., a model with its parameters numerically specified, which is useful for description, prediction and policy purposes. Many believe that the closer to the true causal mechanism a structure is, the more useful, i.e., better, it is. However, the true causal mechanism is likely to be very complicated and the more complex a model is the less useful it is likely to be. In order to concentrate on the issues relevant to the two applied econometric methods described in the previous paragraph let us limit the class of models we are considering to the same level of simplicity (for instance, involving equal number of estimated parameters). Will the a priori or the experimental method produce the most useful model or that closest to the truth? On the basis of usefulness probably the a priori method is better since, presumably, it will have been set up with the use in mind. On the surface, though, the experimental approach should produce a truer model since it uses the data as a way of selecting the model. However, it has been questioned whether it is a valid statistical procedure to use the data to select the model.

In order to judge this issue we need to have a stochastic model which can be considered to be true. Econometric theory is based on such a model which is justified in three ways (1) either all causal relations are inherently stochastic or (2) the combined effect of errors in variables can be expected to follow a probability distribution or (3) causal relations are basically deterministic, but the stochastic term represents the combined effect of a large number of variables which cannot be included explicitly. Which of these one accepts depends very much on one's philosophical bent. If one accepts (3) it is useful to distinguish between the absolute truth, i.e., the whole deterministic truth, and the stochastic truth, i.e., the model econometric theory uses. This latter type of truth can be thought of as that model which would be agreed on by all (provided each could set some or all of the parameters equal to zero). With this true model at hand we can now see whether it is possible to choose between models on the basis of the data. If all the models can be considered to be special cases of the true model, then it is possible to develop formal tests of validity. Malinvaud (1966) gives the following example. Suppose we have to choose a consumption function specification from the following

$$C_t = a_0 Y_t + a_1 Y_{t-1} + b + \epsilon_t \qquad (7.1)$$

$$C_t = a_0 Y_t + cC_{t-1} + b + \epsilon_t . \tag{7.2}$$

In this case the following true model can be concocted

$$C_t = a_0 Y_t + a_1 Y_{t-1} + cC_{t-1} + b + \epsilon_t \tag{7.3}$$

and vigorous tests based on the data be designed.

Tests on the coefficients of (7.3.) will provide the test of specification. Notice that for a coefficient such as a_0 which appears in all specifications the significance tests will be different depending upon whether (7.3) or one of the other models is used. This suggests that significance tests for a trial and error approach are not just a matter of using the standard tests based on the current hypothesis. Indeed it has been shown that the levels rise in the case of one trial and error procedure which can be handled formally. A simple example can be constructed by adding the following possible consumption function specification to the three above.

$$C_t = a_0 Y_t + b + e_t \tag{7.4}$$

In the case where one has to choose between (7.1) and (7.4) Malinvaud (1966, p. 220) suggests the following procedure. Test whether $c = 0$ in (7.3) (at level of significance α_1, say) and then test whether $a = 0$ in (7.1) (at level of significance α_2, say). If these tests are positive, accept (7.4). However, he shows that the level of significance for the whole procedure is not α_1 nor α_2 but approximately $\alpha_1 + \alpha_2$. This illustrates how a trial and error method in econometrics can affect the interpretation of the standard errors calculated from the conventional formulae. This particular case has the special feature of all the competing specifications being special cases of the true hypothesis. Normally the situation is not as simple as this. For instance, the differences may centre on the form of the relationship. The statistical properties of the experimental method in general are not known, but it would seem that significance statements must be affected and that the more experimentation there is the less meaningful the quoted standard errors.

It seems the difference between the two methods then can be stated in this way. The a priori approach sets forth a maintained hypothesis rather like a religious belief. The statistical inferences stemming from it are valid provided one is of the same faith. The experimental approach appeals to non-believers, but is not based on rigorous statistical method. Faced with these two stark alternatives econometricians choose a position somewhere in the middle and all experiment to some extent. It is incorrect though to hide the degree of experimentation and act as if the final specification was the first to be considered. Thus, in fact, there are not two methods but one, though it will help to bring out the elements of the method if we continue with our comparison of the "two methods".

One of the criteria of the experimental approach is "plausibility". Knowledge of plausible values can be construed as a priori information and so should be incorporated into the maintained hypothesis. If one is prepared to reject certain models or structures regardless of what results stem from the data then it makes sense to do this before estimation or testing takes place. Thus the only difference between the two methods on this account is whether the a priori information is handled formally or not. In the earlier chapters we have illustrated a number of ways this can be done within the framework of classical statistics. With the development of Bayesian methods in econometrics it is hoped that more a priori information will be capable of formal treatment; in the meantime there is still a great deal of a priori information that can only be used via the "plausibility" criterion.

Another difference in the two methods stems from the weight given to the two types of information. The experimental approach obviously asks more from the data than the a priori approach. If it is felt that the available data are of very poor quality, little faith can be put in the experimental method. It is sobering to remember that economic data usually involves large measurement error, small number of observations, low variability and considerable multicollinearity. When standard econometric techniques are used on this type of data the results must be suspect. Thus, when conflict arises between the results based on statistical information, one has to decide which information deserves most faith.

To sum up this discussion, it appears that neither of the two extremes of applied econometrics can be upheld. Although on statistical grounds we would prefer to be able to set up a maintained hypothesis on the basis of which we would choose the specification before going on to estimate it, this is in general not possible and so some experimentation is necessary. The specifications that are considered should incorporate formally any a priori information available, but given the present state of econometric methods, this may also be impossible. An informal method of experimentation and judging the 'plausibility' may be the only method of choosing both the model and structure, although it must be borne in mind that the significance statements are affected.

At the beginning of this discussion we eliminated the criterion of simplicity in order to concentrate on the other issues. One of the standard criteria of applied econometrics is the goodness of fit usually measured by R^2. The square of the multiple correlation coefficient represents the proportion of the variance of the dependent variable explained by the systematic part of the model. If R^2 is to be used as a criterion perhaps we should pause to consider how much of the statistical data we should expect to explain. Indeed, in wider context, how much of all the information and each particular type, statistical and a priori, should we expect to explain? Obviously the closer we are to the absolute truth the more information of each type will be satisfied. However, we can hardly expect to approach the absolute truth. If we turn our attention to the stochastic truth, then there is no reason to believe that the variance of the disturbance term should be necessarily small and hence choosing a model in which the sample residual variance is small, is not necessarily to be encouraged. A model or structure which satisfies all the available information, both statistical and a priori, is likely to be complex. For simple models we should not expect as good fits to the data and to the a priori information as we expect for more complex models. Conventionally the first aspect is accounted for by adjusting the multiple correlation coefficient according to the number of parameters estimated. There is no corresponding adjustment for the a priori information. When models involve different dependent variables, e.g., log y instead of y, then even the comparison of R^2 is not straight forward (see Goldberger 1964, p. 217). The comparison of models of differing degrees of complexity, involving different degrees of information, forces us back to the usefulness criterion. Very few empirical studies consider this point; most empirical studies seem to imply that models should satisfy all information regardless.

Although we have concluded that some experimentation is necessary, the importance of a prior specification, both of the systematic and stochastic parts, should still be emphasised. We end this chapter with a few illustrations taken from the earlier chapters. The chapter on inventories produced an example, where two models (see sections 5.8.2 and 5.8.3) have the same estimating equation. In fact, the interpretations of the empirical results are in direct conflict. To resolve the conflict one has to make a decision on the plausibility of the two models rather than on any empirical evidence. A similar case arose in the consumption function chapter where the life cycle and permanent income are so similar and the data is so poor that it is impossible to decide between the two on the basis of the data. We also reported two studies (see section 4.6.9 and 2.6.9) which illustrate the different conclusions that can be drawn when the stochastic specifications are different. On the whole econometricians have to rely upon the data to indicate the appropriate stochastic specification believing that economic theory, since it is based on exact models, has nothing to offer with regard to a priori knowledge on the stochastic term. Barten's interesting work on stochastic utility functions (see section 3.3.2d) suggests that this is too pessimistic. Zellner,

Kmenta and Drèze (see section 6.4.4) also show the important implications for estimation, that the interpretation of the disturbance term in a production function model has.

The theme of this book has been to stress the a priori information in applied econometrics. It is in this aspect that the author feels future development will come. Goldberger (1964, p. 1) refers to econometrics as composed of mathematical economics, econometric theory and empirical econometrics. We have already seen some development of stochastic economic theory in the first of these fields, and some development of Bayesian methods, in the second. Hopefully, more progress will be made in these fields and the results become widely available to applied econometricians.

REFERENCES

Abramovitz, M., 1950. Inventories and business cycles. Studies in Business Cycles, vol. 4 (National Bureau of Economic Research, New York).

Allen, R.G.D., 1937. Mathematical Analysis for Economists (MacMillan & Co. Ltd., London).

Almon, S., 1965. Econometricia, vol. 33, pp. 178–196.

Anderson, W.H. Locke, 1967. Business fixed investment: a marriage of fact and fancy. In: Ferber (1967) pp. 413–425.

Ando, A., see Modigliani and Ando (1960).

Ando, A., E.C. Brown, J. Kareken and R. Solow, 1963. Lags in fiscal and monetary policy. In: Commission on Money and Credit, Stabilization Policies (Prentice-Hall Inc., Englewood Cliffs, New Jersey).

Ando, A. and F. Modigliani, 1963. American Economic Review, vol. 53, pp. 55–84.

Andrews, W.J., see Marschak and Andrews (1944).

Arrow, K.J., H.B. Chenery, B.S. Minhas and R.M. Solow, 1961. Review of Economics and Statistics, vol. 43, pp. 225–250.

Arrow, K.J., see Murata and Arrow (1965).

Ball, R.J. and P.S. Drake, 1963. The Manchester School, vol. 31, pp. 87–101.

Ball, R.J. and P.S. Drake, 1964. International Economic Review, vol. 5, pp. 63–81.

Barten, A.P., 1964. Econometrica, vol. 32, pp. 1–38.

Barten, A.P., 1968. Econometrica, vol. 36, pp. 213–251.

Baumol, W., 1959. Economic Dynamics, 2nd edition (MacMillan, New York).

Beckmann, M.J., see Sato and Beckmann (1968).

Belsley, D.A., 1969. Industry Production Behaviour: The Order Stock Distinction (North-Holland, Amsterdam).

Bischoff, C.W., 1969. Review of Economics and Statistics, vol. 51, pp. 354–368.

Black, J., 1969. Economica, vol. 36, pp. 310–313.

Branson, W.H. and A.K. Klevorick, 1969. American Economic Review, vol. 59, pp. 832–849.

Bronfenbrenner, M. and P.H. Douglas, 1939. Journal of Political Economy, vol. 47, pp. 761–785.

Brown, E.C., see Ando et al. (1963).

Brown, M. and J.S. de Cani, 1963a. International Economic Review, vol. 4, pp. 289–309.

Brown, M. and J.S. de Cani, 1963b. Review of Economics and Statistics, vol. 45, pp. 386–394.

Brown, M., 1966. On the Theory and Measurement of Technological Change (Cambridge University Press, Cambridge).

Brown, M., ed., 1967. The Theory and Empirical Analysis of Production. Studies in

Income and Wealth, vol. 31. Conference on Research in Income and Wealth (National Bureau of Economic Research, New York).
Brumberg, R.E., see Modigliani and Brumberg (1954).
Bruno, M., 1962, A Note on the Implications of an Empirical Relationship between Output per Unit of Labour, the Wage Rage, and the Capital-Labour ratio. Mimeograph. Stanford University, July.
Carter, H.O., see Halter et al. (1957).
Chau, L.C., see Zellner et al. (1965).
Chenery, H.B., see Arrow et al. (1961).
Childs, G., 1967. Unfilled Orders and Inventories: A Structural Analysis (North-Holland, Amsterdam).
Chow, G.C., 1960. Econometrica, vol. 28, pp. 591–605.
Chow, G.C., 1968. Quarterly Journal of Economics, vol. 82, pp. 403–418.
Clemhout, S., 1968. Review of Economic Studies, vol. 35, pp. 91–104.
Cohen, K.J., see Modigliani and Cohen (1958).
Courchene, T.J., 1967. Canadian Journal of Economics, vol. 33, pp. 325–357.
Cramer, J.S., 1969. Empirical Econometrics (North-Holland, Amsterdam).
Davis, T.E., 1952. Review of Economics and Statistics, vol. 34, pp. 270–277.
De Cani, J.S., see Brown and de Cani (1963a,b).
De Leeuw, F., 1962. Econometrica, vol. 30, pp. 407–423.
Dhrymes, P.J., 1965. Review of Economics and Statistics, vol. 47, pp. 357–366.
Dhrymes, P.J. and M. Kurz, 1967. Investment, dividend and external finance behaviour of firms. In: Ferber (1967) pp. 427–467.
Diamond, P., 1965. Review of Economic Studies, vol. 32, pp. 161–168.
Douglas, P.H., 1948. American Economic Review, vol. 38, pp. 1–41.
Douglas, P.H., see Bronfenbrenner and Douglas (1939).
Drake, P.S., see Ball and Drake (1963, 1964).
Drèze, J., see Zellner et al. (1966).
Duesenberry, J.S., 1949. Income, Savings, and the Theory of Consumer Behaviour (Harvard University Press, Cambridge, Massachusetts).
Duesenberry, J.S., 1958. Business Cycles and Economic Growth (McGraw-Hill, New York).
Duesenberry, J.S., O. Eckstein and G. Fromm, 1960, Econometrica 28, 749–809.
Duesenberry, J.S., G. Fromm, L.R. Klein and E. Kuh, 1965. The Brookings Quarterly Econometric Model of the United States (Rand McNally & Co., Chicago, North-Holland, Amsterdam).
Eckstein, O., see Duesenberry et al. (1960).
Eisner, R., 1958, American Economic Review, vol. 48, pp. 972–990.
Eisner, R., 1964. Capital expenditures, profits and the acceleration principle. In: Conference on Research in Income and Wealth. Models of Income Determination. Studies in Income and Wealth, vol. 28, pp. 137–176. (National Bureau of Economic Research, New York).
Eisner, R., 1965. Realization of investment anticipations. In: Duesenberry et al. (1965) pp. 95–128.
Eisner, R., 1967. American Economic Review, vol. 57, pp. 363–390.
Eisner, R. and R. Strotz, 1963. Determinants of business investment. In: Commission on Money and Credit. Impacts of Monetary Policy (Prentice Hall Inc., Englewood Cliffs, New Jersey) pp. 59–233.

Eisner, R. and M.I. Nadiri, 1968. Review of Economics and Statistics, vol. 50, pp. 369–382.

Evans, M.K., 1967a. Journal of Political Economy, vol. 75, pp. 335–351.

Evans, M.K., 1967b. Review of Economics and Statistics, vol. 49, pp. 151–164.

Ferber, R., 1953a. A Study of Aggregate Consumption Functions, Technical Paper No. 8. (National Bureau of Economic Research, New York).

Ferber, R., 1953b. University of Illinois Bulletin, vol. 50, pp. 1–140.

Ferber, R., ed., 1967. Determinants of Investment Behaviour. A Conference of the Universities – National Bureau Committee for Economic Research (National Bureau of Economic Research, New York).

Ferguson, C.E., 1965. American Economic Review, Papers and Proceedings, vol. 55, pp. 296–305.

Fisher, F.M., 1962. A Priori Information and Time Series Analysis: Essays in Economic Theory and Measurement. (North-Holland, Amsterdam).

Fisher, F.M., 1969. Econometrica, vol. 37, pp. 553–577.

Fletcher, L.B., see Lu and Fletcher (1968).

Friedman, M., 1957. A Theory of the Consumption Function (Princeton University Press, Princeton, New Jersey).

Friedman, M., 1958. Journal of Political Economy, vol. 66, pp. 545–549.

Friend, I. and R. Jones, 1960. A Study of Consumer Expenditures, Incomes, and Savings: Proceedings of the Conference on Consumption and Savings (University of Pennsylvania, Philadelphia).

Frisch, R., 1932. New methods of measuring marginal utility. Beiträge Ökonomischen Theorie (J.C.B Mohr, Tübingen).

Fromm, G., see Duesenberry et al. (1960, 1965).

Gamaletsos, T., see Goldberger and Gamaletsos (1967).

Geisel, M.S., see Zellner and Geisel (1968).

Godley, W.A.H. and J.R. Shepherd, 1965. National Institute Economic Review, no. 33, pp. 35–42.

Goldberger, A.S., 1959. Impact Multipliers and Dynamic Properties of the Klein–Goldberger Model (North-Holland, Amsterdam).

Goldberger, A.S., 1964. Econometric Theory (John Wiley & Sons, New York).

Goldberger, A.S., 1967. Functional Form and Utility: A Review of the Consumer Demand Theory. Social Systems Research Institute, University of Wisconsin: Systems Formulation, Methodology and Policy Workshop Paper 6703.

Goldberger, A.S., see Theil and Goldberger (1960).

Goldberger, A.S., and T. Gamaletsos, 1967. A cross country comparison of consumer expenditure patterns. Social Systems Research Institute (University of Wisconsin, Systems Formulation, Methodology and Policy Workshop Paper 6706) in: European Economic Review, 1970, 357–400.

Goldsmith, R.W., 1955. A Study of Saving in the United States (Princeton University Press, Princeton, New Jersey).

Green, H.A.J., 1964. Aggregation in Economic Analysis, An Introductory Survey (Princeton University Press, Princeton, New Jersey).

Griliches, Z., 1957. Journal of Farm Economics, vol. 39, pp. 8–20.

Griliches, Z., 1966. Journal of Political Economy, vol. 74, pp. 100–101.

Griliches, Z., 1967a. Econometrica, vol. 35, pp. 16–49.

Griliches, Z., 1967b. Production functions in manufacturing: some preliminary results. In: Brown (1967) pp. 275–322.

Griliches, Z., 1968. Review of Economics and Statistics, vol. 50, pp. 215–234.

Griliches, Z. and D.W. Jorgenson, 1966. American Economic Review, Papers and Proceedings, vol. 56, pp. 50–68.

Griliches, Z. and N. Wallace, 1965. International Economic Review, vol. 6, pp. 311–329.

Griliches, Z., G.S. Maddala, R. Lucas and N. Wallace, 1962. Econometrica, vol. 30, pp. 491–500.

Grunfeld, Y., 1960. The determinants of corporate investment. In: A.C. Harberger, ed., The Demand for Durable Goods (University of Chicago, Chicago) pp. 211–266.

Grunfeld, Y., 1961. Econometrica, vol. 29, pp. 397–404.

Hall, R.E. and D.W. Jorgenson, 1967. American Economic Review, vol. 57, pp. 391–414.

Halter, A.N., H.O. Carter and J.G. Hocking, 1957. Journal of Farm Economics, vol. 39, pp. 966–974.

Huang, D.S., see Zellner et al. (1965).

Hickman, B.G., 1965. Investment Demand and U.S. Economic Growth (The Brookings Institution, Washington).

Hickman, B.G., 1966. Investment demand in the sixties, in: The Economic Outlook for 1966, Thirteenth Annual Conference on the Economic Outlook, November 18–19, 1965 (University of Michigan, reprinted by The Brooking Institution).

Hicks, J.R., 1946. Value and Capital, 2nd ed. (Oxford University Press, Oxford).

Hildebrand, H. and T.C. Liu, 1965. Manufacturing Production Functions in the United States, 1957. An Inter-industry and Inter-state Comparison of Productivity. (The New York State School of Industrial and Labour Relations, Cornell University, Ithaca, New York).

Hirsch, A. and M. Lovell, 1967. The Structure of Expectations. Mimeograph. Graduate School of Industrial Administration, Carnegie Institute of Technology, July 1st. See forthcoming: Sales Anticipation Inventory Behaviour (Wiley & Sons, New York).

Hoffman, R.F., see Sato and Hoffman (1968).

Houthakker, H.S., 1955–6. Review of Economic Studies, vol. 23, pp. 27–31.

Houthakker, H.S., 1957. Econometrica, vol. 25, pp. 532–551.

Houthakker, H.S., 1960. Econometrica, vol. 28, pp. 244–257.

Houthakker, H.S., 1965. Econometrica, vol. 33, pp. 277–288.

Houthakker, H.S., see Prais and Houthakker (1955).

Houthakker, H.S. and L.D. Taylor, 1966. Consumer Demand in the United States 1929–70. Analyses and Projections (Harvard University Press, Cambridge, Massachusetts).

Johnston, J., 1961. Quarterly Journal of Economics, vol. 75, pp. 234–261.

Jones, R., see Friend, I. and R. Jones (1960).

Jorgenson, D.W., 1965. Anticipations and investment behaviour. In: Duesenberry et al. (1965) pp. 35–92.

Jorgenson, D.W., 1966. Econometrica, vol. 34, pp. 135–149.

Jorgenson, D.W., see Hall and Jorgenson (1967).

Jorgenson, D.W. and C.D. Siebert, 1968. American Economic Review, vol. 58, pp. 681–712.

Jorgenson, D.W. and J.A. Stephenson, 1967. Econometrica, vol. 35, pp. 169–220.

Jorgenson, D.W., 1969. Review of Economics and Statistics, vol. 51, pp. 346–353.

Kadane, J.B., see Maddala and Kadane (1967).

Kareken, J., see Ando et al. (1963).

Kendrick, J.W., 1961. Productivity Trends in the United States (Princeton University Press, Princeton, New Jersey).

Kendrick, J. W., 1964. Comment on Solow. In: Conference on Research in Income and Wealth, The Behaviour of Income Shares. National Bureau of Economic Research (Princeton University Press, Princeton, New Jersey).

Klein, L.R., 1946. Econometrica, vol. 14, pp. 93–108.

Klein, L.R., 1950. Economic Fluctuations in the United States, 1921–1941. Cowles Commission Monograph 11 (John Wiley and Sons, New York).

Klein, L.R., 1953. A Textbook of Econometrics (Row Peterson, Evanston).

Klein, L.R., 1960, The efficiency of estimation in econometric models. In: R.W. Pfonts, ed., Essays in Economics and Econometrics. A Volume in Honour of Harold Hotelling. (University of North Carolina, Chapel Hill) pp. 216–232.

Klein, L.R., see Duesenberry et al. (1965).

Klevorick, A.K., see Branson and Klevorick (1969).

Kmenta, J., 1964. Econometrica, vol. 32, pp. 183–188.

Kmenta, J., 1964. Econometrica, vol. 32, pp. 183–188.

Kmenta, J., 1967. International Economic Review, vol. 8, pp. 180–189.

Kmenta, J., see Zellner et al. (1966).

Koyck, L.M., 1954. Distributed Lags and Investment Analysis (North-Holland, Amsterdam).

Kuh, E., 1963, Capital Stock Growth: A Micro Econometric Approach (North-Holland, Amsterdam).

Kuh, E., see Duesenberry et al. (1965).

Kuh, E., see Meyer and Kuh (1957).

Kurz, M., see Dhrymes and Kurz (1967).

Kuznets, S., 1942. Uses of National Income in Peace and War, Occasional Paper no. 6 (National Bureau of Economic Research, New York).

Leser, C.E.V., 1955. Econometrica, vol. 23, pp. 442–446.

Lintner, J., 1967. Corporation Finance: Risk and Investment. In: Feber (1967).

Liu, T.C., 1963. Econometrica, vol. 31, pp. 301–346.

Liu, T.C., see Hildebrand and Liu (1965).

Lomax, K.S., 1949. The Manchester School, vol. 17, pp. 146–162.

Lomax, K.S., 1950. Journal of the Royal Statistical Society, vol. 113, pp. 346–351.

Lomax, K.S., 1953. Bulletin of the Oxford Institute of Statistics, vol. 15, pp. 147–150.

Lovell, M.C. , 1961. Econometrica, vol. 29, pp. 293–314.

Lovell, M.C., 1964. Determinants of inventory behaviour. In: Models of Income Behaviour. Conference on Research in Income and Wealth. Studies in Income and Wealth, vol. 28. National Bureau of Economic Research (Princeton University Press, Princeton, New Jersey) pp. 177–231.

Lovell, M.C., 1967. Sales anticipations, planned inventory investment and realizations. In: Ferber (1967) pp. 537–579.

Lovell, M.C., see Hirsch and Lovell (1967).

Lu, Y.C. and L.B. Fletcher, 1968. Review of Economics and Statistics, vol. 50, pp. 449–452.

Lucas, R.E., 1963. Substitution Between Labour and Capital in U.S. Manufacturing 1929–58, unpublished Ph.D. thesis, University of Chicago.

Lucas, R.E., 1967. International Economic Review, vol. 8, pp. 78–85.

Lucas, R.E., see Griliches et al. (1962).

Mack, R.P., 1948. Reviews of Economics and Statistics, vol. 30, pp. 239–258.

Mack, R.P., 1956. Consumption and Business Fluctuations. A Case Study of the Shoe Leather Hide Sequence. Studies in Business Cycles, vol. 7 (National Bureau of Economic Research, New York).

Maddala, G.S., 1965. Differential Industry Effects on Differential Factor Effects of Technological Change. Memo 36. (Research Centre in Economic Growth, Stanford University, March).

Maddala, G.S. and J.B. Kadane, 1967. Econometrica, vol. 35, pp. 419–423.

Maddala, G.S., see Griliches et al. (1962).

Malinvaud, E., 1966. Statistical Methods of Econometrics (North-Holland, Amsterdam).

Marschak, J., 1953. Economic measurements for policy and prediction. In: W.C. Hood and T.C. Koopmans, eds., Studies in Econometric Method, Cowles Commission Monograph 14 (John Wiley & Sons, New York) pp. 1–26.

Marchak, J. and W.H. Andrews, 1944. Econometrica, vol. 12, pp. 143–205.

McKinnon, R.I., 1962. Econometrica, vol. 30, pp. 501–521.

McKinnon, R.I., 1963a. The CES, Production Function Applied to Two Digit Manufacturing and Three Mining Industries for the United States, unpublished.

McKinnon, R.I., 1963b. Factor Price Changes and Production Function Estimation. Mimeograph Stanford University.

Meyer, J.R. and R.R. Glauber, 1964. Investment Decisions, Economic Forecasting and Public Policy (Harvard University Press, Boston).

Meyer, J.R. and E. Kuh, 1957. Review of Economics and Statistics, vol. 39, pp. 380–393.

Mills, E., 1962. Price Output and Inventory Policy (John Wiley & Sons, New York).

Minasian, J.R., 1961. Journal of Political Economy, vol. 69, pp. 261–270.

Minhas, B.S., see Arrow et al. (1961).

Modigliani, F., 1949. Fluctuations in the Saving–Income Ratio: A Problem in Economic Forecasting. In: Conference on Research in Income and Wealth. Studies in Income and Wealth, vol. 11 (National Bureau of Economic Research, New York) pp. 369–441.

Modigliani, F. and A. Ando, 1960. The permanent income and the life cycle, hypothesis of saving behaviour: comparison and tests. In: Friend and Jones (1960) vol. 11, pp. 49–174.

Modigliani, F., see Ando and Modigliani (1963).

Modigliani, F. and R.E. Brumberg, 1954. Utility analysis and the consumption function. In: K.K. Kurihara, ed., Post-Keynesian Economics (Rutgers University Press, New Brunswick. New Jersey) pp. 277–319.

Modigliani, F. and K.J. Cohen, 1958. The significance and uses of ex ante data. In: M.J. Bowman, ed., Expectation Uncertainty and Business Behaviour (Social Science Research Council, New York) pp. 151–164.

Modigliani, F. and M. Miller, 1963. American Economic Review, vol. 53, pp. 437–443.

Modigliani, F. and M. Miller, 1967. Estimates of the cost of capital relevant for investment decisions under uncertainty. In: Ferber (1967) pp. 179–213.

Modigliani, F. and O.H. Sauerlender, 1955. Economic expectations and plans of firms in relation to short term forecasting. In: Short Term Forecasting. Conference on Research in Income and Wealth Studies in Income and Wealth, vol. 17. National

Bureau of Economic Research (Princeton University Press, Princeton, New Jersey) pp. 261–359.
Mundlak, Y., 1966, Review of Economics and Statistics, vol. 48, pp. 51–59.
Murata, Y. and K.J. Arrow, 1965. Unpublished results of estimation of elasticities of substitution for two digit industries from inter-country data for two periods. Reported in Nerlove (1967).
Murti, V.N. and V.K. Sastry, 1957. Econometrica, vol. 25, pp. 205–221.
Nelson, R.R., 1965. Review of Economics and Statistics, vol. 47, pp. 326–328.
Nagar, A.L., see Theil and Nagar (1961).
Nerlove, M., 1965. Estimation and Identification of Cobb-Douglas Production Functions (Rand McNally and Co., Chicago, North-Holland, Amsterdam).
Nerlove, M., 1967. Recent empirical studies of the CES and related production functions. In: Brown (1967) pp. 55–122.
Orr, L.D., 1967. International Economic Review, vol. 8, pp. 368–373.
Pashigian, P.B., 1965. International Economic Review, vol. 6, pp. 65–91.
Powell, A., 1966. Econometrica, vol. 34, pp. 661–675.
Prais, S.J. and H.S. Houthakker, 1955. The Analysis of Family Budgets (Cambridge University Press, Cambridge).
Resek, R.W., 1966. Review of Economics and Statistics, vol. 48, pp. 322–333.
Rowe, D.A., see Stone and Rowe (1957, 1962).
Sandee, J., ed., 1964. Europe's Future Consumption (North-Holland, Amsterdam).
Sastry, V.K., see Murti and Sastry (1957).
Sato, R. and M.J. Beckmann, 1968. Review of Economic Studies, vol. 35, pp. 57–66.
Sato, R. and R.F. Hoffman, 1968. Review of Economics and Statistics, vol. 50, pp. 453–460.
Sato, T., see Tsujimura and Sato (1964).
Sauerlender, O.H., see Modigliani and Sauerlender (1955).
Shepherd, J.R., see Godley and Shepherd (1965).
Siebert, C.D., see Jorgenson and Siebert (1968).
Simon, H., 1956. Econometrica, vol. 24, pp. 74–81.
Smith, V.E., 1945. Econometrica, vol. 13, pp. 260–272.
Solow, R.M., 1957. Review of Economics and Statistics, vol. 39, pp. 312–320.
Solow, R.M., 1960a. Econometrica, vol. 28, pp. 392–406.
Solow, R.M., 1960b. Investment and technical progress. In: Arrow, K.J., S. Karlin and P. Suppes, eds., Mathematical Methods in the Social Sciences, 1959. Proceedings of the First Stanford Symposium (Stanford University Press, Stanford, California) pp. 89–104.
Solow, R.M., 1962. American Economic Review, Papers and Proceedings, vol. 52, pp. 76–86.
Solow, R.M., 1964. Capital labour and income. In: Conference on Research in Income and Wealth, The Behaviour of Income Shares (National Bureau of Economic Research, Princeton University Press, Princeton, New Jersey) pp. 100–128.
Solow, R.M., see Arrow et al. (1961).
Solow, R.M., see Ando et al. (1963).
Soskice, D., 1968. Review of Economics and Statistics, vol. 50, pp. 446–448.
Spiro, A., 1962. Journal of Political Economy, vol. 70, pp. 339–354.
Stekler, H.O., 1969. Review of Economics and Statistics, vol. 51, pp. 77–83.
Stephenson, J.A., see Jorgenson and Stephenson (1967).

Stone, R., 1954a. The Measurement of Consumer's Expenditure and Behaviour in the U.K. 1920–1938. Vol. 1 (Cambridge University Press, Cambridge).
Stone, R., 1954b. The Economic Journal, vol. 64, pp. 511–527.
Stone, R., 1962a. The Manchester School, vol. 30, pp. 1–14.
Stone, R., 1962b. A Computable Model of Economic Growth. Department of Applied Economics, University of Cambridge: A Programme for Growth, vol. 1 (Chapman and Hall, Cambridge) pp. 28–33.
Stone, R., 1964. The Manchester School, vol. 32, pp. 79–112.
Stone, R., 1966. The changing pattern of consumption. In: R. Stone, ed., Mathematics in the Social Sciences and Other Essays. (Chapman and Hall, London) pp. 190–203.
Stone, R., and D.A. Rowe, 1957. Econometrica, vol. 25, pp. 432–443.
Stone, R., and D.A. Rowe, 1962. The Manchester School, vol. 30, pp. 187–201.
Strotz, R., see Eisner and Strotz (1963).
Taylor, L.D., and T.A. Wilson, 1964. Review of Economics and Statistics, vol. 46, pp. 329–346.
Taylor, L.D., see Houthakker and Taylor (1966).
Theil, H., 1954. Linear Aggregation of Economic Relations (North-Holland, Amsterdam).
Theil, H., 1964. Optimal Decision Rules for Government and Industry (North-Holland, Amsterdam).
Theil, H., 1967. Economics and Information Theory (North-Holland, Amsterdam) pp. 37–46.
Theil, H. and A.S. Goldberger, 1960. International Economic Review, vol. 2, pp. 65–78.
Theil, H. and A.L. Nagar, 1961. Journal of the American Statistical Association, vol. 56, pp. 803–805.
Tsujimura, K. and T. Sato, 1964. Review of Economics and Statistics, vol. 44, pp. 305–319.
Verhülst, M.J., 1948. Econometrica, vol. 16, pp. 295–308.
Wallace, N., see Griliches and Wallace (1965) and Griliches et al. (1962).
Walters, A.A., 1963. Econometrica, vol. 31, pp. 1–66.
Walters, A.A., 1968. An Introduction to Econometrics (MacMillan, London).
Watts, H.W., and J. Tobin, 1960. Consumer Expenditures and Capital Account. In: Friend and Jones (1960) vol. 2, pp. 1–48.
Wilson, T.A., see Taylor and Wilson (1964).
Zellner, A., 1957. Econometrica, vol. 25, pp. 552–566.
Zellner, A., and M.S. Geisel, 1968. Analysis of Distributed Lag Models with Applications to Consumption Function Estimation. A paper read to the European Meeting of the Econometric Society in Amsterdam.
Zellner, A., J. Kmenta and J. Drèze, 1966. Econometrica, vol. 34, pp. 784–795.
Zellner, A., D.S. Huang and L.C. Chau, 1965. Econometrica, vol. 33, pp. 571–581.
Zellner, A., and M.A. Geisel, 1968, Analysis of distributed lag models with applications to consumption function estimation. To appear in: Econometrica, November 1970.

AUTHOR INDEX

R

S

T

V

W

Z

SUBJECT INDEX

A

B

C

D

E

F

G

H

I

L